Studien zur Außereuropäischen
Christentumsgeschichte
(Asien, Afrika, Lateinamerika)
―――――――
Studies in the History of Christianity
in the Non-Western World

Herausgegeben von / Edited by
Klaus Koschorke & Johannes Meier

Band 37 / Volume 37

2023
Harrassowitz Verlag · Wiesbaden

Wei Jiang

"True Catholicism" in Colonial South Asia

The Independent Catholics in Ceylon and India
in the late Nineteenth and Early Twentieth Centuries

2023

Harrassowitz Verlag · Wiesbaden

Printed with the financial support of the German Research Foundation (DFG).

Cover Art: Pages from the periodical *The Independent Catholic*, published in Colombo from 1892 to 1896.

This work is licensed under the Creative Commons Attribution-ShareAlike 4.0 (BY-SA) which means that the text may be used for commercial use, distribution and duplication in all media.

For details go to: https://creativecommons.org/licenses/by-sa/4.0/deed.en.

Creative Commons license terms for re-use do not apply to any content (such as graphs, figures, photos, excerpts, etc.) not original to the Open Access publication and further permission may be required from the rights holder. The obligation to research and clear permission lies solely with the party re-using the material.

Bibliographic information published by the Deutsche Nationalbibliothek
The Deutsche Nationalbibliothek lists this publication in the Deutsche Nationalbibliografie; detailed bibliographic data are available on the internet at https://www.dnb.de/.

For further information about our publishing program consult our website
https://www.harrassowitz-verlag.de/

© by author.
Published by Otto Harrassowitz GmbH & Co. KG, Wiesbaden 2023

ISSN 1611-0080 ISBN 978-3-447-11847-7
eISSN 2197-4829   eISBN 978-3-447-39282-2
DOI: 10.13173/1611-0080   DOI: 10.13173/9783447118477

Table of Contents

Preface 9

Introduction 13
1. A Global and Local History of the Buona Morte Church 13
2. Structure of the Book 16
3. Archives and Electronic Sources 22

Chapter 1: Catholicism and European Colonialism in Ceylon 27
1. Ceylon at 1500 29
   1.1 Geography and Polities 29
   1.2 Sinhalese and Tamil Languages 30
   1.3 Sinhalese Buddhism 31
   1.4 Hinduism 32
   1.5 Islam 33
2. Christianity During the Portuguese Intervention 34
   2.1 Political Presence 34
   2.2 The Missionary Enterprise 37
      2.2.1 Nestorians in Ceylon According to Cosmas 37
      2.2.2 Conversion and Competition 38
   2.3 Indigenous Christians in Mannar, Negombo and Colombo 40
3. Underground Catholics in Dutch Ceylon 43
   3.1 Dutch Control of Ceylon 43
   3.2 Oratorians and Underground Christians 44
4. Christianity in British Ceylon 47
   4.1 Ceylon as a "Model Colony" and Laboratory of Modernity 47
   4.2 The Oratorian Conundrum 50
      4.2.1 Challenges to the Goan Missionaries in Ceylon 50
      4.2.2 The Social Context of the Decline of the Oratorians 52

Table of Contents

Chapter 2: *Padroado* Controversies in South Asia ... 55

Vignette – The Consequences of the *Padroado* Controversies ... 55

1. A Brief Overview of Literature on the Debates on *Padroado* in South Asia, 1853–1940 ... 57
   1.1 The Capuchins, the New Society of Jesus Against the *Padroado* ... 57
   1.2 Hull and the Bombay Mission History, 1929–1930 ... 59

2. From Early Modern Solutions to the Modern Challenges ... 62
   2.1 *Padroado Real*: A Legal and Political History ... 62
   2.2 The Rise of the *Padroadists* in South Asia and the Concordats ... 64

3. Definition of Schism ... 66

4. Failed Communications ... 68

5. *Padroadists* in Bombay and Goa ... 69
   5.1 Bombay ... 69
   5.2 Final Efforts: The Assembly in Panjim (Goa) in 1886 and Lisboa Pinto's Voyage to Portugal ... 74

Chapter 3: Ecumenical Catholicities in the Nineteenth Century ... 79

1. A Triumphant and Controversial Episcopal Consecration ... 79

2. Vilatte and His Failed Pursuit of a Catholic Reform Before 1892 ... 81

3. The Anglican Communion and the Search for a Primitive Catholicity ... 86

4. The Jacobites in the Context of the Thomas Christians in South Asia ... 88

5. The Independence and Reunion Movements Among the Syrian Christians in the Nineteenth Century ... 89

6. Alvares' Syrian Orthodox Identity and His Reception in Various Churches ... 96
   6.1 *A Supremacia Universal* as an "Identity Document" ... 96
   6.2 An Expansion of the Independent Catholic Church: The Ordination of Alexander Steward in 1900 ... 100

Chapter 4: Ceylon I:
The Roman Catholic Portuguese Mission in Ceylon, 1837 to 1887 ... 103

1. João Bonifácio Misso and the Catholic Lay Unrest in Colombo ... 105
   1.1 Burghers ... 105
   1.2 Bonifácio Misso's Turn from a Pro-Roman to a Pro-*Padroado* Catholic ... 107
   1.3 *Padroado* Groups Outside Colombo: Negombo ... 110
   1.4 The Burgher Community of Misso and the Portuguese Consul General in Colombo 1845–1864 ... 113

2. The Church in Mannar 114
   2.1 Miguel Filipe Mascarenhas in Mannar and Mantotte 114
   2.2 The Indo-Portuguese Legacy in Mannar and Mantotte 117
   2.3 A Reaction to the First Vatican Council in the Vicariate of Jaffna 118
   2.4 The Development of the Portuguese Mission in the 1870s 120

Chapter 5: Ceylon II:
The Independent Catholic Mission 1887–ca. 1900 123

1. Decisive Years, 1884–1888 123
   1.1 Despair, 1884–1887 123
   1.2 The Establishment of the Independent Catholic Mission
       in February 1888 126
   1.3 Turning to the Syrian Church of Malabar in June 1888 128

2. Members, Sociability, and Rivalry 132
   2.1 Members 132
   2.2 Glimpses of Daily Life 135
   2.3 Lisboa Pinto and His Social Integration in Colombo 136
   2.4 Liturgy and Feasts 139
   2.5 Rivalry With the "Romanists" 142

3. Decline 143
   3.1 Complaints Against Alvares 143
   3.2 Demands of Priests 143
   3.3 Last Days in the Twentieth Century 145

Chapter 6: India:
Indian Representations of the Independent Catholic Mission in Ceylon .. 147

1. Alvares: An Indian Prelude 148
   1.1 The Unruly Alvares Before 1877 148
   1.2 Conflicts With the Archbishop of Goa From 1877 to 1882 150
   1.3 Alvares' Career as a Journalist From 1882 to 1895 156

2. Indian Reactions to the Syrian Archbishop and His
   Independent Catholic Mission 157
   2.1 Alvares' Trials in 1890, 1895, and 1906 157
   2.2 Goan Representation of the Indian-Ceylon Independent Catholics 162
   2.3 Goan Representations of the Syrian Character of the
       Independent Catholic Mission 165

3. Expansion in Madurai 167

Chapter 7: *The Independent Catholic* in the Ceylon Public Sphere 173

1. *The Independent Catholic* as a Cradle of Trade Unionism:
   A Literature Review 173
2. The Printing Press in Nineteenth Century Ceylon: Boom and Impacts 178
   2.1 Journalism Boom 178
   2.2 Call for a National Church 181
3. *The Independent Catholic* and Its Local and Global Perceptions 184
   3.1 The Feuille *Independent* 184
   3.2 Clifton Press 185
   3.3 Perceptions in Ceylon, India and Beyond 187
4. *The Independent Catholic*'s Importance 191

Conclusion 193

Appendices 201

Appendix 1: Lists of Names 203

Appendix 2: Inscriptions of Grave Stelæ in the
Church of Our Lady of Good Death 211

Bibliography 213

Illustrations 239

Preface

While most of the writing was done in Bonn, this book would have been impossible without the immense help and support I received during my archival research and fieldwork in India, Sri Lanka, and the United Kingdom between 2017 and 2018.

The bulk of the archival sources on Antonio Alvares was found in the State Central Library of Goa, whose former director Dr. Carlos M. Fernandes and librarian Ms. Maria Ana Paiva kindly granted me access to the newspaper repositories. The historians Dr. Celsa Pinto and Ms. Maria Lourdes Bravo da Costa not only generously shared their expertise, but also invited me to participate in Goan feasts. Ms. Lilia de Souza's altruistic help was essential for me to work efficiently at the Catholic Archive of Goa in the Archbishop's Palace, Panjim. Ms. Arti Mayekar-Fernandes at the Xavier Centre of Historical Research patiently attended to all my requests concerning rare books and newspapers. Professor Pratima P. Kamat and Professor Koshy Tharakan at the University of Goa inspired me with their publications and invaluable advice. Fr. Cosme Jose Costa at the Society of the Missionaries of St Francis Xavier in Pilar generously shared his unpublished writings with me. The six weeks I spent in Altinho together with Prof. Ananya Chakravarti was unforgettable and I am indebted to her friendship. Ms. Philomena Lydia Fernandes and Dr. Jason Keith Fernandes gave me precious insights into the recent past of Goa.

In Mangalore, Fr. Rajesh Rosario at St Joseph's Seminary and Fr. Denis Prabhu at the Bishop's House of Mangalore carefully guided me into their archives, libraries, and their communal life. Dr. C. L. Furtado, Emeritus Bishop of the Church of South India, broadened my understanding of Christianity in Karnataka.

Fr. Selvaraj Aruldoss SJ, and Fr. Leonard Fernando SJ, at St. Joseph's College (Autonomous), Tiruchirappalli, enlightened me with their publications and kindly allowed me to pursue research at the Jesuit Madurai Province Archives in Shembaganur.

The Malankara Orthodox Syrian Church (MOSC) provided enormous support to my research at multiple levels and across India and Sri Lanka. The St Mary's Orthodox Church in Ribandar, Goa, welcomed me in their Qurbanas and on the occasion of joyful receptions. In Brahmavar, I am most grateful to Fr. Noel Lewis, Fr. Abraham Kuriakose, and Fr. Lawrence David Crasta, who offered me endless resources and cares when I travelled alone. In Kottayam, Dr. Meladathu Kurian Thomas taught me the history of the Old Seminary and introduced me to the Church History Association of India. In Devalokam I was received by the late Catholicos Baselios Marthoma Paulose II, thanks to the intervention of his secretary Fr. Aswin Fernandis. Mr. Sujith Varghese George guided me across Kerala and Tamil Nadu by showing me the sites of former missions of the Independent Catholics. He and his family provided me incredible hospitality and intellectual inspirations. His skills in management also made a joint adventure possible, namely organising a cross-confessional conference on the history of the Independent Catholics, that took place successfully in Colombo in November 2018. I am indebted to authors like Dr. Ajesh Philip, Mr. George Alexander, Mr. George

K. Kurian for their excellent research on the biography of Antonio Alvares and his missionary work. I am also grateful to Mr. Ancil Mathew in Goa, Fr. Markose Geevarghese in Tiruchirapalli, and Fr. Jerry Varghese in Devalokam for their trust and friendship.

In Sri Lanka, I thank Prof. G.P.V. Somaratna and Dr. Prabo Mihindukulasuriya at Colombo Theological Seminary, for their warm hospitality and scholarly guidance for my first encounter with Sri Lankan Christianity. Mr. Yuren Athukorala, former archivist at the Department of National Archives of Sri Lanka helped me retrieve misplaced issues of *The Independent Catholic* newspaper. In Colombo, I received immense attention and sponsorship from the Roman Catholic Church. Fr. Joy Mariaratnam CMF demonstrated a genuine interest in regard to the history of the Buona Morte Church and took on organisational responsibilities for the Colombo conference. Leading Catholic historians such as Fr. Jayalath Balagalla OP, Fr. Xystus Kurukulasuriya, and Fr. Gnanamuhu Pilendra, helped to extend my research beyond Colombo towards Ampitiya, Kandy, Negombo, and Jaffna. The sisters of the Society of the Divine Saviour at Buona Morte Church, especially Sr. Helen Lambert, Sr. Vasanthini Dionysius, and Sr. Ranjana Silvapulle, lodged me in their convent, so that I could relate the past of the Independent Catholics of Ceylon to its religious neighbourhood of today. Fr. Aloysius Pieris SJ, kindly explained to me the development of Catholic theology during my visit to the Tulana Research Centre in Kelaniya. I am deeply grateful to Mr. Neil D'Silva for openly sharing memories of his family past. Mr. Stan Devotta provided precious local contacts and devoted substantial time to my exercise of oral history. Mr. and Mrs. Abraham Alex from the MOSC twice provided free accommodation when I conducted research in Colombo. My special thanks are extended to Mr. Ismeth Raheem for his expertise in art and architecture and his patience in teaching me the history of the Muslims in Sri Lanka.

In London I thank Abba Seraphim for elucidating to me the history of the Orthodox Church in the UK and for his kind interest in my project. The Lambeth Palace Library provided essential sources for my study on René Vilatte.

In Germany, I must thank the Syro-Malankara community in Bonn and Fr. Joseph Chelamparambath for inviting me to their Qurbanas and taking keen interests in my research on the history of the Syrian Church of Malabar all over the years of this project.

Many colleagues read the full version or part of the book manuscript, especially on occasion of the following three workshops in Bonn: "Independent Catholicism in South Asia" (January 25 to 26, 2019), "Independent Catholicism in South Asia and the Philippines" (August 29 to September 1, 2019) and "Independent Catholicism in Asia and Beyond Around 1900" (January 23 to 25, 2020). They are Paolo Aranha (Rome), Meladathu Kurian Thomas, Sujith Varghese George, Lawrence David Crasta, Megan Thomas (University of California, Santa Cruz, USA), Philipp Kuster (Ludwig-Maximilians-Universität Munich), Francis Gealogo (Ateneo de Manila University, Philippines), Scott Maclochlainn (Universität Göttingen), Adrian Hermann (Universität Bonn), Andreas Krebs (Universität Bonn), Peter-Ben Smit (Utrecht University), Klaus Koschorke (Ludwig-Maximilians-Universität Munich), and Rochelle Pinto (Bangalore). I am deeply grateful to all for their candid comments and suggestions.

Last, but not least, this study emerged out of a research project funded by the German Research Foundation (DFG) from 2016 to 2021. The title of the project was "Independent Catholic Movements in Late 19th and Early 20th Century Asia: The 'Independent Catholics of India, Goa, and Ceylon' and the 'Iglesia Filipina Independiente' in the Context of Religious, Political, and Social Movements of Emancipation in Colonial Modernity" (PI: Prof. Dr. Adrian Hermann). The project was conducted at the Department of Religion Studies at the Forum Internationale Wissenschaft of the University of Bonn, where I worked as a Post-Doctoral Researcher from 2017 to 2020 in collaboration with Adrian Hermann. This study is one of the project's major results, a pioneering study of the "Independent Catholic Mission" and "Independent Catholic Church" in Ceylon around 1900. The periodical of this movement, *The Independent Catholic*, which appeared in Colombo from 1892–1896, describes itself on its masthead as a paper published "in the interest of True Catholicism", which provides the inspiration for the title of my book.

For copyediting work on the manuscript I thank Doris Westhoff, Philip Kuster, Aaron Vowinkel, and Laila N. Riedmiller. I also thank all my former colleagues at the Department of Religion Studies at the Forum Internationale Wissenschaft of the University of Bonn, in particular Sónia Lopes Belabbes, for their friendship and constant support. Special thanks are due to Klaus Koschorke and Paolo Aranha for their invaluable comments on the project and during the preparation of this book.

Wei Jiang

Zürich, April 2022

Introduction

1. A Global and Local History of the Buona Morte Church

Towards the east end of Belmont Street in the hustle and bustle of the district of Colombo 12 stands a Roman Catholic church fully painted in a brilliant blue. Its silhouette against the bright sun blurs with the crystal tropical sky. The church is built in a modified neoclassical style marked by a colonnade façade with a triangular pediment sided by two bell towers.[1] Two golden angels stand apart above them, with their crescent wings pointing upward to the remote endlessness. Over their shoulders and trumpets one sees from afar the gigantic Colombo Lotus Tower – an eloquent symbol of Chinese geopolitical influence – dominating the skyline of the capital of a country where over 70% of the population practices Buddhism. With a small oculus window the pediment ascends to a white budded cross atop. In the middle of the façade, the visitor can read "Buona Morte Church 1847", an odd Anglo-Italian hybrid[2] bewildering those searching for the historical site of Our Lady of Good Death, the cathedral of the Independent Catholic Mission in Ceylon, Goa, and India during the late nineteenth and mid-twentieth centuries.[3]

This church, now a substation of St. Sebastian parish, is located in an area where the overwhelming majority of the inhabitants today is Muslim.[4] The gate of the churchyard is the southern end of Oilman Street, where two golden-domed Mosques call tens of thousands of residents, merchants, shopkeepers, and tuk-tuk drivers living in the neighbourhood to their daily worship. Every morning many parents bring their children into the Buona Morte churchyard to attend the St. Sebastian Muslim Maha Vidyalaya, a Sinhala middle school and perhaps the only Muslim school in Colombo whose name honors a Catholic saint. St. Sebastian is the common patron saint of two other Catholic parishes near Buona Morte, all three established during the first half of the nineteenth century and located north of a canal also named after the Roman martyr. The designation St. Sebastian was likely first used by the Portuguese to name a bastion, built together with the ones named after St. Stephen and the

---

1 An undated photo of the church has been published in ABBA SERAPHIM, *Flesh of Our Brethren* (London 2018), 210. The photo shows a porch attached to the entrance of the church and a balcony in front of the pediment. It is not clear when and why the porch and the balcony were dismantled.
2 The linguistic uncertainty surrounding the church becomes even more obvious when looking at Google Maps, where this place of worship is identified by the nonsensical form "Bourna Mote church" (last access on 28 December 2021).
3 Several authors described their encounters with this church and their enduring interests in its past. A. PHILIP / G. ALEXANDER, *Western Rites of Syriac-Malankara Orthodox Churches* (Kerala 2018); G.K. KURIAN, *Saint Alvares Mar Julius* (Ribandar, Panaji, Goa 2013); SERAPHIM, *Flesh of Our Brethren*.
4 See the catalogue of churches of the Archdiocese of Colombo (https://archdioceseofcolombo.lk/parishes, last accessed on 30 December 2021).

Mother of God (*Madre de Deus*) in northern Colombo.[5] During the second half of the seventeenth century, the Dutch reworked the rich water system of the city by constructing the St. Sebastian canal so as to better connect two important bodies of water in the north, namely Beira Lake and the Kelani Ganga River. For the last two decades, the St. Sebastian middle school has rented the Buona Morte churchyard, integrating a vibrant Muslim life into a diminished Catholic space. The inter-religious relations have not always been idyllic. Recurrent tensions arise when youngsters resort to violence and cause disturbances to the only residents of the site of Buona Morte, the Salvatorian Catholic nuns, whose Mother Mary's Convent and Nursery are attached to the south end of the churchyard. Few attend the daily mass in the evening, but individuals constantly walk in to pray. A highlight of the year is the church festival on 12 August, when hundreds of parishioners gather for a procession, often joined by curious neighbours of all religious backgrounds.

Unlike any other Catholic church in Colombo, Buona Morte has a rather peculiar history which will be unraveled in this book. It all started with the urban transformations that took place since the start of the British colonial era. The western wall of the churchyard separates the Catholic premises from those of the Attorney General's Department of the Supreme Court of Sri Lanka, established in 1801 in a district named Hultsdorf or Hulftsdorp, after General Gerard Pieterszoon Hulft (1621–1656), Governor General of the Dutch Indies. The British legal center attracted a flow of lawyers, translators, clerks, and printers, establishing professional businesses but also buying private property to settle there. Some of the thriving new neighbours were labeled "Dutch burghers". The term "burgher" is a Dutch noun and, as is obvious to speakers of Germanic languages, covers the semantic spectrum of "citizen" and "town dweller". The expression was used to indicate people of mixed European and Sri Lankan descent (Sinhala or Tamil), normally professing Roman Catholicism, Calvinism, Anglicanism, but even Buddhism in some exceptional cases.[6] Their European ancestry was primarily Portuguese and Dutch, with some elements from other European nationalities, including Germans who had been serving under the Dutch East India Company. On 21 February 1845, the British authorities granted a piece of land in Belmont Street to a group of Burghers to build on it a chapel dedicated to Our Lady of Good Death.[7] The leader of this group, the Catholic surgeon Dr. John Bonifacio Misso (1797–1864), was the first Consul General of Portugal in Ceylon and an adamant supporter of *Padroado*, the royal patronage of the Portuguese crown over the Catholic missions in Asia. When the chapel was inaugurated in 1847 (if the date on the church façade is reliable), Misso could hardly foresee how his initiative would result in an irreversible antagonism with the Roman Catholic authorities in Ceylon. It would have been beyond his wildest imagination that this chapel would trigger unexpected ecumenical innovations and international academic interest for now already over 170 years.

I visited Sri Lanka for the first time in February 2018, with the purpose of collecting archival sources on the Independent Catholic Mission, also known as the Latin branch of what at that time was called the Syrian Orthodox Church of Antioch in Malabar. This Latin community once spread across British Ceylon and India and was present even in Portuguese

---

5   R.L. BROHIER / I. RAHEEM, *Changing Face of Colombo, 1505–1972*. Covering the Portuguese, Dutch, and British Periods (Colombo 1984), 16.
6   T.J. BARTHOLOMEUSZ, "Buddhist Burghers and Sinhala-Buddhist Fundamentalism", in: T.J. BARTHOLOMEUSZ / C.R. DE SILVA (eds.), *Buddhist Fundamentalism and Minority Identities in Sri Lanka* (Albany 1998, 167–185).
7   Original documents about the land deed are still to be found, but some details have been mentioned in B. BARCATTA, *A History of the Southern Vicariate of Colombo, Sri Lanka, Being Also the History of the Apostolate of the Sylvestrine-Benedictine Monks in the Island*. Vol. 1 (Ampitiya 1991), 446.

Goa. My research was funded by a *Deutsche Forschungsgemeinschaft* (DFG) project entitled "Independent Catholic Movements in Late 19th and Early 20th Century Asia: The 'Independent Catholics of India, Goa, and Ceylon' and the 'Iglesia Filipina Independiente' in the Context of Religious, Political, and Social Movements of Emancipation in Colonial Modernity", hosted at the University of Bonn from 2017 to 2020. Before coming to Colombo, I had spent two months working at various archives and libraries in Goa, as well as visiting the former Independent Catholic Mission in Kalianpur, today belonging to the Malankara Orthodox Syrian Church (MOSC) Diocese of Brahmavar, in the state of Karnataka. On my trip southwards along the Malabar coast, I visited the Roman Catholic Diocese of Mangalore and the MOSC Headquarter and Seminary in Kottayam, talking to priests, historians, and lay researchers, from whose knowledge I started to combine, as pieces of a jigsaw puzzle, the various phases and turns in the history of the South Asian Independent Catholics. However, my first encounter with the former and only cathedral of the entire Independent Catholic movement in South Asia was a totally different experience. The dilapidated church I saw in Colombo could not be compared to any of the churches I had seen before in India, either Catholic or Orthodox. Today, it is marginalised by a Muslim majority and dwarfed by the main judicial landmark of the country. The parish priest, Father Joy Mariaratnam, a Claretian missionary from Jaffna, was preoccupied with the disturbances occurring in his church, but he also showed a great interest in its puzzling history. Since 2009, researchers from Kerala, Tamil Nadu, and Goa have made significant progress in tracing the living memories of the Independent Catholics in Colombo and Mannar. At the same time, Malankara Orthodox Syrian Bishops had cordial meetings with the Archbishop of Colombo, receiving permission to celebrate Holy Qurbanas (i.e. Eucharistic functions) according to the Western Syrian rite at the altar of the Buona Morte Church, each time attracting great attention among the parishioners. After we were introduced to each other, Father Joy and I initially envisaged hosting an ecumenical lecture at the Buona Morte Church or Saint Sebastian Parish, reconciling Orthodox and Roman Catholic memories of the place, while highlighting the Catholic presence in the multi-religious neighbourhood. After six months of preparation and following the expansion of my archival research on the eastern coast of South India, in the state of Tamil Nadu, this initial plan had grown and developed into something much bigger, namely an international conference eventually held at the Colombo auditorium hall of Caritas, the Roman Catholic relief agency, in November 2018. Different from conventional conferences, centered on a well-defined confessional protocol, "A Global and Local History of Buona Morte Church" involved a wide spectrum of Christian denominations, and consequently sparked more questions and doubts than anyone alone could answer and solve. Scholars from various Churches in Sri Lanka and India, including the Malankara Orthodox Syrian, the Roman Catholic, the Anglican, and various Protestant denominations were encouraged to shed light from their own perspectives on the little known Buona Morte Church in Colombo in particular, as well as on the condition of Christianity in Ceylon during the British colonial era in general. It was on that occasion that I, originally specialised on early modern Church History, started to realise the enormous sources, global entanglements, and ecumenical complexities of a nineteenth century church movement such as the Independent Catholics. Most of all, our DFG-project, originally conceived merely for academic purposes in Germany, had by then acquired a new dimension, contributing to the elaboration of a public memory by communities eager to retrieve roots and pass them on to future generations.

As every other corner of Colombo, a historical site like the Buona Morte Church can disclose forgotten, unexpected, and occasionally even enigmatic stories from the colonial past. None of those stories can be told, however, in a vacuum and without reference to the racial, religious, and ethnic conflicts of Sri Lanka lasting until today. On Easter Sunday 2019, five months after our Buona Morte conference, Sri Lankan Christians, citizens of other faiths, and international tourists suffered in a series of terrorist suicide bombings that ultimately caused 269 deaths and at least 500 injuries. The first bomb exploded in the shrine of Saint Anthony in Kotahena, Colombo, where Father Joy Mariaratnam was celebrating Mass at 8:25 am.[8] Father Joy survived at the altar but not so the 93 Catholics who were participating in the rite. One year later, on 20 March 2020, the Sri Lankan government announced a nation-wide lockdown due to the COVID-19 pandemic. Since then Masses were broadcast on TV and online, while only 12 faithful could attend the Easter Sunday Mass in person at St. Anthony's shrine that year.[9] Compared to these recent events, my research into a nineteenth century minoritarian Christian movement like Independent Catholicism might seem connected only very indirectly to alarming issues such as Islamic terrorism or the emergence of regional forms of religious nationalism that undermine the rights of minorities such as the Christians, representing 7.4% (2012 census) of the population in a predominantly Buddhist Sri Lanka, while amounting to a mere 2.3% (2011 census) in India, whose much praised democracy is ever more challenged by Hindu extremism.

However, precisely the tragedies that occurred in Sri Lanka after the end of the civil war in 2009 call for a greater attention to a plurisecular Christian presence, considered only in a limited way in both classic and recent works on the ethnic conflicts and the modernisation processes on the island.[10] The available narratives on Sri Lankan Christian history are mainly written within denominational frameworks and tend to leave out schismatic figures as well as internal discord and/or failed reforms. It is therefore a priority for this book to contextualise our case study along various scales of time, space, and historiography, drawing on conflicting evidence and linking processes occurring in a global space, ranging from Ceylon to Great Britain, passing through Turkey and Italy, and reaching up to North America. In this way, this book aims at contributing to a new perspective for interpreting the history of Christianity in British Ceylon rather than at merely developing a minor footnote in the history of Global Christianity.

2. Structure of the Book

The passage of the Buona Morte Church from being a *Padroado* Catholic church since 1847 to becoming an Independent Catholic cathedral in 1888 epitomizes the development of the Roman Catholic Church in South Asia during the British colonial era. When Ceylon became a British colony at the end of the eighteenth century, the Roman Curia started to reorganise the ecclesiastical jurisdiction in British India and Ceylon, conferring the *Padroado* churches to the Roman Congregation of Propaganda Fide, i.e. the Papal secretariate for missions. The Goan priests loyal to the Portuguese *Padroado*, who had kept the Catholic faith in Ceylon

---

8 "Sri Lanka holds mass amid high security, forces look for suspects" on *Aljazeera*, 28 April 2019 (https://www.aljazeera.com/news/2019/04/sri-lanka-holds-mass-high-security-forces-suspects-190428103355234.html, last accessed on 28 December 2021).
9 "Easter Sunday in Sri Lanka this year was sombre" on *News In Asia*, 13 April 2020 (https://newsin.asia/easter-sunday-in-sri-lanka-this-year-was-sombre/, last accessed on 28 December 2021).
10 K.M. DE SILVA, *Reaping the Whirlwind*. Ethnic Conflict, Ethnic Politics in Sri Lanka (New Delhi 1999); N. WICKRAMASINGHE, *Sri Lanka in the Modern Age*. A History of Contested Identities (New York 2014); S. SIVASUNDARAM, *Islanded*. Britain, Sri Lanka, and the Bounds of an Indian Ocean Colony (Chicago 2013).

alive throughout the Dutch colonization, were now supposed to leave their churches. The Catholics of Ceylon were entrusted to new missionaries, particularly from France, Italy, and the German-speaking world. Like the aforementioned Dr. Misso, thousands of Catholics across South Asia publicly refused the decision of the Holy See and protested against the acquiescence to the Roman decrees shown by the Archbishopric of Goa. A wave of local divisions spread throughout the Catholic milieus in India and Ceylon, particularly among the Western-educated native elites. In 1886 pro-*Padroado* factions in Bombay and Goa organised a delegation and sent the medical doctor Pedro Manuel Lisboa Pinto (1857–1898) to Europe to present a petition to Pope Leo XIII (r. 1878–1903) and the King of Portugal Dom Luís I (r. 1861–1889) for retaining the *Padroado* jurisdiction in South Asia. The indifferent attitudes Lisboa Pinto encountered in Europe led to the ultimate disappointment of even the staunchest Asian *Padroado* supporters. Following a historical trajectory still to be fully explored, Antonio Francisco Xavier Alvares (1836–1923), a suspended Goan Catholic priest who had formulated the delegation plan in 1886, decided to leave Goa and embrace the Syrian Orthodox Church in Kottayam (Travancore), where he received the title of Apostolic Prefect in 1887 from the Metropolitan Mar Dionysius VI (1858–1934) before eventually being consecrated as "Julius I, Archbishop of Ceylon, Goa, and India (excluding Malabar)".

Merging his personal antagonism against the Roman Catholic authorities with the traditional hostility of the Saint Thomas Christians to Latinization, particularly since the Coonan Cross Oath uprising in 1653, Alvares gave origin to an Oriental Orthodox community following the Latin rite. The Independent Catholic Mission, first established at the Cathedral of Our Lady of Good Death in 1888, became part of the history of the Malankara Orthodox Syrian Church, by then still ruled from the Anatolian monastery of Mardin by the Patriarch of Antioch of the Syrian Orthodox. Alvares and his fellow Goan priest Luis Mariano Soares (c. 1858–1903) embarked on an expansion drive, moving from the first mission centres in Colombo and Mannar, towards parishes in Bombay, Travancore, and Madras previously entrusted to the *Padroado* jurisdiction. Their advancement threatened both the local Jesuits as well as the Anglican missionaries of the Church Mission Society, who reported to Rome and London respectively, complaining of the proselytism promoted by the "Goan schismatics" or "Jacobites", derogatory labels imposed on Alvares and Soares. In the face of opposition from the Propaganda priests and due to increasing problems such as lack of discipline, disobedience, liturgical tensions, local caste conflicts as well as insufficient financial support from the Malankara authority in Kottayam, most of the missions declined since the early twentieth century, with the only exception of the Kalianpur mission, which survived and in 2010 was elevated to the Diocese of Brahmavar, erected by Baselios Marthoma Didymus I, Catholicos of the Malankara Orthodox Syrian Church (r. 2005–2010).

Independent Catholicism in India and Ceylon was a minoritarian Christian movement, which emerged in South Asia during the nineteenth century and was connected in intricate ways with a global development known as Old Catholicism that opposed the process of Roman centralisation marked particularly by the First Vatican Council (1869–70). Thanks to new means of transportation and communication, as well as to a modernised printing industry, the Independent Catholics gained a certain reputation in the Christian world. Eccentric Catholic groups in Britain, North America, and Italy were attracted by the redefined Catholicity proposed by the Indo-Ceylonese Independent Catholics, claiming a universal supremacy of the Apostolic See of Antioch against the pretensions of Rome. A number of European men approached the Independent Catholic Mission seeking priestly ordination, and even episcopal consecration, so as to pass on the Apostolic lineage that Alvares had received from the Roman Catholic Church. Some were successful in their queries. The most significant case was the episcopal consecration of the French priest Joseph René Vilatte (1854–1929) in Colombo in 1892, celebrated by Alvares and three Syrian Orthodox Bishops from Malabar. Vilatte established a link between the Indo-Ceylonese Independent Catholics and the Old Catholic Church in Switzerland and Holland. With the latter he had tried to promote the first Old Catholic mission in Wisconsin, USA, but had eventually failed. As a consequence, through the assimilation of Vilatte and his North American mission, the movement of the Independent Catholics in South Asia became part of global ecumenical practices and cross-confessional rivalries, involving Old Catholics, Anglicans, Syrian Orthodox in the Ottoman Empire and in Travancore, not to mention Roman Catholics. Through the development of the Wisconsin Independent Catholic mission, Vilatte furthermore passed on his Apostolic lineage, inherited from Alvares, to Europe, America, and Africa, where various forms of Independent Catholicism continue to exist even today.

Based on the abovementioned chronology, this book is divided into three parts. The first presents historical contexts and reviews the existing historiography. The second part is a tentative narrative of the history of the Independent Catholic movement in Ceylon and India, whereas the final part offers a thematic discussion of central issues concerning the movement.

Chapter 1 examines the history of Catholicism in Ceylon, as marked by three European interventions, namely by Portuguese (1506–1658), Dutch (1658–1796), and British (1796–1948) colonialism, offering a longue durée perspective to the emergence of the Independent Catholics in the late nineteenth century. The Portuguese era is studied with a focus on the first Catholic conversions that occured in Mannar, Negombo, and Colombo, places which would provide the bulk of the Independent Catholics in the nineteenth century. The Dutch era is examined to highlight how Catholicism resisted and did not fade away during this period, when the Calvinist Dutch Reformed Church was the official Christian denomination. Our look at the British era will help to understand why the Goan Oratorians, as the only Catholic missionary body that had been active in Ceylon throughout the Dutch period, failed to satisfy the needs of the local Catholics when religious freedom was proclaimed by the British authorities in the nineteenth century. The Oratorian missionaries had helped to consolidate a Portuguese *Padroado* identity among the native Christians by maintaining a connection with Catholic communities in India. The decline of the Oratorians in Ceylon in the nineteenth century, which coincided with the rise of the discontent Catholic group in Colombo led by Misso, has been considered as the outcome of a failed administration. However, the rampant racism that the European missionaries beheld towards the Indian and Ceylonese priests and laymen played an important role in provoking distrust and rebellion. Similarly, racism would be found in other contexts such as the very *Padroado* controversies that will be studied in the second chapter.

Chapter 2 examines the origins of the Independent Catholics from a Roman Catholic point of view, in relation with the *Padroado* controversies in South Asia. It is a widely accepted presumption that these served as a catalyst of Misso's initiative in the 1840s as well as of Alvares' movement in the 1880s, because both figures self-identified as *Padroadists*, i.e. supporters of the *Padroado* against the transfer of jurisdiction to the Roman Congregation of Propaganda Fide. This assumption will be assessed carefully in the historiography developed both on the *Padroado* questions as well as on the St. Thomas Christians. The chapter furthermore examines related terms such as "*Padroadist*" and "Goan schism", and analyses the content of the *Concordats* signed between Rome and Portugal in 1838, 1856, and 1886. These agreements led to an internal division within the native Catholics across South Asia, irritating in particular Western-educated priests and laymen, who had developed a sense of autonomy and demanded direct communication with the religious and political authorities in Europe. The final part of the chapter examines the concrete *Padroadist* communities centered in Bombay and Goa, overlooked by historians who have written on the *Padroado* in general. In particular, we examine the exemplary case of the *Padroadist* family of Pedro Manuel Lisboa Pinto and his uncle José Camilo Pinto, who were surgeons and intellectuals at the same time, editing several English and Portuguese newspapers in Bombay and Colombo. The chapter ends with an analysis of the failed *Padroadist* delegation to Europe led by Lisboa Pinto in 1887. This important initiative is studied through a conference held by the delegates, whose proceedings were published in Goa in October 1886 and have so far been unknown to historians. Lisboa Pinto's unsuccessful mission marked the end of all hopes of the South Asian *Padroadists* for a solution within a Roman Catholic framework, hence opening up the exploration of alternative ways of being Catholic.

Chapter 3 analyzes the Independent Catholic movement in the context of nineteenth-century ecumenical history. We start with a reconstruction of Vilatte's initial contacts with Alvares, highlighting a common pursuit at redefining Catholicity, shared by both the Belgian Christian migrants in Wisconsin and the *Padroadists* in Ceylon. Our analysis shows that Vilatte's various attempts at forming an alliance with the Episcopal Church in America and the Old Catholic Church in Switzerland, before his final affiliation with the Ceylonese Independent Catholics, were not contingent acts, but rather the outcome of a conscious reflection on possible alternatives to the growing Roman centralisation, to be found in various ecumenical ventures undertaken in the Protestant and Orthodox worlds. The chapter continues with a brief review of three sets of ecumenical relations that can be connected to and compared with the Independent Catholics in Ceylon. In the first place, the Anglican Oxford Movement in its relation with the Roman Catholic Church; secondly, the Anglican Communion and the Oriental Orthodox Church both in Turkey and India; finally, the Old Catholic Church and the Eastern and Oriental Churches. In the end, the chapter offers a preliminary analysis of a little-known Portuguese pamphlet published by Alvares with the title *A supremacia universal* (Colombo, 1898), in which he manifested his own interpretation of Catholicity through a condemnation of the universal supremacy claimed by the Papacy. This pamphlet has to be considered in connection with Alvares' correspondence in that same year 1898 with the Anglican Benedictine monk Fr. Ignatius of Jesus (born Joseph Leycester Lyne, 1837–1908), so as to discern a vision that the Indo-Ceylonese Independent Catholicism beheld towards an extension of its mission to England.

Chapter 4 offers a revisionist history of the *Padroadist* movement in Ceylon from 1840 to 1887, highlighting three regions, namely Colombo, Negombo, and Mannar, the last of which comprised the majority of those who would become Independent Catholics by the end of the nineteenth century. The chapter starts with a discussion of the terms "Dutch Burghers", "Portuguese Burghers", and "Portuguese" in their proper historical contexts and stressing the native connotations that those identities gradually adopted. New archival findings reveal a shift of attitude of Misso from a pro-Roman to a pro-*Padroado* position, after he assumed the function of Portuguese Consul General in Colombo in 1845. Moving beyond Colombo, we can see that in Negombo, the *Padroadist* protest against the Propaganda missionary, represented by Vicar Apostolic Giuseppe Maria Bravi (1813–1860), was involved with protests against a fishing fee charged by the Church. The Negombo case suggests a double horizon in the *Padroado* controversies: on the one hand, at a macro-level, there was certainly a protest against the centralizing attempts promoted by the Papacy, also by means of the Propaganda

Fide authorities; on the other hand, the banner of *Padroado* was also waved in contexts of very local tensions between ethnic and caste groups. Our third case study shows that the unrest in Mannar and Mantote was triggered by requests, for instance by a certain Miguel Filipe, for a Goan missionary leadership defending *Padroado* against the competing claims of the Vicariates of Jaffna and Colombo, who represented the Roman authority on the spot. In the northern regions of Ceylon, the local Christians, both Tamil and Sinhala speakers, were moulded by a distinctively Portuguese form of Catholicism, epitomised by the devotion to the Portuguese Saint Anthony of Padua or Lisbon (1195–1231), as well as to the first Goan Oratorian missionaries to Ceylon, namely Joseph Vaz (1651–1711) and Pedro Ferrão. The former was beatified in 1995 and canonised in 2015, whereas Ferrão's thaumaturgic powers are associated with the shrine of Our Lady of Madhu, established by him and today one of the most important sites of Marian devotion for Sri Lankan Catholics. The chapter ends with a discussion of a very rare pamphlet, presenting a Tamil and English translation of a speech allegedly delivered by the Catholic Bishop Josip Juraj Strossmayer (1815–1905) during the First Vatican Council, in which the prelate criticised the concept of Papal infallibility. We infer that this pamphlet, though published by the Wesleyan Methodist missionaries in Jaffna, was addressed to the Catholics involved in the Goan schism, hence it can be considered a symbolic step in the passage from a jurisdictional to a doctrinal dissent within the Roman Catholic community.

Chapter 5 looks at the Independent Catholic congregation in Hultsdorf, Colombo, centered around the Buona Morte Church. It details its integration into the local community during the first decade of its existence, namely from the establishment of the Mission in 1888 to the death of Lisboa Pinto in 1898. Articles published in the Bombay-based Portuguese newspaper *O Anglo-Lusitano* in 1887 reveal how the *Padroado* congregation in Colombo, led by the trustee Stephen Silva, dispatched various petitions to Portugal and Rome and requested help from Bombay, until Alvares and Lisboa Pinto agreed to revitalise the Colombo congregation by migrating to Ceylon between August and October 1888. Soon after the Independent Catholic Mission was announced in Colombo, Alvares and Soares travelled to Mannar and Mantotte to visit the northern alliances of the Colombo congregation. Those churches had long-term disputes in court with the Catholic Diocese of Jaffna over lands and church properties until a final decision was taken in favour of the Independent Catholics in 1894. Despite pressure and excommunications by the Archbishop of Colombo, the congregation at Our Lady of Good Death continued to grow in number, all the while building relationships with the Colombo middle class, including the Governor of Ceylon, foreign consuls, Muslims merchants, social reformers, printers, authors, medical doctors, and musicians. Their official monthly *The Independent Catholic* addressed readers who pursued careers as civil servants, but also had an impact on consumers, with adverts suggesting to buy American Singer sewing machines that were allegedly superior to German devices. A report published in the daily newspaper *The Ceylon Independent* on Lisboa Pinto's birthday celebration in 1898 sheds light on the lifestyle of the Independent Catholics as reflected in their furniture and musical tastes. The high percentage of Muslim or "Moor" guests invited to the gathering reveals close Christian-Muslim relations in the neighbourhood of Hultsdorf, quite surprising considering today's tense inter-religious context. The last section of the chapter deals with the reasons for the decline of the Independent Catholics in Ceylon at the beginning of the twentieth century.

Chapter 6 contributes to the existing scholarly literature on Bishop Alvares with newly found archival sources from Lisbon, Goa (Panjim and Pilar), Kodaikanal (Shembaganur),

London, and Rome, including new findings on his pamphlets and monographs as well as the newspapers he edited. A record in the archive of the Society of the Missionaries of St. Francis Xavier in Pilar, Goa, reveals the unruly character of the then 37-year-old Alvares, who abandoned the apostolic experiment developed by an association of missionaries in Nova Goa in 1873. Instead, he embarked on a journalistic career, becoming editor of the Diocesan newspaper of Goa, *A Cruz*, until he was suspended by the newly appointed Archbishop António Sebastião Valente (1846–1908) in 1882. This event marked the start of a recurrent and violent persecution of Alvares for the following two decades. We cross-check the pastoral letters issued by the Archbishop with the corresponding articles published in *A Cruz*, in order to fathom the actual reasons for Alvares' suspension, beyond generic accusations of disobedience addressed to the Goan priest. The chapter further analyzes the visits that, by 1886, Alvares had made to three Tamil-speaking cities, namely Trichinopoly, Tanjore, and Nagapattinam, then to Colombo in Ceylon, as well as to the Malayalam-speaking city of Alappuzha (in today's Kerala). In each place, Alvares interviewed local Catholics of both genders and from different social backgrounds on their opinions on the *Padroado* and Propaganda Fide missionaries. He was equally interested in the concrete ways of how they ministered to the local faithful in daily life. As a priest and journalist, Alvares was among the few *Padroado* experts who had studied the question in situ, whereas the majority of authors from the Roman Catholic authorities relied on paperwork and local intermediaries. The chapter ends with a presentation of Alvares and Soares' missions in the Tamil-speaking regions in the 1890s. Thanks to Jesuit records we can show that the Independent Catholic rebellion was often related to caste conflicts. This is another aspect entirely unknown to the existing historiography on Alvares and his movement.

Chapter 7 presents a thematic discussion of Independent Catholicism in Colombo in relation to the early history of the local labour movement and the emergence of a lively press in nineteenth-century Ceylon. We first revisit V. K. Jayawardena's 1972 book *The Rise of the Labor Movement in Ceylon*, in which she attributed the emergence of trade unionism to the newspaper *The Independent Catholic*, the official organ of the Independent Catholic Mission in Colombo. Our analysis is embedded in the development of the printing press in Ceylon from the Dutch era to the "information explosion" during the British era, when religious and commercial institutions engaged to an unprecedented extent in publishing and journalism in all native languages, further sharpening the local religious differentiation and even leading to new conflicts. Similarly, *The Independent Catholic* was an arena of controversial statements, in the first place against the Roman Catholic Church, but also against Protestants. In the following sections, the chapter analyses the origins, publishing processes, and circulation of *The Independent Catholic.* An exploration of the Clifton Press, which printed the journal in 1892–1894, suggests that the Independent Catholics might have had close relations with other social groups, such as the Theosophists, and activists of a temperance movement who particularly targeted *arrack*, the typical South Asian liquor produced from the fermented sap of coconut palm flowers. The last section delves into the global exchanges connected to *The Independent Catholic,* through which the minoritarian Christian movement centered in Hultsdorf gained visibility not only in journals published in different languages in Ceylon, but also in Portuguese, Malayalam, and English newspapers in Goa, Travancore, England, Wales, New York, and Cleveland.

3. Archives and Electronic Sources

The present book is the fruit of research in archives and libraries in five countries, namely in Portugal, the United Kingdom, Vatican City, India, and Sri Lanka.

The *Arquivo Diplomático e a Biblioteca do Ministério dos Negócios Estrangeiros, Lisboa*,[11] or the *Diplomatic Archive and Library of the Ministry of Foreign Affairs of Portugal*, has incorporated the full collection of the *Arquivo histórico da Embaixada de Portugal junto a Santa Sé*, or the *Historical Archive of the Portuguese Embassy to the Holy See*, previously held in Rome. According to a typed descriptive index entitled *Catálogo do Arquivo histórico da Embaixada de Portugal junto a Santa Sé* available in the archive, this large collection has at least 73 *caixas*, or boxes, concerning the Portuguese Church and missions in Europe, Africa, America, and Asia from the 16th to the 20th century. The *caixas* 33, 34 and 35 are under the title of *Diocese do Oriente*, whereas the *caixas* from 36 to 45 concern *Padroado do Oriente*, with subdivisions such as *Sobre a Concordata de 1857* (caixas 36–37), *Ratificação da Concordata* (caixas 37–38), *Revisão da Concordata-Assuntos do Padroado* (caixas 39–40), *Execução da Concordata* (caixas 41–43) and *Acordos d'abril de [19]28 e [19]29* (caixas 44–45). The thousands of pages in this collection have not yet been studied by historians on the *Padroado* controversies due to the limited access they had once on the premises of the Portuguese Embassy to the Holy See in Rome. These documents deserve further research in comparison with other important Vatican collections, particularly in the Archivio della Congregazione per l'Evangelizzazione dei Popoli de Propaganda Fide, which will be dealt with below. I systematically consulted *caixas* 36 to 44, covering various original petitions sent by the *Padroadists* in Colombo, Mannar, and Mantotte in 1884, as well as various reports by the Catholic Bishops in Ceylon and Goa concerning the activities of Alvares.

The *Biblioteca Real da Ajuda* in Lisbon holds an autographic letter by Lisboa Pinto, dated 22 April 1887, one week before he gave a speech at the Sociedade de Geografia de Portugal.[12] The archival location suggests that this letter was likely addressed to the King of Portugal. No document has been found in response to his petition.

The *Biblioteca Nacional de Lisboa* holds copies of several rare newspapers published by Alvares in Goa, such as *A Cruz* (1876), *Times of Goa* (1885), and other Goan newspapers that extensively reported on Alvares and the Independent Catholics in Ceylon, such as the Margao (Goa)-based weekly *O Ultramar* (September 1897 to February 1898, incomplete).

The Library of the Sociedade de Geografia de Lisboa holds several rare pamphlets published by *Padroadist* authors in India, including the prolific anonymous author R. M. P. from Bombay, these initials representing Vicente Salvador Rodrigues, Júlio Menezes, and Pedro Manuel Lisboa Pinto.[13] Lisboa Pinto was elected a member of the Sociedade and his lecture given on 30 April 1887 was included in the official proceedings *Actas das Sessões* of the

---

11 On a description of the archive in relation with the *National Archive of Portugal Torre de Tombo* see J. SERRÃO / M.J. DA SILVA LEAL / M. H. PEREIRA (eds.), "Ministério dos Negócios Estrangeiros", in: *Roteiro de Fontes da História Portuguesa Contemporânea*. Arquivo Nacional da Torre do Tombo. Vol. 2 (Lisboa 1984, 221–257).
12 J.M. FLORES, *Hum curto historia de Ceylan*. Quinhentos anos de relações entre Portugal e o Sri Lanka (Lisboa 2001), 149; F.G. CUNHA LEÃO (ed.), *O Índico na Biblioteca da Ajuda*. Catálogo dos manuscritos relativos a Moçambique, Pérsia, India, Malaca, Molucas e Timor (Lisboa 1998), 330.
13 A. M. DA COSTA, *Dicionário de literatura goesa*. Vol. 3 (Macau 1998), 105.

Sociedade in the same year, before being published as a *separata* by Typographia do Jornal do Commercio [sic] in Lisbon.[14]

The *Lambeth Palace Library* is the official library of the Archbishop of Canterbury, and the principal archive of the Church of England. It holds rich documents on the relations between the Church Mission Society and the Syrian Orthodox Church in Kottayam. What concerns our research most are those records on the controversies over the alleged proselytism of the Syrian Church, especially on Vilatte, who would later be classified by Anglican theologians as an *Episcopus vagans* of modern times, namely, one of those "wandering bishops" who "have been consecrated bishop in an irregular or clandestine manner or who, having been regularly consecrated, have been excommunicated by the Church that consecrated them and are in communion with no recognized see".[15] Alvares had been unknowingly involved in debates on the authenticity of Vilatte's episcopal consecration, as compiled in the *Documents Proving the Validity of The Episcopal consecration of J. Renatus Archbishop Vilatte* (London, 1901), before concerns over *episcopi vagantes* were raised up in the Lambeth Conferences in 1920 and again in 1958.[16] Alvares also aroused the attention of the Anglicans due to his correspondence with the Anglican Benedictine monk Fr. Ignatius, published in the Welsh newspaper *Western Mail*. These original printed pamphlets, manuscripts, and newspaper clippings are conserved in collections named after two Archbishops of Canterbury, namely Frederick Temple (in office 1896–1902) and Randall Thomas Davidson (in office 1903–1928).[17]

The Archivio della Congregazione per l'Evangelizzazione dei Popoli de Propaganda Fide is particularly relevant to our research because of the documents in the collection *Scritture riferite nei Congressi, Indie Orientali* (abbr. SC Indie Orientali), with reference to the years between 1887 and 1890 (Vols. 32–35), in which dozens of letters from the Archbishops of Colombo and the Apostolic Delegates reported on the Goan schismatics in Ceylon and India.[18] Some of these documents concerning Colombo, Mannar, and Negombo have already been published in an English translation in Vito Perniola's *The Catholic Church in Sri Lanka: The British Period* in volumes VII to VIII, and XII, dated from 1884 to 1899.

The *Archivio storico della Congregazione per le Chiese Orientali*, is the repository of collections entitled *Soriani del Malabar*, comprising reports and letters by the Apostolic Delegate of the East Władysław Michał Zaleski (in office 1887–1916) which originally belonged to the Archives of Propaganda Fide.[19] References to the Independent Catholics in Ceylon are rare in comparison with those concerning the Syrian Churches in Malabar. Yet an English-Syriac certificate of a priestly ordination owned by the Goan priest at Colombo, the Vicar Joseph Xavier Botelho, is of particular significance, for it represents the Syriac orientation

---

14 The owner of *Jornal do Commercio* was Luís de Almeida e Albuquerque (1819–1906), former mayor of Lisbon in 1876-1877. See a footnote on Albuquerque in M.M. AUGELLO / M.E.L. GUIDI, *The Economic Reader*. Textbooks, Manuals and the Dissemination of the Economic Sciences during the 19th and Early 20th Centuries (Abingdon 2012), 211.
15 F.L. CROSS / E.A. LIVINGSTONE (eds.), *The Oxford Dictionary of the Christian Church* (Oxford 2009), 555.
16 H.R.T. BRANDRETH, *Episcopi Vagantes and the Anglican Church*, 2nd ed. (London 1961), 5.
17 An online catalogue of manuscripts in the Lambeth Palace Library is available through the *Database of Manuscripts and Archives*, Church of England Record Centre, (https://archives.lambethpalacelibrary.org.uk/CalmView/advanced.aspx?src=CalmView.Catalog, last accessed on 28 December 2021).
18 N. KOWALSKY / J. METZLER (eds.), *Inventory of the Historical Archives of the Congregation for the Evangelization of Peoples or "De Propaganda Fide"* (Rome 1988).
19 On an introduction to the archive see A. REBERNIK / G. RIGOTTI / M. VAN PARYS, O.S.B. (eds.), *Fede e martirio. Le chiese orientali cattoliche nell'Europa del Novecento. Atti del Convegno di storia ecclesiastica contemporanea, Città del Vaticano, 22–24 ottobre 1998* (Città del Vaticano 2003).

of the Independent Catholics even though the Latin language and the Latin rite were kept for liturgy and prayers.

The British Library keeps several publications authored by Alvares and Lisboa Pinto, in both Portuguese and English, more copies of which are difficult to find even in Indian and Sri Lankan archives. The Library also has miscellaneous papers on Goa and Ceylon, often bound under topics such as "Roman Catholic controversies", as described by early librarians. In particular, there are several anonymous publications against the Independent Catholics in Ceylon, providing information beyond the official documents produced by the Mission.

The Cambridge University Library has a photocopy of a printed letter by the Independent Catholic Mission of Ceylon, addressed "To His Holiness Ignatius A. Messias, Patriarch of Antioch and the East", dated in Colombo, 10 November 1900. This photocopy was presented to Cambridge in 1980 by the Metropolitan of Glastonbury, who owned the original letter. Another original letter is conserved at the Archives of the Monastery of Mor Hananyo (Dayro d-Mor Hananyo in Syriac, Daryülzafaran Manastırı in Turkish), which might have more documents from Ceylon (but which could not be consulted for the present study).

The Xavier Center of Historical Research belongs to the Goa Jesuit Province of the Society of Jesus, and is located in Alto Porvorim, Goa.[20] It holds an extensive collection of Goan and Bombay newspapers, such as *O Ultramar*, *O Anglo-Lusitano*, *The Examiner*, and pamphlets donated by private owners including the influential politician, legal scholar, and bibliophile José António Ismael Gracias (1857–1919),[21] and a leading Catholic Brahman family in Margao, the da Costas, founders of *O Ultramar*. A volume binding 17 works on the *Padroado* controversies entitled *17 opúsculos sobre Padroado*, published in Bombay, Colombo, and Lisbon from 1844 to 1888 respectively, is of particular importance. Some of them were not easy to retrieve in their original publication places, for instance three letters by José Camilo Pinto published in Bombay in 1886. In the Center there are other precious items related to Alvares' activities in 1886, for example records of two speeches. In August of that year he gave a lecture (*Prelecção*) at the town hall of the municipal council (*paços da Câmara municipal das Ilhas*) of Ilhas de Goa (today's Tiswadi) on the current political situation. Later in October he gave a talk at a meeting (*comicio*) of the Delegation of the *Padroado* in the East in Panjim, during which Lisboa Pinto's mission to Europe in 1887 was decided. Surprisingly, the proceedings of the first lecture carry a three-page document folded into the middle of the pages. It is a printed report given by Alvares, dated in Goa in 1908, to the Chancellor José Maria de Sousa Horta e Costa (1858–1927), the Governor General of the State of Portuguese India in 1907–1910. Attached to the report was a list of 32 cholera patients across Goa whom Alvares had treated successfully during the year 1907. All three documents have previously been unknown to historians and will be analysed for the first time in this book.

The Goa State Central Library holds the most important printed sources on nineteenth-century Goan history. The journals used for the present book include *O Brado indiano* (1894–1895), *A Cruz* (1879–1882), *A Verdade* (1882–1885), *Oriente* (1929), and *O Boletim official* (1880–1910), in addition to a sizeable number of treatises on the *Padroado* controversies published in the nineteenth and twentieth centuries.

---

20 See a brief introduction in T.R. DE SOUZA, "Xavier Centre of Historical Research", in: B. M. GUPTA (ed.), *Handbook of Libraries, Archives & Information Centres in India*. Humanities Information Systems and Centres. Vol. 9, Part 2 (Delhi 1985), 239–242.

21 Ismael Gracias was the director of the *Biblioteca Pública de Nova-Goa* in 1892–1895. S.A. LOBO, *O Desassossego goês. Cultura e política em Goa do liberalismo ao acto colonial*, PhD Thesis (Lisboa 2013), 94.

In the Church Archive of Goa, previously known as the *Arquivo da Cúria Patriarcal de Goa*[22], the volumes entitled *Edicts* (*Portarias*), collected during the time of Archbishop of Goa António Sebastião Valente from 1882–1895, are of particular importance. They contain copies of the edicts and pastoral letters issued by the Archbishop. They also encompass letters on Alvares' suspension in 1882 with detailed explanations. In addition to these official letters, there is also a collection named *Separate papers* (*Papéis avulsos*) that contains original letters sent from parishes in Goa giving information on Alvares' itineraries with astonishing detail.

Surprisingly, my two months research in the *Directorate of Archives and Archaeology of Goa*, better known as *Historical Archives of Goa* yielded only scarce findings on Alvares in the collection of *Monções do Reino,* the state papers that form the bulk of the archive. Among the limited findings is a reply from the Secretariat of the State of Marine and Overseas Affairs in Lisbon from 1882, annulling the suspension that Valente had issued on the Diocesan journal *A Cruz* and its editor Alvares. It was also possible to find some references to his fellow Portuguese priest Avelino da Cunha, who visited Goa from Ceylon in 1890, without being charged by Goan authorities for jurisdictional transgression.

In the Jesuit Archives of Madurai Province, located in Shembaganur (near Kodaikanal), in the state of Tamil Nadu, I used *La mission du Maduré: historique de ses pangous* (Trichinopoly, 1914) by the French Jesuit and historian Léon Besse (1853–?), in which Alvares and Soares's missionary work was recorded as a transgression to the Jesuit jurisdiction. Previous Jesuit scholars catalogued specific documentations, of which two are essential for my research, namely a descriptive list of the "Diary of the Madurai Mission" prepared by Besse, and "Historical notes on the Tinnevelly District" composed by Adrian Caussanel (1850–1930). Several parish diaries dated to between 1895 and 1897 shed light on Soares' active missions in various villages such as Periyathalai in Tuticorin, and Kalugumalai in Thoothukudi.

In the National Archives of Sri Lanka, I consulted mainly two journals, namely the monthly *The Independent Catholic* (1892–1896, incomplete), and the daily *The Ceylon Independent* (1898). Both are essential sources for reconstructing the history of the Colombo Independent Catholics in particular during the years 1892 to 1898.

There are other archival sources that have not been explored at all, or only in a limited way, due to restricted access and the time limitations of this project. This monograph uses only few documents from the *Archivio della Congregazione per la Dottrina della Fede* in Rome, previously known as the Roman Inquisition, in which official papers on excommunications of the Goan "schismatic" priests could be kept. Two other religious archives in Rome, namely the Archives of the Sylvestrine General Curia and the Archives of the General Curia of the Oblates of Mary Immaculate, could yield additional information. Both religious orders were active in the Diocese of Jaffna and the Archdiocese of Colombo respectively since the nineteenth century. According to the Italian Sylvestrian monk and historian Beda Barcatta, the archives of Montefano, near Fabriano in Italy, have a manuscript entitled *History of the Independent Catholicism in Ceylon* by a certain Ph. Caspersz. Another copy of the same document is likely deposited at the Archives of Montefano, Ampitiya, near Kandy in Sri Lanka. According to Barcatta, the *History* is also related to certain documents held in the collection *General Correspondence*, at the Archives of the Diocese of Kandy, Sri Lanka.[23] It

---

22   M.L. ABRANTES, *Arquivo da Cúria Patriarcal de Goa* (Goa 1993).
23   B. BARCATTA, *A History of the Southern Vicariate of Colombo.* Vol. 1, 497, notes 52 & 60.

was not possible to access a copy of this document. Other important archives and collections include the Archives of Archbishop's House in Colombo, Archives of the Jaffna Bishop's House, Maharashtra State Archives in Mumbai, Archives and Historical Research Department of Tamil Nadu, and Catholic parish records in the Diocese of Mangalore, in addition to private collections owned by previous Independent Catholic families and today's Malankara Orthodox families in Kerala. Sources in those repositories may be useful for further research in this field.

I used two databases for consulting historical English newspapers:
- *The Guardian* Archive (https://theguardian.newspapers.com)
- The British Newspaper Archive (https://www.britishnewspaperarchive.co.uk)

I have browsed *The Tablet* (1890–1906), *Western Mail* (1893–1897), *The Guardian* (1890–1908), *The Homeward Mail* (1906), *The Irish news and Belfast morning News* (1907), and *The Northern Whig* (1903), in which references to the Independent Catholics in Ceylon have been found.

I also made use of several digital collections available online for free, as well as of the Digital Humanities projects at the British Library containing manuscripts and publications on and from Goa and Jaffna, including:
- The *Internet Archive* (https://archive.org)
- The Digital Repository @ HKUL owned by The University of Hongkong Libraries (https://digitalrepository.lib.hku.hk)
- "Archival records from Creating a digital archive of Indian Christian manuscripts", the Endangered Archive Project, at *The British Library* (https://eap.bl.uk/project/EAP636)
- "Preservation of the manuscripts of the Jaffna Bishop's House (1850-1930)", the Endangered Archive Project, at *The British Library* (https://eap.bl.uk/project/EAP700)
- "Anti-colonialism and religious independence in the Philippines around 1900: Preserving the archival records of the early history of the Iglesia Filipina Independiente", an Endangered Archive Project at *The British Library* (https://doi.org/10.15130/EAP855)

Chapter 1:
Catholicism and European Colonialism in Ceylon

In November 1900 the Independent Catholic Mission in Colombo sent a petition to the Patriarch of Antioch and head of the Syriac Orthodox Church Ignatius Abded Mshiho II (1895–1903) with a review of the development of the Church across Ceylon and India in the last 13 years. The report was written in a poignant tone. When the Independent Catholics joined the Syriac communion under the Antiochian jurisdiction in 1888, they counted 500 members residing in Colombo, 3000 in Mannar, and 500 in Kallianpur (who then moved to nearby Brahmavar, in the Udupi district), taken care of by a handful of priests. A particular problem that the church faced consisted in the fact that the two Ceylonese missions were then in shortage of ministers who could celebrate sacraments according to the Latin liturgy. The clergymen who worked there had often neglected their mission by constantly travelling to India, or had even abandoned their Independent Catholics to join the Chaldean Church. Not specified in the petition but as revealed in other sources, the Vicar Luis Mariano Soares (1858–1903), once in charge of the Tamil speaking missions in Mannar and then in Dindigul, left to join the Syro-Chaldean Church around 1898. After his schism, a Sinhala man named W. M. Talayaratna was ordained in Colombo and sent to the Mannar mission. Hence the Independent Catholics in Ceylon requested that Kottayam and Mardin supply additional priests.[1]

The original copy of the printed letter of November 1900 is conserved in the Archives of the Monastery of Mor Hananyo (Dayro d-Mor Hananyo in Syriac, Daryülzafaran Manastırı in Turkish), close to the city of Mardin, in southern Turkey.[2] It represents a very rare self-statement of the Independent Catholics, reporting their general size, albeit with some approximation. The importance of the document lies in the contrast to other estimates of size, considering that the Roman Catholic Bishops in Ceylon tended to depict the "Goan schismatics" – this was the derogatory name they were called – by using a very diminutive figure of just 12–17 families,[3] in order to relieve the Congregation of Propaganda Fide from grief concerns about the tensions and dissent among the Christians in Ceylon. For the same reason, we may also question whether the Independent Catholics inflated their numbers. A large community would definitely impress the Antiochian Patriarch and convince him of the urgency of sending priests to the Ceylon mission. At any rate, if we can give some credit to the figures boasted by the petitioners, or at least to the relative proportions of the three missions within the island, it is quite striking to notice that the literature on the Independent Catholics in South Asia has

---

1   "To His Holiness Ignatius A. Messias, Patriarch of Antioch and the East", dated in Colombo, November 10, 1900. 3 pages. A photocopy of this letter was presented by the Metropolitan of Glastonbury to the Cambridge University Library in 1980, where I accessed it.
2   W. TAYLOR, *Narratives of Identity*. The Syrian Orthodox Church and the Church of England 1895–1914 (Newcastle upon Tyne 2013), 134.
3   Theophilus Andrew Melizan to Propaganda Fide, dated in Colombo, 16 November 1894, in: V. PERNIOLA, *The Catholic Church in Sri Lanka*. The British Period. Vol. 8: 1887–1899. The Archdiocese of Colombo (Dehiwala 2004), 484.

been overwhelmingly focused on the Colombo and Kallianpur missions, leaving the North Ceylon mission – i.e. three quarters of the entire Church – as *terra incognita*. Who were those Mannarites? Why and how did they become Catholics and then Independent Catholics? In order to generalise these questions and gain a chronological understanding of Independent Catholicism as first and foremost a local movement, it is necessary to review the Catholic Church history in Ceylon, especially surrounding Colombo and Mannar, from the first converts in the sixteenth century until the Independent Catholic Mission emerged in the late nineteenth century.

This chapter examines the history of Catholicism in Ceylon in a chronological sequence marked by three European interventions, namely Portuguese (1506–1658), Dutch (1658–1796) and British (1796–1948) colonialism, in various local polities. During these four and a half centuries, Roman Catholicism went through a cyclical fluctuation in terms of ecclesiastical development. The Catholic faith was first introduced to Ceylon by European missionaries under the military protection of the Portuguese crown. Conversions gradually extended to the hinterlands where the local kings practiced Buddhism or Hinduism as their official religions. The extension of the Catholic missionary work was interrupted when the Dutch East India Company (*Vereenigde Oostindische Compagnie*, VOC) overtook the Portuguese power in the mid-seventeenth century. Catholic missions withdrew and their adherents were partially converted to the Calvinist Church. However, the Dutch ban on the Catholic Church was not thoroughly implemented. A new religious body according to the model of the Congregation of Oratory of Saint Philip Neri established by Brahman secular priests arrived clandestinely from Goa, resuming ministry among the underground Catholic Ceylonese as well as the Catholic soldiers serving in the Dutch army. Due to their presence, a total of 343 churches and chapels were extant when the British government replaced Dutch colonial rule in 1796 and granted freedom of conscience and worship to the Roman Catholic Church.[4]

Despite religious toleration, the Catholic Church in British Ceylon, now entirely ministered by Goan priests, faced unprecedented turmoil from within, much more severe than the challenges deriving from inter-religious tensions. A strife took place between a form of Catholic patriotism emerging in the Eurasian (Ceylon-European and Indo-Portuguese) communities, and a European praxis inherited from the early modern conventions of Church-State relations. The latter was at the origin of the *Padroado* controversies, affecting all Catholic regions that had once belonged to the Portuguese royal patronage and now fell under British colonial administration. In Ceylon in particular, the restoration of a legal status to the Catholic Church at the threshold of the British rule required a readjustment of the Catholic jurisdiction to the political status quo. On the one hand, the island had been a British "crown colony" since 1815, on the other hand the Catholic ecclesiastical authorities were still bestowed on the Portuguese crown despite its political absence from the island. In reaction to the *Concordats* signed between Portugal and the Holy See, there emerged a climate of discord among the Catholics in South Asia. The Indian and Ceylonese clergymen and laymen were offended by the reduced Portuguese jurisdiction and the strengthened direct Roman control. Those pro-*Padroado* activists were united by a Portuguese patriotism that brought together several Indo-Portuguese and Sri Lankan Eurasian groups (Dutch Burghers, Paravas, Karāvas) of different professions and social classes. They pointed at the corruption in the

---

4   V. PERNIOLA, *The Catholic Church in Sri Lanka*: The British Period. Vol. 1: 1795–1844. The Colombo Vicariate (Dehiwala 1992), 10, note 2: "Report of the mission of Ceylon", dated in Goa 16 December 1797.

Roman bureaucracy and distrusted the other European (Italian, French, and German speaking) missionaries, who were now sent by Rome to replace the Goan missionaries in Ceylon. The Independent Catholics were among the most controversial pro-*Padroado* activists for their radical refusal of Papal authority.

The historical context of the Independent Catholic movement is the main concern of this chapter. In the following four sections we will sketch the contours of the Catholic presence in Ceylon from 1500 to 1900, the timeframe in which the three colonial systems are to be examined in relation to Catholic developments. As an exercise of socially grounded Church history, here we try to clarify social status, castes, and races of both the missionaries and the indigenous Christians. Geographically we prioritise Colombo, Negombo, and the northern regions of Jaffna and Mannar – strongholds of the pro-*Padroado* movement and the Independent Catholic movement – so as to delve into the local contexts to map ethnic and caste tensions.

1. Ceylon at 1500

1.1. Geography and Polities

Sri Lanka or (before 1972) Ceylon, a large teardrop-shaped island, is located in the northern tropical area, separated by the narrow Palk strait from the Indian subcontinent. The island receives rain every year by two monsoons, the Southwestern between April and June and the Northeastern between mid-October to mid-February. The former is abundant and determines a Wet Zone in the western and southern regions of the island, whereas the relative scarcity of the latter provokes a nine-month long drought in the northern and eastern parts.[5] The seasonal rhythm of the monsoons called for the creation of irrigation channels at least since the first century BC.[6] Some time before, around the third century BC, Theravada Buddhism was introduced to Sri Lanka, being promoted by the kings of Anurādhapura, a city in the Dry Zone. In the following centuries the island was frequently conquered by Pandyan and Chola rulers coming from the Tamil country, so that the Sinhala kings were eventually driven further into the southwestern Wet Zone.[7] The division of dry and wet zones was particularly influential in the formation of a culture of irrigation, through which water scarcity was effectively tackled. While early polities and religious centers in the island emerged in the Dry zone, thanks to the advanced water-management and irrigation systems, the difference in rainfall later became a less influential factor in the history of the island, while factors such as access to overseas trade gained in importance. Due to the invasions from South India, in addition to malaria and natural disasters, the Sinhalese kingdoms that flourished in the Dry

---

5   V. PERNIOLA, *The Catholic Church. The British Period.* Vol. 1: 1795–1844. The Colombo Vicariate (Dehiwala, Sri Lanka 1992), 10, note 2: "Report of the mission of Ceylon", dated in Goa on 16 December 1797.
6   R.A.L.H. GUNAWARDANA, "Irrigation and Hydraulic Society in Early Medieval Ceylon", (*Past & Present* 53, 1971, 3–27).
7   According to Rhoads Murphey, until the thirteenth century the Sinhala kingdoms preferred the Dry Zone despite its difficulties. See his article "The Ruin of Ancient Ceylon" (*The Journal of Asian Studies* 16/2, February 1957), 182–183. A collection of studies on the end of the Rājarata kingdom is published in K. INTIRAPĀLĀ (ed.), *The Collapse of the Rajarata Civilization in Ceylon and the Drift to the South-West.* A Symposium (Peradeniya 1971).

Zone declined and were unable to maintain their agricultural irrigation schemes.[8] Changes in economic structures favoured the seaborne trade, leading to an increasing reliance on several trading groups, first dominated by the Arab and then the European merchants.

By 1500 Ceylon was fragmented into three strong political units and several smaller principalities. The kingdom of Kōṭṭe was the largest and most powerful political entity thanks to the development that occurred under the reign of Parākramabāhu VI (1412–1467). This polity could count on a flourishing agriculture, and the royal treasure depended primarily on land revenue rather than maritime trade.[9] The Kingdom of Kandy (Kaṇḍi) in the central area of the island was then a weak power engulfed by several strong rivals, such as the Kingdom of Gampola. The northern part of the island was occupied by the Kingdom of Jaffna under the Hindu dynasty of the Āryacakravarti since the 13th century.[10] However, during the 15th century there was a gradual decline of the Āryacakravartis, in the light of the rise of the Vijayanagara Empire in South India and the consolidation of Kōṭṭe. Standing between this latter royal city and Jaffna were the Tamil Vaṇṇi chieftaincies.[11] External trade, handled mainly by Muslim merchants, remained "much less productive than the traditional sources of revenue such as land taxes and revenue from grain".[12] Nonetheless, by the fourteenth century, Muslim traders gained influence in the royal court and in the local economy, as the Sinhalese monarchs sought new sources of revenue.[13] For instance, Malayālam-speaking Muslims (known as Māppiḷas) and Tamil Muslims "were virtually enjoying a monopoly of the Indo-Sri Lanka trade until the arrival of the Portuguese".[14] These so-called "moors of the land" (*mouros da terra*, in Portuguese) or Ceylon moors, including the powerful Muslim merchants of Gujarat, were seen as formidable rivals by the Europeans as soon as they set foot in South Asia. Commercial rivalry, as much as religious differences (Roman Catholics vs. Muslims), set apart the old and the new actors in the Indian Ocean trade.

1.2. Sinhalese and Tamil Languages

By the beginning of the sixteenth century, Sri Lanka was ruled by people who spoke two Indic languages, namely Sinhala and Tamil. A small community of hunter-gatherers called *väddās* might have been the aboriginal people who first settled on the island.[15] The Lankan chronicles attest to an early Aryan conquest under the leadership of a warrior nobility, giving origin to the Sinhala community. Modern historians, however, stress economic factors – the

---

8 N. ATTYGALLE et al. (eds.), *History of Ceylon*. Vol. I: From the Earliest Times to 1505, Part II: From the Coḷa conquest in 1017 to the arrival of the Portuguese in 1505 (Colombo 1960), 713–725.
9 K.M. DE SILVA, *A History of Sri Lanka* (London 1981), 97; A. SCHRIKKER, *Dutch and British Colonial Intervention in Sri Lanka, 1780–1815. Expansion and Reform* (Leiden 2007), 16; G.P.V. SOMARATNA, *The Political History of the Kingdom of Kotte, 1400–1521* (Colombo ²2016).
10 S. PATHMANATHAN, *The Kingdom of Jaffna* (Colombo 1978).
11 On the Vanni chieftaincies see D.G.B. DE SILVA, "Hugh Nevill Memorial Lecture – II: New Light on Vanniyās and their Chieftancies based on Folk Historical Tradition as found in Palm-Leaf Mss. in the Hugh Nevill Collection" (*Journal of the Royal Asiatic Society of Sri Lanka* 41, 1996, 153–204); K. INTIRAPĀLĀ, "The Origin of the Tamil Vanni Chieftaincies of Ceylon" (*Journal of Humanities* 1/2, July 1970, 111–140). On the Gampola Kingdoms see DE SILVA, *A History of Sri Lanka*, 88.
12 DE SILVA, *A History of Sri Lanka*, 90.
13 A. BANDARAGE, *Colonialism in Sri Lanka*. The Political Economy of the Kandyan Highlands, 1833–1886 (Berlin 1983), 53.
14 M.A.M. SHUKRI (ed.), *Muslims of Sri Lanka*. Avenues to Antiquity (Beruwala 1986), 123.
15 P. PEEBLES, *The History of Sri Lanka* (Westport 2006), 7.

richness of gems in Ceylon for instance – as a luring attraction for the Indian traders.[16] From a social-linguistic point of view, Sinhala is part of the Modern Indo-Aryan family of languages, related to Hindi, Marathi, and Bengali spoken on the subcontinent. Hypotheses hold that the Sinhala people came originally either from the north-eastern or the north-western parts of India.[17] Despite its wide South Asian connections, Sinhala developed exclusively in Ceylon. In contrast to Sinhala, Tamil belongs to the Dravidian language family and is not a language exclusive to Sri Lanka, actually having its main diffusion in the Tamil areas on the south-eastern edge of the Indian subcontinent. Suppositions have been made on the possible identification of the *nāgas* mentioned in prehistoric Ceylon, with an early Tamil-speaking population.[18] The Pali chronicles Mahāvaṃsa (written in the 6th century AD) and Cūḷavaṃsa (a sequel to the Mahāvaṃsa up to the 19th century) paid great attention to the Tamil communities that gave origin to the Anuradhapura Kingdom (4 BC–11 AD). The geographical proximity between Jaffna, the Mannar archipelago, and the Coromandel Coast explains why the northern point of the island was so prone to invasions. Two Tamil empires – Coḷa and Pāṇḍya – turned Ceylon into a province of theirs. Following a longue durée line, the British encroachment in Ceylon started by extending the Madras Presidency to this northern tip of the country. Significant Tamil migrations took place throughout history and gave rise to multiple divisions among the Tamil speakers, according to location, caste, religion, and social status.[19] By 1500 Tamils were the majority in the Kingdom of Jaffna and the chieftaincies of Vanni. As Pali and Sinhala were adopted by Sri Lankan Buddhists, Tamil became associated with Hinduism and Islam. Thanks to Muslim Tamil merchants, the Kingdom of Jaffna was well connected in the seaborne trade, up to Malabar, the Coromandel Coast of India, and beyond.[20] The north/Tamil and southwest/Sinhala division of Ceylon was noticed by the first Portuguese visitors in the early sixteenth century. In fact, these ethno-geographical contrasts of Ceylon also left their mark on the spread of Christianity in the following centuries.

1.3. Sinhalese Buddhism

As Richard Gombrich has written about Sri Lanka, "Theravāda Buddhism has dominated the religious and cultural life of the country throughout its recorded history".[21] In fact, during the first thousand years of the Common Era, Buddhist institutions on the island played a central role in keeping the tradition alive, making the Sinhalese identity enduringly entangled with that religion.[22] In particular in the eleventh and twelfth centuries, Sri Lanka was also part of larger Buddhist networks in the Bay of Bengal, with missions being sent for example to Bodhgaya by King Vijayabahu I (1039–1110) and connections established with Burma.[23]

---

16   DE SILVA, *A History of Sri Lanka*, 6–8.
17   For a concise history of the language see D. CHANDRALAL, *Sinhala* (Amsterdam 2010), 1–6.
18   S. PATHMANATHAN, *The Kingdom of Jaffna*. Part 1: Circa A.D. 1250–1450 (Colombo 1978), 14.
19   For a detailed introduction into the role of Tamils in the early history of Sri Lanka see M.D. RAGHAVAN, *Tamil Culture in Ceylon*. A General Introduction (Colombo 1971), 1–39.
20   A review of the historical contacts between the Malayalam speakers of various castes with Sinhalese is found in K.C. SANKARANARAYANAN, *The Keralites and the Sinhalese* (Madras 1994).
21   R.F. GOMBRICH, *Theravāda Buddhism*. A Social History from Ancient Benares to Modern Colombo (London ²2006), 138.
22   GOMBRICH, *Theravāda Buddhism*, 138.
23   T. FRASCH, "A Buddhist Network in the Bay of Bengal. Relations Between Bodhgaya, Burma and Sri Lanka, c. 300–1300", in: C. GUILOT et al. (eds.), *From the Mediterranean to the China Sea*. Miscellaneous Notes (Wiesbaden 1998, 69–92), 73–74, 83–91.

Nevertheless, throughout the centuries, Buddhism and its central institution, the Sangha, the community of monks, sometimes prospered and sometimes experienced times of decline.[24] With the downfall of the Sinhalese Polonnaruva kingdom (1055–1212) at the beginning of the 13th century, Buddhism faced one of a number of historical crises. A lack of discipline within the Sangha was believed to be responsible for the loss of royal patronage and endorsement, as well as loosened ritual celebrations and even the decrepitude of shrines.[25] Equally problematic were numerous schisms across the centuries, furthered by Mahayanist, Tantric, or Hindu external influences.[26] By the sixteenth century, due to the Christian inroads and various waves of Hindu migrations, Buddhism was under pressure, culminating in a loss of the "indigenous ordination tradition", which was only reestablished in the 18th century through a mission from Thailand.[27] This new Siam-derived monastic order (*Siyam Nikaya*) traces its lineage to the monk Upali, the leader of that mission in 1753.[28] At the same time, Sinhalese popular religion was always influenced by Hindu traditions, so that it combined Buddhist values and cosmology with a veneration of pan-Hindu deities with a "strong South Indian coloration".[29] The Sinhalese society at the time, almost wholly rural and agricultural "consisted of a rice-growing peasantry, various craftsmen (metal-workers, potters, etc.), a few service personnel (washermen, load-carriers, etc.) … and the Sangha".[30] In such a society, the village temple with the resident monk(s) served as the center of the religious life, functioning both as ritual specialists and as central educators as well as preservers of the intellectual tradition.[31] When the Portuguese and the first Catholic missionaries reached Ceylon in the sixteenth century, the monks, next to the local sovereigns, were unavoidable counterparts to any temporal and spiritual expansion.

1.4. Hinduism

In today's Sri Lanka, the religious center that arguably "attracts the most indigenous visitors and is the greatest focus of interest and emotion is Kataragama".[32] This shrine in the southeast corner of the island is frequented by Buddhists but also by affiliates of all other religious traditions. As a "center of Hindu-Buddhist syncretism", it is considered by Gombrich and G. Obeyesekere "a great melting pot of Sri Lanka society".[33] The site points to the importance of Hindu influences on the religious landscape of the island, with a complex that houses the main shrine of Kataragama Deviyo (also called Skanda in the Sanskrit Puranas, or Murugan by the Tamil people), as well as shrines for Ganesha, Vishnu, and the Buddha among others.[34] John C. Holt has argued that "generations of immigrants and mercenaries representing a

---

24 GOMBRICH, *Theravāda Buddhism*, 139.
25 ATTYGALLE et al., *History of Ceylon*, 745.
26 K. MALALGODA, *Buddhism in Sinhalese Society, 1750–1900*. A Study of Religious Revival and Change (Berkeley 1976), 27.
27 GOMBRICH, *Theravāda Buddhism*, 139.
28 MALALGODA, *Buddhism in Sinhalese Society*, 144.
29 GOMBRICH, *Theravāda Buddhism*, 144.
30 GOMBRICH, *Theravāda Buddhism*, 143.
31 GOMBRICH, *Theravāda Buddhism*, 143, 146–147.
32 R.F. GOMBRICH / G. OBEYESEKERE, *Buddhism Transformed*. Religious Change in Sri Lanka (Princeton 1988), 163. On a similar and important plural site see R. BASTIN, *The Domain of Constant Excess*. Plural Worship at the Munnesvaram Temples in Sri Lanka (New York 2002).
33 GOMBRICH, *Buddhism Transformed*, 163, 168.
34 GOMBRICH, *Buddhism Transformed*, 165.

plethora of castes from various regions of South India have brought [...] [to Sri Lanka] a kaleidoscope of religious myths and rites reflective of Hindu worldviews contemporary in the locales of their origins".[35] The most important of these are the four guardian deities of Sinhaladvīpa (i.e. the Sri Lanka island) in the kingdom of Kandy, combining the three Hindu deities – Kataragama Deviyo, Pattini, and Viṣṇu – with Natha Deviyo, deriving from Avalokiteśvara in Mahayana Buddhism. Historical traces of these complex relationships can be found in many of the important Sri Lankan textual sources. In the *Mahāvaṃsa* and *Cūḷavaṃsa*, the epic chronicles of Sri Lankan history, King Parakramabahu I (1153–1186), widely regarded as a great patron of Theravada Buddhism, is described also as a patronizer of Hindu temples, making him a "master patron of both Buddhist and Hindu establishments, the supreme imperial overlord of all communities".[36] Between the twelfth and the sixteenth century, various parts of Hindu tradition, in particular the cult of Vishnu, became part of Sinhala Buddhist culture and of local conceptions of kingship. After the end of the Polonnaruva era in the thirteenth century,[37] this influence even increased, going beyond the royal courts, and can be detected "in some exemplary compositions of classical Sinhala literature, in the design and ornamentation of architecture, and in the popular cultic practices of Buddhist monasticism".[38] One can therefore identify a variety of patterns, rituals, and aspects of Hindu worship that "have been woven into the fabric of this Buddhist religious culture".[39] According to Holt, this points to "a deeply wrought ambivalence to the Hindu presence throughout Sinhala history".[40] The "Hindu permeation of Sinhala culture" was particularly discernible in the sixteenth century, when, during the reign of Bhuvanekabahu VII (1521–1551), Brahman pundits were serving the king, and one such advisor was even sent as an ambassador to Portugal.[41] When Parakramabahu VI died in 1467, the Sangha's influence on the Kotte royalty was waning, so that by 1500 and at the time of the Portuguese arrival, "the upper strata of Sinhalese society were more or less becoming Hinduized".[42] At the same time, at various times in history, members of the Sangha objected to such worship of the Gods, as for example in the fifteenth-century *Budugunalamkaraya*, "perhaps the wittiest protest of all", in which the eminent monk Vidagama Maitreya decried the uselessness of Brahmanical ritual and the inferiority of these Hindu Gods.[43]

1.5. Islam

By 1500 the adherents to Islam in Sri Lanka were mainly descendants from early migrations from the Arab world and from southern India. The island's relation with the Arab world dates back to at least the ninth century, when Ibn Khurradadhbih mentioned Sri Lanka as "Sarandib" in his book *Kitāb al-Masālik wa-l-mamālik* ("Book of Routes and Kingdoms")

---

35 J.C. HOLT, "Hindu Influences on Medieval Sri Lankan Buddhist Culture", in: M. DEEGALLE (ed.), *Buddhism, Conflict and Violence in Modern Sri Lanka* (London 2006, 38–66), 39.
36 J.C. HOLT, *The Buddhist Vishnu*. Religious Transformation, Politics, and Culture (New York 2004), 37–39.
37 On Hindu temples at Polonnaruva see also S.A. MEEGAMA, "South Indian or Sri Lankan? The Hindu Temples of Polonnaruva, Sri Lanka" (*Artibus Asiae* 70/1, 2010, 25–45).
38 HOLT, *The Buddhist Vishnu*, 47.
39 HOLT, *The Buddhist Vishnu*, 31.
40 HOLT, *The Buddhist Vishnu*, 33.
41 HOLT, *The Buddhist Vishnu*, 47.
42 H.B.M. ILANGASINHA, "A Study of Buddhism in Ceylon in the Fifteenth and Sixteenth Centuries (Circa 1400–1600)", Ph.D. Thesis (London 1972), 375, quoted in: HOLT, *The Buddhist Vishnu*, 47.
43 HOLT, *The Buddhist Vishnu*, 58.

in ca. 845. In other Arabic works, the island was called either 'Siyalan' or 'Sahilan'. Thanks to easy maritime connections between the Mediterranean Sea, the Red Sea, the Persian Gulf, and the Indian Ocean, islamicised Arab merchants reached Sri Lanka during their eastward mercantile expansion up to China. According to a 10th century account by Ibn Shajriyar, Sri Lankans had sent a messenger to Medina when Muhammad was still alive. The messenger did not achieve his mission before the prophet passed away. But he succeeded in enquiring on the doctrine thanks to a meeting with Caliph Umar (633–644).[44] This direct but short-lived contact however did not lead to an islamisation of the entire Lankan island, but the multiplication of Arab trading in the following centuries provided a solid foundation for the emergence of Muslim communities in the coastal towns. Around 940 the Caliph of Baghdad sent a learned religious teacher named Khalid Ibn Abu Bakaya to Sri Lanka, where he organised the Muslims of Colombo into a community. Muslims, referred to as "Yon" in medieval Sinhala sources,[45] resided in Colombo and in all other main port cities in Ceylon, while they were less prominent in the hinterland and mountainous areas, which were dominated by Buddhist Sinhalese.[46] In the fifteenth century the Māppiḷas, the Malayāḷam speaking Muslims, became the main competitors with the Portuguese for the ports between the Malabar Coast and the western coast of Ceylon.[47]

2. Christianity During the Portuguese Intervention

2.1. Political Presence

The year 1505 was the foundation for the Portuguese encounter with Sri Lanka.[48] In that year King Manuel of Portugal ordered his Viceroy of India, Francisco de Almeida, to search for Sri Lanka, about whose wealth enthusiastic accounts circulated widely. The first news of the "sea of Ceylon" (*mar de Ceilão*) reached Lisbon in the summer of 1499 with the fleet of Vasco da Gama. The captain who had landed in Calicut (today's Kozhikode) in 1498 reported that an island nearby called *Cillam* produced cinnamon. More importantly, a well-informed Ashkenazi Jew named Gaspar da Gama, who had been converted to Catholicism, claimed in front of the Portuguese King that Ceylon was an island of Christians ruled by a Christian King. Opposite to Ceylon was a place called Coromandel (*Chomandarla*), known for its

---

44 L.S. DEWARAJA, *The Muslims of Sri Lanka. One Thousand Years of Ethnic Harmony, 900–1915* (Colombo 1994), 24–25.
45 SOMARATNA, *The Political History of the Kingdom of Kotte*, 167.
46 M.M.M. MAHROOF, "Muslim Under Portuguese and Dutch Occupation 1505–1796", in: M.M.M. MAHROFF et al. *An Ethnological Survey of the Muslims of Sri Lanka. From Earliest Times to Independence* (Colombo 1986), 44–46.
47 J.M. FLORES, "The Straits of Ceylon, 1524–1539: The Portuguese Mappilla Struggle over a Strategic Area", in: S. SUBRAHMANYAM (ed.), *Sinners and Saints. The Successors of Vasco da Gama* (Delhi 2000, 57–74).
48 In 1978 Chandra Richard de Silva discussed discrepancies regarding the year of the Portuguese arrival to Ceylon. Having compared the Portuguese chronicles by Fernão Lopes de Castanheda (first published in 1552–61, reprinted in 1883) and Fernão de Queyroz (manuscript completed in 1688 and first published in 1914), the historian supported the statement of the British scholar Donald William Ferguson, who had maintained 1506 to be the correct year. See the full analysis in C.R. DE SILVA, "The First Visit of the Portuguese to Ceylon 1505 or 1506?", in: I. PREMATILEKE / L. VAN LEEUW (eds.), *Senarat Paranavitana Commemoration Volume* (Leiden 1978, 218–220); D.W. FERGUSON, "The Discovery of Ceylon by the Portuguese in 1506" (*Journal of the Royal Asiatic Society Ceylon Branch* 19/59, 1907, 284–363).

abundance in pearls.⁴⁹ The luring spices, precious stones, and the alleged Christian presence justified the organisation of an expedition to Ceylon. In 1506 the son of the Viceroy, Lourenço de Almeida, accidentally arrived in Galle during his attempt to intercept Muslim traders in the Maldives, merely 800 km from the southwestern part of Ceylon.⁵⁰ At that time, the Muslim traders had started to circumvent the armed Portuguese interference by sailing to Sumatra, Malacca, and Bengal for purchasing pepper and cinnamon, to be traded up to the Red Sea and beyond.⁵¹ The Portuguese engaged more substantially with the Ceylon trade beginning in the 1520s, with a focus on cinnamon, a commodity then of high value in the European market. In 1507 Lourenço de Almeida and his crewmen were received by the King at the city of Kōṭṭe and granted 400 *bahars* of cinnamon per year.⁵² To celebrate the successful treaty the Captain ordered the Portuguese coat of arms engraved on a rock, upon which a small chapel was erected in the name of Saint Lawrence. A certain Fr. Vicente celebrated the first Mass on the island. He wished to stay for evangelical purposes but was ordered to return to Cochin until a more convenient relation was achieved with the Sinhalese.⁵³

Cinnamon was a native plant, exclusively available from Sri Lanka. Before the European intervention in the Indian Ocean it did not enjoy the same reputation as the other two "traditional" produces – arecanut and coconut, both highly sought-after in the Asian market. Revenue charged on traders of the latter two items constituted the bulk of the finances of Kōṭṭe as well as of the Kandyan kingdoms. By then, the planting and supply of cinnamon were attributed to the caste of *salāgamas*, the cinnamon peelers.⁵⁴ In Europe, cinnamon was mainly used as a condiment as well as a heating drug.⁵⁵ Due to its medical and therapeutic values, cinnamon became popular among lower social classes who benefited from the relatively lower price. Cinnamon enjoyed its popularity and profitability until the second half of the sixteenth century and its loss in value contributed to the decline of Portuguese maritime power.

The sixteenth century witnessed a variety of diplomatic methods used by the Portuguese with the local sovereigns, ranging from initial acquisitive attitudes, in order to obtain a sufficient supply of cinnamon, to a full-fledged territorial occupation. The stability of the trading monopoly was guaranteed by diplomatic negotiations with the Kingdom of Kōṭṭe. The early treaties revealed a bond with the Sinhala king as both friend and vassal. On the one hand, the Viceroy of India and the non-Christian King of Kōṭṭe were paired by a stated friendship (*amizade*). On the other hand, the Sinhala king was a vassal subject to the Crown of Portugal. This relation was reflected in the internal crisis of Kōṭṭe. In 1521 the royal family was split by an inheritance war among three princes. The Portuguese provided military aid to the eldest

---

49 J.M. FLORES, *Os portugueses e o Mar de Ceilão. Trato, diplomacia e guerra (1498–1543)* (Lisboa 1998), 101–102.
50 C.R. DE SILVA (ed.), *Portuguese Encounters with Sri Lanka and the Maldives. Translated Texts from the Age of Discoveries* (Farnham 2009), 1.
51 P. DA TRINDADE, *Conquista espiritual do Oriente. Das coisas que as frades menores da Província de S. Tomé fizeram na conversão dos infiéis desde a ilha de Ceilão até as de Japão*. Vol. 3 (Lisboa 1962), 12.
52 A *bahar* was a measure of weight of about 400–500 pounds. See T. ABEYASINGHE, *Portuguese Rule in Ceylon, 1594–1612* (Colombo 1966), 227.
53 F. DE QUEYROZ, *The Temporal and Spiritual Conquest of Ceylon*, trans. Simon Gregory Perera, 1st ed. 1930. Vol. 1, Book 1–2 (New Delhi 1992), 182.
54 DE SILVA, *A History of Sri Lanka*, 97.
55 This use of cinnamon-wood (*pao da canela*) was explained by GARCIA DA ORTA in 1563 in his *Coloquios dos simples e drogas da India*, ed. by F.M.C. DE MELLO FICALHO (Lisboa 1891), 210. See a study on the quality of Ceylon cinnamon by a Brazil-born botanist and priest in J.M. DA CONCEIÇÃO VELOSO, *Memoria sobre a cultura do laureio cinamomo vulgo canelleira de Ceilaõ* (Lisbon 1798).

son Bhuvanekabahu, who had his influence in the capital city of Kōṭṭe. In return they were given 300 *bahars* of cinnamon.[56] The power of Bhuvanekabahu's younger brothers Mayadunne and Madduma Bandara was based in Sitawaka and Rayigama respectively. The increased dependency of Bhuvanekabahu on the Portuguese created evangelical opportunities for the Franciscan missionaries, who gained trust among the royal families in Kōṭṭe and started conversions. The Portuguese mobilised a Sinhalese embassy to Portugal in 1554, led by the prince Maha Bandara or Dharmapala, grandson of Bhuvanekabahu. In 1557 Dharmapala was converted to Christianity, but this action led to his downfall, as a non-Buddhist could not reign over the Sinhala kingdom. The heirless Dom João Dharmapala chose to bequeath Kōṭṭe to the Portuguese crown on 12 December 1580, a step that was at the time regarded by Philip II of Spain, by then also king of Portugal, as an annexation.[57] The Portuguese took over the palace of Kōṭṭe, becoming the new rulers of the land.

Using both political maneuvers and military forces, the Portuguese went on to conquer the Sitawaka kingdom in 1581 and coveted a territorial expansion to the interior and to the north of the island. However, their attempts of annexing the Jaffna peninsula and archipelago had started already in the 1560s. The Viceroy Constantino de Bragança invaded the Jaffnapatnam kingdom but failed, being consoled only by the acquisition of Mannar. This town rose to be an important port for the Portuguese because of its strategic position, both for the exploitation of the pearls banks stretching between Tuticorin to northern Sri Lanka, and for the shipping route in-between Chilaw, Cape Comorin, and the Palk Strait. Nonetheless, Jaffna was still a coveted place because of its reputation as a lucrative site for the exportation of elephants, which had become an important commodity through handlers in kingdoms in the west and in the Vanni chieftaincies. From 1582 onwards, the Tamil King in Jaffna started to pay tribute to the Portuguese, first with elephants and then with other valuables.[58] This short-lived tributary system came to an end when André Furtado de Mendonça killed the ruler of Jaffna in 1591 and replaced him with Pararasa Sekeran, a new ruler who was at Portuguese disposal. With the annexation of Jaffna, the Portuguese entered a new phase in their relation with Ceylon. No longer a commercial group with limited and scattered interests along the coastal lines, they became the territorial rulers of most of the island. Within two decades from 1594 the Portuguese achieved this transition from traders to colonisers.

Until 1594 the kingdom of Kandy remained a weak Sinhala power, under pressure from Kōṭṭe and Sitawaka. Well protected in the mountainous area of central Ceylon, it remained at peace with the Portuguese. In 1594 a Sinhalese renegade from Portuguese service called Konappu Bandara, who reverted from Catholicism to Buddhism, seized the throne of Kandy. His subjects, however, only considered him a usurper. The Portuguese saw this occasion as a chance to expand their control to the vast central part of the island. In 1518 they had built a fort in Colombo, and later on they transformed what had previously been a village with a cinnamon field into a fortified city and the principal port of the island. By 1580, when the Portuguese had abandoned many ports along the *Carreira* from Goa to Cochin and Ceylon, Colombo was saved due to its high local income but also as a strategic path towards the interior island.[59] Following the loss of Ormuz in 1623 and Malacca in 1641, the fall of Ceylon

---

56 ABEYASINGHE, *Portuguese Rule in Ceylon*, 10.
57 DE QUEYROZ, *The Temporal and Spiritual Conquest of Ceylon*, 26; G.D. WINIUS, *The Fatal History of Portuguese Ceylon*. Transition to Dutch Rule (Cambridge, Massachusetts 1971), 6–7.
58 T. ABEYASINGHE, *Jaffna under the Portuguese* (Colombo 1986), 2.
59 N. PERERA, *Society and Space*. Colonialism, Nationalism, and Postcolonial Identity in Sri Lanka (Oxford 1998), 26–27.

to the Dutch in 1656 was a great loss to the Estado da Índia, because "Ceylon represented by far the largest and richest single possession in Asia of the Portuguese king; its captain-general was second in standing only to the viceroy himself."[60]

2.2. The Missionary Enterprise

2.2.1. Nestorians in Ceylon According to Cosmas

The earliest written evidence of Christianity in Ceylon is recorded in a Greek work entitled Χριστιανική Τοπογραφία, namely *Christian Topography*. The author of this text allegedly is a certain Cosma Indicopleustes, a sixth-century merchant from Alexandria, who lived as a monk.[61] Since the seventeenth century, there have been many debates about his identity, priesthood, and the different versions of the text.[62] However, scholars have hardly cast doubt on the religious authenticity of the author, whose remarks on cosmology and doctrine clearly suggest his adherence to Nestorianism.

Christian Topography was written in Greek and accompanied with illustrations. The purpose of the author was to represent the earth in resemblance to the tabernacle of the ancient Israelites.[63] The work also collected information on India and 'Taprobane', the Greek name for Sri Lanka: "The island has also a church of Persian Christians who have settled there, and a Presbyter who is appointed from Persia, and a Deacon and a complete ecclesiastical ritual."[64]

Little is known about the Nestorian Christians in Ceylon, except the findings of a Persian cross engraved on a column fragment in Anuradhapura.[65] Unlike the Jesuits' discovery of the Nestorian legacy in China, the presence of Persian Christianity in Ceylon was not known to the missionaries in Portuguese Ceylon, or at least no written record has been found on this yet.[66] However, it is not illogic to infer frequent visits of Syrian Christians from Malabar to

---

60 G.D. WINIUS, *The Fatal History of Portuguese Ceylon*. Transition to Dutch Rule (Cambridge 1971), ix.
61 For a full English translation see INDICOPLEUSTES COSMAS, *Kosma Aiguptiou Monachou Christianike Topographia = The Christian Topography of Cosmas, an Egyptian Monk*, ed. John Watson McCrindle, 1st edition in 1897 (London 2017). An erudite version in French is W. WOLSKA-CONUS (ed.), *Topographie Chrétienne* (Paris 1968–1973)..
62 P. MIHINDUKULASURIYA, "Persian Christians of the Anuradhapura Period", in: P. MIHINDUKULASURIYA / I. POOBALAN / R. CALDERA (eds.) *A Cultured Faith. Essays in Honour of Prof. G. P. V. Somaratna on His Seventieth Birthday* (Colombo 2011, 225–244). See an early historiography in McCrindle's introduction in J.W. MCCRINDLE (ed.), *The Christian Topography of Cosmas* (Cambridge 2010), i–xxvii, and updated literature on Cosmas Indicopleustes's biography and the latest discovery on the versions of the manuscripts in S.A. FALLER, "The World According to Cosmas Indicopleustes – Concepts and Illustrations of an Alexandrian Merchant and Monk" (*The Journal of Transcultural Studies* 1, 2011, 193–232), 193–199.
63 A good analysis on the illustration is available in W. WOLSKA-CONUS, "La 'Topographie Chrétienne' de Cosmas Indicopleustès. Hypothèses sur quelques thèmes de son illustration" (*Revue des études byzantines* 48/1, 1990, 155–191).
64 COSMAS, *Kosma Aiguptiou Monachou Christianike Topographia*, 365.
65 For a recent review of the Nestorians in Ceylon see P. MIHINDUKULASURIYA, *The Nestorian Cross and the Persian Christians of the Anuradhapura Period* (Kohuwela 2012).
66 Contrary to their ignorance about an early Christian presence in Ceylon, the Jesuits in 17th century China promoted the exploration of Nestorian and Jewish history in medieval China, where the evidence of antiquity was used to attract the attention of potential converts. M. NICOLINI-ZANI, "Jesuit Jingjiao: The 'Appropriation' of Tang Christianity by Jesuit Missionaries in the Seventeenth Century", in: L. TANG / D.W. WINKLER (eds.),

Ceylon. Evidence on the Keralite-Sinhala connections, even before the diffusion of Buddhism, has been provided convincingly by K. C. Sankaranarayanan, who also inferred occasional trade visits by Nestorian Christians from Ctesiphon (in today's Iraq), who even settled in Sri Lanka and Kerala.[67] We can contrast the uncertainty in regard to the Nestorian presence in pre-modern Ceylon with the frequent contacts that took place in the nineteenth century, thanks to the dynamic expansion of the Syrian Christian banks and firms across Malabar and Ceylon.[68] The potential connections between the Syrian bankers or merchants in Ceylon and the members of the Independent Catholics are still to be explored.

2.2.2. Conversion and Competition

As in other Portuguese *feitorias,* or fortified trading posts in Asia, the progress of the missionary work was intertwined with military advancement. In Ceylon, well-educated missionaries were trusted by the royal family to tutor their heirs, a situation that often led to the conversion of princes. The Franciscans were by the early 16th century the first and foremost religious order in Ceylon and played an essential role in the Portuguese diplomatic relations with the royal family of Kōṭṭe. From a certain Fr. Vicente who served as chaplain of Lourenço's fleet to Ceylon in 1506 to the despatch of the first Franciscan mission to Ceylon led by João de Vila de Conde in 1543, conversions took place at moderate intensity because the Portuguese had not yet secured diplomatic relations with Kōṭṭe. In 1531 João Vaz de Monteiro, a secular priest from Setubal, became the first Vicar of Ceylon.[69] According to Fernão de Queirós (1617–1688), author of a fundamental history of Ceylon written after the Portuguese holdings in the island were taken over by the Dutch[70], thousands of curious Buddhists came to see the Church in the Colombo Fort.[71] Only after Vila de Conde arrived in Ceylon did a massive conversion movement start among the Sinhalese. The first Franciscans adopted a method of vertical conversion, with priority being given to the conversion of Kings and princes.[72] The missionaries' evangelical zeal provoked the Viceroy of India João de Castro, who accused them of trying to convert King Bhuvanekabahu "by force or by importunate urging", all threatening to damage the peaceful cinnamon trade.[73] After having failed to baptise the King of Kōṭṭe, the Franciscans continued the vertical method with the Sinhala-speaking Karāvas (*Careas*), by first converting the *mudaliyars*, or headmen.[74] A breakthrough occurred when Dharmapala, last king of the Kingdom of Kōṭṭe, was eventually converted and

---

Hidden Treasures and Intercultural Encounters. Studies on East Syriac Christianity in China and Central Asia (Wien 2014, 225–240), 229.
67 SANKARANARAYANAN, *The Keralites and the Sinhalese*, 63.
68 M.A. OOMMEN, "Rise and Growth of Banking in Kerala" (*Social Scientist* 5/3, 1976, 24–46).
69 S.G. PERERA, "João Vaz Monteiro. The earliest Portuguese Tombstone in Ceylon" (*Ceylon Literature Register* 4, 1935, 233–241).
70 See the critical analysis by T. ABEYASINGHE, "History as Polemics and Propaganda. An Examination of Fernão de Queiros' 'History of Ceylon'" (*Journal of the Royal Asiatic Society Sri Lanka Branch* 25, 1980, 28–68).
71 A. WRIGHT, *Twentieth Century Impressions of Ceylon. Its History, People, Commerce, Industries, and Resources* (London 1907), 269.
72 C. GASTON PERERA, "The First Evangelical Mission of the Franciscans to Ceylon" (*Journal of the Royal Asiatic Society of Sri Lanka* 53, 2007), 153.
73 V. PERNIOLA, *The Catholic Church in Sri Lanka. The Portuguese Period. Vol. 1: 1505–1565* (Dehiwala 1989), 192. João de Castro to João III, dated in Diu, 16 December 1546; C. GASTON PERERA, *The Portuguese Missionary in 16th and 17th Century Ceylon. The Spiritual Conquest* (Colombo 2009), 233–234.
74 See the origin of the Karāva caste and their presence in the sixteenth century in M. ROBERTS, *Caste Conflict and Elite Formation. The Rise of a Karāva Elite in Sri Lanka, 1500–1931* (Cambridge 1982), 18–34.

baptised in 1557. His conversion certainly became an example and encouragement for the nobles and the women in the court.[75] Upon learning of their success at converting allegedly seventy-thousand people, the Portuguese King João III praised the Franciscan Custodian of India for the sincerity demonstrated by the native converts.[76] As the church historian Vito Perniola analysed, the statistics provided by the Franciscans might be inflated due to their concerns in regard to the possible dispatch of other religious orders to Ceylon. The rapid progress of conversion is substantiated by a relatively reliable calculation reported in 1631. At that point the Order of St Francis had fifty churches with 71.074 Christians.[77]

Most missionaries to Ceylon had travelled in a circular itinerary across Goa, and the Malabar and Coromandel coasts. As we have seen, the first known Portuguese missionary to Ceylon, Fr. Vicente, came to India with the expedition of Pedro Álvares Cabral (1467–1520) in 1501 before joining Lourenço's troops to the Maldives.

The Asian "conquests" of the Portuguese in 1514 fell under the ecclesiastical jurisdiction of the newly created Diocese of Funchal, in the Atlantic island of Madeira. The Dioceses of Goa and Cochin were established in 1533 and 1557 respectively, providing the Catholics in Asia with a nearer centre of ecclesiastical leadership. In 1557 Goa was also elevated to the rank of Archdiocese, therefore creating the first Roman Catholic Metropolitan jurisdiction based in Asia. The territorial extension of the new dioceses was enormous. The Diocese of Cochin included all of Kerala, the Fishery Coast, the Coromandel Coast, Orissa, Bengal, Pegu (in today's Myanmar), but most significantly the Island of Ceylon.[78] Similarly, the Archdiocese of Goa had direct jurisdiction not only over the Konkan coast, but even as far as the Persian Gulf and Eastern Africa. The wide jurisdictional extension of the Portuguese dioceses in Asia indicates that missionaries and laymen of different communities circulated in large networks connecting the various Portuguese port cities, transferring information across large spaces.

Since the Portuguese were unable to infiltrate the Kandyan kingdoms, the religious missions were focused on the fishermen castes who resided in the coastal regions and provided services to the Portuguese. In a way, the fishermen castes were the very foundation for the missionaries to secure their evangelical work in Ceylon. We will further analyse this in the following section on native agency.

The fact that the Franciscans maintained a predominance, if not a monopoly, in many mission fields in the sixteenth century set a foundation for a wide-ranging conflict within the Catholic Church. Jurisdictional clashes among religious orders can be found also in contemporary missions in Japan and China, where the Jesuits established a monopoly and were then requested by the Franciscans to open their areas to all religious orders.[79] In fact, clashes between religious orders would be a longue durée pattern of the missions in Asia. In the seventeenth century a new terrain of contention would emerge with the competition between the *Padroado* and Propaganda Fide. Finally, in the nineteenth century, a third source of tension

---

75 For a thorough analysis of the conversion of the Sri Lankan royal families see A. STRATHERN, *Kingship and Conversion in Sixteenth-Century Sri Lanka*. Portuguese Imperialism in a Buddhist Land (Cambridge 2007).
76 PERNIOLA, *The Catholic Church in Sri Lanka*. The Portuguese Period. Vol. 1, 356. D. João II to Francisco de Chaves OFM, dated in Lisbon, 20 March 1557.
77 Perniola believed it to be three thousand instead of seventy thousand in 1556. PERNIOLA, *The Catholic Church in Sri Lanka*. The Portuguese Period. Vol. 1, 347–348.
78 A. DA SILVA RÊGO, *O Padroado Português do Oriente*. Esbôço histórico (Lisboa 1940), 16.
79 ABEYASINGHE, *Portuguese Rule*, 195.

would be represented by the spread of nationalism among the missionaries sent from Propaganda, for instance between Italians (at the time of the *Risorgimento* process of national unification) and French.

A direct consequence of the missionary rivalry in the early modern time was the regional split of the Ceylon Church. The initial missionary monopoly of the Franciscans was fundamentally challenged only in the second half of the sixteenth century, when Jesuits, Dominicans, and Augustinians were eventually allowed to come in. With the expansion of the Portuguese territories the demand to send more missionaries to Ceylon was rising. The Viceroy Ayres de Saldanha proposed to the king of Portugal to send Jesuits to work in Kandy, whereas the Franciscans would remain in their current missions, placed in prosperous areas.[80]

While the religious orders working in Asia were all subject to the Portuguese *Padroado*, this did not mean that all missionaries were also of Portuguese origin. Among the four religious orders (Jesuits, Franciscans, Augustinians, and Dominicans), the Jesuits in Ceylon hailed from a large variety of regions, just as it was the case in other places in their Malabar province. A catalogue of 1620 reveals that only 8 out of 17 Jesuits active in Ceylon were actually born and educated in Portugal, and thus *reinóis* (born in the *Reino,* the "Kingdom" of Portugal). The rest were Portuguese born in Cochin, Colombo, and Ormuz, or other Europeans coming from Italy or Flanders. Remarkably, at least two Jesuits were born from mixed marriages, with a Portuguese father and an Asian mother.[81] Among the Franciscans Paulo da Trindade, the Franciscan chronicler who visited Ceylon in the 1620s and was born in Macao to a probably non-Portuguese mother, is worth mentioning.[82] The rather diversified origins of the missionaries point to the fact that the missionaries and native Christians understood neither the notion of a "Portuguese" Church, nor being "Portuguese" the same way we understand them today. The concept of *Portugueseness* needs to be carefully studied according to variable contexts, considering in particular how nationalism emerged as a driving force in Europe during the nineteenth century. This will be discussed later in the section on the British period, observing how mixed identities of "Catholic" and "Portuguese" were redefined and negotiated within the *Padroado* movement at that time.

2.3. Indigenous Christians in Mannar, Negombo and Colombo

In this section we focus on the cities of Colombo, Mannar, Jaffna, and Negombo, where a concentrated Christian community emerged in the sixteenth and seventeenth century.

Mannar played a crucial role in the Catholic Church in Ceylon in the early Portuguese period. By 1546 only five Franciscans and two other priests were active on the Island.[83] Some had already visited the northern region. Due to the small number of missionaries, necessarily laymen, and particularly catechists, played an essential role not only in the management of

---

80 ABEYASINGHE, *Portuguese Rule*, 193.
81 V. PERNIOLA, *The Catholic Church in Sri Lanka*. The Portuguese Period, Vol. 3: 1620–1658 (Dehiwala 1991), 34–35. This is a list of Jesuits in Ceylon dated 1621.
82 V.R. GOMES TEIXEIRA, "Fr. Paulo da Trindade, O.F.M., Cronista Macaense" (*Review of Culture / Revista de Cultura* [Macau] 28, 2008), 8.
83 Some of them had reached Mannar Island and made conversions. The presence of early Franciscans in Mannar and their conversions has been recorded in an eighteenth-century Tamil poem and chronicle entitled *Yalpana-Vaipava-Malai*. For a critical analysis of the work see S. GNANA PRAKASAR, "Sources of the Yalpana-Vaipava-Malai" (*Ceylon Antiquary and Literary Register* 6, 1921, 135–141).

the community, but often even in the very creation of missions, in a process of "self-Christianization".[84] If native agency was essential, Perniola stressed that in the early decades an impulse to obtain conversions did not come primarily from the missionaries, to the point that Portuguese "lay officials showed almost greater keenness than friars on converting people."[85] Even in the case of the Jesuit missions in Ceylon, the initiative was local. In 1543 the pearl fishermen of Mannar learnt that Francis Xavier had gained a reputation as a preacher among the Paravas in Tuticorin and Madurai. They sent people to invite him to visit their village in Mannar across the Strait. In 1544 a deputation went from Mannar to the port city of Punnaikayal, with the hope to invite the Jesuit to their island.[86] In the end it was Francisco Coelho, an Indian priest, who made the visit to Mannar on behalf of Xavier.[87]

It is not yet clear how these Parava Christians grew in their scale and influence. However, their presence had certainly triggered the suspicion of Chekarasa Sekaran, the Rajah of Jaffna, who was convinced that their conversion would lead to an allegiance of the Mannar people to the Portuguese. By that time Mannar was subject to Jaffna and paid tributes to the Rajah. Five thousand soldiers were sent to Mannar and killed those who admitted to having converted to Christianity, in a number of about 600 to 700.[88] Xavier, after having heard the news, travelled to Goa to persuade the Governor Martim Affonso de Souza that an immediate punishment was required on the Rajah, otherwise the Christian enterprise would become hopeless. Xavier's suggestion rekindled the Portuguese intention of occupying Mannar. In 1560 Constantino de Bragança's final conquest of Mannar was considered to be a retaliation for the earlier persecution of the local Catholics.[89] After Mannar's annexation by the Portuguese, the Viceroy sent a letter to Manoel Rodriguez Coutinho, the captain of the Fishery Coast, inviting the Christians there to cross the Strait to Mannar, because the "Holy Martyrs [had] purchased it" for the Christians.[90] Some of the Fishery Coast Catholics arrived in Mannar and worked for its fortification. The capture of Mannar strengthened the Christian identity of the local Christians, who now had gained protection from both the Portuguese and the Indian Paravas, against their Tamil king. By 1634 there were seventy Portuguese married in Mannar, most likely to local women. They were given land in some depopulated villages in Mantotte, where they settled down.[91] Little is known about the descendancy of those Portuguese. However, in some way this might be part of the remote origins of the Portuguese identity of the *Padroado* supporters in local churches in Mannar and Mantotte that would later be so important under British rule.

In the Indian context the Paravas shared a partial similarity with the Syrian Christians in Malabar, because both were communities engaged in a thriving trade, respectively pearls and

---

84 K. KOSCHORKE et al. (eds.), *A History of Christianity in Asia, Africa, and Latin America, 1450–1990*. A Documentary Sourcebook (Grand Rapids 2007), 25; S. GNANA PRAKASAR, *A History of the Catholic Church in Ceylon* (Colombo 1924), 42.
85 PERNIOLA, *The Catholic Church*. The Portuguese Period. Vol. 1, xii.
86 J. WICKI (ed.), *Documenta Indica*, vol. III (1553–7) (Roma: Monumenta Historica Soc. IESU, 1945), 238–239, 252–253.
87 G. SCHURHAMMER / E.A. VORETZSCH, *Ceylon zur Zeit des Königs Bhuvaneka Bahu und Franz Xavers, 1539–1552*. Quellen zur Geschichte der Portugiesen, sowie der Franziskaner- und Jesuitenmission auf Ceylon (Leipzig 1928), 135.
88 A.J.B. ANTONINUS, *The Martyrs of Mannar*. From Authentic Documents (Mannar 1944), 7.
89 D. BARTOLI, *Dell'Historia della Compagnia di Giesù: l'Asia*. Parte Prima (Rome 1653), 716.
90 ANTONINUS, *The Martyrs of Mannar*, 42.
91 PERNIOLA, *The Catholic Church in Sri Lanka*. The Portuguese Period. Vol. 3: 274.

spices.⁹² However, the social status of the two communities differed noticeably, as the Syrian Christians enjoyed a rank analogous to the one of the Nayar warriors, whereas the Paravas were low-ranking fishermen, comparable with Tamil-speaking Muslim weavers, as well as other fishermen and traders on the Coromandel Coast.⁹³ The conversion of the Paravas to Christianity in the first half of the sixteenth century was closely associated with the clientage system that the Portuguese established strategically on the Malabar Coast. In the Ceylon context, the Tamil-speaking Paravas were often compared with the Sinhala-speaking Karāva in the South. Both were indigenous groups important to the Portuguese in Ceylon, and both belonged to the lower classes of the society.⁹⁴ It is still to be explored how the two groups interrelated in the Catholic Church, especially when members of both communities joined the *Padroado* party in the British era. There might be common structural factors that led both groups to choose and defend the same partisan affiliation.

In Jaffna the Franciscans and the Jesuits made rapid progress in the seventeenth century, turning the region into a majoritarian Catholic realm. By 1634 the former were in charge of forty churches and the latter of fifteen. Christians belonged mainly to the Balala, Karāva, and Chando castes.⁹⁵

Negombo became another stronghold of the Karāva Catholics towards the end of the Portuguese era. This port city is situated thirty kilometers northwards from Colombo and was connected to it by an ancient canal, dating back to the eighth century and used for the transportation of cinnamon.⁹⁶ Since the seventeenth century the Catholics rose to the majority of the local population. Many of the fishermen lived in Duwam, a small island across the lagoon from Negombo.⁹⁷ It became even more noticeable when the VOC fleet, led by François Caron (1600–1673), took control of the city in 1644.⁹⁸ In Catholic chronicles and hagiographies Negombo gained the status of a symbol of persecution, in a line of continuity with the Martyrdom of Mannar.⁹⁹ The Dutch initially repressed Catholicism and imprisoned priests. Many Catholics allied with the Dutch and joined in the crackdown on their own churches. Meanwhile other religious communities, namely Buddhists and Hindus, took advantage of the situation to demolish the Catholic places of worship.¹⁰⁰

---

92 On the trading activities of the Thomas Christians, compared to the ones of other communities in South India, see P. MALEKANDATHIL, 'Dynamics of Trade, Faith and the Politics of Cultural Enterprise in Early Modern Kerala', in: M.V. DEVADEVAN (ed.), *Clio and Her Descendants*. Essays in Honour of Kesavan Veluthat (New Delhi 2018, 157–198).

93 S. BAYLY, *Saints, Goddesses and Kings*. Muslims and Christians in South Indian Society, 1700–1900 (Cambridge 2003, 1st ed. 1989), 321.

94 For an introduction to the migrant groups of Karāva, Parava, Durāva, Salāgama, and Mukkuvā communities, see ROBERTS, *Caste Conflict*, 21–30. On conflicts between the Karāva and Paravas see J. WICKI (ed.), *Documenta Indica*, vol. III (1553–7) (Roma: Monumenta Historica Soc. IESU, 1945), 34–5.

95 PERNIOLA, *The Catholic Church in Sri Lanka*. The Portuguese Period. Vol. 3: 280. From A. BOCARRO, *Livro das plantas de tôdas as fortalezas, cidades e povoações do Estado da India Oriental*, ed. by A. B. DE BRAGANÇA PEREIRA. Tomo 4, Vol. 2 (Goa 1937).

96 J.E. TENNENT, *Ceylon*. An Account of the Island, Physical, Historical, and Topographical, with Notices of Its Natural History, Antiquities and Productions. Vol. 1 (London 1860), 143.

97 R. RAJPAL KUMAR DE SILVA / W.G.M. BEUMER, *Illustrations and Views of Dutch Ceylon 1602–1796*. A Comprehensive Work of Pictorial Reference with Selected Eye-Witness Accounts (London 1988), 281.

98 D. HABERLAND, "François Caron and His Description of Japan" (*Review of Culture / Revista de Cultura* [Macau] 28, 2008, 70–85), 76–77.

99 J.E. TENNENT, *Christianity in Ceylon*. Its Introduction and Progress under the Portuguese, the Dutch, the British, and American Missions; with an Historical Sketch of the Brahmanical and Buddhist Superstitions (London 1850), 59.

100 PERNIOLA, *The Catholic Church in Sri Lanka*. The Portuguese Period. Vol. 3, 326.

The development of the Catholic mission in Colombo during the Portuguese era was quite different from that of Mannar. In 1518 the Portuguese captain Lopo Soares obtained permission from the King of Kōṭṭe to build a fort in Colombo. For decades, the Portuguese were confined to the fort and conversions in the city increased only slowly. The most interesting feature of Portuguese Colombo was possibly not so much its religious and military architecture, but rather its hybrid demography. Biedermann argues that Colombo experienced a burgeoning of *casados moradores* (married settlers), who were nominally "Portuguese", even though they were mostly Christians of mixed blood. In 1630 there were 350 *casados* assigned to military service in defence of Colombo. This number has to be multiplied by at least five times, if women and children are taken into account. In addition to these "Portuguese", there were also 1500 armed servants from diverse ethnic groups. There also were 2000 so-called "Black" soldiers, excluding the Sinhalese men in arms.[101]

3. Underground Catholics in Dutch Ceylon

3.1 Dutch Control of Ceylon

In contrast to the development of Portuguese control in Ceylon, Dutch rule over the island relied to a much lesser degree on the assistance from a religious force – which would have been the Calvinist Dutch Reformed Church. Cinnamon was still a main reason for the Dutch's enterprise on Ceylon, and the emphasis on securing a lucrative business led the VOC to seek greater efficiency and profit from their trade and land possessions.[102] Indifferent to the indirect rule of the Portuguese, who relied on establishing bonds with the local administration, the Dutch Company developed a rule gradually more centralised, so as to control the entire plantation economy and make the tax system better organised. On one hand the VOC allocated castes to specific labour in the cinnamon plantations, providing them with privileges. On the other hand, the Dutch chose to depend on the *mudaliyārs*, the headmen of each caste or ethnic group for the collection of taxes, promoting their social mobility.[103]

The Dutch competed fiercely with the local rulers and indigenous chiefs for a better control of agriculture. A noticeable case was the strife for the paddy lands cultivated along the Attanagalu Oya River and the Kelen River, on the Western part of the island. By the mid-eighteenth century the VOC gained dominance over those fields and aimed at achieving a higher productivity than under the indigenous chiefs.[104] The Company waged open wars against the Kingdom of Kandy, but never gained direct control. In 1766 the VOC and Kandy signed a treaty that secured the former's right to peel cinnamon freely in the Kandyan territories. Meanwhile the Dutch territorial possessions increased at the expense of the native kingdom.[105] The Dutch emphasis on the southwestern regions of Galle and Colombo was due

---

101 Z. BIEDERMANN, *The Portuguese in Sri Lanka and South India*. Studies in the History of Diplomacy, Empire and Trade, 1500–1650 (Wiesbaden 2014), 132–133.
102 M. DOS SANTOS LOPES, "'Ao cheiro desta canela': Notas para a história de uma especiaria rara", in: J.M. DOS SANTOS ALVES / C. GUILLOT / R. PTAK (eds.), *Mirabilia Asiatica* (Wiesbaden 2003), 55.
103 SCHRIKKER, *Dutch and British Colonial Intervention*, 33–35, 40–41.
104 N.R. DEWASIRI, *The Adaptable Peasant*. Agrarian Society in Western Sri Lanka under Dutch Rule, 1740–1800 (Leiden 2008), 60–61.
105 SCHRIKKER, *Dutch and British Colonial Intervention*, 39.

to the local cinnamon production, while the interest in the control of Jaffna had to do with its strategic position in the Indian ocean trading networks.

Within the Dutch period, some important changes occurred in regard to the ethnic composition of the island. A new ethnic group emerged among those who entered into mixed marriages with the Dutch soldiers, as well as with the Portuguese. Dutch Colombo rose to be the second largest settlement of the VOC in Asia after Batavia. In 1749 almost 32 percent of the 1648 VOC employees were born in Asia. This means that it was the local-born who staffed the administration and the warehouses. This merger of ethnicities, beginning in the Portuguese era, continued into the late seventeenth century. In 1684 there were 678 children of Calvinist Christian inhabitants in Colombo, of whom only 84 had two European parents, accounting for 12 percent.[106] As a consequence, a layered society was emerging. However, in the lower reaches of the Christian society, the boundaries between the various groups tended to be fluid. As Denis B. McGilvray observed, there were almost no Dutch Burghers who could actually boast a Dutch origin. Intermarriages between the Dutch Burghers and the Portuguese Burghers were very common.[107]

3.2 Oratorians and Underground Christians

In 1642, the Dutch East Indian Company issued Statutes in Batavia prescribing Reformed Christianity as the official religion:

> No other religion will be exercised, much less taught or propagated, either secretly or publicly, than the Reformed Christian Religion as it is taught in the public Churches of the Netherlands.[108]

However, this rule was not observed uniformly in all the Catholic areas that were captured by the Dutch. A small number of priests was allowed to serve a still large number of Catholics. This limited toleration minimized the risk of a rebellion of the Catholics, but also much reduced the vitality of the Catholic missions. Beyond Ceylon, this was the case in Cochin, occupied by the Dutch in 1663. Five Franciscans were still allowed to continue the ministry for 8,000 Catholics that remained in the city. The Dutch authorities also allowed that, between Quilon and Cape Comorin, eight Jesuits continued their work with the Catholics scattered in thirty-nine villages.[109]

However, the VOC did not apply this relatively benign policy in Ceylon, which had been completely conquered by 1658. After the last Portuguese were expelled from Jaffna, the Company issued a *plakaat* stating that "anyone who harboured a Roman Catholic priest or who even failed to denounce one whose whereabouts he happened to know would be liable to the death penalty."[110] Boudens describes this as an equation of the Portuguese and the Catholics in the understanding of the Dutch.[111] This implies that the convergence of the two

---

106 U. BOSMA / R. RABEN, *Being 'Dutch' in the Indies*. A History of Creolisation and Empire, 1500–1920, trans. W. Shaffer (Singapore 2008), 39.
107 D.B. MCGILVRAY, "The Portuguese Burghers of Eastern Sri Lanka in the Wake of Civil War and Tsunami", in: J.M. COSTA DA SILVA FLORES (ed.), *Re-Exploring the Links*. History and Constructed Histories between Portugal and Sri Lanka (Wiesbaden 2007), 325.
108 R. BOUDENS, *The Catholic Church in Ceylon under Dutch Rule* (Roma 1957), 73.
109 BOUDENS, *The Catholic Church*, 74.
110 BOUDENS, *The Catholic Church*, 74.
111 BOUDENS, *The Catholic Church*, 75.

identities, one based on the loyalty to a previous ruler, and another one of religious nature, might have been strengthened and enhanced due to their prohibition.

Once the Portuguese missionaries were no longer allowed in the Dutch colony, the authorities of the *Padroado* resorted to clerics that could operate disguised among the native population. In the context of an expanding native clergy within Goa and the other territories of the Estado da Índia, a newly established religious community of Goan Brahman priests was of importance. Founded by Fr. José Vaz (1651–1711), this was a Congregation of the Oratory of Saint Philip Neri, whose headquarters were in the Goan *Convento da Cruz dos Milagres*.[112] The first Congregation of the Oratory had been founded in Rome in 1575 by Filippo Neri (1515–1595), a remarkable figure in the religious history of Italian Renaissance. Most known as "the saint of joy", Neri was also considered a "Christian Socrates" for his maieutic method and rooting in a concrete daily life.[113]

In contrast to the contemporary Jesuits, Theatines, and Barnabites, all established in the sixteenth century, the members of the Oratory were secular priests living under obedience but bound by no formal vows, as required for entering other religious orders.[114] The Oratorians were united with their fellow communities in different regions merely by the observance of the rules of Filippo Neri, not by an overarching organisation. Such a relatively flexible and decentralized administration derived from the very concerns of Neri, who gave priority to the survival of individual communities rather than to a success on a large scale. This principle allowed for the establishment of congregations in very different conditions, ranging from Europe to Mexico,[115] Goa, and Ceylon. In the nineteenth century a Congregation of the Oratory would be founded in England by the ex-Anglican John Henry Newman (1801–1890), who has been proclaimed saint in 2019.[116]

Starting with Vaz since 1687, scores of priests of Konkani Brahman origin penetrated Ceylon and undertook a fruitful clandestine apostolate.[117] These missionaries were highly

---

112 The main printed documentary source on this crucial religious community is M. DA COSTA NUNES, *Documentação para a história da Congregação do Oratório de Santa Cruz dos Milagres do clero natural de Goa* (Lisboa 1966). On the origin of the Congregation in Goa see S.G. PERERA, *Historical Sketches* (Colombo 1962), 212–225. While a comprehensive scholarly biography of Vaz is still missing, it is still useful the hagiography by S. G. PERERA, *Life of the Venerable Father Joseph Vaz. Apostle of Ceylon* (Galle 1953).
113 L. BOUYER, *The Roman Socrates. A Portrait of St. Philip Neri* (London 1958); L. PONNELLE / L. BORDET, *Der heilige Philipp Neri und die römische Gesellschaft seiner Zeit (1515–1595)*. Festgabe zum 500. Geburtstag des hl. Philipp Neri (Bonn 2015).
114 A fundamental reference on the history of the Congregation of the Oratory is A. CISTELLINI, *San Filippo Neri, l'Oratorio e la Congregazione Oratoriana. Storia e Spiritualità* (Brescia 1989), 3 vols.
115 The Oratorian mission in Mexico was led by the Spanish Juan Antonio Perez de Espinosa (1676–1747). D.A. BRADING, *Church and State in Bourbon Mexico* (Cambridge 2002, 40–61). Inspired by Filippo Neri's Oratory was also the highly influential Congregation of the Oratory of Jesus, established in France by Pierre de Bérulle in 1611. See Y. KRUMENACKER et al. (eds.), *L'Oratoire de Jésus. 400 ans d'histoire en France* (11 novembre 1611–11 novembre 2011) (Paris, 2013).
116 A synthesis on his life and thought is offered by I. KER, *John Henry Newman. A Biography* (Oxford, 2009).
117 K. KOSCHORKE, "Holländische Kolonial- und katholische Untergrundkirche im Ceylon des 17. und 18. Jahrhunderts", in: U. VAN DER HEYDER / H. LIEBAU (eds.), *Missionsgeschichte, Kirchengeschichte, Weltgeschichte. Christliche Missionen im Kontext nationaler Entwicklungen in Afrika, Asien und Ozeanien* (Stuttgart 1996, 273–280); I.G. ŽUPANOV, „Goan Brahmans in the Land of Promise. Missionaries, Spies and Gentiles in the 17th–18th Century Sri Lanka", in: J. FLORES (ed.), *Portugal – Sri Lanka. 500 Years* (Wiesbaden 2006, 171–210). While the most famous Goan Oratorians were Brahmans, it has to be verified whether subjects from other castes (and particularly from the Charados) were eventually admitted, for instance at the beginning of the nineteenth century. See Â.B. XAVIER, "Purity of Blood and Caste: Identity Narratives among Early Modern Goan Elites", in: M.E. MARTÍNEZ, M. HERING TORRES, AND D. NIRENBERG (eds.), *Race and Blood in the Iberian World* (Münster 2012, 125–149).

effective religious specialists, but often also gifted writers and polyglots, able to compose spiritual works in different relevant languages. The most famous missionary writer was by all means Fr. Jácome Gonçalves (1676–1742), active in the first half of the eighteenth century and celebrated for his Sinhala and Tamil works.[118] The literary tradition and talent continued even later, with a figure like Fr. Gabriel Pacheco, who composed works in Tamil, Sinhala, and Dutch.[119] The achievements of the Oratorians, both pastoral and cultural, appear particularly striking considering the efforts made by the Dutch authorities to curb their clandestine activities. From the minutes of the Calvinist Consistory of Dutch Ceylon – held in the Wolvendaal church, ironically very near to what became a century later the Independent Catholic centre of Hultsdorp – we can sense the impotence of the Calvinist leaders in converting the "Popish" faithful, while even the Dutch colonial authorities were inclined pragmatically to a de facto toleration of the Catholic practices.[120]

The pioneering work by Vaz and his companions was accredited by Pope Clement XI, who officially entrusted the mission of Ceylon to the Congregation of the Oratory in 1706.[121] It is widely acknowledged that Saint José Vaz, canonized in 2015, was rightly proclaimed "Apostle of Ceylon", inasmuch as without his activity and that of his many Goan confreres, Catholicism could have faded away from the island.

In the history of Christianity in Ceylon, the Goan Oratorians' impact was not only limited to their years of actual service, but had a posthumous influence far beyond their suppression in 1838, both in Portuguese India and in British Ceylon. We will show several instances of such an enduring influence with respect to Ceylon and its "schismatic" movement. Our assumption is that, during the time of repression under the Dutch, the Catholics of Ceylon joined their attachment to the old faith and religious practice in an indissoluble way with a special devotion towards the Goan Oratorian priests. In fact, in addition to their missionary zeal, these Oratorians were also remarkable intellectuals, not only well versed in Portuguese and Latin, but also highly respected in cultural terms to be entrusted with seminary teaching tasks in Goa.[122]

In the eyes of the Catholics in Ceylon, those Goan priests were possibly no less "Portuguese" than those European missionaries who worked there in the early seventeenth century. However, further reflection is required to understand to which extent the Ceylon Catholics considered the Oratorians also distinctively Goan or Indian.

---

118 A classical biography of Gonçalves is the one by S.G. PERERA, *Life of Father Jacome Gonçalvez* (Madura 1942). The Sinhala and Tamil works of Gonçalves have been studied recently by A. FERNANDOPULLE, *A Critical Study of the Works of Fr. Jacome Gonsalves (1676–1742)* (Colombo 2017); A. FERNANDOPULLE, *Father Jacome Gonsalves, Sinhala Christian Literary Hero. A Study of the Sinhala Literary Works of Fr Jacome Gonsalves (1676–1742)* (Colombo 2000).
119 A.C. DEP, *The Oratorian Mission in Sri Lanka, 1795–1874. Being a History of the Catholic Church, 1795–1874* (Colombo 1987), 22. Gabriel Pacheco was ordained priest in 1773, as stated by R. STREIT, *Bibliotheca Missionum*. Vol. 6: Missionsliteratur Indiens, der Philippinen, Japan und Indochinas, 1700–1799 (Roma 1964), 225.
120 In this respect, a gold mine still to be explored is K. KOSCHORKE (ed.), *The Dutch Reformed Church in Colonial Ceylon (18th Century)*. Minutes of the Consistory of the Dutch Reformed Church in Colombo Held at the Wolvendaal Church, Colombo (1735–1797), trans. S.A.W. Mottau (Wiesbaden 2011).
121 See the report of the mission of Ceylon by Carlo Tomaso Maillard de Tournon, dated in Malacca, 26 August, 1704, published by V. PERNIOLA, *The Catholic Church in Sri Lanka. The Dutch period*, Vol. I: 1658–1711 (Dehiwala 1983), 252–253. See the papal decree in DA COSTA NUNES (ed.), *Documentação para a história*, 299–305.
122 T.R. DE SOUZA, *Discoveries, Missionary Expansion, and Asian Cultures* (New Delhi 1994), 172.

Finally, our emphasis on the Oratorians should also take into consideration significant removals and erasures. A major effect of the Dutch conquest of Portuguese Ceylon was the expulsion of the Catholic missionaries who, until 1658, were primarily Franciscans and Jesuits.[123]

4. Christianity in British Ceylon

4.1. Ceylon as a "Model Colony" and Laboratory of Modernity

This section aims to sketch briefly the elements that characterised the colonial dynamic of Ceylon from the end of the eighteenth to the late nineteenth century, right before our protagonists – Alvares and Dr. Lisboa Pinto – arrived in Colombo in 1888 respectively from Goa and Bombay. Despite later political divisions between post-colonial states, it is necessary to understand the economic and social transformations, and the religious situation in nineteenth-century Ceylon in the connections, similarities and, for sure, also in the contrasts between this Crown colony and the complex patchwork of the British *Raj*.

The British occupation of Ceylon in 1796 was an effect of the colonial competition around the globe between Britain and France, with the once expansionist Dutch Republic now being squeezed between much bigger players. In 1780 the Fourth Anglo-Dutch War broke out, as a consequence of the Dutch support to the rebellious American colonies. In 1782–1783 the port of Trincomalee on the north-eastern coast of Ceylon was taken away from Holland and fought over by the British and the French. Dutch sovereignty over the port was restored in 1783 by the Treaty of Versailles. The sensitivity of Trincomalee for the British derived from the fear that a French control of that strategic harbour, as much as the one of Galle, might easen attacks against British possessions in India.[124] However, the Dutch recovery of Trincomalee was short-lived, as in 1795 – following Napoleon's invasion of Holland and the subsequent creation of a satellite Batavian Republic – the British took over the port with the aim of preventing a French occupation. This turn of events was justified by the "Kew Letters", with which the exiled *Stadtholder* William V (resettled precisely in Kew) requested George III to protect the Dutch possessions in Asia against the French. By 1796 the British had expanded their "protection" from Trincomalee to the rest of Dutch Ceylon. In the intention of the *Stadtholder*, the British protection was meant to be provisional and should end in a restoration of the status quo, as soon as the French threat had ceased. However, "from the beginning the British had set their mind on using the Kew Letters to conquer Ceylon".[125]

---

123 On the Franciscans, see the recent study by C.G. Perera, "The First Evangelical Mission of the Franciscans to Ceylon" (*Journal of the Royal Asiatic Society of Sri Lanka* 53, 2007, 153–202). A classical work on the Jesuit apostolate is S.G. PERERA, *The Jesuits in Ceylon (in the XVI and XVII Centuries)* (New Delhi 2004, 1st ed. Madura 1941).
124 K.M. DE SILVA (ed.), *History of Ceylon*. Vol. 3: From the Beginning of the Nineteenth Century to 1948 (Colombo 1973), 6–7; E. MEYER, "The Specificity of Sri Lanka. Towards a Comparative History of Sri Lanka and India" (*Economic and Political Weekly* 31/7, 1996), 396.
125 SCHRIKKER, *Dutch and British Colonial Intervention*, 132.

The British achieved what had eluded both the Portuguese and the Dutch, namely subjugating even the Kingdom of Kandy, the internal region of Ceylon that had remained independent since the end of the fifteenth century.[126] The process took place in less than two decades. After an unsuccessful campaign in 1803–1805, the British were able to conquer the mountainous polity in 1815, exiling King Sri Wickrama Rajasinghe to the Vellore Fort (falling within the Madras Presidency). A rebellion was effectively squashed in 1817, ensuring British control over the entire island, which had been upgraded to the status of Crown Colony in 1815. In fact, "Ceylon was considered by the imperial government to be its 'model colony'. It provided the pattern for crown colony government in the early nineteenth century".[127] The subjugation of the entire island of Ceylon distinguished the British expansion from all previous European attempts at control in the region.[128] Such a fundamental territorial difference, as well as other changes in administrative practices and in technology, allowed for a particularly intense colonial domination. In fact, the British control of Ceylon was characterized by a much more direct and immediate rule than the one practised in British India.[129] In the latter, a fundamental feature were the princely states that "comprised two-fifths of south Asia's territory and about one-fifth of its population at the time when the British Crown took over the control of the remaining provinces from the English East India Company in 1858".[130] As a "pax Britannica" was imposed throughout South Asia, the strategic relevance of Trincomalee against potential threats faded away, and Colombo gained greater importance. The British diverted their attention from securing a stronghold in the Bay of Bengal that could protect their interests in India to a much broader domination over the Indian Ocean, projected from what is even today Sri Lanka's capital city. Such an external projection was paired by internal consolidation and interconnection. Colombo and Kandy were linked by road in 1831 and by railway in 1867, so that "the Up-Country, until then quite isolated from the lowlands, looked unrecognisable in the space of a few decades".[131]

During the nineteenth century Ceylon drastically changed its economic profile and position in international trade. In an effort to implement "modernity" and capitalism, the British authorities disrupted a traditional social and economic mechanism. In 1832 took place the abolition of the system of *rājakariya* ("service to the king"), by which

> the king could command military services in case of national emergency and labour services in the construction of roads and other works of public utility. Since the service was attached to the land and not to the individual, whoever enjoyed a given extent of land had to supply the labour due, or provide a substitute.[132]

---

126 The military strategies that allowed Kandy to resist for 220 years to European colonialism are analysed by C. WICKREMESEKERA, *Kandy at War*. Indigenous Military Resistance to European Expansion in Sri Lanka 1594–1818 (Colombo 2004).
127 M. JONES, *Health Policy in Britain's Model Colony*. Ceylon, 1900-1948 (New Delhi 2004), 18.
128 K.M. DE SILVA, "Resistance Movements in Nineteenth Century Sri Lanka", in: M. ROBERTS (ed.), *Sri Lanka. Collective Identities Revisited*. Vol. 1 (Colombo 1997), 145; SILVA (ed.), *History of Ceylon*. Vol. 3, 12–13.
129 J.C. HOLT (ed.), *The Sri Lanka Reader*. History, Culture, Politics (Durham 2011), 230–231.
130 W. ERNST / B. PATI, "People, Princes and Colonialism", in W. ERNST / B. PATI (eds.), *India's Princely States. People, Princes and Colonialism* (New York 2007, 1–14), 1.
131 WICKRAMASINGHE, *Sri Lanka in the Modern Age*, 29.
132 L.S. DEWARAJA, "Revenues of the King of Kandy" (*Journal of the Sri Lanka Branch of the Royal Asiatic Society* 16, 1972, 17–24).

In other words, the *rājakariya* was a Sri Lankan version of the *corvées* exacted in premodern feudal Europe. In the eyes of reform-minded British officers such as William MacBean George Colebrooke (1787–1870), the requirements of *rājakariya*

> hindered the development of agriculture and commerce by their interference with normal occupations. They denied the people the chance of changing their form of work or migrating from the district in which they lived. They reduced the people to a state of serfdom, and compelled Government to preserve distinctions of race and caste in order to get its work done and to deny equal rights to all its subjects.[133]

Another major change occurred in relation to the cultivation and export of cinnamon. As K. M. de Silva has effectively observed, "the lure of cinnamon brought the VOC to Sri Lanka and throughout the period of its rule in the island's maritime regions, the protection of the cinnamon monopoly was its great passion".[134] The cinnamon monopoly was inherited in 1802 by the English East India Company, passing in 1822 directly into the hands of the colonial government.[135] The monopoly was eventually abolished in 1833 but, with the imposition of export duties to compensate the revenue loss, the cinnamon of Ceylon was defeated by international competition. It "never recovered the position it enjoyed in the years before 1833; it survived as a minor crop controlled by Sri Lankan plantation owners and smallholders, and subject to widely fluctuating market conditions".[136]

The British commitment to the liberalisation of the economy, even if it could lead to immediate negative consequences, shows a distinctive ideological persuasion. In this sense it is not even inappropriate or anachronistic to speak, as N. Biziouras does, of a "minimal state" based on "a low level of subsidies" and "minimized state ownership in different economic activities"; a state that "insisted upon balanced budgets (and often achieved budget surpluses)", and used "low levels of indirect taxation for revenue purposes".[137] Ceylon became a laboratory for the implementation of liberal economic doctrines, in a way that recalls familiar developments that occurred in the late 20th and early 21st centuries.

Responding to the demands of a global market, plantations were created in the internal regions of the island that had just come under British control. Initially there was a great expansion of coffee plantations, taking the role that had once belonged to cinnamon. In fact, the British launched an extensive programme of road construction to facilitate the large-scale production of coffee in the Kandyan regions.[138] Due to a relative shortage of Sinhalese peasants, around 10,000 immigrant labourers came to Ceylon from the 1820s and 1830s to work

---

133 G.C. MENDIS, *Ceylon under the British* (New Delhi 2005, reprint of the 3rd ed. of 1945), 53.
134 SILVA, *A History*, 161.
135 SILVA, *A History*, 239.
136 SILVA, *A History*, 271.
137 N. BIZIOURAS, *The Political Economy of Ethnic Conflict in Sri Lanka. Economic Liberalization, Mobilizational Resources, and Ethnic Collective Action* (London 2014), 34.
138 E. MEYER, "Labour Circulation between Sri Lanka and South India in Historical Perspective", in: C. MARKOVITS / J. POUCHEPADASS / S. SUBRAHMANYAM (eds.), *Society and Circulation. Mobile People and Itinerant Cultures in South Asia, 1750–1950* (London 2006), 71–72.

on the coffee plantations.[139] These migrant workers originated mainly from the Madras Presidency and included primarily Tamils, in addition to the pre-existent Tamil-speaking communities in Ceylon, quite different in social profile.[140]

However, the Coffee Leaf Disease in the late 1870s and early 1880s devastated the coffee monocultures, so that there was a reorientation towards another cash crop of global and ubiquitous impact, namely tea.[141] The labour-intensive regime of the tea plantations led to a recruitment of further workers from India. A distinctive feature of the migrants to Ceylon, as well as to Malaya and Burma, was that, contrary to what happened in the Caribbean and elsewhere, they were not formally subject to an indenture regime and were, at least in theory, 'free' in their relations with the employers.[142] It is important to recall that between 1834 and 1900, 92.2% of all Indian emigrants went to Ceylon, Malaya, and Burma, in a situation that could not be defined in proper terms as "indenture".[143]

Ceylon, as a "model colony" of the British Empire, showcased a massive shift from traditional socio-economic relations towards a capitalist modernity defined by the West. Within a limited and constrained geographical space, Ceylon experienced an intense transformation that was also highly attractive to South Asian intellectuals and professionals who were seeking new venues for their careers.

4.2. The Oratorian Conundrum

4.2.1. Challenges to the Goan Missionaries in Ceylon

If so significant had been the work of the Oratorians since the end of the seventeenth century, the situation took a very different turn by the beginning of the nineteenth century, in the context of the British domination. On the one hand, the Catholics could finally count on an official policy of religious toleration, proclaimed already in 1796.[144] However, despite the improved political situation, other serious problems had to be dealt with. In fact, the nineteenth-century Oratorian missionaries in Ceylon received considerable criticism from contemporary European missionaries and from local Christians. They also have been judged sternly by the greatest expert on Sri Lankan Church history, the Jesuit scholar Vito Perniola (1913–2016). In the introduction to his monumental *The Catholic Church in Sri Lanka: The British Period*, Perniola argued that a lack of administration and an incapability of adapting to the demand for English education were among the main reasons for the decline of the Order in Ceylon:

---

139 R. WENZLHUEMER, "Indian Labour Immigration and British Labour Policy in Nineteenth-Century Ceylon" (*Modern Asian Studies* 41/3, 2007, 575–602), 576–580.
140 P. PEEBLES, *Social Change in Nineteenth Century Ceylon* (New Delhi 1995); P. PEEBLES, *The Plantation Tamils of Ceylon* (London 2001).
141 R. WENZLHUEMER, *From Coffee to Tea Cultivation in Ceylon, 1880–1900. An Economic and Social History* (Leiden 2008).
142 WENZLHUEMER, "Indian Labour Immigration", 575–602. A recent comparative study of the indenture of Indian migrant workers is M.S. HASSANKHAN / L. ROOPNARINE / H. RAMSOEDH (eds.), *The Legacy of Indian Indenture*. Historical and Contemporary Aspects of Migration and Diaspora (Abingdon 2016).
143 S.S. AMRITH, "South Indian Migration, c. 1800–1950", in: J. LUCASSEN / L. LUCASSEN (eds.), *Globalising Migration History. The Eurasian Experience (16th–21st Centuries)* (Leiden 2014), 122.
144 PERNIOLA, *The Catholic Church in Sri Lanka*. The British Period, Vol. 1, 1.

> The Oratorian priests, the successors of those who had heroically withstood the persecution of the Dutch in order to minister to the Catholics, had become almost an amorphous group with hardly any initiative, satisfied with a minimum concern for the spiritual welfare of the people of whom they were put in charge year in and year out at the beginning of the month of September. The system of changing the missionaries every year from one mission to another was a further element of stagnation. No priest succeeded in fostering strong links with a Christian community; no shepherd ever had a good knowledge of his sheep.[145]

A milder attitude can be found only in earlier works such as the one of the self-taught historian Arthur Cletus Dep (a former Deputy Inspector General of the Sri Lanka police), who resorted to an apologetic tone in his history of the Oratorians in Ceylon.[146] The little known Sylvestrian Benedictine Fr. Lawrence Hyde, whose short history was published by his confrere Fr. Bede Barcatta, also provided a positive representation of the Goan missionaries in Ceylon.[147] Perniola's critique cast light on a real and undeniable administrative decay of the Oratorians, but at the same time failed to indicate the colonial context conducive to the decline of the Order, a unique missionary body of native clergymen active across South Asia at an age of high colonialism and racism. Nonetheless, Perniola's negative view also allows us to revise certain excessively eulogistic remarks. For instance, according to Dep, the Oratorian missionaries sent from Goa to Ceylon had been destined to stay there for life, representing a sacrifice of an entire existence. While this might have been true in early modern times, the rule had definitely been altered by the nineteenth century and the Goan priests indeed had the possibility to return to their homeland eventually.[148]

A common misconduct that the Oratorians were often accused of concerned their toleration of allegedly superstitious practices. The Italian Oratorian Orazio Bettacchini immediately identified such abuses among local Catholics shortly after his arrival in Ceylon in 1845:

> In order to obtain favours, they [local Catholics] put a rope around the neck of the statue of the Saint; throw it into water and ill-treat it badly uttering, at the same time, all sorts of profanities against the Saint, who, they say, is thus brought to grant many favours which he would not grant, were he to be treated kindly (will he grant out of fear what he would not grant out of love?).[149]

The theological justification given by the Goan priests was based on the idea of an afterlife compensation to an unfulfilled desire: "St Anthony did not obtain the grace of martyrdom, which he desired, while he was still alive, now he is happy to be despised." In the eyes of Bettacchini, this practice was rooted in Buddhist or Hindu practices. However, the same practice was already mentioned in a seventeenth century travelogue by a French diplomat, François La Boullaye-Le-Gouz, who travelled to India in 1664. When he was en route with the French Capuchin missionary Zenon de Beaugé (1603–1687), the priest received news

---

145 V. PERNIOLA, *The Catholic Church in Sri Lanka*. The British Period. Vol. 2: 1845–1849. The Vicariates of Colombo and Jaffna (Dehiwala 1995), xiii.
146 DEP, *The Oratorian Mission*.
147 According to Barcatta, Hyde was biased in favour of the Oratorians. L. HYDE, "A Short Historical Review of the Sylvestrine Monks in Ceylon from 1845 to 1920", ed. BEDE BARCATTA, original in 1920, 15, n.24. A digital copy is accessible at http://www.osbsrilanka.org/wp-content/uploads/2014/09/A-Short-Historical-Review-by-Fr.-Lawrence-Hyde-OSB.pdf (last accessed on 2 January 2022).
148 DEP, *The Oratorian Mission*, 12.
149 Bettacchini's letter to the Congregation of Propaganda Fide, dated in Colombo, 9 July 1845, transcribed and published in PERNIOLA, *The Catholic Church in Sri Lanka*. The British Period. Vol. 2, 28.

about the detention of his confrere Ephrem de Nevers († 1695), by the Inquisition of Goa. The reason was that Ephrem preached to the Portuguese Catholics in Madras reproaching them for their custom of beating and trampling upon the statue of Saint Anthony of Padua. Such a reproach had been misrepresented as a sort of Protestant critique to the veneration of saints. This seventeenth-century report makes it plausible that the custom of torturing statues of saints had a Portuguese origin, rather than stemming from any Indian religions.[150]

Another common problem faced by the Oratorians was not specific to them, but rather was connected with the prejudices spreading among Europeans, including missionaries, during that century. While racist discourse has a long history[151], in the nineteenth century prejudices merely based on skin colour and physical appearance often became part of a generalized common sense and reached the level of generalized ideology. If the Jesuit Visitor Alessandro Valignano (1539–1606) had warned already in the late sixteenth century against the admission of Indians to the Society of Jesus using proto-racist arguments[152], a new level was reached by men such as Giuseppe Maria Bravi OSB (1813–1860), the first Vicar Apostolic of Ceylon of European origin:

> They are Indians and thus by nature they are incapable of any perseverance; they are low, proud and fickle. The best of them, the most holy, do not succeed in correcting themselves of these defects. I am inclined to think that there is not a single exception in the whole of India, though one may have been educated in Rome or in London or Paris. When they are united and when the occasion is favourable, the black skin asserts itself irresistibly.[153]

The novelty of such a judgement, an attitude that became widespread throughout the 19th century, stands out clearly if we consider that the very first Vicar Apostolic of India, and one of the first ever appointed by the Pontifical Congregation de Propaganda Fide, had been a "brown man", the Goan Brahman Mateus de Castro (1594?–1679) in the first half of the seventeenth century.[154]

4.2.2 The Social Context of the Decline of the Oratorians

In this section we analyse the challenges that the Oratorians faced in the final phase of their presence in Ceylon. The single most important cause of Oratorian decadence had to do with developments occurring in Europe. In 1828 a civil war broke out in Portugal between the

---

150 F. LA BOULLAYE-LE-GOUZ, *Les voyages et observations du sieur de La Boullaye-Le-Goulz* (Paris 1653), 223. See also L. MIROT, "La vie et les aventures d'un Capucin auxerro-nivernais aux Indes: le Père Ephrem de Nevers" (*Buletin de la Section de Géographie du Comité des Travaux historiques et scientifiques* 60, 1945, 45–69); F. RICHARD, "Ephrem de Nevers et Zénon de Baugé, premiers auteurs français d'ouvrages en tamoul" (*Moyen- Orient et Océan Indien* 6, 1989, 151–163).
151 F. BETHENCOURT, *Racisms*. From the Crusades to the Twentieth Century (Princeton 2013).
152 See P. ARANHA, "Gerarchie Razziali e Adattamento Culturale: La 'Ipotesi Valignano'", in: A. TAMBURELLO / M.A.J. ÜÇERLER / M. DI RUSSO (eds.), *Alessandro Valignano S.I., Uomo del Rinascimento. Ponte tra Oriente ed Occidente* (Roma 2008), 76–98.
153 V. PERNIOLA, *The Catholic Church in Sri Lanka*. The British Period. Vol. 3: 1850–1855. The Vicariates of Colombo and Jaffna (Dehiwala 2003), 4. Bravi to Propaganda, Colombo, 15 January 1850.
154 See recently P. ARANHA, "Early Modern Asian Catholicism and European Colonialism, Dominance, Hegemony and Native Agency in the Portuguese Estado da Índia", in: K. KOSCHORKE / A. HERMANN (eds.), *Polycentric Structures in the History of World Christianity / Polyzentrische Strukturen in der Geschichte des Weltchristentums* (Wiesbaden 2014, 285–306).

Absolutist party (*absolutistas*) led by Dom Miguel I (1802–1866, r. 1828–1834) and the progressive liberal party (*constitucionalistas*), represented by Dona Maria II (1819–1853) but actually under the direction of her father Dom Pedro (1798–1834). The religious orders, allied with the defeated *Miguelistas*, received punishment when Dom Pedro triumphed in 1833.[155] A decree was issued on 5 August of that year, extinguishing all male religious orders in Portugal and in its Empire, as well as forbidding the admission of novices to the female congregations. Such a political upheaval, a sort of new earthquake shaking Lisbon, had echoes even in remote places, where Catholics had been subject to the *Padroado Real* of the Kingdom of Portugal since the sixteenth century. In Goa, the suppression of religious orders and confiscation of their houses led to an utter devastation of all the Catholic institutions across South Asia that had been staffed until then from the capital of the *Estado da Índia*. The Oratorians in Ceylon could not count anymore on confreres coming from Goa to replace them. In 1836 the last batch of Oratorians came from Goa to Ceylon, so that the mission counted eighteen members in that year.[156] From that moment onwards, the churches in Ceylon would still be considered part of the *Padroado*, but would have to be staffed by diocesan priests, many of which would likely be former members of religious orders such as the Oratorians. One of these was Mateus Caetano, former Oratorian and then secular priest, who became Vicar General of Ceylon and died in 1874 at the age of 68 years.[157]

If the political upheaval in Portugal was the primary factor damaging the missions in Ceylon, the specific evolution of the colonial society posed further challenges. Education was the issue at stake. It cannot be claimed that the Oratorians had not paid attention to this aspect, as in 1836 there were already 101 schools for Roman Catholic pupils in the island, out of which fourteen were in Colombo.[158] However, the rapid development of English education promoted by the Anglican and Protestant churches put the Catholic missionaries under unbearable pressure. The Goan priests, who were in charge of Tamil-, Sinhala-, and Portuguese-speaking communities and who had also produced important literary contributions in those languages, did not react promptly to the advent of an English cultural hegemony, for a lack either of preparation or interest. The Oratorians, and the missionaries who followed them, did not satisfy the desire of many Catholics in Ceylon to have their children educated according to an English model. At that time, a group of laymen in the Church even criticised the Goan priests for not being competent in preaching sermons in English (at least once a month) in addition to Portuguese, Sinhala, and Tamil.[159] Already at that time a community of English-speaking Catholics was emerging (including for instance Irish soldiers serving under the British colonial government), but the Goan missionaries were unable to cope with their new demands. Among these dissatisfied Catholics was the already mentioned John Bonifácio Misso, who according to the Vicar Apostolic Bettacchini was a leading physician in the island and served as private doctor to several Oratorians in Colombo at that time.[160]

A third critical aspect of the late Oratorian mission, in addition to the suppression of the religious congregations and the challenges of English education, lay in the internal split between a "conservative" and "progressive" party. The former, despite the "betrayal" of Portugal against its religious, was still loyal to the *Padroado* and believed that new clerical recruits

---

155 V. NETO, *O Estado, a Igreja e a Sociedade em Portugal. 1832–1911* (Lisboa 2001), 45–52.
156 PERNIOLA, *The Catholic Church in Sri Lanka. The British Period.* Vol. 1, 167–168.
157 DEP, *The Oratorian Mission*, 88.
158 PERNIOLA, *The Catholic Church in Sri Lanka. The British Period.* Vol. 1, 187.
159 PERNIOLA, *The Catholic Church in Sri Lanka. The British Period.* Vol. 1, 180.
160 BARCATTA, *A History of the Southern Vicariate*, 269.

could only be sent from the dioceses of Cochin and Goa. The "progressive" Oratorians, namely those willing to adapt to new situations, were willing to receive English-speaking priests and actually requested them from Mons. Daniel O'Connor (1786–1867, r. 1834–1840), Vicar Apostolic of Madras. While Misso and many more Catholics (possibly two thousand and mostly Burghers) supported the "progressive" faction among the Oratorians, the Holy See appointed the "conservative" Fr. Vicente do Rosario as Vicar Apostolic of Ceylon in 1841, against the "progressive" confrere Fr. Caetano Antonio. These conflicts on appointments and the *Padroado* would come to a head in the later half of the 19th century.

Chapter 2:
Padroado Controversies in South Asia

Vignette – The Consequences of the Padroado Controversies

February 1895. It had been almost a decade since the *Concordat* of 1886 had been signed between Portugal and Rome as an end to the jurisdictional rearrangement of the *Padroado* in Asia. As in other parts of the Catholic world in South Asia, the pro-*Padroado* party in Bombay and Ceylon had lost its momentum. One year before, Antonio Francisco Xavier Alvares had been arrested in Goa, not for his support of the *Padroado* (which he had given up in 1887), but for his claim to be a bishop of the so-called Jacobite Syrian Church, suspicious to the Roman Catholic Church. The "Goan/Portuguese schism" stopped appearing in high frequency in the correspondence between the Congregation of Propaganda Fide and the Bishops and Apostolic Delegates in Asia. It seemed as if the century-long controversy was moribund and the anger gave way to other ecclesiastical concerns, as well as to life-threatening emergencies such as recurrent plague epidemics in India. However, the long and wide impact of the *Padroado* Controversies had a knock-on effect, as observed by the Apostolic Delegate of the East Indies, Władysław Michał Zaleski (in office 1892–1916), who was at that time a critic of the nomination of native Bishops in the Suriani Catholic Church in Malabar.[1] His claims were not unpopular in the Catholic Church in the nineteenth century. It was believed among the European missionaries that the Suriani clergymen did not have proper formation and were not even proper true Catholics, so that none of them were worthy candidates. However, the issue was even more complex. The Polish Bishop also attributed the Suriani demand for native Bishops to the influence of the *Padroado* anarchy and the Goan schism. In his view, the Suriani Catholics were contaminated by the malign legacy of the schismatic *Padroado* priests from the Latin rite Church:

> *Padroado* has infused in the people a spirit of rebellion and of insubordination to ecclesiastical authority and also towards the Holy See. This sad heredity of *Padroado* is a danger for the Church in India.[2]

---

1 Suriani is derived from the "Syriac" and refers to the Christian community of the Malabar Coast established in the first century AD. On the difference of Suriani and Nazrani Catholics see C. VARICATT, *The Suriani Church of India. Her Quest for Autochthonous Bishops (1877–1896)* (Kottayam, 1992), 1–2. For a discussion of the Nazrani Orthodox see M.K. THOMAS, *The Way of St. Thomas. A Brief History of The Malankara Orthodox Syrian Church* (Kottayam 2012), 14–43.
2 VARICATT, *The Suriani*, 388–389. The original letter is found in the Archivio della Congregazione per le Chiese Orientali (ACCO), Rubrica 109, Soriani del Malabar Varia (1894–1897) fol. 49v. Kandy 8 February 1895, Zaleski to Cardinal M. Ledóchowski, Prefect of the Congregation of Propaganda in Rome.

Zaleski was new to the Portuguese/Goan schism, unlike Christophe Bonjean OMI (in Ceylon 1857–1892). As the first Archbishop of Colombo, Bonjean had worked for forty years in both Jaffna and Colombo Dioceses and had witnessed the emergence of dissident *Padroado* groups scattered in disconnected regions of the island since the 1840s, before they transformed into the first Independent Catholic Mission in 1888. As for Zaleski, he had learned about most of the vicissitudes of the *Padroado* debates in Asia only from the written memories and the voice of his predecessors. When he arrived in India and Ceylon in 1892 as a new Apostolic Delegate for the East Indies, the turmoil of the ex-*Padroadists* in Colombo after having joined the Syrian Orthodox Church since 1888, had become part of the conflicts that Rome had with the Saint Thomas Christians in Malabar. Thanks to the hindsight of Zaleski, we can discern more easily the interconnectedness of local resistance within the Catholic Church in South Asia during the nineteenth century, despite different contexts and diversified reasons. Zaleski's comment also shows the entanglement of multiple dichotomies: the Asian and the European, the Portuguese and the Roman, the Latin and the Syrian rites. In fact, the tensions were not confined to the Catholic Church. A spirit of rebellion and unconformity was shared and inherited commonly by the Christian churches in South Asia across denominational divisions.

This chapter on the Portuguese *Padroado* examines how this historical process was related to the emergence of the Independent Catholics in Ceylon and India. In the first place, we will briefly review the scholarly literature of the "*Padroado* controversies" in South Asia from the mid-nineteenth to the mid-twentieth centuries, covering the zenith of those conflicts until the eventual solution of the issue in 1929. The Carmelites in Bombay and Jesuits initiated a denunciation of *Padroado* through publications in Italian and English in 1853, with the hope to further limit the *Padroado* jurisdiction as prescribed in the *Concordat* of 1838. The initial debate and the follow-up developments were studied by the English Jesuit historian Ernest R. Hull, in a narrative epitome written from a Propaganda Fide perspective. According to this Jesuit author, the schism led by Antonio Alvares after 1886 was not associated with the general discussion on the *Padroado* and Propaganda conflicts. Secondly, we give a brief review of the institution of *Padroado* in pre-modern time, relating to and comparing with the various tensions concerning the *Padroado* controversies during the nineteenth century. Thirdly, we highlight essential terms such as "*Padroadists*" and "schism", as interpreted by Hull from the point of view of the Holy See. This is to be contrasted to the grassroot representations of "Propaganda (Fide) missionaries" held by the Indo-Portuguese Catholics. Fourthly, we continue exploring the mistrust or misunderstandings between Rome and South Asia by looking at the intermediate roles of the Apostolic Vicars. Fifthly and lastly, we try to sketch the *Padroado* community in the metropolis of Bombay, where the *Padroado* media centre in the subcontinent was based. We focus on a *Padroadist* family in that city, from which two medical doctors, José Camillo Lisboa and his nephew Pedro Manuel Lisboa Pinto, gained experience through practice of journalism and leadership in social movements. The development of the *Padroado* movement in Bombay was an example and an inspiration for that of Ceylon, until the latter decided to separate from the Catholic Church in 1888.

1. A Brief Overview of Literature on the Debates on Padroado in South Asia, 1853–1940

1.1 The Capuchins, the New Society of Jesus Against the Padroado

During the nineteenth century, debates on *Padroado* emerged across regions which were hitherto or had been under Portuguese colonial rule in Asia and Africa.[3] In the Catholic sources, written in Latin, Portuguese, Italian, and French, the defence of the *Padroado* jurisdiction in South Asia was often labelled by the Roman Catholic authors as the "Goan schism", while defenders were called "Goan schismatics". In the case of the Independent Catholics, Alvares and his congregation in India and Ceylon were also called "Jacobite schismatics" for their recourse to the Syrian Orthodox communion.[4]

At the beginning of the nineteenth century, the Portuguese royal patronage (*Padroado*) faced unprecedented challenges in the Portuguese overseas missions. In the course of the century, with the decline of Portuguese power in Asia and Africa, turmoil over the *Padroado* came to its zenith because of the convergence of several tensions, such as conflicts between church and state, between colonial powers, between liberalism and conservatism, and most of all between those labelled as "white" and "dark"-coloured races. Already in the seventeenth century, the Portuguese *Padroado* and its defenders such as the Portuguese bishops and the Society of Jesus, came into jurisdictional clashes with other European institutions and organisations, such as the Spanish *patronato*,[5] the Roman Congregation of Propaganda Fide, and the Missions Etrangères de Paris[6] and alike. Popes, kings, bishops, and theologians were then the main players in the conflicts over *Padroado*, while European missionaries in Asia travelled back to Europe in order to lobby in different courts, with native testimonies in favour of their arguments. With few exceptions, neither the native clergy nor the laity participated in these negotiations.[7] However, thanks to new means of transportation and communication, especially the mail network established within the British Empire in the nineteenth century, discussions in public media multiplied in metropolises such as Bombay, Madras, and Colombo, extending also to Portuguese India.[8]

---

3 On the *Padroado* debates in Congo see J.I. NKULU BUTOMBE, *La Question du Zaire et ses Répercussions sur les Juridictions Ecclésiastiques.* 1865–1888 (Kinshasa 1982).
4 See references to "the weak party of the Jacobite schismatics" in a letter from André-Théophile Mélizan, archbishop of Colombo to Propaganda Fide, Colombo, 16 November 1894, translated in PERNIOLA, *The Catholic Church in Sri Lanka*, vol. 3, 484.
5 On the Spanish patronage in the Philippines, see F.J. MONTALBÁN, *Patronato español y la conquista de Filipinas con documentos del Archivo General de Indias*, Bibliotheca Hispana Missionum IV (Burgos 1930).
6 This history has been reflected on from various perspectives. Studies from the Roman institutional point of view have been collected in J. METZLER (ed.), *Sacrae Congregationis de Propaganda Fide memoria rerum*: 350 anni a servizio delle missioni 1622–1972, 3 vols. (Rom 1971–1976). An excellent study from the Portuguese and Jesuit viewpoints is found in A. VASCONCELOS DE SALDANHA, *De Kangxi para o Papa pela via de Portugal*: Memória e documentos relativos à intervenção de Portugal e da Companhia de Jesus na questão dos ritos chineses e nas relações entre o imperados Kangxi e a Santa Sé, 3 vols (Macau 2002).
7 A noticeable exception was Bishop Matheus de Castro (1594–1679) of Goan Brahman origin, who travelled to Rome and negotiated with the Congregation of Propaganda Fide for the rights of the native clergy in India. See recently in P. SOUZA FARIA, "Mateus de Castro: Um bispo 'brâmane' em busca da promoção social no império asiático português (século xvii)" (*Revista Eletrônica de História do Brasil* 9/2, 2007, 31–43).
8 See an analysis of the communication system in British India in D. HEADRICK, "A Double-Edged Sword: Communications and Imperial Control in British India" (*Historical Social Research* 35/1, 2010, 51–65).

Two religious orders played a leading role in the struggle for an amendment to the *Concordat* of 1838. These are the Capuchins in the Apostolic Vicariate of Bombay and the Jesuits of the mission of Madurai in South India. The New Society of Jesus, re-established in 1814 after the suppressions decreed between 1759 and 1773, returned to India no longer subject to the Portuguese *Padroado*, but firmly under the supervision of the Congregation of the Propaganda Fide. The new Jesuit missions in India were subject to different European Jesuit provinces. The English Province of the Jesuits first sent missionaries to Bengal, where a Mission was founded in 1834. It was followed by the Madurai Mission in 1838, staffed by the French Toulouse Province. The Jesuits from the Upper German Province undertook the Bombay Mission in 1858. Jesuits from the Belgium Province initiated a second Bengal Mission in 1859. Italian Jesuits from the Venetian Province undertook the Calicut-Mangalore Mission in 1878. Goa, that had been the very center of the Jesuit presence in Asia in the early modern times, became once again a mission only in 1890, supported by the Portuguese Province. Finally, a Mission was established in Patna in 1919, thanks to the North-American Jesuits of Missouri.[9] Almost all of these Jesuit Missions encountered vehement resistance from the Indo-Portuguese priests and laymen loyal to the Portuguese *Padroado* rooted in the territories of the new Missions.

Mons. Anastasius Hartmann (1803–1866), a Swiss Capuchin who was Apostolic Vicar of Patna and Administrator of the Apostolic Vicariate of Bombay, took action against the bishop of Macao, Jerónimo de Mata, when the latter visited Bombay in 1853. The Portuguese prelate performed ordinations of a large number of candidates, and gave a sermon attacking the Propagandists in Bombay. In 1853 Hartmann sent the Italian confrere Ignazio Persico (1823–1895) to Rome, so as to promote a revision of the *Concordat* of 1838 and further limit the Portuguese jurisdiction in the British colonial territories.[10] Persico's mission found a manifesto in the book, also published in 1853, under the title *The Goa Schism: Being a Short Historical Account of the Resistance Made by the Indo-Portuguese Clergy to the Institution of Apostolic-Vicariates in British India.* This work was a collaboration made between Persico and William Strickland.[11] This English Jesuit had worked at the Madurai Vicariate Apostolic since 1847, before joining the Jesuit Bombay Mission in 1854.[12] Both authors shared in this text the personal experiences that they had with the "schismatic priests" in the two Missions. Persico later also published an Italian memoir, calling public attention to the Indo-Portuguese schism.[13] Persico later became the Secretary of the Congregation of Propaganda Fide (in office 1891–1893), so as to initiate a revision of the *Concordat* of 1838.[14]

---

9 See a brief introduction to the establishment of the New Society in India in L. FERNANDO, 'Jesuits and India', *Oxford Handbooks Online* (published online in November 2016 and last accessed on 2 January 2022).

10 See a detailed study on Persico's biography with an informative historical context in D.C. SHEARER, "Ignatius Cardinal Persico, O.F.M.Cap. (1823–1895)" (*Franciscan Studies* 10, 1932, 53–137). A brief biography is also given in *Bibliotheca missionum: Missionsliteratur Indiens u. Indonesiens, 1800–1909* (Aachen 1965), 194.

11 I. PERSICO / W. STRICKLAND S. J., *The Goa Schism*. Being a Short Historical Account of the Resistance Made by the Indo-Portuguese Clergy to the Institution of Apostolic-Vicariates in British India (Dublin 1853). In 1852 Strickland had published *The Jesuit in India: Addressed to All Who Are Interested in the Foreign Missions* (London 1852).

12 Strickland and later German Jesuits' transfer to Bombay marked the establishment of the New Society in that city. On the movement of the Jesuits from Europe and from the Bengal and Madurai Missions in 1853 to 1856 see A. VÄTH, *Die deutschen Jesuiten in Indien*. Geschichte der Mission von Bombay-Puna 1854–1920 (Regensburg 1920), 68–81.

13 *Memoria sullo scisma Indo-Portoghese che si presenta al pubblico da un missionario delle Indie Orientali Italia.*

14 HULL, *Bombay Mission History*: Vol I, 420–426.

In the same year of 1853, the Jesuit Lorenzo Puccinelli (1819–1872), belonging to the Madurai Mission, published in Rome three memoirs collected under the title *Lo scisma Indo-Portoghese al giudizio degli Imparziali*.[15] Puccinelli, based in Tuticorin, had been an experienced missionary on the frontline of the local competition with the *Padroado* priests on the Fishery Coast. He was sent to Rome in 1852 to report on the unruly Goan priests troubling the Madurai Mission. In Rome he became secretary of the Apostolic Vicar of Verapoly, the Discalced Carmelite Luigi di Santa Teresa Martini (1809–1883), assisting in the discussions on the Catholics in Malabar and their petitions for native bishops. Puccinelli also participated in the Portuguese-Vatican negotiations that led to the *Concordat* of 1857. In the following decades and until the beginning of the twentieth century, the Jesuits in the Madurai mission had to deal with a puzzling development of the earlier *Padroado* unrest, in the form of an unprecedented expansion of Syrian Christianity, through a rather unique Latin branch of the Syrian Orthodox Church.

1.2 Hull and the Bombay Mission History, 1929–1930

Entering the early twentieth century, the debates on *Padroado* came to a final appeasement. Towards the end of 1920s, historians who had witnessed the vicissitudes from different perspectives tried to give a general overview. In 1940, António da Silva Rêgo, former missionary to Macao and distinguished missionary historian, regarded three works as general references to the topic: the second volume of the *History of the Catholic Church in India* on the years 1652–1924, by a Bombay priest, Manoel Francis X. D'Sa, the *Bombay Mission History* by an English Jesuit in Bombay, Ernest Hull[16], and Rêgo's own *O Padroado Português do Oriente: esbôço histórico*. These works were no longer part of the *Padroado* debate itself, but a partisan viewpoint was still explicit in their interpretations, hence the complexity of this history.

Ernest Reginald Hull S. J. (1863–1952) was born in England and joined the Society of Jesus at the age of 23. He was called to the Jesuit Bombay mission after having worked in Scotland and Ireland.[17] Between 1908 and 1913 he worked as editor of the official newspaper of the Bombay Diocese, *The Bombay Examiner*, through whose printing press he published dozens of pamphlets and monographs. Meanwhile, he was also appointed as archivist and secretary of the archbishop of Bombay, gaining exclusive access to the historical sources. His two-volume *History*, covering the periods 1534–1858 and 1858–1923 respectively, was the outcome of "a series of 43 articles published in *The Examiner* between 1908 and 1910; followed by another series of 15 articles containing the particular history of single places and institutions, published between 1910 and 1915", in addition to "the task (undertaken in 1920) of pulling to pieces the Diocesan Archives of Bombay and Poona".[18] Hull's extensive re-

---

15 L. PUCCINELLI, *Lo scisma Indo-Portoghese al giudizio degli Imparziali Memorie Tre* (Roma 1853). See Puccinelli's biography in C.E. O'NEILL AND J.M. DOMÍNGUEZ (eds.), *Diccionario histórico de la Compañía de Jesús*. Vol. 4: Piatti–Zwaans (Roma 2001), 3256–3257.
16 E.R. HULL, *Bombay Mission History: With a Special Study of the Padroado Question*, Vol. 1: 1534–1858, Vol. 2: 1858–1890 (Bombay 1927–30).
17 C.E. O'NEILL, *Diccionario histórico de la Compañía de Jesús*. Costa Rossetti–Industrias, vol. 2 (Madrid 2001), 1966–1967; J. BEAUMONT, *Roads to Rome. A Guide to Notable Converts from Britain and Ireland from the Reformation to the Present Day* (South Bend 2010), 218.
18 HULL, *Bombay Mission History*, Vol. 1, 1.

search into specific locations, and his panoramic view of church history were initially prepared for a general history of the Vicariate of Bombay including its surrounding areas. It became, however, "apparent that a very large portion of the history involved a detailed study of the conflict between *Padroado* and Propaganda; and this not as a mere local question, but one which extended over the whole of India, and even the entire East." Hull spoke of "*Padroado* questions", a term that had been used by Leo Meurin in his pamphlet entitled *Padroado question*. As a consequence, he writes, "the present history has a twofold aspect, the one local and particular, the other universal." Clearly, Hull treated the Archdiocese of Bombay as an archetype of the *Padroado* conflict. In fact, this archdiocese found its ultimate origin in events that occurred soon after the creation of Propaganda Fide in 1622. In 1637 this new Roman congregation established the Apostolicate Vicariate of the "Idalcan" (i.e. of the Sultanate of Bijapur, ruled by the Adil Khan dynasty), entrusted in 1637 to the Brahman prelate Mateus de Castro. In 1669 the ecclesiastical jurisdiction was redefined as Vicar of the Great Mogul, and in 1820 it became finally the Vicariate of Bombay, elevated to archdiocese in 1886.

With the transfer of Bombay from the Portuguese crown to Charles II of England in 1661, the ecclesiastical jurisdiction on the region had to be negotiated between three European parties, namely the Kingdom of Portugal in relation to its Padroado claims even on ceded territories, the Holy See and obviously the Kingdom of Great Britain (since its institution in 1707). To a certain extent, this was a central issue throughout the vicissitudes of the Vicariate of Bombay, as demonstrated in Hull's meticulous chronological survey on the individuals responsible for the mission. It is through these individual actions and correspondence that we can identify the *Padroado* activists' networks from Bombay to other parts of South Asia.

Interestingly, Hull did not consider Antonio Alvares and the Independent Catholics a part of the *History* of the *Padroado* controversies. In the section on the long-term consequences of the Torres affair, he explicitly stated that: "The Alvarez [sic] schism which caused some disturbance in Ceylon after 1886 has nothing to do with our history."[19]

We have not been able to find further explanations or studies by Hull on the so-called "Alvarez schism". A possible reason is that the renegade Alvares joined the Syrian Orthodox Communion in 1886–1887, turning his back on the *Padroado* alliance in Goa and Bombay. This abrupt break is attested to in various articles against the *Padroado* published in Alvares' English newspaper in Colombo, *The Independent Catholic* (1892–1896), but also reported substantially in the Bombay-based *Padroadist* newspaper *O Anglo-Lusitano* (1886–1955). Possibly because of a stance against both the Papacy and the *Padroado*, Hull no longer considered Alvares and his Independent Catholic Mission a part of an internal cleavage of the Roman Catholic Church, but an external one in relation to the Orthodox Church of Antioch. Hence the "Alvares schism" became something that had more to do with the broader context of the Roman Catholic controversy with the St Thomas Christians in Malabar. Hull's attitude towards Alvares contradicted most other authors in relation to Alvares's role in the general development of the Goan schism. Hull's view on Alvares was opposite to what Christian Masillamani Agur, the Anglican lay historian and Office Manager at the British Resident's

---

19 HULL, *Bombay Mission History*, Vol. 1, 260.

Office (1884–1904) in Trivandrum expressed in his fundamental work entitled *Church History of Travancore*.[20] In Part II of this tripartite book, Agur discusses both Alvares and the Independent Catholic Mission as concerning the "Roman Catholic Church", in particular as part of his analysis of the two *Concordats* signed between Lisbon and Rome in 1857 and 1886. According to him, the very foundation of the Independent Catholics, which he believed were mainly constituted of the "Bharatar community", lay in their dissent from the "*Concordats* and the Hierarchy and they resisted the Pope's efforts to suppress the Double Jurisdiction."[21]

The pro-*Padroado* literature was produced mainly by Indo-Portuguese elites in Bombay, Goa, and Ceylon, including three authors from Bombay – Vicente Salvador Rodrigues, Júlio Menezes, and Pedro Manuel Lisboa Pinto under the pseudonym R.M.P., and later on the Goan Lopes Alpoim.[22] These were Hull's polemical targets, so that Alvares' "apostasy" appeared rather as a different issue. However, to complicate furthermore the analysis, we need to consider a fundamental point made recently by Giovanni Vian. This Italian historian has discovered a report sent by the Apostolic Delegate Zaleski in 1909, analysing the spread of Modernism, and specifically of "disciplinary modernism" in India. Rather than being a challenge on Biblical exegesis or on the alleged conflict of modern science with Catholic doctrine, this "disciplinary modernism" consisted in

> the despise of ecclesiastical authority, of canon law and liturgical rites; the tendency to judge the decisions made by bishops, and to relate with them, and speak about them with little respect; an excessive charity towards Protestants, and a certain vanity to show oneself as having "latitudinarian and liberal ideas".[23]

What is most striking is that, according to Zaleski, the very Jesuit Ernest Reginald Hull had been "the Precursor of Modernism in India". Vian observes that, in order to contrast Hull's negative influence, the Apostolic Delegate made all efforts to remove the English Jesuit from his position as redactor of the *Bombay Examiner*, so that the latter had to give up in 1913, after five years of service. In the light of these circumstances, unknown to the previous historiography on 19th–20th century Catholicism in India, we can sense an interesting paradox: the Modernist Ernest Reginald Hull fought against the *Padroado* supporters, among whom emerged also a fringe movement, namely Alvares and the Independent Catholics, that eventually promoted some other form of Catholic Modernism.

---

20 C.M. AGUR, *Church History of Travancore* (Madras 1903). He is also the author of *History of the Protestant Church in Travancore* (Madras 1903). A biography of Agur can be found in the blog "Milestones of Kanyakumari" by P. Babu Manohran (http://milestonesofkanyakumari.blogspot.com/2015/05/remarkable-church-historian-mrchristian.html, last accessed on 5 January 2022).
21 C.M. AGUR, *Church History of Travancore* (New Delhi 1990), 367.
22 On this literature see A. DA SILVA RÊGO, *O padroado português no Oriente e a sua historiografia (1838–1950)*. Subsídios para a história portuguesa 15 (Lisboa 1978).
23 G. VIAN, "Indie Orientali, Indocina, Oceania: Il modernismo in mondi lontani', in: C. ARNOLD / G. VIAN (ed.), *The Reception and Application of the Encyclical Pascendi. The Reports of the Diocesan Bishops and the Superiors of the Religious Orders until 1914*, Studi di Storia 3 (Venezia 2017, 231–245).

2. From Early Modern Solutions to the Modern Challenges

2.1 Padroado Real: A Legal and Political History

The *Padroado Real* was a fundamental agreement between the Holy See and the Kingdom of Portugal (later the First Republic of Portugal in 1910–1926) on the ecclesiastical jurisdiction and management of its metropolitan territory and, most significantly, of the overseas lands occupied and annexed by the Lusitan state. In substance, the Pope ceded certain ecclesiastical rights to a Catholic monarch – the most important prerogative possibly being a right of presentation of episcopal candidates, to be then approved by the Holy See – in order to ease the diffusion of the faith in regions that were distant from Rome and could not easily be taken care of directly by a pontiff. At the root of the *Padroado* controversies there was a disagreement on the nature of the Roman cession to the Portuguese monarch: were certain rights alienated permanently or merely entrusted temporarily and conditionally? Did any revision in the *Padroado* arrangement require merely a decision on behalf of Rome, did the Portuguese party have a right to be consulted, or did it even need to consent explicitly, on account of the expenses that had been incurred previously in the exercise of the patronage functions? In fact, the entire financial support of the church apparatus in the Portuguese overseas territories depended on the royal budget, as the Lusitan armies also militarily defended the Christians in Asia against attacks by "infidel" (i.e. Muslim) or "pagan" (e.g. Hindu and Buddhist) kings. In the previous chapter we have seen an interesting example, namely the conquest of Mannar as an act of retaliation against an anti-Christian persecution, and as a means to defend the Christians from possible future attacks.

Almost contemporary to the Portuguese *Padroado Real* was the Spanish *Patronato Regio* that the popes granted to various Iberian Kings, even before Castilla and Aragon underwent a personal unification in 1492.[24] The *Patronato* jurisdiction extended to the Western and Eastern Indies when the Castilian King became the head of a globally extended Iberian empire.[25]

As Carl Schmitt has clearly synthesized in relation to Spain,

> The *papal missionary mandate* was the legal foundation of the conquista. This was not only the pope's position, but also that of the Catholic rulers of Spain, who recognized the missionary mandate to be legally binding. Above all, they emphasized the duty of the mission in their many instructions and orders to their admiral, Christopher Columbus, and to their governors and officers. [...] In the December 1501 bull *Piae devotionis*, the pope transferred Church tithes to Catholic rulers and, in return, imposed upon them the maintenance of priests and churches. [...] In an August 1508 bull, he established the patronage of the Spanish rulers over the churches in America.[26]

The Royal patronage has to be understood as an institution created to respond to the globalisation of the Roman Catholic Church, on the basis of a heritage of medieval canon law and

---

24 J. GARCÍA ORO and M.J. PORTELA SILVA, "Felipe II y el Patronato Real en Castilla" (*La Ciudad de Dios* CCXIII, 2000, 530–532).
25 I.T.P. LEE, "La actitud de la sagrada congregación al Regio Patronato", in: J. METZLER (ed.) *Sacrae Congregationis de Propaganda Fide memoria rerum: 350 anni a servizio delle missioni...1622–1972*, vol. I.1 (Rome 1971, 353–438); F.J. MONTALBÁN, *Patronato español y la conquista de Filipinas con documentos del Archivo General de Indias*, Bibliotheca Hispana Missionum IV (Burgos 1930).
26 CARL SCHMITT, *The Nomos of the Earth* (New York 2006), 111.

a political theory that assumed a fundamental difference between Christian and non-Christian political spaces, and that stipulated for the Pope the role of arbiter between Christian kings.[27] It was on the basis of this legal framework that the Holy See could draw a line (*raya*) between the expansion areas reserved for Portugal and the ones destined to Spain. Once this imperial line was drawn, then it was also possible to ascribe specific ecclesiastical rights to each monarchy within its own reserved territory.

The Royal patronage in regard to overseas "conquests", devised just before the Reformation, was shaken by the latter in its canonical and theoretical foundations. The Pope could cede only rights that he enjoyed, but the existence of those very rights was denied by the Protestants, for whom the Pope was at most a lapsed and sinful bishop of Rome, but never the head of the universal church or a binding arbiter among Christian sovereigns.

The ever-growing questions in regard to the royal patronage vividly reflected the changing balance between church and state, as well as the competition between different temporal powers. The new Roman Congregation of *Propaganda Fide*, created in 1622 with the purpose of strengthening the direct control of the Holy See over the global missions, would inevitably interfere with the Iberian royal patronage in areas such as the supervision over the various missionary religious orders, as well as the concrete and effective exercise of episcopal functions, with Apostolic Vicars competing with territorial bishops.

If a dimension of intra-European tension is undeniable in the development of the royal patronage system, it ultimately impacted the Christians of non-European regions in the first place. In those areas the emergence of a Catholic identity among the native faithful also implied a positioning vis-à-vis the national identities of the colonizers, either Portuguese or Spanish. A mixed identity was preeminent among Catholics with an interracial background, such as the Dutch and Portuguese Burghers. In fact, those "people inbetween", to use Michael Roberts' definition of the Eurasians in Sri Lanka, contrasted themselves to those who developed a more local identity.[28]

It is generally assumed that Prince Henry the Navigator's (1394–1460) maritime expansion westwards into the unknown Atlantic and the coasts of North Africa was a continuation of the anti-Muslim *Reconquista* of the Iberian Peninsula. However, when the Portuguese expanded to the non-Muslim lands deep south in Africa, the legitimacy of the conquest itself was inevitably questioned. In the light of the advantages that the Portuguese expansion even in non-Muslim areas could bring to the expansion of Catholicism, the Holy See did not hesitate in granting special rights to the Lusitan kings, as Administrators and then Great Masters of the chivalric Order of Christ (successor in Portugal since 1319 to the Templars, abolished in 1310), in the newly conquered lands.[29] In 1418 Pope Martin V (1368–1431), in his *Res Publica Christiana,* called for a new crusade against the *Mouros* in North Africa and granted the establishing of the Diocese of Ceuta, a city conquered by Dom João I (1391–1438) in 1415. In 1442 Eugene IV (1383–1447) used for the first time the term *ius patronatus* to

---

27 SCHMITT, *The Nomos of the Earth*, 91.
28 M. ROBERTS / I. RAHEEM / P. COLIN-THOMÉ, *People Inbetween*. The Burghers and the Middle Class in the Transformations within Sri Lanka, 1790s–1960s, vol. 1 (Ratmalana Sri Lanka 1989).
29 The pope perpetually entrusted the mastership of the Order of Christ to the Portuguese Crown in 1551. Before that moment, members of the royal family of Avis had been administrators or great masters of the Order on a circumstantial basis. On the general history of the Order see recently I.L. MORGADO DE SOUSA E SILVA / F. ANGIOLINI (eds.), *A ordem de Cristo (1417–1521).* Militarium ordinum analecta 6 (Porto 2002).

indicate the jurisdiction of the Order of Christ over the territories discovered and conquered in the Atlantic.[30]

The privileges of Portugal were gradually specified by the popes, following the steps of the Portuguese expansion from Ceuta to Cabo Bojador and beyond. The concept of *Padroado Real* was better defined particularly by bulls of Nicolas V (1397–1455) and Callixtus III (1478–1458), while scholars consider the 1534 Bull *Aequum reputamus* by Paul II as the most complete definition of *Padroado Real*.[31]

2.2 The Rise of the Padroadists in South Asia and the Concordats

According to Sebastião Rodolfo Dalgado, "*Padroadist* is a term coined in Indo-Portuguese to denote one who is under the spiritual jurisdiction of Bishops nominated by Portugal, or one who defends the right of the Portuguese nation to ecclesiastical patronage in British India". It was generally used in opposition to *Propagandista*: "a missionary or convert of the Roman Catholic congregation of the Propagation of the Faith".[32]

Throughout the nineteenth century the Catholic Church in India experienced a condition of latent or open schism, due to the conflict between communities pledging allegiance either to the *Padroado Real* of Portugal or to the Congregation of Propaganda Fide. This jurisdictional conflict dated back to the seventeenth century, shortly after the establishment of Propaganda Fide in 1622. Since the beginning of the eighteenth century, with the expansion of British colonization in South Asia and with the decline of Portuguese influence in India, the churches under the *Padroado* were gradually transferred to Propaganda Fide and the direct control of the Holy See. The suppression of male religious orders and the freeze imposed on female congregations in Portugal and its empire, together with a break of diplomatic relations between the Holy See and Portugal from 1833 to 1841, created the conditions for inflicting a radical blow to the *Padroado* system. The Holy See took over in the space left vacant by the Portuguese authorities, with Gregory XVI appointing new Apostolic Vicars in 1834 (Calcutta and Madras) and in 1836 (Pondichéry and Ceylon), and eventually publishing in 1838 the Brief *Multa præclare*, by which the *Padroado* jurisdiction in the territories that were beyond Portuguese sovereignty was de facto abolished. More precisely, in a provisional way and as long as a different decision was not taken by the Holy See,

---

30 L.M. JORDÃO, ed., *Bullarium patronatus Portugalliae regum in ecclesiis Africae, Asiae atque Oceaniae: Bullas, brevia, epistolas, decreta actaque Sanctae Sedis ab Alexandro III ad hoc usque tempus amplectens,* Vol. I (1171–1600), (Lisboa 1868), 20. The Bull *Etsi suscepti,* published on 9 January 1443 by Eugene IV, defined the extent of the *jus patronatus* in the following terms: "et administratori praedicto, necnon pro tempore existentibus Magistro ac fratribus ejusdem militiae, quod terras, possessiones et alia mobilia et immobilia bona quaecumque in regnis ac dominiis Regis Portugaliae pro tempore existentis, et quibuslibet aliis locis consistentiaque praefatae militiae per quosvis Christi fideles donari vel alias per eam justis modis acquiri contingerit, acceptare et cum similibus quibus alia in ipsis regnis bona nunc habet et possidet immunitatibus, libertatibus, privilegiis, modis atque formis retinere, ac etiam singulas, quarum *jus patronatus* [my highlighting] ei Christo fideles donaverint vel in ipsum, transtulerint ecclesias recipere, necnon sub modis, et cum privilegiis, quibus ecclesiam de Casevel Ulixbonensis dioecesis tenet, etiam retinere...".

31 M. DA CRUZ, "O Padroado", 239–241.

32 DALGADO, *Portuguese Vocables in Asiatic Languages*. From the Portuguese Original of Monsignor Sebastião Rodolfo Dalgado, trans. Anthony Xavier Soares (New Delhi 1988), 248, 302.

a. the territories in the Diocese of São Tomé de Meliapor that had not been yet committed to a Vicar Apostolic were to be united into the Apostolic Vicariate of Madras;
b. the territories in the Diocese of Cranganore and Cochin that had not yet been delivered to a Vicar Apostolic were to be united into the Apostolic Vicariate of Malabar, based in Verapoly
c. the "region of Malacca beyond the Ganges" would be entrusted to the Vicar Apostolic of Ava and Pegu.[33]

De facto, the ancient bishoprics of Cochin (established in 1557) and São Tomé de Meliapor (erected in 1606), as well the archbishopric of Cranganore (indicated as a mere diocese in the *Multa Præclare,* even though it was rather an archbishopric without suffragan sees, established in 1616, and heir to the Archdiocese of Angamale that had been created in 1599), lost all their territories and became mere titular sees, as if they were dioceses *in partibus infidelium.* The resistance against this Papal decision was vigorous throughout Asia, leading to a situation of open and ubiquitous division, the so-called "Goan Schism".[34] The term "schism" has to be placed in quotation marks, as it was used more in a polemical sense than in canonical terms. In fact, the authority of the Pope was not questioned in principle by the supporters of the *Padroado*. This division was described in the following terms in an English Catholic journal in 1851, with obvious sympathies for Propaganda Fide:

> The Goa clergy, then in possession of all our [= Catholic] ancient churches in India, refused to acknowledge any orders from Rome which were not forwarded through their own government [i.e. approved and registered by the Portuguese Chancery]; they rose in open resistance, opposed in every possible way the return of the European missioners [sic], and positively refused all obedience to the Bishops and Vicars-Apostolic appointed by Rome. Hence what is termed the Goa schism.[35]

The divisions were particularly violent in a region that the *Multa Præclare* had not considered specifically, namely the Archdiocese of Goa. The territory of Bombay also fell under the leading episcopal see of the *Padroado*, in competition with the Apostolic Vicar of the "Great Moghul", renamed as Apostolic Vicariate of Bombay in 1832. As even Rome did not specify what should happen in that region, veritable jurisdictional campaigns were waged from both sides so as to draw one or the other parish under each one's episcopal jurisdiction. It is precisely in this tense atmosphere in Bombay that Dr. Lisboa Pinto, the later Independent Catholic activist, grew up.

To put an end to such scandalous divisions, the *Concordat* of 1857 repealed the main norms of the *Multa Præclare* and partially re-established the traditional *Padroado* jurisdiction in areas beyond direct Portuguese sovereignty.[36] In relation to the ecclesiastical jurisdiction in South Asia (other norms regulated the situation of Southeast Asia and China), the

---

33 An English translation and summary of *Multa Præclare* can be found in HULL, *Bombay Mission History*, Vol.1, 238–244.
34 A partisan but detailed presentation of the schism is provided by M.-T. DE BUSSIERRE, *Histoire du Schisme Portugais dans les Indes* (Paris 1854).
35 ANONYMOUS, "Mission and Vicariate Apostolic of Madura, East Indies" (*The Rambler: A Catholic Journal of Home and Foreign Literature Politics, Science, Music and the Fine Arts* 8, 1851, London), 85.
36 RÊGO, *O padroado português*, 29–30.

approach chosen for the settlement consisted of an acknowledgement and formalization of the situation de facto existing on the ground:

1. A paritetic commission would define the borders of the suffragan dioceses depending on the Metropolitan See of Goa, ascribing to those *Padroado* bishoprics the territories that de facto acknowledged the Goan authority.
2. For the first time since the creation of Propaganda Fide, a provision would be made for the erection in South Asia of a new diocese subject to the *Padroado*, to be carved out from the territory belonging to the Archdiocese of Goa.

However, this arrangement was eventually not enacted. The commission for the delimitation of the diocesan borders did not conclude its work, as the Holy See did not appoint its own delegate. At the same time, doubts were raised on the actual capacity of Portugal to provide sufficient missionaries and means for the pastoral care of the immense territories. Conflicts continued to divide the Roman Catholic Church in South Asia, until a new *Concordat* was signed in 1886, granting to the archbishop of Goa the status of Patriarch of the East, with metropolitan jurisdiction over the newly established Diocese of Damão (retaining also the formal title of the suppressed archbishopric of Cranganore), as well as over the Dioceses of Cochin and São Tomé de Meliapor. These bishoprics were subject to the traditional discipline of the *Padroado*, with bishops presented by the Portuguese Crown and then appointed by the Pope. These *Padroado* dioceses would exist side by side with the relevant Apostolic Vicariate, hence leading to situations of double jurisdiction. This twofold arrangement was even clearer in the new regime of "semi-*Padroado*" that was intended for the dioceses of Bombay, Mangalore, Quilon, and Madurai (then shifted to Tiruchirapalli). In the case of episcopal vacancy, the bishops of each metropolitan area would prepare a list of three names, to be forwarded to the Portuguese government (via the archbishop of Goa), who would then select a candidate and would present him to the Holy See for appointment.[37] While this complicated system of double jurisdiction led to more friendly relations between Rome and Lisbon, it was not accepted by hardline *Padroado* supporters, those who were more *Padroadist* than the *Padroado* hierarchy itself.

In the light of the last *Concordat*, the Apostolic Vicariate of Colombo was promoted to an Archbishopric by Leo XIII (1878–1903). Antonio Agliardi (1832–1915) was appointed as the Apostolic Delegate to the East Indies in 1884, so as to announce the new arrangement for the Catholic Church in India and Ceylon. Upon his arrival in Colombo in December 1886, Agliardi faced a strong opposition, expressed both in Goa and in Ceylon.

3. Definition of Schism

In 1908, in an exploration of the term later also published in his *Bombay Mission History*, Hull tried to clarify the meaning of "schism", ranging from technically precise definitions to the rather loose meanings that the term acquired in the South Asian controversies on the 19th century *Concordats*. He distinguished seven aspects:

1. In ordinary English, and in other European languages, the word "schism" is often used to mean no more than a split or division of allegiance in a community which holds the same

---

37 RÊGO, *O Padroado português*, 30–33.

religious faith and practice [...]. In this general sense no one will deny that, at least after 1838, a state of schism existed in India wherever the Vicars-Apostolic and the Padroado were in actual conflict; and in this sense no one can raise any objection against the use of the word.

2. As soon however as one of the two parties begins to call the other "schismatic", the word loses its colourless meaning, by assigning the blame to one side. So also with the terms "Goanese schism" or "Indo-Portuguese schism" which undoubtedly imply that the fault of the schism lay with the Portuguese [...]

3. Schism in its strictest ecclesiastical sense is a crime of rebellion against the authority of the Church, such as injures the unity of the Church. It does not necessarily mean that the theoretical supremacy of the Holy See is professedly denied – for this would be out-and-out heresy. But it does mean that the Pope's right is ignored and disregarded and acted against, and therefore *constructively* denied, i.e., in practical effect. [...]

4. A schism in the strict ecclesiastical sense reaches its consummation only gradually. Its earliest stage may be a refusal to obey the orders of some local Ordinary, or resistance to the execution of some Papal decision by the Ordinary; so that the conflict is at first of a local character only. But when the Holy See steps in and backs up the local Ordinary, or issues a decree enforcing the point, the conditions for schism begin to ripen. As such resistance often rests on the supposition that the orders in question are unjust, or have been given under a misapprehension, time must always be allowed for proper representations or appeals to be made. [...]

5. Now the question at issue is whether, after the *Multa praeclare* of 1838, the conditions existed which would justify the application of the term "schism" in its strict ecclesiastical sense to those of the Padroado party who refused allegiance to the Vicars-Apostolic? The authorities at Rome, as we see from several documents, did apply the word "schism" to the situation; but the simple use of the word need not have meant more than schism in the ordinary sense –*viz.*, a jurisdictional split detrimental to the unity of the faithful. There is one document, however, (already cited), which goes further. It states that all are bound to submit to the Vicars-Apostolic in the regions assigned to them, and that the continued refusal to do so will carry with it a liability to be pronounced schismatics by the Holy See. This was in 1839 [...]

6. Of course canon law contemplates the possibility of mistaken and unjust judgments even in the highest ecclesiastical courts; and it is on this possibility that the position of the Padroado party in 1838 and following years will be seen to rest. The royal Patronage was granted in such terms that it could not be abrogated without the consent of the King of Portugal; and this consent had not been obtained. [...]

7. One of the arguments used in pamphlet literature was that the Padroado clergy could not have been in schism because they never denied the supreme authority and rulership of the Holy See. This argument ceases to be conclusive when we realise that such a denial, if made, would not be schism but heresy. For schism does not consist in denying the authority of the Church, but in rebelling against its exercise and disobeying its enactments. [...][38]

First published in the newspaper of the Bombay Diocese *Examiner* (24 October 1908), those seven points aimed to be an authoritative interpretation of "the mind of the Holy See".[39] From a historical point of view, the first Goan resistance to the *Concordat* of 1838 marked the start of an open schism in the Catholic Church in South Asia, but surely not to the extent of the Great Schism in 1054 between the West and East Churches, nor the English Reformation.[40] Hull's pioneering work on the *Padroado*-Propaganda conflict in South Asia, based on a careful compilation of official documents, inspired later scholars even on the opposite side, such as António da Silva Rêgo.

---

38 Partial quotation from HULL, *Bombay Mission History*, Vol.2 1858–1890, 120–123.
39 HULL, *Bombay Mission History*, Vol. 2, 124.
40 HULL, *Bombay Mission History*, Vol. 2, 122.

What stands at stake is the differentiation between physiological tensions within the Catholic Church and an outright violation of the unity of the Church, particularly in terms of disobedience to the Pope and to his decisions. Hull's seven points describe a wide space between these two poles, but his nuances did not apply only to South Asia, but even to other regions. For instance, even the emergence of the Old Catholic movement took place on a continuum of division from the Roman Catholic Church. In the next sections we look at the communication networks of the *Padroadists* and their concrete lives and actions.

4. Failed Communications

In 1881 the Delegation Apostolic of the East Indies was created by Leo XIII with the purpose of handling the *Padroado* conflicts in India and Ceylon. The first delegate was Antonio Agliardi (in office 1884–1887), who first came to India in 1884 to report on the episcopal arrangement according to the *Concordat* of 1857. Since then, the delegates became essential intermediaries between the native Catholics in Asia and the prelates in Rome. One function of the Apostolic Delegate was to provide updated reports about the *Padroado* party with original evidence, such as newspapers articles and pamphlets. Through this channel, Rome was able to measure the pulse of Catholic public opinion in South Asia. On 21 December 1888 the Secretary of State Cardinal Mariano Rampolla del Tindaro (1843–1913) wrote to the successor of Agliardi, the Apostolic Delegate Andrea Aiuti (in India in the years 1877–1890), commenting on an issue of the Bombay-based weekly *O Anglo-Lusitano*. This letter was published one month later in that same newspaper in an English translation. Rampolla criticised the laymen's involvement in religious matters and demanded that the Apostolic Delegate reprove the Bombay newspaper:

> For every one knows that in the Catholic Church it is not permitted to laymen to mix themselves in discussions regarding religious matters, and to raise protests, even in the shape of petitions, against acts emanating from the Holy See and by it declared definitive after long and careful deliberation. To pretend to instruct the Bishops and the Supreme Pontiff Himself in what they should do for the good of souls and to preserve justice; to say that the Supreme Pontiff was not well informed when He prescribed certain rules of conduct to the faithful; to declare that the acts of the Supreme Pontiff determining the exercise of the ecclesiastical jurisdiction were issued without the knowledge of places and circumstances of time, and in violation of the rights of others, or that they are not binding on the consciences of the faithful is a crime of intolerable presumption, and manifests the plan of sowing schism in the Church.[41]

Rampolla was clearly reacting to the recent visit of Pedro Manuel Lisboa Pinto to Lisbon, as delegate of the association for the Defence of the Portuguese Patronage in the East. During his stay in Lisbon in 1887 the Bombay doctor sent a letter to Pope Leo XIII. Neither having received replies from Portugal nor from Rome, Lisboa Pinto eventually returned to India. Only a few months later, he gave up the *Padroado* enterprise and joined the Independent Catholics in Ceylon. Rampolla did not meet Lisboa Pinto and likely did not reply to his request. Since the Secretary of State did not visit India or Ceylon, he relied on his local informants, namely the Propaganda bishops, the Vicars Apostolic, and most of all the Apostolic Delegates. With this system of validation of information, the communication pattern in regard to the *Padroado* questions in South Asia did not differ significantly from the one that

---

41 "Cardinal Rampolla's Letter" (*O Anglo-Lusitano*, 31 January 1889), 4.

occurred even in the early modern age. Even though telegrams were used frequently, and Indian newspapers were constantly sent to Rome as direct evidence of rebellious ideas spread on the subcontinent, it is necessary to indicate an imbalance between the Roman knowledge of the local church affairs and the wide horizon that the Indian Christians had acquired. In the pro-*Padroado* newspapers one could see a great interest in world news and international political affairs. The very title of *O Ultramar*, for instance, given to a pro-*Padroado* newspaper printed in Margao (Goa), was not merely a reference to the Goans themselves as "overseas" citizens, but also to their concern for the rest of the world. Almost all newspapers that were published by the *Padroadists* in Goa and Bombay, as far as we could consult them, had world news as a main section, in addition to commentaries on ecclesiastical and political issues occurring at the local level.

5. Padroadists in Bombay and Goa

5.1 Bombay

The nineteenth century witnessed the rise of Bombay, from an ordinary emporium situated in the Gujarat and Konkan littoral trading networks, to the status of *Urbs prima in India* (the prime city in India) whose economic power and cultural impact were, by the end of the century, next only to the capital of the British Raj in Calcutta. Two main factors supporting its economic growth were the opening of the Chinese markets in 1813 and the American Civil War in 1861–1865. Encouraged by the world markets, the Gujarat commercial families, who had consolidated their commerce with the East India Company during the eighteenth century, expanded the sale of raw cotton and opium to other countries. With a flow of affluence pouring into the city, the population, urban transportation, public health, and education had undergone a radical development since the middle of the century. The 1864 Census counted a total number of 816,562 inhabitants in the city, out of which 71 percent were Hindus, 17.87 percent Muslims, 6.03 percent Parsis, with the remaining 6.1 percent representing a variety of Europeans and other ethnic minorities.[42] In the meanwhile, port facilities expanded to accommodate major steam shipping companies. By 1847 nine lines were created to transport passengers from Bombay to Colombo, Surat, and Karachi. Two decades later, the opening of the Suez Canal in 1869 made Bombay even more viable for international traders, transforming it into a main port in global itineraries.[43] In 1845 the British government opened the Grant Medical College to educate native medical doctors with Western medical knowledge. The generous provision of stipends and free studentship attracted a large number of Parsi students from relatively poor families, but also new migrants, especially the Goan Catholics. By 1864 Goan students represented 30 percent of all students in the College.[44] In addition to the university and the various governmental colleges of medicine, arts, and science, a number of Christian institutions were opened up to facilitate the formation of a heterogeneous body of English-speaking intelligentsia from non-*Shetia* (or non-merchant) backgrounds.[45]

---

42 C.E. DOBBIN, *Urban Leadership in Western India. Politics and Communities in Bombay City, 1840–1885* (London 1972), 8.
43 P. KIDAMBI, *The Making of an Indian Metropolis. Colonial Governance and Public Culture in Bombay, 1890–1920* (Aldershot 2007), 19.
44 DOBBIN, *Urban Leadership*, 48.
45 DOBBIN, *Urban Leadership*, 154–172.

Notwithstanding the low percentage in the total population, Goans in Bombay achieved high visibility in medical and educational careers. The nineteenth century also witnessed a rise in number of the Goans in Bombay. Ever since the British crown had taken over the island-town from the Portuguese empire, the Catholics in Bombay had seen a decline in numbers and vitality due to the many restrictions imposed by the British. In 1720 the British authorities expelled all the Portuguese Catholic missionaries from the city, while handing over the Catholic jurisdiction to the Carmelites sent by Propaganda Fide.[46] This certainly created tensions between the new religious order constituted of non-Portuguese missionaries, and the Indo-Portuguese Catholics that had strong feelings of Lusophone patriotism, as the latter were reluctant to surrender to the former's authorities. The affected communities increased, as between 1774 and 1812 the East India Company expanded the boundaries of Bombay southwards to Salsette, Caranja, and Baçaim, territories that the Marathas had conquered from the Portuguese in 1739. By the early nineteenth century about 35,000 Catholics lived in Bombay. Though mainly of Indian origin, they were described as "Portuguese Catholics" or "Native Catholics" in English.[47] By the 1830s a steady flow of Goan citizens migrated into Bombay seeking fortune in the flourishing cotton market. In the meantime, a sense of friction began to develop between the existent Catholic Indian community and the newcomers from Goa, complicating furthermore the "Portuguese" identity of the Catholics living in the region.[48]

It was in these circumstances that the jurisdictional conflict between *Padroado* and Propaganda Fide, apparently only involving temporal and religious powers in Europe, provided an occasion for the already polarized Catholics to question the forms of their Christian belonging and the European decisions they were confronted with. It even created a space for debates in the public sphere.

Any Goan living in Bombay during the second half of the nineteenth century could hardly ignore José Camillo Lisboa (1823–1897), a medical doctor and president of the Grant Medical College, known as one of the leaders in the allegiance to the *Padroado* across India and Ceylon. Lisboa was a professor of Western medicine, and a botanist with considerable influence in Goan intellectual circles across India, Ceylon, and Europe.[49] Born in Assagão in the district of Bardez in northern Goa, Lisboa went to Bombay to study medicine and was enrolled in Grant Medical College, established in 1845, as one of its first students. After having completed due courses in five years, he was given a position as lecturer to teach anatomy while practicing as a surgeon at Sir Jamsetjee Jejeebhoy Hospital. He was acknowledged as one of the first Indian doctors studying leprosy. Lisboa also exhibited talents in administration. He served as president of the Grant College Medical Society for ten years and as president of the Medical Union for four years.[50] The foundation of Grant Medical College was

---

46 HULL, *Bombay Mission History*, Vol. 1, 27–63.
47 A. SANTIAGO FARIA / S.L. MENDIRATTA, "Goans and East-Indians: A Negotiated Catholic Presence in Bombay's Urban Space" (*InterDISCIPLINARY Journal of Portuguese Diaspora Studies* 7, 2 July 2018), 47.
48 See for instance P.V. GOMES, "'Bombay Portuguese': Ser ou não ser português em Bombaim no século XIX" (*Revista de História das Ideias* 28, 2007, 567–608).
49 An informative genealogy of Dr. Lisboa can be found online at https://www.geni.com/people/Dr-Jos%C3%A9-Lisboa/6000000010149969469, last accessed on 2 January 2022. A recent study on José Camillo Lisboa and his wife's activities in Bombay can be found in F.L. VICENTE, "Portuguese-Speaking Goan Women Writers in Late Colonial India (1860–1940)" (*Portuguese Studies Review* 25/1, 2017), 324–327. A very recent profile of Lisboa in regard to medical history is offered by M. FRENZ "To Be or Not To Be … a Global Citizen: Three Doctors, Three Empires, and One Subcontinent" (*Modern Asian Studies*, 2020, 1–42).
50 F.X. GOMEZ CATÃO, "Aldeia de Assagão (Goa) Subsídios Para a Sua História": 340.

owed to initiatives of the Indian Medical Service, an association of British doctors who promoted Western medicine in the British colonial city by establishing sanitary and vaccination facilities as well as hospitals and medical schools.[51] The imposition of a Westernised medical system derived from a conviction commonly shared by the British doctors towards the native traditional medicine. According to Charles Morehead, one of the founders of the College and a professor beneficial to Lisboa, "the native practice of medicine was indeed a glaring blemish in the midst of a government professing enlightenment."[52] Nonetheless, students were not totally prohibited from exploring Indian medical knowledge. For instance, at the Grant College Medical Society in 1851, Lisboa and his colleagues discussed about Indian remedies applied to the skin.[53] Lisboa dedicated himself to botanic research and published extensively in journals of the Bombay Branch of the Royal Asiatic Society and the Bombay Natural History Society. Two grasses are named after him: Tripogon Lisboæ and Andropogon Odoratus Lisboæ, the latter of which is believed to have been discovered by his wife and colleague Júlia Rodrigues Lisboa (?–1926). Mrs. Lisboa was also a member of the Bombay Natural History Society and independently published research papers.[54] Her only known article entitled "Short notes on the odiferous grasses (Andropogons) of India and Ceylon, with a description of a supposed new species", published in 1889, was enough to inscribe her name on the list of Western European Women scientists in the nineteenth century.[55]

José Camillo Lisboa epitomized the most successful Goans, who immigrated to Bombay and integrated into the upper echelon of the local intelligentsia. He became a syndic of the University of Bombay (est. 1857), after the medical faculty of Grant Medical College joined in the degree-granting system of that university in 1862. Around 1890, Lisboa was elected a member of the Acadêmia das Ciências de Lisboa in Portugal, an institution created by Queen Maria I of Portugal in 1779 to promote sciences and fine arts, adding up to the first two Indo-Portuguese intellectuals in that association, José Gerson da Cunha (1844–1900) and Julio Gonsalves, both from Bombay.[56] Lisboa and his wife were well-travelled across the globe. During the second half of 1888 the couple made a trip across Europe visiting Genoa, Paris, Bordeaux, Marseille, Madrid, Lisbon, Naples, Rome, and London. Various newspapers such as *Ultramar, Sud-Express,* and *Gazeta de Portugal* followed the footsteps of the couple, praising them as "the first class of the high society of Bombay".[57] Lisboa was also known for his philanthropic work, especially through donations to schools in his hometown of Bardez in Goa.

Lisboa's reputation went far beyond the Bombay medical circle. Some Goan intellectuals regarded him as a leader of the *Padroado* movement in Bombay, together with his nephew Pedro Manuel Lisboa Pinto (1856–1898), who dedicated himself to the *Padroado* campaign in Ceylon.[58] Lisboa's participation in Goan and Bombay politics started as early as his commencement of academic career. He was a co-founder of a political weekly called *Abelha de*

---

51 For a historical sketch of the Service see the preface in Lieutenant-Colonel D.G. CRAWFORD, *Roll of the Indian Medical Service 1615–1930*. Vol. 1 (London 1930): vii–ix.
52 M. RAMANNA, *Western Medicine and Public Health in Colonial Bombay, 1845–1895*. (Delhi 2002), 10.
53 M. RAMANNA, *Health Care in Bombay Presidency 1896–1930* (Delhi 2012), 158.
54 "The Late Dr. J. C. Lisboa" (*Lancet*, Volume 149, Issue 3851, 19 June 1897), 1719.
55 The paper is mentioned in M.R.S. CREESE, *Ladies in the Laboratory II*. West European Women in Science, 1800–1900; a Survey of Their Contribution to Research (Lanham 2004), 274.
56 "Indian intelligence" (*The Indian Magazine* by National Indian Association in Aid of Social Progress and Education in India 337, July 1890), 385.
57 "O Sr. Doutor Lisboa" (*O Ultramar*, 7 December 1888), 4.
58 GOMES CATÃO, "Aldeia", 342.

Bombaim (1848–1857), edited by Luís Caetano de Menezes, from Pirna, Bardez.[59] He even took up the editorial job when Menezes underwent troubles.[60] In 1862, Lisboa participated in a movement against the hitherto governor of Goa, Count of Torres Novas (r.1855–1864), for his alleged manipulation of the council election in Bardez in that year.[61] One of the tensions was centred on a journal entitled *Estrella do Norte,* which published criticism of the Count. Fearing the suspension of that journal, Lisboa committed himself to protect it. Upon return from a trip to Europe, he paid 600 rupees to clear the debts of that journal preventing it from being shut down by the governor. Lisboa paid for articles from the Margao newspaper *O Ultramar* to be reproduced in the *Bombay Times* and in two journals in Britain, so as to reveal the scandal to other Indo-Portuguese readers.[62] More details about Lisboa's engagement in the Bombay-Goa political connectivity are still to be explored. It is nevertheless enough to observe that Lisboa, together with his countrymen in Bardez and in Bombay, fought against individual abuses of power, typically by the Portuguese governors, so as to protect the electoral rights of local Goan candidates, as they felt no less Portuguese than the people in Portugal. Lisboa's protest against the Portuguese dignitaries in Goa did not contradict his loyalty to the King of Portugal, as the *Padroadists* sustained hope that the authorities in Lisbon and Rome would agree with them as soon as direct communication was established through modern media. Lisboa's social capital must have gained him a wide influence across political boundaries. At the heydays of the *Concordat* of 1886, he sent telegrams and letters to all the *Padroado* communities in Madras, Ceylon, and Cochin, while sending pamphlets at his own cost. When he travelled to Damão, remnant of the Northern Province of the Portuguese State of India, Lisboa convinced the Catholics there to send a representation to the local governor, requesting that *Padroado* be retained and a Diocese of Damão be created. Lisboa also participated in events organised in favour of *Padroado*. He wrote to all *Padroado* groups in India to organise petitions to the authorities and councils in Goa and in Portugal.[63]

Lisboa was not alone in his campaign. In the spring of 1885, rumours spread in India that Rome would abolish the Portuguese *Padroado* outside Goa, hence Bombay would be ministered by the missionaries from Propaganda Fide. On 12 April 1885, Bombay *Padroadists* organised an assembly at the Framji Cowasji hall in the city. The assembly was convened by the Portuguese consul F. Meyrelles Canto e Castro.[64] Out of the ten members of the central committee, six were medical doctors.[65] Having been elected in that number, Lisboa gave a main speech to the assembly that is comparable to three other Portuguese letters that he composed between 1885 and 1886, addressing an anonymous contact in Lisbon. The four accounts summarized the merits and successes of the Padroado missions in the progressive conversion in various regions in India, but also the maintenance of the missions that, since the establishment of the Portuguese patronage had extended from Japan and Macao to India.

---

59 A.M. DA CUNHA, "A Evolução do Jornalismo na Índia Portuguesa" (*A Índia Portuguesa* 2, 1923), 513.
60 "O. Sr. Dr. J. C. Lisboa" (*O Ultramar*, 26 March 1887, Anno 29, N°1460), 3, cf. footnote 57.
61 *Analyse do folheto intitulado "O Visconde de Torres-Novas e as eleições em Goa" impresso em Lisboa no anno de 1861* (Nova Goa 1862).
62 "O. Sr. Dr. J. C. Lisboa" (*O Ultramar*, 26 March 1887, Anno 29, N°1460), 3.
63 "O. Sr. Dr. J. C. Lisboa" (*O Ultramar*, 26 March 1887, Anno 29, N°1460), 3.
64 A conference proceeding entitled *Report of a meeting of the Catholics of Bombay subject to the Jurisdiction of the Archbishop Primate of the East, held on the 12th April 1885* (Bombay). A Portuguese version of the same document is entitled *Acta da assemblea dos catholicos de Bombaim; jurisdicionados do Exmo. Arcebispo Primaz d' Oriente reunida em os 12 d'abril de 1885* (Bombaim).
65 *Report of a meeting of the Catholics of Bombay subject to the Jurisdiction of the Archbishop Primate of the East, held on the 12th April 1885* (Bombay), 20.

An argument to further the Portuguese glory was accompanied with an apology against the accusation that "our (Goan) clergy is ignorant". Lisboa quoted remarks from several archbishops of Goa, such as João Crisóstomo de Amorin Pessoa (in office 1860–68) and Aires de Ornelas e Vasconcelos (in office 1874–80), that the Seminar of Rachol, established in 1609 by the Jesuits, had educated native priests not inferior to the "clergy of any diocese of Portugal".[66]

An immediate action of the elected central committee of the Bombay assembly was to send petitions to various European authorities. Meanwhile, they mobilised all their personal resources in Rome, Lisbon, and Goa, displaying the firm determination of the *Padroadists*. Dr. José Nicolau da Fonseca suggested that a petition should be submitted to the Council of Goa (*Camaras de Goa*) and then to Portugal. Dr. Gerson da Cunha sent letters to his contacts in Italy, asking for insights on the manoeuvres put in place by the Congregation of Propaganda Fide against the Portuguese patronage.[67] So far it is unclear how the European contacts of the Bombay *Padroadists'* reacted to these initiatives. Such efforts were carefully observed by their rival Propagandists, especially by Leo Meurin, SJ., then Vicar Apostolic of Bombay:

> In their anxiety for the preservation of the Padroado, our Goanese Christians have been impelled to address themselves not only to the Holy See but also to the Portuguese and English Governments. In fact, [they have sought] the sympathy of any recognised spiritual or temporal authority on behalf of the menaced institution.[68]

The Apostolic Vicar reacted swiftly to the assembly, without even waiting for directives from Rome. Around 1885 Meurin published an English treatise entitled *The Padroado Question*[69], defining the Portuguese patronage as a favour from the papacy, hence not based on intrinsic justice or natural law. While making a summary of the historical development of the *Padroado* in Asia, Meurin carefully distinguished the papal reactions to the two categories of the *Padroadists*, namely the Portuguese crown overtaken by the liberal party, and the Goanese clergy:

> We have not minced matters in speaking of the pretensions of the Crown of Portugal, for the Government which urges those pretensions is an open enemy of the Catholic Church, and we do not consider it our duty to be sparing in our denunciations of those who seek the overthrow of religion. On the other hand, we have carefully refrained from uttering a word to the disparagement of the Goanese clergy. Among them are many excellent priests, pious, learned and zealous men, who make very efficient parish-priests.[70]

Meurin showed an explicit respect to the Goan clergy, treating them as innocent and untainted by the liberal and Masonic influences that ravaged the Portuguese kingdom and that led eventually to the suppression of religious orders in India. The Apostolic Vicar employed this rhetoric not only to reduce his tensions with the Goan dissident minorities, but to degrade their strong patriotic bond to the Portuguese crown. In order to persuade the *Padroadists*,

---

66 *Report of a meeting of the Catholics of Bombay subject to the Jurisdiction of the Archbishop Primate of the East, held on the 12th April 1885*, (Bombay), 8.
67 "O. Sr. Dr. J. C. Lisboa" (*O Ultramar*, 26 March 1887, Anno 29, N°1460), 3.
68 L. MEURIN, *The Padroado Question* (ca. 1885), 2.
69 The treatise does not carry publication dates or locations. I used the copy at the Bibliothek der Philosophisch-Theologischen Hochschule Sankt Georgen, Frankfurt.
70 MEURIN, *The Padroado Question*, 52.

Meurin further explained the papal primacy in the making of various *Concordats* signed with the temporal power of Portugal. In a treatise entitled *The Concordat Question*, Meurin denounced the misunderstanding of papal primacy that featured in an article published in the Goan journal *O Crente*.[71]

To defend themselves, three writers in Bombay – Vicente Salvador Rodrigues, Júlio Menezes, and Pedro Manuel Lisboa Pinto – published their *Observations on the Pamphlet entitled the "Concordat question"* under the pseudonym R. M. P.[72] The authors provided a meticulous analysis of Meurin's text, dividing it into 101 citations so as to elaborate a persuasive point-to-point refutation. As we have seen, Pedro Manuel Lisboa Pinto was a nephew of José Camillo Lisboa and he had also pursued a medical career in Bombay. As the final section of this chapter will demonstrate, Lisboa Pinto extended the Bombay-Goa based *Padroado* campaign to a wider radius up to Ceylon. His voyage to Europe in 1886, as a result of a Goa *Padroado* assembly, will mark a turning point in the *Padroado* enterprise in South Asia and finally divide the trajectories of the once synchronised *Padroado* campaigns. Whereas the Bombay *Padroadists* retained their resentment towards the Propaganda missionaries within the limits of the Roman Catholic Church, the *Padroadists* centred in Ceylon took a radical decision that led to their separation from the church they used to belong to.

5.2 Final Efforts: The Assembly in Panjim (Goa) in 1886 and Lisboa Pinto's Voyage to Portugal

No records have been found to demonstrate the first contacts between Antonio Alvares and José Camillo Lisboa's family. However, Alvares's training at the Jesuit seminary in Bandra, in the suburbs of Bombay, in 1862–1864, and his life-long interest in the treatment of cholera suggest that he must have been connected to Lisboa and Lisboa Pinto on two levels, namely both for a commitment to social progress through public health, and by a personal involvement in the *Padroado* campaigns since his early years as a seminarian.[73]

Encouraged by the Bombay assembly of 1885, Antonio Alvares called for an action in Portuguese India. An assembly took place on 21 October 1886 in the building of the *Direcção das obras públicas* in Panjim. As in Bombay, the main purpose was to make petitions to the various European authorities so as to retain the Portuguese *Padroado* in India and prevent the Holy See from imposing an even more unfavourable new *Concordat*. Differently from the Bombay assembly, half constituted by Goan medical doctors, the seventeen participants of the Goa assembly had diverse backgrounds: five medical doctors and pharmacists, eight landowners and tradesmen, two lawyers and politicians, and two priests and journalists.[74] Caetano Gabriel de Sousa, a landowner from Salvador do Mundo in Bardez, was elected as president of the assembly, and José Maria de Sousa, a lawyer from the island of Goa, as secretary. The assembly elected a central commission led by president Francisco Salvador

---

71 Leo Meurin, The Concordat Question. n.l., ca 1885.
72 A.M. DA COSTA, *Dicionário de literatura goesa* vol. 3 (Macau 1998), 105.
73 In a letter to the governor of Goa dated in Panjim in 1908, Alvares reported his observation of the latest epidemic in Goa and the treatment he offered, based on his life-long experience. He mentioned his seminarian experience in Bandra (Bonderá in Portuguese) in 1862–1864. This letter has a 4-page attachment entitled *Relação dos accomettidos do cholera em Chinchinim, que se acharam sob o tratamento de A. F. X. Alvares, Julio I, desde o dia 16 do mez outubro de 1907*.
74 See Appendix 1.

Pinto, who had previously been president of the Council of Bardez (*Camara Municipal*), hometown of the Lisboa family.

First of all, petitions were sent to the Holy See and the royal court of Portugal, asking them to support the aspirations of the Indian Catholics, by rejecting the latest *Concordat* signed in June 1886, and by establishing a native hierarchy in all the missions in India, Ceylon, and Malacca. To anticipate the arrival of their petitions, the president of this assembly immediately sent telegrams to Rome and Lisbon. Secondly, it was decided to send a delegation to Rome and Portugal. The delegate, eventually identified in the person of Lisboa Pinto, was supposed to inform of the unfortunate situation of the Church in Asia and represent the needs and aspirations of the local Catholics. Thirdly, a petition was also to be sent to Queen Victoria, as Empress of India, explaining that the new *Concordat* had created a new subdivision of the "big Indian family" (*grande familia indiana*) which would result in continuing disorder. Fourthly, to raise further public awareness, telegrams were to be sent to the press in Portugal and British India, informing the public of the purposes of this assembly and asking for their support. Finally, a Central Commission was elected for the implementation of the necessary measures. The same Commission elected Lisboa Pinto as the delegate to embark on the voyage to Europe. As initiator of the assembly, Antonio Alvares coordinated the various subdivisions of the Central Commission.[75]

Until 1887 Bombay *Padroadists* heralded the *Padroadist* movements across India and Ceylon. In reaction to the 1886 *Concordat*, several *Padroadist* groups convened conferences at a local scale, such as the one in Panjim as well as one in Madras in October of the same year. In the library of the Royal Palace of Ajuda in Lisbon, there are also petitions addressed to the King of Portugal by a selected committee of Padroado supporters in Madras in 1885.[76] An earlier petition was sent from Tuticorin in 1870.[77] These petitions hardly received positive feedbacks from Lisbon.

It was in this context that Pedro Manuel Lisboa Pinto emerged as a crucial figure linking the *Padroadist* movements in Goa, Ceylon, and Bombay. Lisboa Pinto was 30 years of age when José Camillo Lisboa entrusted his own clinic in Bombay to him, as the young doctor was considered promising. At that time, Lisboa Pinto received letters from a *Padroadist* group in Colombo, in which they reported on the lack of priests due to the sanctions inflicted by the archbishop of Colombo. In the last letter, the Ceylonese claimed that they were compelled to choose between two options for their future ecclesiastical settlement: either submitting to Bishop Mellus (1831–1908) in Travancore,[78] a prelate from the Chaldean Catholic Church, from whom a schism had allegedly been organised among the Thomas Christians, or alternatively submitting to some Protestant church in Ceylon.[79] Lisboa Pinto was moved by their quest and brought it up at the Goa assembly in 1886. When Lisboa Pinto was selected

---

75 *Acta do comicio de 21 outubro de 1886: Reunion em Nova Goa com os discursos e representações respeito a Egreja Indiana* (Nova Goa: Typographia de *"Times of Goa"*), viii–x.
76 "To His Most Faithful Majesty Don Louis, King of Portugal and Algarves and Royal Patron of the Churches in the East", Biblioteca da Ajuda, 54-X-7, fols. 151r-151v.
77 See its entry registered in F.G. CUNHA LEÃO, *O Índico Na Biblioteca Da Ajuda. Catálogo Dos Manuscritos Relativos a Moçambique, Pérsia, Índia, Malaca, Molucas e Timor* (Biblioteca da Ajuda 1998), 329.
78 Mar Yohannan Elias Mellus (or Milos, Milus) was a bishop of the Chaldean Catholic Church. VARICATT, *The Suriani Church of India*, 20–22.
79 The double option of the Ceylon *Padroadists* was repeated in an article entitled "O padroado" (*O Ultramar*, 5 November 1887), 1: "se Portugal as engeita, passarão ao rito syriaco, ou talvez abraçarão o protestantismo!"

as the "Delegate of the Eastern Catholics of the *Padroado*"[80], he assumed responsibility for both Indian and Ceylon *Padroadists*, as the latter had also sponsored his voyage.

In mid-March 1887 he sailed from Bombay to Lisbon. One week afterwards, the Goan newspaper *O Ultramar* revealed not only the collective decision made at the Goan assembly in 1886, but also the family support behind this cause:

> Mr. Dr. [José Camillo] Lisboa left no stone unturned for the cause of the padroado. The major sacrifice he made for the cause and also for his homeland [*paiz*] is to send his nephew Mr. Dr. Lisboa Pinto to Portugal and Rome so as to advocate the interests of the unfortunate padroadists of Ceylon, whose afflictive requests were irresistible. Mr. Dr. P. Lisboa (son of his brother), who had been in charge of his clinic since four years ago, is now in America.[81] Mr. Dr. Lisboa Pinto replaced him [Dr. P. Lisboa] with great success, as he had become known to the circle of all the patients of his uncle. He [Dr. Lisboa Pinto] therefore sacrificed his career that had so well started. It is certain that the Sinhalese will keep their promise of paying his voyage. Nonetheless, his uncle let him leave without waiting for promised contribution.[82]

Shortly after his arrival in Lisbon, Lisboa Pinto was invited to give a speech at the Society of Geography, which had nominated him as a member. In the meeting scheduled for 30 April, the president of the Society, Antonio Augusto de Aguiar, introduced the Indian guest to the audience. No response from the audience is recorded in the proceedings, other than a brief word of thanks. Aguiar thanked Lisboa Pinto for having spoken with "such touched eloquence" about the "intertwined love of our Indian peoples for Portugal". This love "had triggered in him [Aguiar] with nostalgia the love [=for Portugal] that he himself had felt [i.e. experienced] and verified among those people". On the basis of this experience of his own, Aguiar believed that he could confirm the statement made by Lisboa Pinto about the special affection of the "Indian peoples" for Portugal.[83]

The petition submitted by Lisboa Pinto in favour of the *Padroadists* of India hardly achieved any solid help nor acceptance among the Portuguese of the "Motherland" that he

---

80 The English term was used by Lisboa Pinto in his autograph letter to Pope Leo XIII, dated Lisbon 28 October 1887. APF, *SC Indie Orientali* 32, f.1118r.

81 Dr. P. Lisboa was another nephew of José Camillo Lisboa and held a licence of Medicine and Surgery in Bombay. He had obtained a diploma of the Lying-in Hospital, Dublin, and a Certificate from the Gynæcological Department of the Dublin Rotunda Hospital. See his academic achievement in "Personal Intelligence" (*Journal of the National Indian Association in Aid of Social Progress and Education in India* 179, November 1885), 563–564.

82 "Ve-se do pouco que dito fica, que o sr. dr. Lisboa não deixou pedra por mover pela causa do padroado. O Maior sacrificio, porem, que elle fez por esta causa, que é tambem a de seu paiz, é o de andar sair o seu sobrinho, o sr. dr. Lisboa Pinto, con destino a Portugal e Roma, para ahi advogar os interesses dos infelizes padroadistas de Ceylão, a cujas afflictivas solicitações não teve animo para resistir. O sr. dr. P. Lisboa (filho de seu irmão), que desde ha 4 annos, estava encarregado da sua clinica, acha-se hoje na America; - substituia-o o dr. Lisboa Pinto com bom successo, pois já era conhecido de toda a roda dos pacientes do seu tio. Perde, pois, elle muito na sua carreira, que tão bem tinha encetado. É certo que os singalazes cumprirão a promessa de pagar a despeza da sua viagem; com tudo o tio fel o sair sem esperar pela contribuição promettida." In: "O. Sr. Dr. J. C. Lisboa" (*O Ultramar*, 26 March 1887, Anno 29, N°1460), 3.

83 *Actas das Sessões da Sociedade de Geographia de Lisboa fundada em 1875*, vol. VII (Lisboa 1887), 50. "Sessão de 30 de Abril de 1887". "O sr. presidente agradeceu, em nome da Sociedade, ao sr. Lisboa Pinto, a sua interessante conferencia, dizendo que as palavras em que elle se referira com tão commovida eloquencia ao entranhado amor dos nossos povos indianos por Portugal lhe avivára com saudade o que elle proprio sentíra e verificára entre esses povos, estimando poder corroborar a affirmação do orador." His lecture was published as a pamphlet and as part of the regular proceedings of the Society. See P.M. LISBOA PINTO, *Conferência sobre o Padroado portuguez proferida na Sociedade de Geographia de Lisboa* (Lisboa 1887). Also in *Actas das Sessões*, 51–63.

had hoped for. No concrete action, neither from the Society of Geography, nor from the government came out of his lecture. In the following years, *Padroadists* in Goa and especially in Ceylon had to increase the pressure and take matters into their own hands without hope for direct Portuguese support.

Chapter 3: Ecumenical Catholicities in the Nineteenth Century

1. A Triumphant and Controversial Episcopal Consecration

In the early morning of Sunday 29 May 1892, the Church of Our Lady of Good Death in Hultsdorp, Colombo, was decorated with ferns and evergreens. In the churchyard the flag of the USA, then with 45 stars, was waving among profuse decorations. The band of the *Ceylon Volunteers,* under the direction of its master Albert Ernst Luschwitz, was getting ready for the start of celebrations.[1] Along with them, a large number of attendants, members of the congregation, as well as friends and diplomats, such as the American Consul William Morey and his wife, were arriving, while preparatory prayers were being chanted in the church since 7 o'clock am.[2] At 8:30 the solemn mass of episcopal consecration of the French priest Josef René Vilatte (1854–1929) began. Vilatte had been elected by his Old Catholic congregation in Wisconsin and then approved by the Syrian Orthodox Patriarch of Antioch Ignatius Peter IV. Only a few days before, on 24 May, three Indian bishops had reached Colombo onboard the steamer *Africa*. These were the Archbishop Antonio Alvares, also known as Mar Julius I, and two Metropolitans from Malabar, namely Mar Gregorios of Parumala (1848–1902) and Mar Athanasius Paulos Kadavil (1833–1907). This unprecedented event of the consecration of a European priest at the local Independent Catholic congregation was reported in detail by their monthly journal *The Independent Catholic*:

> Both the consecrating prelate and the Archbishop-Elect took their respective places. Archbishop Alvares robed himself with the alb, stole and cope, and took his seat on the main altar where the mitre and crozier were given to him. The Archbishop-Elect then approached him, and on his knees made the profession of faith by reciting the Nicene creed and answering in a clear voice to the questions put to him by the consecrator. Then, at the communion railings the Bull of Consecration was read out to the congregation by Dr. Lisboa Pinto. It is a short but touching document. Then commenced the solemn high Mass, chanted by Archbishop Alvares, and recited simultaneously on a side altar by the Prelate-Elect. After the Epistles, the palms of the new Archbishop's hands were anointed and the crown of his head. At the moment of consecration, the most Rev. Archbishop Alvares and Their Lordships Mar Athanasius and Mar Gregorius imposed their hands on the head of the Archbishop-Elect, who visibly became pale, and much moved as the words "Accipe Spiritum Sanctum" were pronounced by the three Bishops. He had become an Archbishop.

---

1 The same band used to perform also in the Victoria Park in Colombo where a young audience gathered. SEPTUAGENARIAN [sic], 'Memories Grave and Gay' (*Journal of the Dutch Burgher Union of Ceylon* XXXIX/3, July 1949), 87.

2 William Morey was the American consul in Ceylon from 1877 to 1907. RICHARD MOREY SHERMAN, 'American Contacts with Ceylon in the 19th Century: An Introduction to Their Impact' (*Journal of the Royal Asiatic Society of Sri Lanka*, New Series 35, 1990/1991), 1–8.

At the offertory, Mgr. Vilatte presented to Archbishop Alvares loaves of bread, two little barrels of wine and water and a candle, and then took his place beside the celebrant on the main altar. The mass continued till after the communion, which both prelates partook of.[3]

As stated in the same article, this consecration was viewed by the Indo-Ceylonese Independent Catholics as a "historical event for our island of Ceylon". It certainly boosted their confidence in the daily confrontations in the public media with the Roman Catholic authorities, whose followers constituted the great majority of the Christian population in the British colony. The two parties would insult each other with derogatory attributes such as "Romish" or "Jacobites". The creation of a link to North America through René Vilatte had certainly brought the new Christian community into the social and political spotlight of the local colonial society. Two days before the consecration, both Alvares and Lisboa Pinto had been invited to a reception arranged by the Governor of Ceylon Arthur Elibank Havelock (r. 1890–1895) at the Queen's House.[4] As Alvares expressed already in his first reply to Vilatte in 1889 when the latter enquired on the possibility of episcopal consecration, the Ceylonese church was attempting to achieve a global projection towards the "New World", thereby breaking the constraints imposed by the Roman Catholic authorities, as represented by the person of the French archbishop of Colombo Christophe Ernest Bonjean:

> We from the bottom of our hearts thank God that He has mercifully shown us the way out of the slavery of Rome; and we rejoice to see a large number of Christians making heroic efforts in the same direction as ourselves in the New World. And we feel confident that the good God will deign to mercifully help these holy endeavours […] If the necessary arrangements could be made we would overlook the hardships connected with the voyage and go across the seas to confer the episcopate on such a worthy minister of God as yourself, particularly as Dr. Lisboa Pinto urges us in the strongest terms to forget everything and think of America […][5]

Alvares discerned a resemblance between Vilatte's congregation in Wisconsin and his own movement in India and Ceylon, in that they all shared the "same direction" and the same enemy, i.e. Rome. Such a common polemical target was embedded in the inter-denominational convergences and divergences between the various Christian churches. In the light of Vilatte's consecration, the South Asian Independent Catholics acquired several credits and discredits vis-à-vis other Christians, depending on the perspective of the different churches. First of all, even though the expression "Independent Catholics" had appeared previously, a new understanding of the term passed from South Asia to America, Mexico, the Caribbean, and Africa due to the apostolic succession obtained by Vilatte in Ceylon.[6] Secondly, Alvares' credentials were examined at Lambeth Palace, as the Anglican Church tried to verify the effectiveness of Vilatte's episcopal consecration in Colombo and the ensuing priestly ordinations carried out by him.[7] The relations between the Anglican missionaries and the Syrian Orthodox bishops in Kottayam worsened after Alvares and Villatte ordained several English

---

3 "The Consecration of Archbishop Vilatte" (*The Independent Catholic* 5, May 1892), 3.
4 "Independent Catholics at the Leyee" (*The Independent Catholic* 5, May 1892), 3.
5 Alvares to Vilatte dated on 10 May 1891, partly quoted in P.F. ANSON, *Bishops at Large* (1st ed. 1964. Berkeley 2006), 106.
6 In South Carolina an "Independent Catholic" congregation emerged already in 1819. See J. BYRNE, *The Other Catholics: Remaking America's Largest Religion* (New York; Chichester, West Sussex 2016), 334-5.
7 GEORGE A. KIRAZ, 'The Credentials of Mar Julius Alvares Bishop of Ceylon, Goa and India Excluding Malabar' (*Hugoye: Journal of Syriac Studies* 7/1, 2007, 157–68).

laymen. Thirdly, the substantial expenses for Vilatte's consecration in Colombo heavily burdened the Independent Catholic congregation in Hultsdorp, straining the relations between Alvares on the one hand, and Lisboa Pinto and other laymen on the other. Fourthly, the unexpected agency of the Latin branch of the Syrian Orthodox Church, through priestly ordinations that impacted the Anglicans, gave the Syrian bishops in Malabar a sense of importance and self-confidence that might have contributed to the decision of establishing a Malabar Church in 1912 separate from the patriarch of Antioch.

In this chapter we look at both the historical contexts and the consequences of Vilatte's consecration in Colombo, in relation to the efforts at redefining "Catholicity" undertaken by several Christian churches during the nineteenth century. In the first place, we will assess the contingent character of Vilatte's consecration in Colombo, tracing his individual ecclesiastical enterprise – a peculiar "Catholic reform" – vis-à-vis various Churches, from the Roman Catholic to the Presbyterian, from the Episcopalian to the Old Catholic, before he eventually adopted Independent Catholicism. Secondly, we will examine the causes for Vilatte's "Catholic reform" in the context of the Anglican pursuit for a primitive Catholicism, overcoming the breach in the apostolic tradition caused by the Reformation. Thirdly, we will draw attention to the Anglican interactions with the Syrian Churches, both in the Ottoman Empire and in Malabar. Fourthly, we will highlight the Anglican perception of Vilatte's consecration by the three Indian Bishops of the Syrian Church. Fifthly, we turn to examine the ecumenical relations between the Malabar Churches, summarising the (re)union attempts that the Anglican, Catholic, and Syrian Christian leaders had engaged in back and forth during the nineteenth century. Finally, we will analyse Alvares' own interpretation of Catholicity, as represented in a polemical booklet he composed in the course of the controversy over Vilatte's consecration, namely *A supremacia universal na Egreja de Christo*, published in Colombo in 1898. The section ends with a brief comparison between Alvares and two European figures, Vilatte and an English man named Alexander Westwood Steward, who sought for apostolic succession from the Independent Catholic Church in Colombo.

2. Vilatte and His Failed Pursuit of a Catholic Reform Before 1892

On 15 July 1891, a 37-year-old French priest named Joseph René Vilatte[8] left his congregation of the Precious Blood in the neighbourhood of Dyckesville, in the town of Green Bay,

---

8 There is a rekindled interest in Vilatte among both ecclesiastical authors and lay scholars. An updated summary of his biography can be found in the 4th edition of *The Oxford Dictionary of the Christian Church*. Julie Byrne has written a short but balanced biography of Vilatte in her discussion of the genesis of the term "Other Catholics" in the American *Census of Religious Bodies*, starting from 1890. See BYRNE, *The Other Catholics: Remaking America's Largest Religion* (New York 2016), 100–105. A biographical monograph presenting Vilatte in a denominational perspective as a North American "Community Organizer of Religion" is offered by S.A. THERIAULT, *Msgr. René Vilatte: Community Organizer of Religion, 1854–1929*, 2nd ed. (Berkeley 2012, 1st ed. 1997). J. KERSEY offers a review of the secondary literature ("key sources") in his recent *Joseph-Rene Vilatte (1854–1929): Some Aspects of His Life, Work and Succession* (Roseau, Dominica 2012), 24–30. R. STECK's pamphlet *Monseigneur Joseph René Vilatte: Une vie en image* (n.p. 2013) contains a selection of historical documents, such as a birth certificate and the record of sacerdotal ordination, with original images photographed at various French ecclesiastical archives. One of the most advanced studies on Vilatte appeared in ABBA SERAPHIM's *Flesh of Our Brethren: An Historical Examination of Western Episcopal Successions Originating from the Syrian Orthodox Patriarchate of Antioch*, 2 ed., 1st ed. 2006. (London 2017, 150–252), in which the author used archival sources from both the British Library and the Library of Lambeth Palace. René Vilatte and his fellows Fr. Augustine of the Angels (i.e. Bernard Harding) and the Bishop Paolo Miraglia Gullotti already published their own accounts under the title of *Publications by and about Joseph René Vilatte*

Wisconsin, and set sail from New York to Ceylon. The venture ahead into the Indian Ocean had the same goal as the many voyages he had already made across the Atlantic: to serve the eight thousand Belgian and French Catholics residing by the shore of Lake Michigan, for whom he had been providing first lay assistance and then pastoral care since 1884.[9] Flourishing on fur business, these European descendants lacked proper assistance from the Roman Catholic hierarchy, then dominated by clerics of Irish origin. As was recalled in 1885 by the first Episcopalian archbishop of Fond du Lac, John Henry Hobart Brown (1831–1888), in support of Vilatte,

> [he] resided for a while at Green Bay, a city of this Diocese [Fond du Lac]. In the neighborhood of this place there are settled about 30,000 Belgians. Of these a large number, probably 8,000, are believed to be inclined to the principles of pure primitive Catholicism.[10]

Yet, differently from his previous trips to Europe, Ceylon for Vilatte was an option out of despair. During the previous six years he had hoped to achieve his "Catholic reform"[11], benefiting from the ecumenical dialogue between the American Protestant Episcopal Church and the Old Catholic Church, inasmuch as his small congregations in Green Bay were de facto heavily sponsored and facilitated by the Episcopalian Diocese of Fond du Lac, administered from the homonymous city, which had a Protestant tradition. However, the Belgian and French Catholics were opposed to Anglicanism as much as to "Romanism", hence they demanded Vilatte to be ordained by someone who could unequivocally be considered a real bishop from a Catholic point of view.[12] It was due to these circumstances that Archbishop Brown agreed to Vilatte pursuing his priestly ordination from the Swiss Old Catholic Bishop Eduard Herzog (1841–1924).[13] Brown's long-term plan foresaw that Vilatte, once acknowledged as a legitimate Old Catholic priest, would establish a congregation in communion with the Episcopal Church under the jurisdiction of Fond du Lac.[14] Vilatte obtained full trust from the Swiss Old Catholics and received his priestly ordination from Herzog in July 1885 in

---

and the Old Catholics. (n.l., ca. 1890–1925). Some of Vilatte's English accounts have been included in A.J. QUEEN's *Credo: The Catechism of the Old Catholic Church* (New York 2005, 382–428). S.A. THERIAULT recently published Vilatte's French documents in *Lettres pastorales, mandements, sermons, déclarations et circulaires de Mgr René Vilatte 1892–1925*. (Berkeley 2017). Combined, these recent efforts at a reconstruction of Vilatte in Church history have made significant progress since the first scholarly studies were dedicated to the French man by two acclaimed Anglican authors, namely H.R. TURNER BRANDRETH in his influential *Episcopi Vagantes and the Anglican Church*, 1st ed. in 1947 (Berkeley 2006, 47–69), and P.F. ANSON in his *Bishops at Large*, 1st ed. in London in 1964 (Berkeley 2006, 91–129). On Vilatte now also see C. BURLACIOIU, *'Within three years the East and the West have met each other': Die Genese einer missionsunabhängigen schwarzen Kirche im transatlantischen Dreieck USA-Südafrika-Ostafrika (1921–1950)* (Wiesbaden 2015), 18–21, 189, 202.

9 On the Belgian migrant community in the Great Lakes region see H.R. HOLAND, *Wisconsin's Belgian Community: An Account of the Early Events in the Belgian Settlement in Northeastern Wisconsin with Particular Reference to the Belgians in Door County* (Sturgeon Bay, Wisconsin 1933); B.A. COOK, *Belgians in Michigan* (East Landing 2007).
10 Letter dated 27 May 1885. QUEEN, *Credo*, 385, 383.
11 Vilatte to Bishop John Henry Hobart Brown, mid-December 1884, quoted in WILLIAM M. HOGUE, 'The Episcopal Church and Archbishop Vilatte' (*Historical Magazine of the Protestant Episcopal Church* 34/1, 1965), 35-6.
12 Vilatte, "My relations with the Protestant Episcopal Church" in QUEEN, *Credo*, 416; WILLIAM M. HOGUE, 'The Episcopal Church and Archbishop Vilatte', 37.
13 A biography of this Old Catholic Bishop is offered by WALTER HERZOG, *Bischof Dr. Eduard Herzog: Ein Lebensbild* (Laufen 1935).
14 HOGUE, 'The Episcopal Church and Archbishop Vilatte', 38.

Bern. Since the Lambeth Conference in 1878, the Old Catholic movement was favoured by the Anglicans. Herzog visited England and America and was, among the Old Catholic bishops, a leading admirer of the Anglican Communion.[15] The fact that the archbishop of Utrecht, Johannes Heykamp (1824–1892), addressed Vilatte as "Priest over the Old Catholics in America" implied a recognition at least at a personal level, if not yet as part of an official declaration of communion.[16] However, with the ascension of Charles Chapman Grafton (1830–1912) to the See of Fond du Lac in 1888, Vilatte started to receive harsh criticism from the American Episcopalians in regard to his ambiguous position in ecumenical matters. As the Episcopalian pastor W. B. Maturin argued, "[Vilatte's] manner of carrying on the mission seemed to be nothing more than tricking Roman Catholics out of their papal allegiance by disguising Protestant Episcopalianism under the trappings of Old Catholicism".[17] Caught between the two, Vilatte would appear too Roman to the Episcopalians, and too Protestant to the Old Catholics. Notwithstanding an apologia clarifying his unequivocal dismay over Protestantism and his good intention of being a "medium",[18] the Old Catholics suspended Vilatte's application for episcopal consecration. The archbishop of Utrecht, Johannes Heykamp (r. 1875–1892), made it clear that Vilatte's relations with the Episcopalians were considered unacceptable:

> You may well conceive, dear Father, that we should in no manner have it understood that from the human and material assistance, you should remain in harmony and ecclesiastical relations with a church whose faith is not Catholic, and which is, separate from the center of Catholic unity.[19]

The archbishops gathered at the First International Old Catholic Congress in 1891 in Cologne decided not to consecrate Vilatte, nor to acknowledge him as the only official representative of their Church in North America. On the contrary, in 1897 the Old Catholics entrusted Fr. Antoni Stanisław Kozłowski (1857–1907), a priest who had separated from the Roman Catholic Church in 1895 and briefly collaborated with Vilatte, with the task of opening their first Diocese in America.[20] However, Kozłowski's mandate focused on the Polish immigrants, without special provisions for the Belgians in Wisconsin.[21] Estranged from Utrecht, Vilatte turned to bishop Vladimir Sokolovsky, head of the Russian Orthodox Diocese of Alaska and the Aleutian Islands (r. 1888–1891), which had been based in San Francisco after the Russian Empire sold Alaska to the United States.[22] This move further escalated

---

15 On Herzog's role in the Old Catholic relation with the Anglo-American Church see MARK D. CHAPMAN, *The Fantasy of Reunion. Anglicans, Catholics, and Ecumenism, 1833-1882* (Oxford 2014), 264-95.
16 Heykamp to Vilatte, dated in Utrecht 19 September 1889. QUEEN, *Credo,* 425-6.
17 HOGUE, 'The Episcopal Church and Archbishop Vilatte', 41.
18 "…while on one hand Romanism has added much error and corruption to the primitive faith, Protestantism has not only taken away the Roman errors but also a part of the primitive deposit of faith." VILATTE, "My relations", in QUEEN, *Credo,* 414.
19 Heykamp to Vilatte, dated in Utrecht 21 December 1889, in QUEEN, *Credo,* 426-7.
20 LAURENCE J. ORZELL, 'A Pragmatic Union: Bishop Kozłowski and the Old Catholics, 1896-1898' (*Polish American Studies* 44/1, 1987, 5–24).
21 LAURENCE J. ORZELL, 'Curious Allies: Bishop Antoni Kozlowski and the Episcopalians' (*Polish American Studies* 40/2, 1983, 36–58); QUEEN, *Credo,* 388-9.
22 The coming of Bishop Vladimir triggered violent conflicts in the Russian community of San Francisco. See TERENCE EMMONS, *Alleged Sex and Threatened Violence: Doctor Russel, Bishop Vladimir, and the Russians in San Francisco, 1887-1892* (Stanford, CA 1997).

Grafton's animosity against Vilatte, while creating the potential for a conflict, though eventually avoided, between the Episcopal and Orthodox Churches.[23]

By May 1891 the only archbishop who had replied with sympathy and interest to Vilatte's requests of support was Antonio Alvares, the head of the newly established Independent Catholic Church of Goa, India, and Ceylon, who had promised to confer episcopal consecration to the "worthy minister of God" from Wisconsin after him passing due examination.[24] Alvares was not uninformed on Vilatte's controversial past. As Bishop Grafton came to know about Vilatte's imminent voyage to Ceylon, he sent a telegram to Alvares informing him of Vilatte's attempts with several Churches. Grafton's original telegram has not been located yet, but a letter of his in 1893 reported that the very contact of Vilatte with the Syrian Church was through Antonio Alvares:

> After a time I found he was in correspondence with some clergy in Holland looking to his obtaining the Episcopate from the Archbishop of Utrecht. He also came to me and wanted me to join with him in the effort and proposed to me that he would be my suffragan, having charge of this special work. I addressed letters to the Archbishop of Utrecht and to the Right Rev. Dr. Herzog, who was cognisant of Rene Vilatte's oath of obedience to me, and the Old Catholic Bishops determined not to take action in the matter. Then Rene [sic] Vilatte turned to Bishop Vladimir, the Russian Bishop, then at San Francisco, and sought the Episcopate of him. In the end it came to nought. Then Rene Vilatte sought to make terms with [a] Roman Catholic Bishop, Dr. Kutzer, now Archbishop of Milwaukee, Wisconsin. Rene Vilatte was willing to return to the Roman Communion, but Dr. Kutzer's terms were not satisfactory to him. From what the Archbishop said to me it was clear the Archbishop had little trust in him. It was after he had failed in these directions he turned to Ceylon. He had learnt about the position of the Right Rev. Bishop Alvares through a man named Harding who had formerly been there as a monk under the name of Bro. Augustine of the Angels. Harding is a very worthless character, a notorious drunkard and these two hatched up the scheme between them.[25] When he went to Ceylon I telegraphed to the Archbishop and warned him against the untrustworthiness of Rene Vilatte. I received a letter from a person claiming to be a Vicar-General that no more of my letters were desired. And a letter I had sent was returned to me from Ceylon as being misdirected. I cannot understand why any Eastern Bishop should so desire to antagonise the Anglican Church in America.[26]

Alvares indeed received Grafton's message but refused to accept his advice. In a letter dated 21 November 1898 to Fr. Ignatius of Jesus (born Joseph Leycester Lyne, 1837–1908), head of the Anglican Benedictine Abbey of New Llanthony, Alvares disclosed his understanding of Grafton as being biased and even grudging.[27] Alvares refused to give any credit to the critiques against Vilatte, attributing them to the "colossal audacity" of a "non-Apostolic" Protestant Bishop:

---

23 GLENN D. JOHNSON, 'Joseph René Vilatte: Accidental Catalyst to Ecumenical Dialog', (*Anglican and Episcopal History* 71/1, 2002, 42–60).
24 Alvares' second letter to Vilatte, partly quoted in PETER F. ANSON, *Bishops at Large* (1st ed. 1964, Berkeley 2006), 106.
25 Grafton was referring to Fr. William Bernard Harding, formerly a member of the Roman Catholic order of the Oblates of Mary Immaculate.
26 Lambeth Palace Library, *Davidson* 83, fol. 465r. A printed copy of a letter by the Bishop of Fond du Lac, January 3, 1893.
27 On Father Ignatius' attempt to reintroduce monasticism into the Church of England, see recently HUGH ALLEN, *New Llanthony Abbey: Father Ignatius's Monastery at Cape-y-ffin* (Tiverton 2016).

Having satisfied you on the questions raised, it remained for us to add a few words concerning the questionable conduct of the Protestant Bishop Grafton, of Fond-du-lac, towards Mgr. Vilatte. If he had been a person of thought, he must have ceased his unconscious (unconscientious?) career concerning Mgr. Vilatte since the publication of the memorable ultimatum of the trustees of Dykesville, published in the "State Gazette" of the 11th of November, 1890, and the correspondence that appeared since then between himself and Mgr. Vilatte. And as to the uncharitable remarks of Bishop Grafton criticising the episcopate of Mgr. Vilatte as "colossal audacity" (it) is only a suitable term for a non-Apostolic Protestant bishop, and not to a legitimate Old Catholic Archbishop.

We may, in this connection, inform you that just about the time of Mgr. Vilatte'a arrival in Ceylon we have received a telegraphic message from Bishop Grafton of Fond-du-lac, asking us not to consecrate Mgr. Vilatte. On inquiry, from parties disinterested, and from facts patent to us, we found, to our full satisfaction, that Bishop Grafton was only trying to pay off a private grudge.[28]

Alvares' negative attitude towards Protestantism and the Catholic belief that the Anglican Communion lacked an apostolic lineage might have added credits to Vilatte's application. Yet some other factors contributed to the trust of the Indo-Ceylonese congregation towards Vilatte. A key role was played by the enigmatic English priest (William) Bernard E. Harding, who first introduced the Ceylonese Independent Catholic congregation to Vilatte. Harding had entered the Roman Catholic religious order of the Oblates of Mary Immaculate some time after having been ordained priest. As a postulant of the Oblates, he reached Colombo on 18 October 1884, in a group of six missionaries.[29] In Ceylon he was assigned to the Archdiocese of Colombo, under the authority of his confrère Archbishop Bonjean. For reasons still unknown, Harding left Ceylon, his religious order and even the Roman Catholic Church. Assuming the religious name of Augustine de Angelis, he joined the Society of the Precious Blood that Vilatte and Brother Jean-Baptiste Gauthier (1853–1922) had established in Gardner, Wisconsin, in 1888.[30] Harding's experience in Colombo coincided with the establishment of the Independent Catholic Church. Bonjean's excommunication of Alvares in 1888 must have been widely discussed within the Catholic community and it is possible that Harding contacted the Independent Catholic congregation in Colombo before he travelled to the USA. The experience gained in Colombo for at least five years allowed Harding to discern a strong link between the situations in Colombo and in Green Bay. In 1891 in Wisconsin Harding, together with the Church Trustees Édouard Debecker and Augustin Marchand, made the first contacts with Archbishop Alvares, requesting that Vilatte be consecrated as Archbishop of the Wisconsin mission.[31] A sum of $ 225 was collected in the name of another trustee named Guillaume Barrette for Vilatte's voyage to Ceylon in 1892.[32]

Vilatte landed in Colombo in September 1891. In the following nine months, he was examined by Alvares and his behaviour was observed by the congregation, before the episcopal

---

28 "Mar Timotheos's consecration declared valid and canonical - Father Ignatius a real priest - independent testimony from abroad" (*Western Mail* 7 January 1899), 6. The text between brackets was added by the editor of the *Western Mail*.
29 His arrival in Colombo was reported by *Le Missioni Cattoliche: Bullettino* [sic] *settimanale dell'Opera La Propagazione della Fede* vol. 14/7 (Milano 1885), 7.
30 On Gauthier see *Inventory of Church Archives of Wisconsin: Protestant Episcopal Church in the United States of America: Diocese of Fond du Lac* (Madison, WI 1941), 96, 107.
31 BYRNE, *The Other Catholics*: 108. On Guillaume Barrette (1829-1916), a nephew of a priest of the *Belgian Petite Église* called Clément Barrette, see THÈRIAULT, *Msgr. René Vilatte*: Chapter II "Community organization of Religion among the Belgians and the French-Canadians in Wisconsin 1885-1892", 66-70.
32 THÈRIAULT, *Msgr. René Vilatte*, 113.

consecration was eventually celebrated in May 1892.[33] During those months, he must have found commonalities with the Indian and Ceylonese Independent Catholics in several respects. The Dutch Burgher and Indo-Portuguese Independent Catholics had substantial European ancestry, resembling the origins of the French-Canadian or Belgian-American Catholics. Alvares and Lisboa Pinto on the one hand, and Vilatte on the other, had all had a migration experience. Both Alvares and Vilatte had been antagonised by established ecclesiastical authorities: Bonjean and the Archbishop of Goa António Sebastião Valente for Alvares, and Grafton in the case of Vilatte.[34] The *Padroado* questions in India and Ceylon would make Alvares and Lisboa Pinto identify easily with the Old Catholics of the Union of Utrecht, but also with a minoritarian experience such as *La Petite Église*, a schismatic Catholic Church in France and Belgium within which Vilatte had been born and brought up.[35] Both the Independent Catholics of South Asia and the ones of North America were just starting out, facing challenges but also enjoying enthusiasm for a future still to be written. Finances were certainly a delicate aspect, and their instability affected cross-continental voyages and contacts between sister churches located in different parts of the world.

3. The Anglican Communion and the Search for a Primitive Catholicity

The figure of Joseph René Vilatte represents the initial ecumenical interaction between the Old Catholics and the Episcopal Church of the United States. Vilatte's final affiliation in Ceylon with an original form of Independent Catholicism of Latin rite but in communion with the Syrian Orthodox Church, highlights how the religious reform promoted by Alvares could be perceived as closely related to both the Union of Utrecht and the specific form that Anglicanism had taken in the United States. For our context, one of the most interesting questions concerns the reasons that led Vilatte, born in the *Petite Église*, a minoritarian church that separated from the Roman Catholic Church in reaction to Napoleon's *Concordat* of 1801, to consider the Episcopal Church a valid option for his own quest towards Catholicity.[36] An intriguing factor in Vilatte's approaches to the Episcopal Church was the Catholic heritage that he thought he could find there. Such a retrieval was however highly disputed, so that Vilatte was also compelled to announce his detachment from the Anglican tradition, in order to appease those who – from an exclusivist Orthodox or Old Catholic perspective – were not willing to recognise the apostolic character of the Church of England and its derivations.

Vilatte's hesitation towards Anglicanism had its reasons in the very uncertain basis of Anglican identity. A discerning observer such as John Henry Newman (1801–1890) initially

---

33 Alvares to Fr. Ignatius on 21 November 1898, "Mar Timotheos's consecration" (*Western Mail*, 7 January 1899), 6.
34 On Valente's opposition to Alvares see *infra*, chapter 6.
35 Vilatte's connection with *La Petite Église* has been briefly discussed in BYRNE, *The Other Catholics*, 100. The connection of the St Mary's Church in Duval (Wisconsin) and the Belgian followers of *La Petite Église* has been mentioned in THÈRIAULT, *Msgr. René Vilatte*, 47.
36 A Roman Catholic polemical perspective on this church was offered by JEAN-EMMANUEL B. DROCHON, *La Petite Église: Essai historique sur le schisme anticoncordataire* (Paris 1894). Available at: https://gallica.bnf.fr/ark:/12148/bpt6k9756492c. A classical impartial perspective was offered by Camille Latreille, *L' Opposition Religieuse Au Concordat de 1792 à 1803* (Paris 1910). A massive research on the diffusion of this religious denomination in the early decades of the nineteenth century in a specific regional context is offered by AUGUSTE BILLAUD, *La Petite Église dans la Vendée et les Deux-Sèvres (1800–1830)* (Paris 1982).

defined the Anglican Church as more than English, stressing its alleged foundation on apostolic precedent and echoing ideas and sensitivities already expressed by the High Church Movement of the late seventeenth and early eighteenth century. At a later stage Newman changed his opinion and, by concluding "that Anglicanism was not truly apostolic, but based in national life", he converted to Catholicism in 1845.[37] In contrast, a churchman and Regius Professor of Hebrew at Oxford such as Edward Bouverie Pusey (1800–1892) chose to remain in the Anglican Church, emphasising its rooting in the Apostolic tradition and the doctrine of the Fathers.[38]

Newman and Pusey had both been eminent representatives of the Oxford Movement, namely a High Church current that emerged initially in 1833 as a reaction to an Act of the Parliament, merging the dioceses of the established Church of Ireland, thus reducing its financial burden. Starting with a resistance to this specific issue, a much wider movement led primarily by Anglican intellectuals of the University of Oxford entirely reconsidered the relation of their church both with the pre-Reformation past and with the living traditions of the contemporary Roman Catholic church.[39] Ninety *Tracts for the Times* were published between 1833 and 1841, with the participation of a dozen of authors and a major contribution by Newman. The "Tractarians" articulated an Anglo-Catholic sensitivity, finding concrete development in initiatives such as the revival of religious life. Congregations of Anglican Sisters were founded already in the 1840s, whereas in 1866 the first male order was established, namely the Society of St. John the Evangelist, better known as the Cowley Fathers.[40] The experiment of Llanthony Abbey, undertaken by Fr. Ignatius of Jesus, correspondent of Antonio Alvares, also belongs in this context. If conversions of Tractarians to Roman Catholicism were rather frequent, particularly in the years 1845–1851[41], even the Orthodox Churches appeared to many High Church Anglicans not only as a source of precious inspiration for spiritual renewal, but also as possible outcome to a quest that could not find an adequate expression in the established Church of England. An example among many was set by the Anglican priest Ulrich Vernon Herford (1866–1938), who was consecrated Bishop in 1902 by Mar Basilios, namely Luis Mariano Soares, a former member of the Independent Catholic Church of Ceylon.[42]

---

37 WILLIAM L SACHS, *The Transformation of Anglicanism: From State Church to Global Communion* (Cambridge 1993), 3.
38 A recent approach to Pusey's theology is offered by BRIAN DOUGLAS, *The Eucharistic Theology of Edward Bouverie Pusey: Sources, Context and Doctrine within the Oxford Movement and Beyond* (Leiden / Boston 2015).
39 The literature on the Oxford Movement is obviously very wide. A recent approach is provided by GEORGE HERRING, *The Oxford Movement in Practice: The Tractarian Parochial Worlds from the 1830s to the 1870s* (Oxford 2016).
40 See J. SERENHEDD, *The Cowley Fathers: A History of the English Congregation of the Society of St John the Evangelist* (London 2019).
41 JAMES PEREIRO, 'The Oxford Movement and Anglo-Catholicism', in *The Oxford History of Anglicanism*. Volume III, ed. ROWAN STRONG (Oxford 2017), 187–211.
42 MAR GEORGIUS I, *A Voyage into the Orient Being Extracts from the Diary of the Rt. Rev. Bishop Vernon Herford* (Hove [Anvers], Belgium 1954).

4. The Jacobites in the Context of the Thomas Christians in South Asia

If the Anglo-Catholic section of the Church of England was often strongly attracted to the various Orthodox churches, concrete situations could nonetheless result in tensions, particularly in the broader context of the British Empire. During 1902–1904 mutual accusations of "proselytism" were exchanged in the pages of the London newspaper *The Guardian* concerning the Indian Church affairs in Travancore. In October 1902 the dispute started with an accusation made by the secretary to the Metropolitan of the Jacobite Syrian Church, Mr. E. M. Philip,[43] who called for the Church Missionary Society (C.M.S.) to relinquish several properties and funds. Philip's complaint continued with an account of the alleged Anglican intrusions into the affairs of the Syrian Church, including the disintegration of its unity and interventions in Syrian ritual and doctrine.[44] These official accusations and claims, before having appeared in the London newspaper, had been sent to the C.M.S. Corresponding Committee in Madras and were presented to the archbishop of Canterbury, Frederick Temple (in office 1896–1902), at Lambeth Palace.[45] The Syrian appeal was presented in London by a C.M.S. member and medical doctor named Shapurji D. Bhabha. He was a Gujarati Parsi converted to Presbyterianism.[46] He was introduced by Lisboa Pinto and Antonio Alvares to the Jacobite Syrian Church and then became the representative of that Church in London. He was also said to have been nominated as ambassador of Ignatius Aphrem I Barsoum, the Syriac Orthodox Patriarch of Antioch (1887–1957) in London.[47]

In February 1904 the *Guardian* published replies from two members of the Anglican Diocese of Travancore and Cochin – the Registrar of the Diocese W. J. Richards and the Archdeacon of Kottayam John Caley (in India in the years 1871–1905) – in regard to the earlier accusations made by E. M. Philip. However, at this point the Anglicans did not dwell anymore on vindicating themselves for having been "falsely accused of proselytizing"[48], but rather counterattacked by deploring a series of "disorderly" consecrations and ordinations having been conferred by the Syrian Church on members of the Church of England.

These allegations included:
1. The episcopal consecration of Joseph René Vilatte by three bishops of the Jacobite Syrian Church, to become Archbishop of that Church in America. He had been given the title of Timoteus I on being consecrated in Colombo in May 1892 and later on he ordained several Anglicans on his own initiative.

---

43 E. M. PHILIP was secretary to the Metropolitan of the Jacobite Syrian Church Mar Pulikkottil Joseph Mar Dionysius II, often called Mar Dionysius V (1833-1909). His book entitled *The Indian Church of St. Thomas* was published posthumously in an original English edition in 1950, and later on in a Malayalam translation.
44 *Guardian*, October 1902.
45 Lambeth Palace Library (LPL), Davidson 83, fol. 413r- 429r. *A letter to the secretary to the corresponding committee of the C.M.S. Madras RE the Syrian Church endowment* (Kottayam 1902).
46 ROBIN H. S. BOYD, *A Church History of Gujarat* (Madras 1981), 220.
47 AJESH PHILIP and GEORGE ALEXANDER, *Western Rites of Syriac-Malankara Orthodox Churches* (Kerala 2018), 162. The biography of Dr. Baba [sic] in this book is not accurate.
48 LPL, Davidson 83, fol. 464r. *A statement for The Anglican Episcope, facts and original documents showing proselytizing by the Jacobite Metropolitans of Malabar, and disorderly consecrations by order of the Jacobite Patriarch of Antioch*. February 16th, 1904.

2. The consecration of Henry Marsh Marsh-Edwards, born in Poona and an Anglican priest at the Diocese of Worcester, either by Paolo Miraglia Gullotti[49] or by Vilatte as Bishop of "Caerleon". The consecration took place in Cardiff in 1903.[50]
3. In 1898 Vilatte admitted the already mentioned Joseph Leycester Lyne, namely Ignatius of Llanthony Abbey, to the priestly order.

Among many complaints, the validity of Vilatte's consecration was a central point. A collection of letters and testimonies were gathered by the C.M.S. in this respect. Through these documents, the accusers proved the Syrian Church's firm determination to consecrate the Frenchman, regardless of warnings received from those who were well acquainted with him. Among them, particularly relevant was the already mentioned statement by Grafton, Bishop of Fond du Lac. In the debate over Vilatte's consecration one must discern several chronological and spatial dimensions. First of all, there was a financial debate between a lay secretary to the Syrian Orthodox Bishop in Kottayam on the one hand, and the C.M.S. priests residing in the same city on the other. The focus was a long-term controversy between the two neighbouring churches over funds and properties. Furthermore, the Anglican debaters even expanded to issues external to Malabar proper, by criticising the Syrian Orthodox Church for manoeuvring the episcopal consecration of the "untrustworthy" Vilatte.

5. The Independence and Reunion Movements Among the Syrian Christians in the Nineteenth Century

Since immemorable time, the Syrian Christians in Malabar have shared a belief that the Apostle St Thomas arrived on the Malabar coast and converted the first Christians of the Subcontinent. However, the belief in a common apostolic origin, also testified by the second century Syriac *Acts of Judas-Thomas*, did not suffice to keep the believers united in a single fold.[51] Diverging reactions to external influences led to divisions among the Thomas Christians that persist until today. Over the centuries, as Christian communities of a deep East Syriac tradition established relations first with the Roman Catholic Church, then with the Syrian Orthodox Church (with Western Syriac liturgy), and finally interacted with the Anglican and Protestant Churches in the nineteenth century, both fractionism and ecumenism seemed to be recurrent themes. Very often, fractionism was also intertwined with claims of caste hierarchy and with conflicting historical memories, in the context of a society defined by religious pluralism.[52]

---

49 H.R. Brandreth claimed that Marsh-Edwards was consecrated by Miraglia Gullotti, whereas Anglican authors claim that it was Vilatte. Miraglia Gullotti was consecrated by Vilatte on May 6th 1900 as Bishop of Piacenza. BRANDRETH, *Episcopi Vagantes and the Anglican Church*, 1st Edition 1961 (San Bernardino 2006), 39.
50 The ideological orientation of this bishop can be gleaned from the *Pastoral Letter of the Right Reverend Henry Marsh Marsh-Edwards on the Appalling Advance of Rationalism in the Church of England* (London 1903).
51 References written from the Catholic point of view are MARTIN GIELEN, *St. Thomas: The Apostle of India*, ed. Geevarghese Chediath (Kottayam 1990). A summary of bibliography on St Thomas in India still valuable today is in EUGÈNE TISSERANT, *Eastern Christianity in India. A History of the Syro-Malabar Church from the Earliest Time to the Present Day* (London 1957), 1–8. On the Anglican side, the very W. J. RICHARD who had written against the consecration of Vilatte published *The Indian Christians of St. Thomas, Otherwise Called the Syrian Christians of Malabar. A Sketch of Their History and An Account of Their Present Condition, as Well as a Discussion of the Legend of St. Thomas* (London 1908), 89–94.
52 For an orientation on these entanglements, see G. KOILPARAMPIL, *Caste in the Catholic Community in Kerala. A Study of Caste Elements in the Inter-Rite Relationships of Syrians and Latins* (Cochin 1982); S. BAYLY,

The first external force leading to schisms was certainly the establishment of a Roman Catholic presence in India, in the wake of the creation of the Portuguese *Estado da Índia*. The forced separation of the Malabar Christians from the Church of the East, the imposition of Latin prelates and a process of latinization epitomised by the notorious Synod of Diamper in 1599 led to a major act of resistance half a century later. Following the Coonan Cross Oath of Mattanchery in January 1653, those who revolted against the Portuguese Jesuit bishop Francisco Garcia (1580–1659) came to be known as 'Puthencoor', i.e. "the new group", whereas the opposite party was described as "Pazhencoor", "the old group".[53] The rebels did in fact do something "new". First of all, in May 1653 the Archdeacon Thomas was consecrated bishop (becoming known as Mar Thoma I) by the imposition of hands by 12 priests, through a procedure that was both democratic and canonically dubious.

This became a major problem, once the Thomas Christians in communion with Rome succeeded in 1663 at being placed under the leadership of the first canonically consecrated native bishop of Malabar, namely Palliveettil Mar Chandy (also known as Parambil Mar Chandy or Alexander de Campo, † 1687), who in fact was a cousin of Mar Thoma I. The consecration of the latter was then regularized in 1665 by Mar Gregorios Abdal Jaleel († 1681), Syriac Orthodox Metropolitan Bishop of Jerusalem and delegate of the Patriarch of Antioch. At that point, even from a Roman Catholic point of view, Mar Thoma I could be considered a valid bishop, even though consecrated illicitly. The derivation of the apostolic succession from the Syriac Orthodox Church of Antioch, namely from what the Roman Catholics defined "Jacobites", led to a second fundamental novelty: the 'Puthencoor' shifted, slowly and in a very gradual way, from an Eastern Syriac to a Western Syriac liturgy and tradition. On the other hand, if the Thomas Christians in communion with Rome retained a latinized version of their earlier Eastern Syriac liturgy, there were also Christians who hoped straight away for a reunion with the Church of the East: choosing neither Rome, nor Antioch, they would rather turn their eyes towards Mesopotamia.[54]

The Malankara Syrian Church, as the 'Puthencoor' came to be known, suffered a small schism in 1772,[55] but had to face a far greater challenge at the beginning of the nineteenth century. With the British hegemony on the subcontinent, the influence of the Anglican and Protestant churches became very significant. The Church Missionary Society (C.M.S), an Evangelical Anglican entity founded in London in 1799 with the initial name of Society for Missions to Africa and the East, was established in Cochin in 1816. The C.M.S. hoped that Malankara Christians, heirs of an Apostolic tradition and with a very negative experience of Roman Catholicism, could become partners in a fruitful dialogue with the Anglican and Evangelical missionary enterprise. However, judging from their experience with the Syrian Churches in Asia Minor, the Anglicans found the Indian Church poorly equipped in doctrinal,

---

Saints, Goddesses and Kings. Muslims and Christians in South Indian Society, 1700–1900 (1st ed. 1989, Cambridge 2003); S. VISVANATHAN, *Christians of Kerala*. History, Belief and Ritual among the Yakoba (New Delhi 1999).

53 A classical study on this conjuncture is J. THEKEDATHU, *The Troubled Days of Francis Garcia S.J. Archbishop of Cranganore (1641–59)* (Rome 1972).

54 Mar Gabriel, an East Syrian bishop originally in communion with Rome, came to India in 1705 (or slightly later, as argued in earlier scholarship) and, until his death in Kottayam in 1731, represented a third party between the 'Puthencoor' and 'Pazhencoor'. See I. PERCZEL, "Four Apologetic Church Histories from India" (*The Harp: A Review of Syriac, Oriental and Ecumenical Studies* 24, 2009, 189–211).

55 This led to the creation of the Malabar Independent Syrian Church, a small community existing even today. See J. FENWICK, *The Forgotten Bishops*. The Malabar Independent Syrian Church and its Place in the Story of the St Thomas Christians of South India (Piscataway 2009).

theological, and liturgical terms. The very identity of Jacobite Syrian Christians appeared dubious from a theological point of view. One of the founding C.M.S. missionaries, Claudius Buchanan (1766–1815), was dissatisfied by the concrete development of the Anglican Church among the Thomas Christians of Malabar, as this was "not ... a National Church employ[ing] her influence to greater advantage" but was rather focused on "restoring and building up the ruins of the Syrian Communion in Antioch, in Mesopotamia, and in India."[56] For sure, the agenda of "renovation" included also the establishment of colleges, of a theological seminary in Kottayam, and of printing presses, all initiatives that fitted well with a Protestant missionary agenda. Nonetheless, for the C.M.S. missionaries, the Syrian Church in Malabar had not only suffered physical isolation from the Patriarch in Asia Minor, but had also been contaminated by the influence of the Roman Catholic Church, whose doctrine and ceremonies had "deformed" the Indian Church, and stained its apostolic tradition.[57] The staunch aversion of the Anglican establishment (as distinct from the Oxford Movement) to the Roman Catholic Church, and vice versa, displayed also in South Asia, reflected the ecumenical crisis of the two Churches in Europe, which reached its climax with Leo XIII's declaration of the invalidity of the Anglican Orders with the Bull *Apostolicæ Curæ* in 1896.[58] While the Malankara Church benefitted considerably from the collaboration with the C.M.S., this also led to conflicts between reformers inspired by Protestantism and supporters of the Orthodox tradition. After decades of litigation and vain attempts at reconciliation, an independent reformed Mar Thoma Syrian Church was created in 1889, separating from the Jacobite Syrian Church and maintaining close relation with the Anglican Church, leading to a Concordat of Full Communion in 1961.[59] The Anglican influence in Malabar hardly altered the peace between the patriarch of Antioch and the archbishop of Canterbury. However, a rivalry remained at the level of local churches, between the C.M.S. missionaries and the Malankara Orthodox bishops, as demonstrated in the dispute over Vilatte.

The Roman Catholics in Malabar, often addressed as Suriani or Nazrani Catholics during the nineteenth century, faced multiple challenges at the same time. On the one hand, there was the conflict between Padroado and Propaganda Fide, with the latter being heralded in Malabar by the Discalced Carmelites since the time of the Coonan Cross Oath. The *Padroado* had certainly a particular connection to the Latin Catholics of Malabar, namely with the people who had converted after the arrival of the Portuguese to India.[60] However, there were also many Suriani Catholics under the jurisdiction of the old Padroado archdiocese of Cranganore and the diocese of Cochin.

On the other hand, the Roman Catholics of Malabar were challenged also by external rivals. These were two churches of Eastern Syriac Rites, namely the Chaldean Catholic Patriarchate and the Church of the East, the former in full communion with Rome and the latter

---

56 W.J. RICHARD, *The Indian Christians of St. Thomas, Otherwise Called the Syrian Christians of Malabar. A Sketch of Their History and An Account of Their Present Condition, as Well as a Discussion of the Legend of St. Thomas* (London 1908), 21.

57 W.S. HUNT, *The Anglican Church in Travancore and Cochin, 1816–1916*. Operations of the Church Missionary Society in South- West India, Vol. I (Kottayam 1920), 62.

58 On the preparation of this Bull see A.F. VON GUNTEN (ed.) *La validité des Ordinations Anglicanes*. Les documents de la Commission Préparatoire à la Lettre Apostolicae Curae (Fontes Archivi Sancti Officii Romani 1, Firenze 1997), vol. 1; A. CIFRES (ed.), *La validez de las ordenaciones anglicanas*. Los documentos de la comisión preparatoria de la bula Apostolicae curae (Fontes Archivi Sancti Officii Romani 2, Rome 2012), vol. 2.

59 On this reformed Oriental church, see J. DANIEL, *Ecumenism in Praxis*. A Historical Critique of the Malankara Mar Thoma Syrian Church (Frankfurt am Main 2014).

60 See T. THAYIL, *The Latin Christians of Kerala*. A Study of Their Origins (Bangalore 2003).

accused of being "Nestorian".[61] Since the seventeenth century there was also the fundamental influence of the Syrian Orthodox Church, also known as "Jacobite Church", of Western Syriac Rite and accused by the Catholics of being "Monophysite".[62] During the nineteenth century, the Chaldean Catholic Church continued to claim its jurisdiction over the Thomas Christians in communion with Rome, even though they had been effectively under the *Padroado* and Propaganda Fide since the seventeenth century.

The Chaldean Catholic Patriarch Joseph VI Audo (1790–1878), elected in 1847, was a capable leader and embarked on a reformation of his church in Iraq.[63] Meanwhile, he requested the Holy See to restore a Chaldean jurisdiction over Malabar, so that the Thomas Christians would be ruled by bishops subject to the Patriarch in Mosul, replacing the Apostolic Vicars sent from Propaganda Fide. Before the Holy See could give a pertinent response, Audo sent out two bishops to India, Mar Thomas Rokos in 1860 and then Mar Eliya Mellus (1831–1908) in 1874 to enact this plan starting from Trichur, in the northern region of today's Kerala.[64] Local Catholic priests and laymen in Trichur embraced both Rokos and Mellus. For a long time they had been disappointed by Rome for neglecting their requests for native bishops. A considerable number of *Padroado* priests in Trichur refused to acknowledge the authority of the Apostolic Vicar of Verapoly, the Italian Carmelite Leonardo Mellano di San Luigi (1826–1897), and followed Mellus.

Meanwhile, the Apostolic Vicar Mellano, whose Carmelite Order had been in charge of the Malabar Catholic missions since the seventeenth century, faced a separation movement from its Third Order led by native laymen.[65] In 1876 the Apostolic Vicar of Bombay Leo Meurin was entrusted by Rome to visit Verapoly so as to find a solution to the schism triggered by Mellus. Meurin, however, represented a small fraction of European missionaries, who did favour an independent native Bishop to be elected for the local Catholics. Meurin's position had made him popular among the Suriani Catholics but also a rival to Mellano and many of the Carmelites. Judging from Meurin's reports, the Congregation of Propaganda was still unable to find a solution and eventually sent a second visitor to Malabar. The new visitor, Ignazio Persico (1823–1895), an Italian Jesuit who had worked in the Madurai Mission in the Tamil lands, reached Malabar in 1877. As explained in chapter 2, Persico was experienced in the *Padroado*-Propaganda conflicts among the Tamil Catholics. His report took the side of Meurin and harshly criticised the Carmelites in Malabar:

> Their [i.e. the Thomas Christians] longing for a bishop of their own rite was age-old and had occurred many times. Their demand has grown and become intensive in recent times. This is likely due to the fact that they [Suriani Catholics] are abandoned, no longer being attended by the Carmelites. The Carmelites either have no or little knowledge of the languages, or they ignored the Suriani and even treated them in a way of haughtiness and rudeness. Additionally,

---

61 On the inadequacy of the term "Nestorian" see S.P. BROCK, "The Nestorian Church: A Lamentable Misnomer" (*Bulletin of the John Rylands Library* 78/3, 1996, 23–35).

62 In recent scholarship the term *myaphysism* has replaced the earlier *monophysism,* which is both theologically erroneous (it might apply only to the Christological position of the Eutichians, a group no more existing, whereas it misrepresents all the current non-Chalcedonian churches) and it has a strong derogatory connotation. See S.P. BROCK, "Miaphysite, Not Monophysite!" (*Cristianesimo nella Storia* 37, 2016, 47–51).

63 J. HABBI, "Les Chaldéens et les Malabares au XIXe siécle," (*Oriens Christianus* 64, 1980, 82–107).

64 On Mar Thoma Rokos see P. PALLATH, *Rome and Chaldean Patriarchate in Conflict.* Schism of Bishop Rokos in India (Changanacherry 2017); MAR APREM, *The Chaldean Syrian Church in India* (Trichur 1977), 90–99; on Mellus IBID., 108–115.

65 CHERIAN VARICATT, *The Suriani Church of India.* Her Quest for Autochthonous Bishops (1877–1896) (Kottayam 1992), 15.

the Suriani have an antipathy towards the Apostolic Vicar Monsignor Mellano, who barely paid attention to the Suriani' needs and preferred the Catholics of Latin rites to those of Syrian rites. In fact many schools have been constructed for the Latins, whereas almost nothing for the Suriani. They are totally ignored and abandoned to themselves.[66]

The Malabar Christians, divided by Eastern Syriac, Western Syriac, and Latin rites, saw themselves subject to multiple external rivalries. The antagonism between the Roman Catholic, Anglican, Jacobite, and Nestorian churches had its origins outside Malabar, but had overarching consequences in India. On the other hand, some native bishops of the Jacobite and the Catholic Churches, being exposed to and involved in such conflicts, became aware of the contradiction between the necessity of social reforms in their own communities and the inefficiency of their mother churches in Rome, Mardin, or Mosul, in addressing their status within the British colonial society. During the second half of the nineteenth century, the Malabar churches that refused to follow the Anglican influence went on a path of reunion, in the hope of becoming a single autochthonous church.

Two Church leaders, namely Fr. Emmanuel Nidhiry (1842–1904), Vicar General of the "Northists" in the Apostolic Vicariate of Kottayam[67] and the Jacobite Metropolitan Mar Dionysius V (in office 1866–1909) were the leaders of this movement.[68] Under their joint initiative, a *Nazrani Jathyikya Sangham* or Syrian National Union Association was created in Malabar in 1866, leading in 1887 to the publication of the journal *Nazrani Deepika*. The prime aim of the Association was to promote educational and social reforms for the wellbeing of the Syrian Christians. The rules of that association stated:

> The Syrians of Malabar commonly called Nazranees of St Thomas having been divided into two religious parties called Pazhayacootoocar (people of the ancient party) and Poothencootoocar (people of the recent party) have become two weak fractions as broken members of a body and deprived of the progress in the social status by education, civilization and elevation to high offices which should proceed from national union.[69]

The union aimed at the education of the priests and laymen of both churches following the model of the Catholic system. The two churches purchased properties in the woodland of Kottayam, the heart of the Jacobite Syrian Church, to build a Syrian Christian College on the

---

66 My own translation of an Italian transcription made by CHERIAN VARICATT, based on ACCO, *Acta* 1877–1878, vol.10, f.272. *The Suriani Church of India*, 20, note 84.

67 P. PODIPARA, *The Hierarchy of the Syro-Malabar Church* (Alleppey 1976), 175; A.M. NIDHIRY, *Father Nidhiry, 1842–1904. A History of His Times* (2nd ed., Kuravilangad 2003). The content of the latter book is accessible also from a website dedicated to the bishop: http://www.nidhiry.org/fn.htm. Chapter 13 "Towards Ecumenism". On the distinction between "Northists" (*Vadakkumbhagar*) and "Southists" (*Thekkumbhagar*), see A.M. MUNDADAN, *History of Christianity in India* (Bangalore 1989), vol. 1: From the Beginning up to the Middle of the Sixteenth Century (up to 1542), 95–98.

68 Correspondence between the two has been published by the Syro-Malankara priest historian Thomas Inchakalody in his Malayalam book *The Christian Churches of Kerala* (Trivandrum 1952). For further studies on the Jacobite church in the reunion movement see Thomas Panicker, "Jacobites in Malabar, and Their Reunion Efforts" (PhD Thesis, Rome 1958).

69 "Rules for the Syrian national union association in Malabar". The original document in Malayalam, with an English translation, is kept at ACO, *Scrit. Rif. Malabar* 1878-1889, ff. 1267-1274. I used the transcription published in CHERIAN VARICATT, *Suriani Church of India*, 515.

model of the Jesuit Colleges in India such as the ones dedicated to St Francis Xavier in Bombay and Calcutta, to St Aloysius in Mangalore, and to St Joseph in Tiruchirapalli.[70] The association also sponsored talented students to pursue an advanced education in foreign countries. In particular, it encouraged students and authors to write against two main issues that had been raised unfavourably in regard to Syrian Christians. In the first place, the local language of Malayalam had been accused of corrupting the faith of the Syrian Christians. Secondly, it had been argued that some Syrian Christians had damaged their old faith and morals due to a pernicious influence from the Protestants.[71]

The association was also concerned with the financial maintenance of the Church and suggested a network of merchants with good faith to be established beyond Malabar, as stated in the article 26:

> 26. Likewise the association should have shops and trustworthy merchants in proper places and port-shops in Cochin and Alleppy [sic, today's Alappuzha] with some faithful merchants and some greater shops and good agents in chief towns, as Bombay etc. Merchandise should be conducted with such auxiliaries in [sic] behalf of the association the income of which should be added to the association fund.[72]

Nidhiry and Dionysius' initiative received unanimously unfavorable opinions from the three bishops directly involved with Malabar, namely the Apostolic Vicar of Verapoly Mellano, the former Apostolic Delegate to India Agliardi, and his successor Aiuti. Among the three, Mellano had the richest experience in Malabar, and his comments on the Association's statutes reflected a consensus of the veteran Carmelites. The first and prime objection was based on their conviction that the Jacobite Christians regarded themselves as superior to the Catholics in terms of caste, an opinion that left no room to an association of equal members. Secondly, the administration of the association on the basis of a general vote was contrary to the hierarchical governance of the Catholic Church. Thirdly, a decline of European episcopal authorities would be the unavoidable corollary of such an association run by local clerics. Fourthly, the finances would be a source of recurrent quarrels between the two Churches. Finally, the association might not lead to conversion of the Jacobites, but rather to an apostasy of the Catholics.[73] The Catholic authorities in Malabar were well aware that Suriani fractionism was triggered by claims of caste belonging and superiority as much, or even more than actual theological differences. However, the Carmelites and the Apostolic Vicars were primarily concerned about the risk of losing their control over the Malabar church. They felt threatened by the rising power of the local clerics reunited as one body.

In April 1888, Nidhiry visited Andrea Aiuti, by then Apostolic Delegate to India, who resided in the hill station of Ooty (Ootacamund), on the Nilgiri Mountains. Aiuti stressed the Roman disapproval of the Association and concerns in regard to the financial disputes that a co-founded college might generate in the future. Likely due to Dionysius V's persistence, on 26 April 1888 Nidhiry arranged a second meeting with the Apostolic Delegate, but this time also with Dionysius V and the Apostolic Delegate of Kottayam Charles Lavigne S. J. (1840–1913) in presence. Aiuti reported on this meeting in a letter to Rome and attached five ques-

---

70 VARICATT, *Suriani Church of India*, 519.
71 VARICATT, *Suriani Church of India*, 519.
72 VARICATT, *Suriani Church of India*, 521.
73 VARICATT, *Suriani Church of India*, 262.

tions Dionysius had raised – on Jacobite hierarchy, finance, married priests, rites, and colleges and seminaries – as essential premises for his potential conversion to Catholicism.[74] These questions were studied by the Congregation of Propaganda Fide. A final decision was drawn in Rome on 25 June 1888 ordering Aiuti to encourage the good dispositions of Mar Dionysius.[75] Nidhiry continued to act as a key intermediary in the Roman – Jacobite negotiation, being the only English translator Dionysius trusted. To his surprise, eventually Dionysius reacted negatively to Propaganda Fide' attitude, as he was disappointed by Rome's refusal to his earlier proposal of a lower school to be run by the Syrian National Union.[76] Dionysius' reaction caused more suspicion among the Catholic bishops regarding his sincerity. In 1890 Dionysius won a legal case against the pro-Anglican leader Mar Athanasius in the high court of Travancore, gaining himself an overwhelming support within the Jacobite Church. Dionysius now openly expressed his discontent with Rome in a conversation with Nidhiry. The former reproached the latter for his allegiance with Rome, which he linked back to what he felt had been the wrong decision that the Catholics of Malabar made at the Coonan Cross Oath. In a report to Rome, Aiuti quoted some remarks from Dionysius, in which a tone of despisal towards the Suriani Catholics for their alleged betrayal of their common ancestors was manifest:

> Instead all of you, breaking such an oath again went under Latin bishops and did everything possible to have a native bishop with the sanction of Rome. You have not managed to have any and are still under Latins, although you hear rumours that you hope finally to see your prayers granted. Even so how could one believe your words which are contrary to the experience of around three centuries? It is a great folly to think that I may give my mitre to place under the pillow of the Latin bishops so that they may sleep over it with more confidence. If you render faith to the Latin bishops and try to convert my priests before obtaining a native bishop, you will be considered as a violator of the oath of our ancestors and as an enemy of the freedom and dignity of our nation.[77]

Dionysius was fully aware of the Suriani Catholics' failed appeal to the Roman curia for a native bishop. He described his Syrian party as occupying a wiser and morally superior position, for they had never trusted the 'Latin bishops' from Europe ever since the Oath had been taken at Mattancherry. On the contrary, in Dionysius' perspective, the Antiochian Church had greatly favoured the Suriani native bishops. Fulfiling his function of intermediary, Nidhiry reported on the dilatory responses and lack of communication with Dionysius. In the meantime, a disheartening declaration of Dionysius reached Rome, and it marked the end of the reunion attempts.[78]

So far, the joint enterprise of Nidhiry and Dionysius has been studied mainly according to the Catholic sources. In hindsight, Catholic historians such as Thomas Panicker, Cherian Varicatt, Abraham M. Nidhiry, and Alex Mathew consider this failed reunion as an episode

---

74 VARICATT, *Suriani Church of India*, 266. For an overview of all denominations of the Saint Thomas Christians in the reunion movement see A. MATHEW, "The Reunion Movement among the St. Thomas Christians, 19th and 20th Centuries" (PhD Thesis, Kottayam 2007), in which Dionysius' visit to Ooty, together with Charles Lavigne and Emmanuel Nidhiry, was studied in pages 166–173.
75 VARICATT, *Suriani Church of India*, 267.
76 VARICATT, *Suriani Church of India*, 269.
77 VARICATT, *Suriani Church of India,* 273. Varicatt translated from Italian to English from a report by Aiuti to Simeoni dated on 10 September 1890, in which he quoted remarks from a letter from Nidhiry dated April 18, 1890. ACO, *Scrit. Rif. Malabar* 1890-1892, f. 2154.
78 VARICATT, *Suriani Church of India,* 273.

in a recurrent aspiration to get in communion with Rome, leading eventually to the establishment of the Syro-Malankara Catholic Church in 1930, when a fraction of Malankara Syrian Orthodox led by the Bishop Mar Ivanios (1882–1953) accepted the authority of the Holy See. On the contrary, the Syrian Orthodox records, however, remain unconsidered. Historians from the Orthodox Church, such as E. M. Philip and V. C. Samuel, hardly referred to Dionysius's interactions with the Catholic Church. Further research is required to explore, for instance Nidhiry's and Dionysius' positions, and the contexts in which they made every decision pro and contra the unification process. In particular the Malabar metropolitans' relations with the Patriarch of Antioch, Peter III, who visited India in 1875, has to be taken duly into account.[79]

The ex-Catholic priest Antonio Alvares, future leader of the Independent Catholic Movement, was in touch with Dionysius around 1886 when the latter was still in earnest hope for a Syrian National Union Association of Malabar. Little is known about Alvares' take on this potential unity, but his consecration as "Archbishop of Goa, Ceylon and India excluding Malabar" on 15 July 1889 in Kottayam, with approval of the Patriarch of Antioch, certainly made waves.[80] It displeased at the same time the Archbishop of Goa and the Archbishop of Colombo, as both announced excommunications against the schismatic priest and his followers. The particular action of granting Alvares the title of "Archbishop" was unprecedented to the Jacobite Syrian Church in Malabar, in which there were rather Metropolitans. The apparently hybrid title of Alvares suggests that the very assimilation of the Independent Catholic Movement into the Antiochian Communion must be studied carefully, as the Jacobite Syrian Church in Malabar was in a process of a realignment of its ecumenical relations.

6. Alvares' Syrian Orthodox Identity and His Reception in Various Churches

6.1 A Supremacia Universal as an "Identity Document"

In 1898 Alvares published a Portuguese book entitled *A supremacia universal* with Clifton Press in Colombo.[81] Later on, the author loosely translated the book into English and published it under the title *Universal Supremacy in the Church of Christ,* printed at the same publishing house in Colombo.[82] In 2020 Dr. Kurian Thomas discovered two typewritten manuscripts of the English version, one at the personal collection of Fr. K. G. Thomas Kottathuvila in Adoor, and the other one at the Catholicate Palace Archives at Devalokam, Kottayam.[83] *A supremacia* was Alvares' only book on Church history and Orthodox theology

---

79 V. C. SAMUEL, *Truth Triumphs: An Account of the Life and Achievements of Malankara Metropolitan Vattasseril Geevarghese Mar Dionysius* (Kerala 1986), 16.
80 This consecration will be studied in Chapter 6.
81 A.F.X. ALVARES, JULIO I, *A supremacia universal na Egreja de Christo, provada pela Escriptura, tradição e escritores insuspeitos a Egreja Romana* (Colombo 1898).
82 A.F.X. ALVARES, *Universal Supremacy in the Church of Christ ... Abridged from the Original in Portuguese.* (Colombo 1898).
83 Metropolitan A.F.X. ALVARES MAR YOOLIOS, *Universal Supremacy of the Church of Christ*, ed. by T. KURIAN (Kottayam 2020), 13.

alongside his other booklets on agriculture and pandemics.[84] It was the last one of an Independent Catholic trilogy dedicated to Antiochian supremacy, following Lisboa Pinto's *Antiochia e Roma* (1890) and *A Supremacia romana sem apoio na Biblia, tradição e historia* (1891), composed by Fr. José Xavier Botelho, who defined himself as "Canon of the Cathedral of Ceylon".[85] The latter booklet was written in defence of the former when it had been censored by the Archbishop of Ceylon. As a concluding work, *A supremacia* offers a vantage point to understand not only the theological statements of the Independent Catholic movements, but also the climax of the ecumenical approaches in which the Jacobite Syrian Church positioned herself.

A supremacia universal is written in the form of a dialogue between a layman and a priest, which in the Portuguese original consists of 40 conversations with a specific title for each section. The first conversation or chapter entitled "The state of the question" revealed that the book was made as a reaction to a series of "unjust and brutal" treatments that the Roman Catholic authority in Goa had exerted on Archbishop Alvares.

> Priest. Welcome my friend. I am glad to see you here because you will no doubt be able to give me news of the great religious discussions going on everywhere these days.
> Layman. With pleasure, Rev. Father. In fact I came here to talk on the very subject. When public indignation was roused in the country on account of the unjust and brutal imprisonment of Archbishop Alvares and when subsequently the *Brado Indiano* a Goan newspaper denounced the Universal Supremacy of the Pope as an invention of the VII century and a fraud without any foundation in Scripture or History. … And at their suggestion [some learned priests] I come here as I know that your Reverence besides being a man of learning and research has a library stocked with almost every important ancient and modern work of reference. Pray therefore, Rev. Father, what is Universal Supremacy?[86]

The conversation thus starts with the inquiry of a fictional Roman Catholic priest to a lay friend in regard to the latest discussions concerning religion.[87] The layman refers to the recent persecution that Archbishop Alvares had received in Goa in 1895, three years prior to the publication of this book. Back then Alvares was arrested on the ground of using episcopal insignia despite his excommunication by the Roman Catholic Archbishop of Goa. The suspicion toward Alvares' identity as an Orthodox Bishop stood alongside the censorship of a Portuguese weekly newspaper co-edited by Alvares entitled *O Brado Indiano: semanario politico, industrial e agricola*, which had published articles against the Papal supremacy.[88]

The series of 40 conversations starts as an apology and then extends to a complete anti-Roman argument. Exhaustive quotations from Latin works and a revisionist reading of Church history imply that the target readership was the well-educated Portuguese elite, and

---

84 Pe. A.F.X. ALVARES, *Direcções para o tratamento do cholera* (Nova Goa n.d.); A.F.X. ALVARES, *Directions for the Treatment of Cholera … Second Edition* (Ceylon 1896); A.J.X. ALVARES JULIO 1, *Mandioca* (Bastora 1917).

85 In the frontespice of the booklet, the author was identified as "Presbyterio [Presbytero] Jose Xavier Botelho, Conego da Sé de Ceylão e Secretario de Dom A. F. X. Alvares Julio J. Arcebispo de Gôa, India e Ceylão". The context would suggest that Botelho was basically the parish priest of the Cathedral of Our Lady of Good Death, with the pompous title of "Canon", and without implying necessarily the existence of a proper Cathedral Chapter.

86 ALVARES MAR YOOLIOS, *Universal Supremacy*, 25. I made minor corrections of the English text according to the Portuguese text in ALVARES, JULIO I, *A supremacia universal*, 1.

87 The priest refers to himself as one of "We Roman Catholic priests." ALVARES MAR YOOLIOS, *Universal Supremacy*, 37.

88 See Chapter 6.

in particular the English and Portuguese-speaking Goan priests. The two interlocutors that the text presents are Catholics and admirers of Archbishop Alvares but not yet followers. On various occasions the priest alludes to his education at Rachol seminary, then belonging to the Archdiocese of Goa where Alvares indeed spent three years as seminarian. *A supremacia*, as well as *Antiochia e Roma* heavily relied on a work on Church history entitled *Institutiones historiae ecclesiasticae novi foederis*,[89] written by an Italian Franciscan missionary in the Habsburg Empire named Chiaro Vascotti (1799–1860).[90] First published in Rome in 1851 and written for Franciscan seminarians, the manual reached its 6th edition in Latin by 1889 and was never translated into other languages. The book was abbreviated by Alvares and Lisboa Pinto as *Historia Ecclesiastica;* its content is taught "in all the seminaries in the Catholic world (*orbe*), and we studied it in the Royal Seminary of Rachol."[91] One might infer that *A supremacia* was prepared for the recruitment of Goan missionaries, as it was published when the Independent Catholic movement entered its 10th year and started to face a serious shortage of priests, due to the expansion of the movement.

The 40 conversations or chapters of *A supremacia* (abridged to 32 chapters in the English version) follow a thematic sequence that can be divided into four steps: the equality of all the Apostolic Sees (c. 2–c. 10), a historical overview of the Ecumenical Councils and controversies in the Middle Ages (c. 11–c. 23), a condemnation of the Bishops of Rome for their misconducts (c. 24–c. 34), and the history and status quo of the Asian Church in the Latin Roman and Orthodox churches, observed from the Independent Catholic experience (c. 35–c. 40). There are several aspects worth to be discussed, namely the theoretical tools, the rhetorical strategies, and the author's self-presentation.

As mentioned before, the fictional Catholic priest relies on the textual authority of Catholic authors from both before and after the Great Schism of 1054. He attacks the Roman supremacy by targeting the widely accepted status of the Pope and the Roman Curia. First of all, he eloquently discusses the lack of historical foundations for a "Universal bishop" (*Bispo Universal*),[92] as allegedly claimed by various Church Fathers such as Pope Gregory the Great (540–604) and Boniface III (died in 607). As the priest argues, this claim can be proven also by the most respected Church historians such as Ignace Hyacinthe Amat de Graveson (1670–1733), Paolo Diacono (720–799), Anastasius III (c.810 – 879, also known as "Anastasius the Librarian"), and Cesare Baronio (1538–1607), famous Church historians and Cardinal.[93] For instance Anastasius III, Librarian and Archivist of the Holy See, once remarked that during the first six centuries of the Church there was no one designated as universal bishop or universal patriarch.[94] In a lengthy chapter 5 the priest stresses the equality among the Apostles but also similarly among all Bishops, as "the Apostles were all equal to one another and not one particular was granted to Peter which the other apostles did not likewise receive."[95] He discusses the alleged decadence of Rome on the basis of various textual evidence. He relates the fall of Rome to the narrative of Nebuchadnezzar, Emperor of Babylonia, in the Book of Daniel, where the prophet interprets the King's dream of a huge statue as God's prediction of the rise and fall of the world powers (Daniel 2).

---

89 CLARUS VASCOTTI, *Institutiones historiae ecclesiasticae novi foederis* 1st ed. (Roma 1851).
90 H. BERGMANN, "Vascotti", in *Österreichisches Biographisches Lexikon*, Vol. 15 (Lfg.68, 2017), 188.
91 A.F.X. ALVARES, JULIO I, *A supremacia universal*, 34.
92 A.F.X. ALVARES, JULIO I, *A supremacia universal*, 3.
93 A.F.X. ALVARES, JULIO I, *A supremacia universal*, 5–7.
94 A.F.X. ALVARES, JULIO I, *A supremacia universal*, 3, 5.
95 ALVARES MAR YOOLIOS, *Universal Supremacy*, 43.

Meanwhile, *A supremacia* also draws on random anecdotes for which no reliable sources are provided. In a discussion on St Peter's Chair (*Cathedra Petri*), the priest distinguishes between the two meanings of "chair", namely the seat from which doctrine is taught, and a banal piece of furniture. As St Augustin remarked in a sermon on St Peter's creation of the Antiochian See, the Church had given a feast in honor of "the birth of the chair". Accordingly, this tradition was ubiquitously observed across the ancient Christian world, but faded away in the Western Latin world. Only as late as in 1592 Pope Clement VIII restored this veneration and chose one chair from a repository of relics as the original chair sat on by the Apostle. However, as *A supremacia* argues, the provenance of the chair was discovered through a scandal in the 18th century:

> From the repository of the sacred relics another chair was ordered out to which Roman catholics paid veneration for sixty years, when in the time of Alexander VII, it was noticed that the chair was in the Gothic style and therefore could not possibly belong to the apostolic times. The pope was angry and ordered the gothic chair to be put aside, and a fresh one brought from the inexhaustible repository. There was apparently no objection against this third chair, which accordingly became the chair of St. Peter. Bernini was ordered to have it encased in bronze, and in 1666 it was exalted to a prominent place supported by Fathers of the Church. When in 1795 the French occupied Rome, some of them were promoted by sacrilegious curiosity to examine the chair of Peter. The bronze case being removed, on careful examination these words in Arabic were found on the chair:- There is no God but God. And Mohamad is his prophet![96]

The St Peter's chair being mocked in the story alludes to the wooden chair, still standing in St Peter's Basilica in the Vatican, that Charles the king of West Francia, Italy, and emperor of the Carolingian Empire presented to Pope John VIII in 875. It was believed that Saint Peter had used it. In 1647 Gian Lorenzo Bernini was commissioned to encase the relic furniture in a gilt bronze casing. Back in the nineteenth century, a mockery questioning the authenticity of the venerated holy chair was a part of anti-Catholic discourse. One of the most influential "anti-popery" works of this kind was *The Two Babylons: The Papal Worship reported to be the Worship of Nimrod and his Wife*, by the Scottish Presbyterian Alexander Hislop. First published in 1853, the book was reprinted several times and nowadays has achieved a massive revival online.[97] A similar excerpt on the Quran quotation was borrowed from A *Hand-Book of popery; or Text-Book of Missions for the conversion of Romanists*, a book published in Edinburgh in 1852.[98] As will be studied in chapter 4, the Protestant missions published anti-Catholic pamphlets in English as well as in vernacular languages in Ceylon. It is likely that Alvares, while being a staunch opponent of Protestantism, used Protestant mockeries and satirical arguments so as to attack a common rival: the Roman Catholic Church.

---

96 ALVARES MAR YOOLIOS, *Universal Supremacy*, 79–80.
97 ANTHONY MILTON, "Epilogue: Words, Deeds, and Ambiguities in Early Modern Anti-Catholicism", in EVAN HAEFELI, *Against Popery: Britain, Empire, and Anti-Catholicism* (Charlottesville and London, 2020), 316.
98 ALEXANDER HISLOP, *The Two Babylons,* 5th ed. (New York 2002 [1853]), 198.

6.2 An Expansion of the Independent Catholic Church: The Ordination of Alexander Steward in 1900

Vilatte was not the only European clergyman who sought ordination in the Independent Catholic Church in Ceylon. In 1900 an English man called Alexander Westwood Steward (1876–?) from Grassington in Yorkshire approached Alvares. Steward had been baptised in the Anglican Church, then received confirmation from the bishop of Salisbury, before heading to Chicago where he allied with the Old Catholic Bishop Antoni Kozłowski. He completed a three years' course of Theology at the University of Illinois and returned to England for further studies at Cambridge. In Wolverhampton, he was admitted to an evangelical group named *The Evangelical Brotherhood of the Order of the Christian Faith*.[99] Perhaps through the mediation of Kozłowski, Vilatte or Fr. Ignatius, who had known about the Independent Catholic Church in Ceylon or had direct contact with it, Steward left for South Asia with the hope to receive a priestly ordination from bishop Alvares. His ordination took place at the Church of Our Lady of Good Death in September 1900. Little is known about his stay in Colombo, nor his ensuing contacts with Alvares and the Colombo community. Back in Cambridge in 1901, Stewart wanted to study moral philosophy at the university. He applied to the Anglican Bishop of Ely Alwyne Compton (1825–1906) for a position as curate, i.e. a parish priest, during his future residency at Cambridge. Yet the Archbishop of York William Maclagan (1826–1910) turned down the application.[100] Having failed both in receiving any favour from the Anglican side and in being admitted at Cambridge, Steward turned towards the Roman Catholic Church. In 1902 he entered the Catholic school of St Cuthbert's College in Durham. In the meanwhile, the Bishop of Hexham and Newcastle examined his baptism and priestly ordination and submitted a request for the clarification of "Doubts on ordination" (*Dubia de ordinatione*) concerning his case to the Congregation of the Holy Office in Rome, namely to the heir of the Roman Inquisition. From the Catholic perspective, what mattered most was the validity of Steward's baptism and ordination by Alvares, who was an excommunicated Catholic priest and hence had a dubious claim to apostolic succession.

To our knowledge, Vilatte and Steward were the only two men of European origin that sought for apostolic succession from Antonio Alvares at the Independent Catholic Cathedral in Colombo. A similar case, but not dealt with in this chapter, concerns the ex-Vicar of the Independent Catholic Church in Mannar, Luis Mariano Soares (?–1903), who reconciled with the Catholic Church in 1898 and then became Mar Basilius of the Syro-Chaldean Church of Trichur (namely the community originated by Mar Mellus) with the title of "Metropolitan of India, Ceylon, Mylapore, Socotra, and Messina [sic!]".[101] In 1902 Basilius ordained and then consecrated an English Anglican layman named Ulric Vernon Herford (1866–1928), who later became the founder of the "Orthodox Church of the British Isles" in England.[102] The history of Soares and Herford was comparable to the one of Alvares and Vilatte, but the latter pair certainly had received more international and cross-confessional attention. While further research is required to find out the total number of ordinations that

---

99 "Hexam e Newcastle, Dubia de Ordin. sull' ordinazione dell'anglicano Stewart per le mani dello scismatico goano Alvares. 1902" in ARCHIVIO DELLA CONGREGAZIONE PER LA DOTTRINA DELLA FEDE (ACDF), S.O., *Dubia circa Ordinem sacrum* 1903/7, 6.
100 ABBA SERAPHIM, *Flesh of Our Brethren*, 143.
101 H. S. B. MAR GREGORIUS, I., D. D. Patriarch of Glastonbury, *A Voyage into the Orient Being Extracts from the Diary of the Rt. Rev. Bishop Vernon Herford, Edited with an Introduction, Footnotes, and Appendices* (Hove (Anvers, Belgium 1954), 3.
102 See the diary of Herford in MAR GREGORIUS, *Voyage into the Orient*.

Antonio Alvares granted on non-South Asian clergymen, it is undeniable that many others received lineage through Vilatte across Europe, Africa and America, whose Churches remain active and continue to grow until today. Thanks to Vilatte's intervention, Alvares and his community, scattered across India and Ceylon, became known via newspapers and official reports to a global public, receiving the reputation of being independent Catholic pioneers akin to the model of the Old Catholic Church, which will be discussed more extensively in chapter 7. In contrast, the Roman Catholic authorities and media labelled Alvares as well as Soares as schismatic and rebellious.[103] Yet, in the course of time, both the Anglican and the Roman Catholic Church lost interest in the Goan schismatics. Rather, they became increasingly concerned about those who had inherited the apostolic succession from this movement, like Vilatte, Steward, and Paolo Miraglia Gullotti, especially because at some point in time many of these men sought a reconciliation with the Roman Catholic Church.

The fact that two or potentially more Europeans sought for ordinations from a Syrian Orthodox Church and from Catholic schismatics requires some further reflections. First, the South Asian and European provenance of the three men, Alvares, Vilatte, and Steward cannot squarely be located within the colonial structures that their nationalities suggest. In fact, their very complex national identities and ecclesiastical belongings somehow outweighed the latent racial prejudice, which had predominated in the relation between European missionaries and native clergymen within the Roman Catholic Church. Concretely speaking, Alvares' Brahmin caste had ascribed him to a high social status within the elite Indo-Portuguese communities across the subcontinent, but also benefited his missionary work across ethnic boundaries in the Tamil, Malayalam, Konkani, and Sinhala speaking lands. His profile also included an overseas Portuguese citizenship and later on a British nationality.[104] The life trajectories of the two European men were not less complicated. Vilatte was born in Paris to the minoritarian community of *La Petite Église*, but devoted most of his pastoral work to a Dutch and French speaking community in Wisconsin. Similarly, Steward's quest for being accepted into the apostolic succession was incited during his stay and studies in Illinois, through the influence of the Old Catholic Polish-American Bishop Antoni Kozłowski.

Secondly, all three Christian men worked with a diasporic Christian community that was culturally or politically isolated. A strong motivation for their ecclesiastical reforms was the search of concrete strategies for the spiritual care of faithful facing multicultural challenges. What is interesting to see is that they were looking for such solutions globally. In the colonial public sphere of the time, periodicals and newspapers had made it possible for men like Vilatte and Steward to come to the conclusion that the answers to their troubles lay in far-away Ceylon.[105] They might have read about *The Independent Catholic* through some widely circulated English newspapers, and decided that establishing contacts with this movement might

---

103 The English Catholic weekly *The Tablet* reported on Alvares and his fellows from 1890 to 1906, in regard to the Padroadists and Propagandists (*The Tablet* on 11 October 1890; 10 September 1892), the "Great Ceylon Schism" (on 13 December 1892), the "Independent Catholics" and "Jacobite schism" (on 21 June 1902), the "Mantote schism" (on 9 August 1902), death of Soares (on 15 August 1903), the "questionable ordination" of Vilatte (on 18 August 1906; 25 August 1906; 6 October 1906).
104 By 1906 at the latest Alvares had become a British citizen, while retaining or replacing the Portuguese citizenship. "The Archbishop states that he is a naturalised British subject… He was at the time a Portuguese subject." (*The Homeward Mail*, February 17, 1906), 195.
105 KLAUS KOSCHORKE et al., *'To Give Publicity to Our Thoughts'*. Journale Asiatischer und Afrikanischer Christen um 1900 und die Entstehung einer transregionalen indigen-christlichen Öffentlichkeit / Journals of Asian and African Christians Around 1900 and the Making of a Transregional Indigenous-Christian Public Sphere (Wiesbaden 2018), 234, 241–248.

prove beneficial to addressing the needs in their own communities.[106] The Ceylon–America–Europe connections attest to the "multidirectional transcontinental interactions" that Klaus Koschorke has stressed as requirements for writing a global history of Christianity during the nineteenth century.[107] In order to highlight such polycentric structures, it will be possible and necessary to conduct comparative research on the various anti-Catholic movements that were able to achieve trust and collaboration notwithstanding the geographic barriers.

Thirdly, Alvares' journey from the Catholic to the Syrian Orthodox Church, as well as Vilatte and Steward's Asian interludes, reflected the intensive ecumenical negotiations between the Roman Catholic Church, the Anglican (including the Episcopalian) Church, the Oriental Churches of Syrian and Chaldean rites, and the Old Catholic Church, which created a space for innovations and hybridizations, such as the Latin branch of the Syrian Orthodox Church in Malabar, better known as the Independent Catholic Church in Ceylon and India. In the next three chapters, we will study the prehistory, origin, and development of that new Church in the context of South Asian colonial history.

---

106 On 'church funding through reading newspapers' see also C. BURLACIOIU, *"Within three years the East and the West have met each other"*. Die Genese einer missionsunabhängigen schwarzen Kirche im transatlantischen Dreieck USA-Südafrika-Ostafrika (1921–1950) (Wiesbaden 2015).

107 KLAUS KOSCHORKE, "Transcontinental Links, Enlarged Maps, and Polycentric Structures in the History of World Christianity" (*Journal of World Christianity* 6/1, 2016, 28–56), 42.

Chapter 4:
Ceylon I: The Roman Catholic Portuguese Mission in Ceylon, 1837 to 1887

During the nineteenth century, the Catholic communities in Colombo and Bombay maintained a particular connection. This relationship cannot be understood without a comparative overview of the two metropolitan cities, both under British colonial rule. In 1881 the population of Bombay amounted to 773,196[1], whereas the inhabitants of the Municipality of Colombo were only 110,502.[2] In fact, the population of Bombay corresponded to about one quarter of the population of the whole of Ceylon.[3] In the same year, the population of Madras was 405,848.[4] Colombo was definitely much smaller than the metropolises of the British Raj. However, despite the obvious differences in size, Colombo displayed an ethnic variety and differentiation comparable to a certain extent to Bombay. In this sense, the two cities shared a similarity. A further connection between Bombay and Colombo was historical: the Portuguese past of both cities. Colombo had developed from a Portuguese outpost in the early sixteenth century, while the territory of Bombay had been ceded by Portugal in 1661 as part of the dowry paid on the occasion of the marriage of Catherine of Bragança with Charles II, including various villages that had been part of the *Provincia do Norte*.[5] The inhabitants of Colombo were divided along racial lines. As Nihal Perera observed, the Portuguese established a white, male Christian city that exerted its political power pushing the natives outside.[6] The racial division was comparable to the distinction of a "White Town" and a "Black Town" in Madras and, to a lesser extent, in Calcutta. While in the latter the division between the European and Indian settlements was not marked by specific physical barriers, in Madras there was a wall to separate the ethnic groups, just as in Colombo. Bombay was a different case:

---

1   M. RAMANNA, *Western Medicine and Public Health in Colonial Bombay*, 1845-1895. (New Delhi 2002), 2.
2   Department of Census & Statistics, Ministry of Policy Planning and Economic Affairs, Sri Lanka, *Census of Population and Housing, 2012*, published at http://www.statistics.gov.lk/PopHouSat/CPH2011/Pages/Activities/Reports/FinalReport/FinalReportE.pdf (accessed on 23 March 2022).
3   K.M. DE SILVA, ed., *History of Ceylon*. Vol. 3: From the Beginning of the Nineteenth Century to 1948 (Colombo, 1973), 287. From 1871 to 1881 the population of Ceylon increased by 15% to 2,759,738.
4   SUNIL S. AMRITH, "South Indian Migration, c. 1800-1950", in: JAN LUCASSEN / LEO LUCASSEN (eds.), *Globalising Migration History*. The Eurasian Experience (16th–21st Centuries) (Leiden, 2014), 145.
5   NIHAL PERERA, *Society and Space*. Colonialism, Nationalism, and Postcolonial Identity in Sri Lanka (Colorado, Oxford, 1998), 23-7. On the conflicted transformation of Portuguese Bombay into a British colony, see M.D. DAVID, *History of Bombay*, 1661–1708 (Bombay, 1973).
6   N. PERERA, "Indigenising the Colonial City. Late 19th-Century Colombo and Its Landscape" (*Urban Studies* 39/9, 2002), 1704.

> Because Bombay consisted of a discontinuous series of islands, European and Indian populations were scattered all over the city. This lack of segregation may in part be attributed to the presence of the Parsis, who had much closer relations with Europeans [...].[7]

By the time of the British domination in the 19th century, Colombo was divided into three principal zones, all facing the Beira Lake:

a. The Fort, seat of the colonial administration, was surrounded by the sea externally and by the lake internally.
b. The Pettah, namely the northern area immediately outside the Fort, by the early nineteenth century hosted about 500 families of European descent, mostly with Dutch and Portuguese ancestors.
c. In the Outer Pettah, beyond the Beira Lake, lived non-European communities such as Sinhalas and "Moors".

The Outer Pettah, in particular the neighbourhood of Hulftsdorp, became a popular habitat for "Moors", Dutch Burghers, and Tamils, who migrated from their traditional residential quarters of Colombo, such as Fort and Pettah, but also from other parts of the island.[8]

This chapter is a prelude to history of the advent of the Independent Catholics in Ceylon. In the next three sections we will trace how, since 1838, a separatist tendency emerged and developed in different parishes in Colombo, Negombo, Mannar, and Mantote in defiance of the Episcopal and Papal hierarchy. In the foreground stands the so-called Goan or Portuguese "schismatic" minority, who acted initially as an ethnically and socially heterogeneous group united by a pro-*Padroado* identity, until it assembled in the name of the Independent Catholic Church in 1888. The period to be examined reveals a transition of the "schismatic" objectives from a reform envisaged by the Burgher community within the Ceylon Catholic Church in 1838, to an absolute aversion to the Papal authorities in 1887. These five decades of the resistance movement were to a certain extent a reflection of the drastic changes in the nature of the Church authorities. During the second half of the nineteenth century, both Buddhism and Islam were inspired by a revivalism from within, whereas as a religious minority the Catholic Church saw a change in the ratio of nationalities within its leadership and supply of clergymen. The Italian, Spanish, and French speaking clergymen supplanted all Indian Oratorians in the ministration of Ceylon, as a result of Roman unilateral decisions and *Concordats* negotiated and signed between Rome and Lisbon, in the period between 1838 and 1886. This asymmetry of power was perceived and resented in a shared way by those Indian clergymen and Ceylonese Catholics that refused to obey their newly appointed European superiors, who were hardly versed in Tamil or Sinhala. The rise of the separatist laymen and the decline of the Indian Oratorians were opposite sides of the same coin, implying the early manifestation of an awakened quest for autonomy in the religious sphere of the British Crown colony.

In the first place, we will review the literature on the Congregation of Oratory, with a focus on its initial achievements in form of the underground church during the Dutch hegemony on Ceylon, and then on the challenges this religious community faced in the British colonial setting. The contextual history of the Oratorians in Ceylon is key to understanding

---

7   P. MITTER, „The Early British Port Cities of India. Their Planning and Architecture Circa 1640-1757", *Journal of the Society of Architectural Historians* 45, no. 2 (June 1986), 95–114, specif. 102.
8   K. JAYAWARDENA, *Nobodies to Somebodies. The Rise of the Colonial Bourgeoisie in Sri Lanka* (London 2003).

the origin of the Independent Catholics in ethnic and socio-political terms, as it provided a remote inspiration for the subsequent rise of a self-conscious and self-asserting form of Catholicism. Secondly, we will examine a group of Burgher dissidents in central Colombo who called for educational reforms so as to train members of the community to get jobs in English-speaking offices. The shift of positions within church politics attests to the complexity of the Burgher identities in colonial Ceylon. Finally, we will move to the "schismatic" Goan priests in Negombo and in the Vicariate of Jaffna, who were assisted by hard-line adherents of fishermen castes in Ceylon and by South Indian migrants. These Christians formed a stronghold of the pro-*padroado* faction across South India and Sri Lanka and would become the bulk of the Independent Catholics. In sum, this chapter analyses the contention within the Catholic Church during the five decades that preceded the emergence of the Independent Catholics as a united group.

1. João Bonifácio Misso and the Catholic Lay Unrest in Colombo

1.1 Burghers

Colombo was a city of cultural, ethnic, and religious hybridity. As Nira Wickramasinghe noted, between 1891 and 1921 the Sinhalese inhabitants were less than half of the population of the capital, sharing the urban space with Tamils, Europeans, Muslims, Burghers, and Malays.[9] Such a composite population attracted the attention of European observers. For instance, the Apostolic Vicar Giuseppe Bravi wrote in 1858:

> The population of Colombo is the most varied and curious that one can see, since from the European aristocrats with coaches and horses costing two or three hundred pounds sterling to the poorest, naked Tamils, all kinds of people are met, each one in his own proper dress and speaking his own language. It is hard to move through the streets crowded as they are with Europeans, Ceylonese, Tamils, Indians, Mestizos, Chinese, Kaffirs, Javanese, etc. Everyone professes his own religion and has his own temples, mosques and places of public worship.[10]

A specific neighbourhood in Outer Pettah is of particular importance for the study of the "Independent Catholics" of Ceylon. This is the area defined by the district of Saint Sebastian Hill and the street called Hultsdorf. The name of this communication lane came from General Gerard Pieterszoon Hulft (1621–1656), Governor General of the Dutch Indies.[11] In the Dutch period "Hulftsdorp", meaning "village of Hulft", was the seat of the *dessave* of Colombo, namely the most senior official in the *dessavonij* (Administrative district) of the city.[12] The administrative function of that neighbourhood was confirmed even in the British time, as in

---

9 WICKRAMASINGHE, *Sri Lanka in the Modern Age*, 52.
10 "Bravi's report of his pastoral visitation in Ceylon", Colombo, 6 September 1858, written originally in Italian. See an English translation in V. PERNIOLA, *The Catholic Church in Sri Lanka. The British Period. Vol. 4: 1856-1863*, The Vicariates of Colombo and Jaffna (Dehiwala 2001), 119.
11 Hulft is remembered for his friendly relations with Rajasimha II (in reign 1629–1687), the third king of the kingdom of Kandy, and for his contribution to the total victory over the Portuguese in Ceylon. See K. ZANDVLIET, *The Dutch Encounter with Asia, 1600–1950* (Amsterdam 2002), 160–161; R. RAJPAL KUMAR DE SILVA / W. G. M. BEUMER, *Illustrations and Views of Dutch Ceylon 1602–1796*. A Comprehensive Work of Pictorial Reference with Selected Eye-Witness Accounts (London/Leiden 1988), 430.
12 See https://www.atlasofmutualheritage.nl/en/Hultsdorf.513p#Details (accessed on 23 March 2022).

1801 the Supreme Court of Ceylon was established there. The Catholic Church of Saint Sebastian was founded by Goan Oratorian priests in the neighbouring Silversmith Street in the early nineteenth century.[13] The area was not exclusively Christian, as since the eighteenth century a growing number of "Moors", namely Tamil-speaking Muslims, had settled around the Old Moor Street north to the St Sebastian area. What would eventually become the cathedral of the Independent Catholics, namely the Church of Our Lady of Good Death, was established in the mid-nineteenth century on the side of the Supreme Court, developing gradually from a cemetery to a chapel, and eventually to a public church. The founder of this religious centre was a Burgher physician, Dr. John Bonifácio Misso (or Missó, 1797–1864), Consul General of Portugal in Ceylon in 1845–1864, whose life will be described below.[14]

The Anglican priest Rev. James Cordiner, who came to Ceylon as the Chaplain of the Garrison at the beginning of the nineteenth century, reported that Colombo had fifty thousand inhabitants, out of which the Burghers amounted to three thousand at the most.[15] The Burghers never exceeded one percent of the entire island's population.[16] Notwithstanding their small number, they "occupied a highly important place in the social and economic life of Ceylon".[17] Developing from Portuguese-speaking Eurasians, these "citizens" or inhabitants "of burgh, borough or corporate town" emerged in the Dutch period, the term "Burgher" initially having more of a functional than an ethnic connotation. Afterwards, it was used to indicate locally married Europeans and their descendants.[18] It has been a common practice to distinguish between "Dutch Burghers" and "Portuguese Burghers", also derogatorily referred to as "Portuguese Mechanics".[19] The distinction is questionable, as even the Burgher families "with documented Dutch ancestry, have preserved a significant number of Portuguese cultural traditions up to the present day".[20] Whether their descent was more Portuguese or Dutch, the Burghers had generally been the outcome of the process of creolisation produced by the mercantile "empire" built up by the VOC.[21] However, there are also traces of "Portuguese" who underwent a more "native" route, retaining their Catholic religion while being integrated into a non-European social context. This was the case with the descendants of some Portuguese in the central and eastern parts of the island, in the territories of the Kandyan Kingdom. These communities were usually deprived of pastoral care, so that there was a layman in charge of them, who could say: "I am head of the Church, but not a Padri. I am called in consequence, Saint Christian". These were the words used by a "Portuguese

---

13 The founding year is not clear. Perniola claimed that from 1828 onwards, the Oratorian mission report sent to the Superior in Goa started to enlist not only priests but also churches and parishes. It is in this list that we found the Saint Sebastian Church in Silversmith Street. Another church of the same namesake was in Small Street. PERNIOLA, *The Catholic Church in Sri Lanka*. The British Period. Vol. 1: 1795-1844. The Colombo Vicariate (Dehiwala, Sri Lanka1992), 123.
14 *Lista Geral dos Officiaes e Empregados da Marinha e Ultramar referida ao 1. de Novembro de 1850* (Lisboa 1850), 169. See bibliography.
15 J. CORDINER, *A Description of Ceylon* (London 1807), 40.
16 DENNIS B. MCGILVRAY, "The Portuguese Burghers of Eastern Sri Lanka in the Wake of Civil War and Tsunami", in: JORGE MANUEL COSTA DA SILVA FLORES (ed.), *Re-Exploring the Links*. History and Constructed Histories between Portugal and Sri Lanka (Wiesbaden, 2007), 325.
17 A. SIVARAJAH, *Politics of Tamil Nationalism in Sri Lanka* (New Delhi 1996), 25.
18 G.V. GRENIER, "'Burgher' Etymology and Some Relevant Reflections" (*Journal of the Dutch Burgher Union* 56/1–4, 1966, 25–30).
19 D.B. MCGILVRAY, "Dutch Burghers and Portuguese Mechanics. Eurasian Ethnicity in Sri Lanka" (*Comparative Studies in Society and History* 24/2, 1982, 235–63).
20 MCGILVRAY, "The Portuguese Burghers", 325.
21 ULBE BOSMA / REMCO RABEN, *Being 'Dutch' in the Indies*. A History of Creolisation and Empire, 1500–1920, trans. WENDIE SHAFFER (Singapore 2008).

Cambawadda", named "Jowan Mendoze", of Wahakotte in "Audagodde Corle", Matale district, 8 miles northwest of Nalanda. Mendoze's statement was not dated, but likely given at the beginning of the British domination.[22] Mendoze reported that during the reign of King Kirti Sri Rajasinha (r. 1747–1782) a famine and a plague seized the Kingdom. For reasons still to be uncovered, the King repented for the earlier expulsion of his Christian subjects, claiming that these calamities were a result of the persecutions suffered by the Catholics in the villages of "Waauda", "Calogalla", and Wahakotte. Hence orders were made to restore the churches in those villages. Catholics were since then allowed to practice their religion. Those "Portuguese", as the Kandyans called them, were considered of the same rank as the caste of the Vellalas, Tamil farmers. Jowan Mendoze also declared that the Catholic faith had been transmitted by relying on texts such as a "Singhalese Testament" (i.e biblical translation or paraphrasis in Sinhala) by the Oratorian Jácome Gonçalves and "several prayers written upon olas (i.e. manuscripts on palmyra leaves)". It's quite remarkable that Gonçalves, spelled as "Jacob Gonsalle" (probably a Sinhala rendering), was defined as "a Portuguese Padri (a native of Portugal)", even though we know that he was a Goan Catholic Brahman. This detail might be a piece of evidence supporting the hypothesis that the Ceylonese Catholics saw the Oratorian missionaries more as "Portuguese" than as "Goans" or "Indians". It would be necessary to find further evidence confirming or qualifying this perspective. Further research is also required to understand whether "Portuguese" that had been integrated so much into the Sinhala and Tamil context were eventually considered Burghers or were incorporated into other native communities. At any rate, if the ethnic definition of the Portuguese in the Kandyan region was puzzling, the more Europeanized Burghers represented an even more complex world. This can be sensed precisely in a case like the one of Dr. Misso, whom the Vicar Apostolic Orazio Bettacchini described in 1843 as a man descended from a French family, who had "the characteristics of the French", a comment that the Italian prelate had definitely not meant in a flattering tone.[23] In spite of Bettacchini's "misogallic" representation of Misso, it is confirmed from the family records of the latter that his ancestors had migrated to Ceylon from France by the end of the eighteenth century.[24]

1.2 Bonifácio Misso's Turn from a Pro-Roman to a Pro-Padroado Catholic

The limited historiography in this field has usually assumed that Misso was a *Padroadist* since the beginning.[25] On the contrary, as we can see in the sources, there was a shift from a pro-Roman to a pro-*Padroado* position.

Inside the Church of Our Lady of Good Death one can find several tombs in memory of people associated with that congregation, who died between 1856 and 1875. An inscription on one of them reads:

---

22 *Statement of Portuguese Cambawadda, Jowan Mendoze, of the village of Wohakotto* [i.e. Wahakotte], *in the Audagodde Corle, Matala District, about eight miles N. West of Nalande*, in: W.M. HARVARD, *A Narrative of the Establishment and Progress of The Mission to Ceylon and India founded by the Late Rev. Thomas Coke* (London 1823), 331–332, then edited again by PERNIOLA, *The Catholic Church. The British Period.* Vol. 1, 113–116.
23 VITO PERNIOLA, *The Catholic Church in Sri Lanka.* The British Period. Vol. 2: 1845–1849. The Vicariates of Colombo and Jaffna (Dehiwala, 1995), 381, Bettacchini to Propaganda Fide, 23 July 1843.
24 This was attested to by Mr. Neil D'Silva, the 9th generation descendant of J.B. Misso, in a personal conversation in Colombo on 21 November 2018.
25 A. WRIGHT, *Twentieth Century Impressions of Ceylon. Its History, People, Commerce, Industries, and Resources* (London 1907), 276.

> In Memory of/Sir JOHN B. MISSO/First Consul General/Of Portugal in Ceylon/Born 13th April 1797/Died 7th March 1864/*Have pity on me…/At least you my friends*/JOB. 19th chap 21[26]

The epitaph highlights several aspects of Misso's historical trajectory. First of all, there is no indication of his ethnicity, an omission that might be interpreted as a trace of the not easily definable identity of the Burgher. Secondly, the epitaph makes no reference to Misso's medical profession but specifies only his service as the First Consul General of Portugal, with the honorific title of "Sir" associated with the function. Thirdly, the biblical quotation from the Book of Job has a victimizing tone, hinting at persecutions suffered unjustly by a pious man. A reader might imagine that, just as Job was tested with all sorts of disgraces even though he was righteous in the eyes of God, so also Misso's vicissitudes and difficulties, in the eyes of his kin and supporters, did not result from faults of his, but rather from the actions of a demonic force.

Misso's family milieu, medical studies and early career are yet to be studied in detail. It is known that John Bonifacio Misso was a wealthy man who possessed several properties in Pettah and Outer Pettah, as well as many coaches and six horses.[27] His social status indeed qualified him to become President of the so-called "Roman Catholic Seminary" or "Seminary School" at Wolfendaal, established in 1839 by the first Apostolic Vicar of Ceylon, the Goan Oratorian Mons. Vicente do Rosario.[28] Despite its name, the school was not a "seminary" in the strict sense, as it was not reserved for young Catholics willing to become priests. In fact, it was open to boys of different religious affiliations. In 1839 it counted 68 Catholics, 11 Protestants and 1 Muslim, whereas in 1844 it enrolled 90 Catholics, 60 Protestants, 1 "pagan" (i.e. Buddhist or Hindu) and 1 Muslim.[29] Misso was therefore at the vanguard of an initiative aiming at modernizing the Catholic community and its relations with other groups, with the Protestants being involved to a significant extent. The program of studies was conducted in English and also included Sinhalese, as well as the classical languages of Europe, Greek, and Latin. While it was not surprising that Dutch was not taught, even though it had been the language of government until less than a half century before, the absence of Portuguese could be seen as a strong statement, as if centuries of Luso-Asian religious and cultural heritage did no longer imply any linguistic connotation.[30]

The distance from the Portuguese tradition could also be sensed in the ecclesiastical realm. It is not a coincidence that Misso was at the forefront of a campaign of local Catholics who, between 1837 and 1842, sought to obtain English-speaking European missionaries. In 1842 the French Lazarist André Dumas shipwrecked near Ceylon on his trip back to Europe from China, where he had been stationed for eleven years. Misso invited Dumas to minister in Colombo, even though this was strongly opposed by all the Catholic priests active in the capital city, due to Dumas' prejudices against the Goan clergy in general. Even the "progressive" faction among the Oratorians, whom Misso supported, were against Dumas. Tensions escalated and Misso organized Latin petitions to the Congregation of Propaganda Fide and Pope Gregory XVI, even appending 2100 signatures of Ceylon Catholics so as to denounce

---

26 See Appendix 2.
27 PERNIOLA, *The Catholic Church. The British Period*. Vol. 2, 381. Bettacchini to Propaganda Fide, 23 July 1843.
28 ARTHUR C. DEP, *The Oratorian Mission in Sri Lanka, 1795-1874*. Being a History of the Catholic Church, 1795–1874 (Colombo, 1987), 34; PERNIOLA, *The Catholic Church. The British Period*. Vol. 1, 273.
29 PERNIOLA, *The Catholic Church. The British Period*. Vol. 1, 277, 387.
30 PERNIOLA, *The Catholic Church. The British Period*. Vol. 1, 274.

the alleged vices and shortcomings of the Goan priests and to obtain European missionaries.³¹ However, the appointment of the Goan priest Caetano Antonio, once belonging to the Oratorian "progressive" faction, as new Vicar Apostolic in May 1843, replacing Vicente do Rozario, was a huge disappointment for Misso and his followers. Seeing the danger of a potential schism within the local Church, between the Goan clergy and lay Ceylonese Catholics seeking modernization and European innovations, the newly arrived Italian Oratorian Orazio Bettacchini (1810–1857) visited Misso and got involved in a meeting held in the physician's residence.³² The missionary described the discussion in the following terms:

> They raised endless arguments in order to provoke me, saying that they are not bound to obey. I was able to meet their arguments easily. They strongly complained of the Holy Father and of Your Eminence [= the Cardinal Prefect of Propaganda Fide] saying that, in spite of the fact that they had manifested all their needs and urgent demands of the mission, and that they had asked for a good shepherd, they had been left without any consolation, without a reply, without a provision as if no heed was taken of them.³³

Misso and his supporters were articulating instances of lay leadership within the Church. For instance, in an early petition addressed around August 1837 to the Vicar General of Ceylon and to all the Oratorian missionaries, they had requested that "six respectable laymen" should be included in the council advising the Vicar and given decisional powers "in all pecuniary matters brought before such council".³⁴ Such requests for lay leadership likely derived from their growing influence in the British colonial society, while the Catholic ecclesiastical establishment was not yet able to correspond adequately to new requests of recognition and appreciation. The clerical authorities of Goa did not pay sufficient attention, but even Italian missionaries such as Bettacchini did not satisfy the Ceylon lay leaders, even though they had nurtured great hopes in missionaries coming from Europe. At this point something unexpected, of crucial importance and still not entirely clear, occurred in the Catholic milieus of Ceylon, led in particular by Misso.

An insight into the bewildering turn in Misso's attitude to the Oratorians – his shift from a pro-Rome to a pro-*Padroado* position – is provided by the sharp observations published by the Protestant Rev. Edward J. Robinson:

> The Italian [Bettacchini] again came forward to deny the things alleged, and to pronounce the doctor [Misso] and his associates competent only to "raise a few intellectual mole-hills in the shape of letters and resolutions." It would seem that the reforming physician repented having administered treatment so severe to the fathers of Goa [= the Oratorians]. His indignation appears to have settled at last on the heads of the presumptuous men from Italy. Not a year afterwards he was in correspondence with the Archbishop of Goa and Primate of the East. His grace, in a very comforting letter, distinctly claiming authority over the Roman Catholic mission in Ceylon, promised ultimate humiliation of the Italian upstarts. Little love has since been lost between the schismatic doctor and Father Bettachini, now Lord Bishop of Jaffna.

---

31 The Catholics to Pope, Colombo, 1 December 1842. PERNIOLA, *The Catholic Church*. The British Period. Vol. 1, 311–314.
32 On this member of the Oratory of Città di Castello see N.M. SAVERIMUTTU, *The Life and Times of Orazio Bettacchini. The first Vicar Apostolic of Jaffna Ceylon (1810–1857)* (Rome 1980).
33 Bettacchini to a friend, Kandy, 16 September 1843. PERNIOLA, *The Catholic Church*. The British Period. Vol. 1, 390.
34 PERNIOLA, *The Catholic Church*. The British Period. Vol. 1, 181–182.

One day, in 1847, the bishop's Italian servant was seen in the streets of Colombo wearing a gay livery, not unlike the Consul-General's uniform. Some of Dr. Misso's friends, regarding this as an intentional insult, determined to retaliate. Arrayed in episcopal robes, and paraded with mock dignity about the city, the Consul-General's coachman attracted crowds of people.[35]

We can imagine the humiliation felt by Misso and his adherents seeing that Rome did not respond even to petitions signed by thousands of "respectable laymen", and that the European missionaries actually available on the ground did not show respect and appreciation for such lay agency, calling the Latin representations carefully drafted and addressed to Rome "a few intellectual mole-hills". According to Robinson, Misso's turn toward the Archbishop of Goa and the Portuguese *Padroado* was entirely motivated by psychological factors such as a desire for revenge. This is clearly a critical point, and only further investigation may clarify whether such an interpretation is adequate, partial, or entirely simplistic. What is certain is that until 1843 Misso and his party were hostile to the Goan clergy, but by 1845 the situation had radically changed. If Robinson's witness does not suffice, it is patent that in January 1845 Misso was appointed Consul General of Portugal, with the British government granting its approval in November 1846.[36] In just two years, the leader of a movement critical of the Portuguese *Padroado* had become the official representative of the Kingdom of Portugal in Ceylon.

1.3 Padroado Groups Outside Colombo: Negombo

As already mentioned in chapter 2, upon publication of the Bull *Multa Præclare* in 1838, the bishops of Cochin and São Tomé de Meliapor on the Indian continent had retained their episcopal title but lost all their territory, now assigned to the Apostolic Vicars. The loss certainly triggered resentment in Manoel de São Joaquim das Neves, O.P., then Archbishop of Cranganore (in today's Kerala) and governor of the vacant episcopal see of Cochin, which gave up its jurisdiction over Ceylon to Propaganda Fide in 1834. Well informed of the tensions between the Oratorians and the Bishopric of Cochin, Misso turned to the latter for help, likely by the end of 1843. Das Neves saw in the petition an opportunity to send more *Padroado* missionaries to Ceylon. Fr. Carlo Francisco Rodrigues de Almeida soon arrived in Ceylon in February 1844 with the title of Vicar General. He transformed Misso's house in Belmont Street into a chapel. Those who frequented his chapel were not only the Portuguese Burghers in Colombo, but also some Paravas from Tuticorin, altogether reaching a total number of eighty.[37]

---

35 E.J. ROBINSON, *Romanism in Ceylon, India, and China* (London 1855), 132–133.
36 He was appointed Consul General on 23 January 1845. See *Lista geral dos officiaes e empregados da Marinha e Ultramar, referida ao 1 de novembro de 1850* (Lisboa 1850), 169. From that source we also learn that in 1842 an Antonio de Sousa was appointed as Consul in Calcutta, and that in 1844 a Braz Fernandes was appointed Consular Agent in Bombay. The approval by the Queen of Great Britain, conveyed through the Foreign Office, was announced by *The London Gazette: Published by Authority*, n. 20670, 20 November 1846, 4856. Barcatta mistakenly indicated the date of Misso's appointment as 30 January 1947 [sic!]. BEDE BARCATTA, *A History of the Southern Vicariate of Colombo, Sri Lanka, Being Also the History of the Apostolate of the Sylvestrine-Benedictine Monks in the Island*. Vol. 1 (Ampitiya, 1991), 497, note 55.
37 N.M. SAVERIMUTTU, *The Life and Times of Orazio Bettacchini, the First Vicar Apostolic of Jaffna, Ceylon (1810–1857)* (Rome 1980), 32. Saverimuttu mentioned Almeida as the Vicar General, whereas the document in the *Ceylon Almanac* recorded him only as a simple missionary.

The next year Misso's group appeared in the *Ceylon Almanac* with the title of "Roman Catholic Mission in Ceylon under the patronage of the Queen of Portugal", served by two priests in Colombo. These were P. C. P. da Conceição Vicar General of Ceylon, and G.[C.?] F. Rodrigues de Almeida, taking care of the pastoral needs of no more than one hundred members, attending the Emanuel Chapel (also belonging to Dr. Misso) at Pettah and the house and burial ground of Misso at Belmont Street.[38]

There were some other large pro-*Padroado* groups at the same time during which Dr. Misso started his ecclesial movement in Colombo. These other communities were in Negombo and in Mannar. The former belonged to the Diocese of Colombo and had close relations with Misso's group. The latter was subject to the Vicariate of Jaffna and will be studied separately in the next section.

Negombo became a bone of contention when in 1845 Ceylon was divided in two episcopal jurisdictions, namely the Diocese of Colombo and the Vicariate of Jaffna. The former had a much greater number of Christians than the latter. Therefore, a demographic balance could be achieved only if Negombo belonged to the Vicariate of Jaffna. The city had been a Catholic stronghold since the Portuguese time. By 1858, four missionaries were in charge of the pastoral care of 26,000 Catholics in 39 churches. Over ninety percent of the whole population in the city were Catholics. The congregation was very poor and dependent on subsidies given by the Bishop of Colombo, to whom they nonetheless also paid a "Fish rent". The Apostolic Vicar Bravi in his visitation report in 1858 stated:

> Though all of them are poor, yet they give to the church what they call the Fish Rent. This gives to the fishermen the possibility of selling their catch as soon as they come ashore and they do sell it at a good price to persons who have bidden for this. These very persons make their profit and they are obliged to give a fixed amount to the church. But unfortunately, since the people of this caste are more or less ignorant, it is this sale that is the seed of so many quarrels and of worry and affliction to the Bishop, driving the people to the point of schism. For the men who are aware that they contribute so much for the cult and for anything else connected with the church, become proud and disobedient, and even obstinate on account of their ignorance, and consequently they are usually divided into two or three factions.[39]

Bravi's apologetical remarks on the alleged convenience of the ecclesiastical Fish Rent to the fishermen can be seen as a clue hinting unintentionally at the exploitative political economy on whose foundations the Catholic church was based in certain parts of Ceylon. As for the reference to factionalism, Bravi expanded on it in relation to the Paravas that had migrated from the Tamil to the Ceylon coast:

> Along the coast there are some churches of Paravers [sic] who have come from the continent and have settled down there. As a rule they are attached to their religion but have all the vices of the Tamil race, especially lying and cheating. The fishermen of the main church and of two or three other churches along the coast, though they have adopted Sinhala customs and are known as Sinhala, yet they have kept the language and all the vices of the lower Tamil inhabitants of the continent from where they seem to originate. They have very many of the worst traits of the Sinhala with very little of what is good both in the Sinhala and in the Tamils. And so you will always find some troublemakers among them, who easily become the leaders of some who will rise against the others to take their revenge generally for a wrong suffered or

---

38 PERNIOLA, *The Catholic Church*. The British Period. Vol. 2, 2.
39 Bravi to Propaganda 6 September 1858. PERNIOLA, *The Catholic Church*. The British Period. Vol. 4, 108–109.

out of jealousy. These quarrels have always an impact on the affairs of the church and of religion.⁴⁰

Here the term "affairs of the church and of religion" was probably used by the veteran Italian Bishop as a hint to the Goan schism. In recent times he had interdicted some of the rebels for one or two years. The purpose of the punishment was based on the hope that

> when the old occasions of scandal and the threat of the Indo-Portuguese schism are removed, they [=the local Catholics] will greatly improve, even if they are not completely corrected. A good result of these measures was a fear in others and a humiliation for the more evil ones, though this humiliation seems to be merely external and false, in the manner of the Indo-Portuguese way, for they are never ready to obey except in their own way.⁴¹

The "old occasions of scandal" referred to an incident that occurred in 1845, when the Oratorian priest Caetano Dias sent a request to Propaganda Fide for retaining three churches in Negombo – St. Sebastian, St. Philip Neri and St. Anne – in his administration, i.e. independent from the Apostolic Vicar of Ceylon, by then the Goan Oratorian Caetano António Pereira.⁴² It is not clear if this was a personal initiative of Dias, but he was considered by Bravi a puppet of Caetano Rozario, the secretary of the same Apostolic Vicar Caetano António Pereira, so as to keep the *Padroado* rights on the island.⁴³ In fact, Orazio Bettacchini had already been appointed in August as Pro-Vicar of Jaffna and Coadjutor to the Vicar Pereira, so that it was already assumed that the former, an Italian sent by Propaganda Fide, would soon obtain full episcopal jurisdiction over Jaffna, which in fact happened in September 1847.⁴⁴

Negombo's *Padroado* movements had reasons quite different from those in Colombo or in Mannar. It reminds us that there might have been diverse motives behind the *Padroado* conflict, which was not only an action of disobedience to Rome, but also a separation from other groups in the same Catholic community. In other words, we need to distinguish a vertical and a horizontal dimension in the *Padroado* conflicts: a rebellion against an ecclesiastical centralised power, often unresponsive to local requests sent to Rome, as well as an expression of tensions occurring in different ethnic and caste communities building up the fabric of Ceylonese Catholicism. In this horizontal dimension, the defence of *Padroado* was almost a superstructure giving expression to tensions of socio-economic nature. Under the banner of the *Padroado*, very diverse "dissident" Catholics found a route to fight for the interests of their own communities against other groups. This condition was not restricted to Ceylon, as we will see later on in relation to the Independent Catholic missions in Trichinopoly (today Tiruchirapalli) in Tamil Nadu, in chapter 5, very comparable to the ones in Jaffna and Mannar.

---

40 V. PERNIOLA, *The Catholic Church in Sri Lanka*. The British Period. Vol. 4: 1856–1863. The Vicariates of Colombo and Jaffna (Dehiwala 2001), 109–110.
41 PERNIOLA, *The Catholic Church in Sri Lanka*. The British Period. Vol. 4, 110.
42 PERNIOLA, *The Catholic Church*. The British Period. Vol. 2, 69–70. Caetano Dias to Propaganda 8 November 1845.
43 PERNIOLA, *The Catholic Church*. The British Period. Vol. 2, 71. Bravi to Bettacchini, 10 November 1845.
44 J. ROMMERSKIRCHEN, *Die Oblatenmissionen auf der Insel Ceylon im 19. Jahrhundert (1847–1893)* (Fulda 1930), 5–7.

1.4 The Burgher Community of Misso and the Portuguese Consul General in Colombo 1845–1864

One of the first name lists of this Burgher community appeared in various newspapers in 1843 at their request, on the occasion of their meeting held at John Baptist Daniel's house on 20 October 1843.[45]

It was reported in 1849 that the total number of the "Portuguese schismatics", i.e. the supporters of the *Padroado*, were around 100 to 200 people in Colombo.[46] Members of this small group occupied important positions in the government. P. H. de La Harpe (?–1865) was the first Ceylonese who was appointed as Assistant Superintendent of Police (in 1847).[47] Vincent William Vanderstraaten was the Registrar of the Supreme Court.[48] At the same time, the two were members of the School Committee of the above mentioned "Roman Catholic Seminary".

The pro-*Padroado* position was also marked by explicit spatial arrangements, by efforts at occupying physical and religious space. Misso had originally owned a small place of worship, the Emmanuel Chapel in Pettah, which served as an initial meeting point for his group. A further development occurred on 21 February 1845, when the British authorities granted Misso a piece of land in Belmont Street, Hultsdorf, to build a cemetery on it. This land was later developed into a residence, then in a chapel and finally into a church devoted to Our Lady of Good Death.[49] This was the very church where Misso was eventually buried in 1864, but which – most importantly – decades later became the cathedral of Bishop Alvares.

Misso's commitment to a church perspective framed by the *Padroado* can be illustrated by three episodes that all occurred within a decade. First of all, in 1853, Misso published in Colombo an English version of a Portuguese *Memoir* against the allocution delivered by Pius IX in the Consistory held on 17 February 1851, on which occasion the Pontiff had downgraded the pretensions of the *Padroado*.[50] However, the commitment in favour of the Portuguese rights did not only have a defensive dimension, contesting the alleged encroachment of the Roman authorities. It also implied an effort to ensure that the Portuguese Crown took effective care of the missions on which it claimed inalienable rights. For this reason, in 1854 João Bonifácio Misso intervened to request the dispatch of missionaries to Ceylon and the payment of the arrears due to a certain Fr. Jacob, missionary in Madurai. The Regent Ferdinand II, assisting the underage King Peter V, decreed in August 1854 that two or three priests should be immediately sent to Ceylon, with regular payment of their stipends and with an

---

45 The original meeting proceedings are conserved at the Archive of the Diocese of Kandy and have been reprinted in their original English in PERNIOLA, *The Catholic Church. The British Period*. Vol. 1, 396–402.
46 BARCATTA, *A History*. Vol.1, 455.
47 PERNIOLA, *The Catholic Church. The British Period*. Vol. 1, 257.
48 PERNIOLA, *The Catholic Church. The British Period*. Vol. 1, 290. A Memorial to His Holiness Gregory XVI, Colombo, 9 May 1842.
49 BARCATTA, *A History*. Vol. 1, 446.
50 *Memoir on the Address of His Holiness Pius IX, delivered in the Secret Consistory on 17th February 1851, etc. - Translated from the original in Portuguese, and printed for Senhor João Bonifacio Missó, Consul general of Portugal in Ceylon* (Colombo, 1853), mentioned in INNOCENCIO FRANCISCO DA SILVA, *Diccionario Bibliographico Portuguez: Estudos de Innocencio Francisco da Silva applicaveis a Portugal e ao Brasil* vol. 8 (Lisboa 1867), 365.

active involvement of the Bishop Elect of Cochin. Furthermore, the *Junta da Fazenda* (Treasury Board) should take due care to pay the stipends that had not yet been received by Fr. Jacob.[51]

The third example of Misso's commitment to the *Padroado* is of symbolic nature. On 2 January 1860 he performed the function of godfather in the baptism conferred to a 36-year-old "pagan" called João. The ceremony took place in the most famous church of Goa, the Basilica of Bom Jesus that had once belonged to the Jesuits. The occasion was particularly symbolic, as between 3 December 1859 and 8 January 1860 an exposition of the incorrupt body of St. Francis Xavier took place, the first one ever made since 1782. The godmother of the neophyte was Dona Maria Isabel da Penha Carvalho Goes Pinto, wife of João Ferreira Pinto, judge in the tribunal of the *Relação do Estado*. Some uncertainty concerns the precise identity of the convert. While one source claims that he came from the region of Madurai, namely from the Tamil country, another indication seems more likely, affirming that the convert was "an adult pagan Sinhala (*Chingalá*), servant" of the same Misso.[52] This baptism was among a number of adult baptisms that were celebrated during the month of Xavier's exhibition. The fact that this baptism took place in a moment of heightened public visibility could imply that it must have been noticed widely in Goa. We could even speculate whether on that occasion Misso met any of the future Independent Catholics of Goa. At any rate, the participation of a Consul General of Portugal in the baptism of a "pagan", celebrated during an extraordinary month-long religious ritual, was an apotheosis of *Padroado* symbolism: the "spiritual conquest of the East" being re-enacted in front of the saintly body of the *Goencho Sahib* ("Lord of Goa"), namely that Francis Xavier who, even though it had not inaugurated the Portuguese missionary expansion in Asia, nonetheless had become its very embodied symbol.

2. The Church in Mannar

2.1 Miguel Filipe Mascarenhas in Mannar and Mantotte

The Goan-European missionary rivalry in the Jaffna Vicariate was centred on Miguel Filipe (also spelled as Philipe or Phelipe) Mascarenhas, a Goan secular priest who first came to Ceylon as a subdeacon in 1842.[53] He was initially assigned to the district of Aripo, namely Tenpattu and Vadapattu,[54] whose Tamil spelling suggests their location in Jaffna. In Colombo he allied with the Vicar of the Oratorians and received blame from Misso for his alleged incapacity at measuring up to the ministry's demands. In reaction to these accusations, Mascarenhas signed a *Memorial* addressed to the Congregation of Propaganda Fide in

---

51 CONSELHO ULTRAMARINO PORTUGAL, *Boletim do Conselho Ultramarino*. Legislação Novissima vol. 2 (Lisboa 1869), 546–547.
52 The Madurai origin of the newly baptised João was affirmed in *Annaes do Conselho Ultramarino*. Parte não official, Serie II, (Lisboa 1867), 119. The reference to a "Chingalá gentio" is in *Boletim do Governo do Estado da Índia*, n. 1 (Nova Goa, 3 January 1860), 5.
53 PERNIOLA stated that Philipe came to Ceylon in 1842, according to the first appearance of his name on the 1842 Ceylon Almanac. However, the 1846 Ceylon Almanac indicated his arrival as 1844. See PERNIOLA'S explanation on the discrepancy in his *The Catholic Church. The British Period*. Vol. 1, 331, as well as in his *The Catholic Church. The British period*, Vol. 2, 1, note 2. Miguel Filipe was referred to also in the Tamilized form "Mikel Pilippu". See ROMMERSKIRCHEN, *Die Oblatenmissionen*, 19–23, and 67–68.
54 PERNIOLA, *The Catholic Church. The British Period*. Vol. 1, 2, note 2.

1842.[55] In 1850 Mascarenhas was entrusted with the mission of Mantotte, opposite to the Mannar island. It is not clear how the relation between Mascarenhas and Misso developed in the next two decades. For sure, both became leaders of resistance movements against the same rival – the missionaries sent by Propaganda Fide – in Jaffna and Colombo respectively. From 1888 onwards, the heirs of both Misso and Mascarenhas' experiences together would constitute the bulk of the Independent Catholic movement in Ceylon.

Back in 1850 Miguel Filipe Mascarenhas was a major concern for the Apostolic Vicar of Jaffna. Bettacchini stated in a letter that Mascarenhas had once even invited the Mantotte Christians to demand the Spanish missionary Floriano Oruna to step down from the pulpit from where he was giving a homily. Reacting to this disorder, on 19 March 1850 Bettacchini issued an order of suspension against Fr. Miguel Filipe.[56] The sixfold reasons can be summarised as follows:

1. Because almost every day he got drunk and caused a great scandal among the people.
2. For his horrible way of speaking against Propaganda, against the same Bettacchini and against all the European missionaries. As regards his way of speaking – argued Bettaccini – Filipe could certainly compete with the fishwives of Marseilles.[57]
3. For having plotted to drive away the missionaries sent by Propaganda Fide.
4. For not having made his annual Confession, hence not having complied with one of the five Precepts of the Church. Such an omission – we may observe – would appear extremely scandalous, given that it was imputed to a priest who rather should give a good example to the lay people.
5. For refusing to hear Confessions and give communion and asking those who wanted the Sacraments to go to the European missionaries.
6. For saying that the same Bettacchini, even though he was the Apostolic Vicar of Jaffna, had no jurisdiction whatsoever and that he was not his Superior etc.[58]

Half of the enlisted reasons concerned actual acts of disobedience of Mascarenhas. The other misconducts, such as drunkenness, vulgar manners, and not giving or hearing confessions, have often been attributed to all Goan priests in Colombo. However, the malicious intentions ascribed to the Goan priests were not limited to the ministry of the local Christians. Mascarenhas was considered a trigger of rivalry even among the European priests. In the same letter to Rome, Bettacchini confidentially mentioned that the Coadjutor of the Apostolic Vicar of Ceylon, namely the Italian Silvestrian monk Giuseppe Maria Bravi, had noticeably changed in his attitudes to him after having met Mascarenhas:

> His [Bravi] conduct towards me from the moment he met the Goans has not been such as to deserve any sympathy, and this is known to all the European missionaries. While he wrote to me as a friend, he betrayed me behind my back. It has been my constant impression that he

---

[55] The name Michael Phelipe [sic] was undersigned in the Memorial to Propaganda on 26 November 1842, in: PERNIOLA, *The Catholic Church*. The British Period. Vol. 1, 310.
[56] Bettacchini to Propaganda, Jaffna, 5 June 1848, in: PERNIOLA, *The Catholic Church*. The British period, Vol. 2, 508.
[57] Bettacchini compared Mascarenhas with the fishwives in Marseille, stereotypically represented as foulmouthed, aggressive, and ignorant.
[58] Bettacchini to Propaganda Fide, Jaffna, 9 March 1850. In: PERNIOLA, *The Catholic Church*. The British Period. Vol. 3, 368–369.

influenced the Vicar Apostolic to keep me from Colombo, etc etc., but of this I am not quite sure. The European missionaries have attributed this conduct to motives not quite pure.[59]

In a petition of the Catholics of Jaffna to Rome, Miguel Filipe Mascarenhas was considered one of the "ideal priests", who "are good preachers and live dedicated lives, priests who have laboured to bring us back from our sinful ways; priests who know the local languages and who are acquainted with our local customs".[60] Spectacularly opposite was the representation given by his adversaries. According to them Mascarenhas, a Goan demagogue, "raised the standard of rebellion, summoned the leading Catholics, got them drunk, gave money to many of them, and prevailed upon many to promise on oath that they would not abandon him till death".[61] Attention should be given to the reference of Mascarenhas corrupting leading Catholics. In fact, the Goan priests active in Jaffna and Mannar gained a good income from the local churches. By the end of 1848 four Goan priests – Noronha, Zefirino Godinho, Mendoza, and Miguel Filipe Mascarenhas – were in possession of three rich churches within the territory of the Jaffna Vicariate. The church with the highest revenue was the one dedicated to St Anne in Kalpitiya.[62]

The extent of material and spiritual resources at stake can explain why this northern region of Ceylon became a special stage for the evolution of the conflict between *Padroado* and Propaganda. In light of the *Concordat* of 1857, three churches in northern Ceylon fell under the double jurisdiction of both the *Padroado* and Propaganda Fide.[63] Reacting to this situation, in 1865 the Goan priests remaining in northern Ceylon filed a lawsuit with regard to those three churches. These were the church of Pallimunai in Mannar, the church of Parappankandel of Sankulam, and the Marathi Kannatty church in Mantotte, all desiring to be under the ecclesiastical jurisdiction of Goa.[64] Further research is required to ascertain whether the lawsuits were successful.

In addition to lawsuits, the "Portuguese" priests could also resort to diplomacy and negotiations in order to expand their sphere of influence. For instance, in the 1860s Mascarenhas gained control even of the shrine of Our Lady of Madhu in Mannar, under the condition that he submitted to the Vicar Apostolic of Jaffna the annual revenue of that church.[65] This passage is remarkable inasmuch as the church of Our Lady of Madhu, dedicated to the Assumption of the Blessed Virgin, has today become one of the most famous shrines of the island, attracting Catholics from all over the country. Even in the second half of the 19th century the shrine had an obvious importance, considering that, by 1868 for instance, there were around 7,000 Catholics on the island of Mannar, a remarkable figure.[66]

---

59 Bettacchini to Propaganda Fide, dated in Jaffna, 9 March 1850. In: PERNIOLA, *The Catholic Church*. The British Period. Vol. 3, 368.
60 Petition of the Catholics of Jaffna, 1845. In: PERNIOLA, *The Catholic Church*. The British Period. Vol. 2, 71.
61 The Oblates of Mantotte-Mannar to Propaganda, 18 October 1865. In: PERNIOLA, *The Catholic Church in Sri Lanka*. The British Period. Vol. 5: 1864–1875, The Vicariates of Colombo and Jaffna (Dehiwala 2001), 386.
62 Oruna to Propaganda, Kalpitiya 8 November 1848. In: PERNIOLA, *The Catholic Church*. The British Period. Vol. 2, 539.
63 The Oblates of Mantotte-Mannar to Propaganda 18 October 1865. In: PERNIOLA, *The Catholic Church*. The British Period. Vol. 5, 389.
64 The Oblates of Mantotte-Mannar to Propaganda 18 October 1865. In: PERNIOLA, *The Catholic Church*. The British Period. Vol. 5, 389.
65 Bonjean to Propaganda 8 February 1870. In: PERNIOLA, *The Catholic Church*. The British Period. Vol. 5, 430.
66 Bonjean to Propaganda 10 March 1868. In: PERNIOLA, *The Catholic Church*. The British Period. Vol. 5, 426.

Some of the churches in Jaffna and Mannar were incorporated into the Independent Catholic mission after 1888, but were then under legal process until the 1890s. We will discuss this issue in chapter 5.

2.2 The Indo-Portuguese Legacy in Mannar and Mantotte

A fundamental question to address is why the local Catholics in northern areas such as the ones of Mannar and Mantotte had a special inclination towards the "Portuguese" priests, even though this meant going against the Vicars Apostolic sent by the Pope through Propaganda Fide. A plausible hypothesis is that this attitude was rooted in the evolution of Ceylonese Catholicism during the Dutch era, namely was a very effective and vital heritage of the Oratorian missionaries at that time. We find further evidence supporting this hypothesis precisely in the shrine of Our Lady of Madhu. Christophe-Ernest Bonjean, third Apostolic Vicar of Jaffna (r. 1868–1883) observed that local Christians had a special veneration to an unknown priest and his grave, who founded the shrine at the beginning of the eighteenth century.[67] The missionary was the Goan Oratorian Pedro Ferrão, who came to Ceylon in 1696. Being a contemporary to Joseph Vaz, Ferrão's missionary work had gained him the name of *Samanassu*, meaning Angel or Angelic Father. He died in 1721 in Puttalam, on the northwest coast of Ceylon, but was buried in the shrine that he had founded. People claimed that his grave in Madhu had performed numerous miracles, especially healing from snake bites. In 1879 Bonjean confirmed the miracles at the shrine, stating that it "is asserted that the great virtue in that earth is not something natural but something due to the intercession of the Blessed Virgin and of that priest [i.e. Ferrão]".[68] Since the *Padroado* priests in 19th century Ceylon were in a line of continuity with the 18th century Oratorian missionaries, working undercover at a time of anti-Catholic policy pursued by the VOC administration, we can clearly detect that the adversaries of the Apostolic Vicars could count on inherited spiritual and thaumaturgic assets. In a shrine like the one devoted to Our Lady of Madhu, the legitimacy and entitlement of the Goan priests rested upon the supernatural sanction given by the miracles of a powerful saint (although one not yet canonised) such as Pedro Ferrão. Hence, we can infer here a potential clash between different forms of ecclesiastical legitimation: on the one hand the institutional and global one of the Apostolic Vicars, based on their pontifical commission, especially at a time in which allegiance to Papal infallibility was becoming a distinguishing mark of Roman Catholicism; on the other hand the highly localised, often thaumaturgic one of the Oratorian missionaries, transmitted to the later missionaries supporting the *Padroado* against Propaganda at the time of the *Concordats*. It is therefore not surprising that local Christians had a strong affection for the Goan priests, who felt encouraged to repeatedly return to Ceylon in spite of all difficulties. Even the fiercest foes of the Goan priests did not deny their popularity among the local Catholics. Bonjean frankly admitted that

> in these missionary countries [South Asia] it would be odious to oppose a priest, even a Goanese priest, who might baptize pagans, whatever their domicile might be. The fact, however, of having baptized a pagan would not give a Goanese any jurisdiction either over the person of the pagan or over the place where that person lived. But if the people happen to get accustomed to seeing some Goanese working under the jurisdiction of the Vicar Apostolic, seeing the affection

---

67 Bonjean to Propaganda 8 February 1879. In: PERNIOLA, *The Catholic Church*. The British Period. Vol. 5, 431.
68 Ibidem.

the masses still have for the Goanese and their secret desire to see them return, it could be that this could lead to certain problems which it would be good to foresee and to forestall.[69]

Bonjean's dilemma derived from the necessary acknowledgment that the Goan priests were actually quite effective, not only taking care of the existing Catholics, but even being able to obtain new conversions among the "pagans", the Buddhists and the Hindus. However, under the new arrangements between Portugal and the Holy See, the fact of having converted certain people would not imply for the Goan priests the recognition of their spiritual jurisdiction over the neophytes. The Vicars Apostolic could not easily renounce the fundamental assistance of the Goan priests, but on the other hand even incorporating them within the Roman ranks would cause problems. We can imagine that Bonjean's fear was ultimately that the attempt to co-opt the adversaries, the ever too popular Goan priests, would not lead to their progressive neutralisation and extinction as a separate group, but rather to their takeover of the Roman missionary infrastructure in Ceylon. In other words, what Bonjean probably meant and feared was that the Goan priests working under the Apostolic Vicars would not be harmless "hostages" but rather a most dangerous Trojan horse, leading to the ultimate conquest from within of Catholic ecclesiastical power in Ceylon.

Our emphasis on the agency and power of the Goan priests has to be balanced with a consideration of the actual circumstances faced by the local faithful. Roman Catholic records suggest that the Christians actually did not discard the European missionaries, especially when the Goan priests were not able to provide sacraments timely. Driven by an urgent demand of liturgical and spiritual care, the jurisdictional division did not stop families from resorting to priests of whatever affiliation, when baptism, prayers on the sick, last anointing, and viaticum were required.[70]

2.3 A Reaction to the First Vatican Council in the Vicariate of Jaffna

In 1871 a Tamil pamphlet, with a parallel English translation, was published in Jaffna by a certain Wesleyan Methodist missionary. It was the double translation of the speech allegedly delivered by Josip Juraj Strossmayer (1815–1905), Bishop of Đakovo, during the First Vatican Council. The English title was *Bishop Strossmayer's Great Speech in the Vatican Council, Rome*. In fact, it was publicly known that Strossmayer had been a vocal opponent to the declaration of Papal infallibility and that Pius IX had a terrible opinion of him.[71] However, while the speech published in Jaffna attempted to attack the declaration of infallibility, in fact it also contested the notion of Papal primacy, thus falling totally outside the boundaries of Catholic doctrine. It used a Catholic bishop as spokesperson for non-Catholic arguments, and not merely for polemics against ultramontanism.[72]

Unsurprisingly, the speech was apocryphal. It had originally been circulating in Italian, being then translated into German and other European languages. Its appearance in Jaffna,

---

69 Note of Bonjean, Jaffna, 20 January 1883. In PERNIOLA, *The Catholic Church in Sri Lanka*. The British Period. Vol. 5: The Vicariates of Colombo, Jaffna, Kandy, 1883–1886 (Dehiwala 2001), 27.
70 The Oblates of Manotte-Mannar to Propaganda, Manttota, 18 October 1865. In: PERNIOLA, *The Catholic Church*. The British Period. Vol. 5, 390.
71 A. KADIĆ, "Bishop Strossmayer and the First Vatican Council" (*The Slavonic and East European Review* 49/116, 1971, 382–409); G.M. CROCE, "Un 'famigerato Vescovo Antifallibilista [sic]': Pio IX e Il Vescovo Strossmayer dopo la fine del Vaticano I" (*Archivum Historiae Pontificiae* 35, 1997, 161–181).
72 R. BOUDENS, *Catholic Missionaries in a British Colony*. Successes and Failures in Ceylon 1796–1893, (Immensee 1979), 123–129.

not only in English but even in Tamil, signalled in the first place the fierceness of the religious competition between Catholics and certain Protestant groups in British Ceylon. In fact, decades later, the Wesleyan Methodists did profit from the divisions between the Catholics, as in 1908 some villages in the vicinity of Mannar broke away from the Roman Church and joined that Protestant denomination, under the leadership of the English missionary Rev. W.C. Bird.[73]

However, the pamphlet had a further and deeper dimension. By being published at a time of latent schism between the supporters of the *Padroado* against the European missionaries sent by Propaganda Fide, it also escalated the polemics between Catholics in Ceylon to an unprecedented level. In fact, the Wesleyan Methodist missionaries contended with articles in local newspapers that the speech was indeed authentic, so that the publication of the pamphlet offered a space of doctrinal debate for opposed parties within the Catholic Church. Further research is required to understand what was the concrete reception of this text, and of similar arguments possibly conveyed by other means, as the Catholics in Ceylon were divided along jurisdictional lines. It is likely that it would have been of greater interest to the Catholics than to the Protestants to know that a Catholic bishop was sharply criticising a newly declared doctrine of the Roman Church. Therefore, we can assume that the primary recipients of the text were precisely the Tamil- and English-speaking Catholics of Ceylon.

The pamphlet can be considered as a symbolic step in the passage from a jurisdictional to a doctrinal dissent within the Ceylon Catholic community. It is necessary to stress that the conflicts between *Padroado* and Propaganda Fide, raging since the mid-seventeenth century, had never implied contentions on a dogmatic level, but rather had concentrated on opposed interpretations of Canon Law, vis-à-vis the definition of the relevant ecclesiastical authority in specific areas. The Protestant missionaries that came to South Asia following the victories of the VOC against the Portuguese challenged Catholicism from without, proposing a "reform" that called into question the ritual structure of the communities. More than a mere "reform", the passage from Roman Catholicism to the Calvinist model of *predikanten* (pastors) like João Ferreira d'Almeida (1628–1691), or even to the less unfamiliar Lutheran framework proposed by the Tranquebar missionaries since the beginning of the eighteenth century, meant a radical revolution of practices and, to a lesser extent, also of beliefs.[74] The Catholic communities in South Asia, and primarily in South India, had been divided during the eighteenth century by the Malabar Rites controversy, concerning the extent to which Christianity could and had to be adapted in the missions of Madurai, Mysore, and the Carnatic. However, the controversy on the Malabar Rites concerned ritual adaptations and the compatibility of caste with Christian morals, not dogmas and articles of faith.[75]

---

73 G.G. FINDLAY/W.W. HOLDSWORTH, *The History of the Wesleyan Methodist Missionary Society*. Vol. 5 (London 1924), 50.

74 Ferreira de Almeida has been studied recently by Luis Henrique Menezes Fernandes, in various essays and most extensively in his unpublished doctoral thesis "Diferença da Cristandade. A controvérsia religiosa nas Índias Orientais Holandesas e o significado histórico da primeira tradução da Bíblia em Português (1642–1694)" (Universidade de São Paulo, 2016). A fundamental orientation on the history of the Tranquebar mission is offered by A. GROSS / Y.V. KUMARADOSS / H. LIEBAU (eds.), *Halle and the Beginning of Protestant Christianity in India*, 3 vols. (Halle 2006).

75 Paolo Aranha is completing a systematic history of the Malabar Rites controversy. A preliminary assessment can be found in P. ARANHA, "The Social and Physical Spaces of the Malabar Rites Controversy", in: G. MARCOCCI / W. DE BOER / A. MALDAVSKY / I. PAVAN (eds.), *Space and Conversion in Global Perspective* (Leiden / Boston 2014), 214–232.

Indeed, during the seventeenth and eighteenth century, the Catholic Church had been divided also on doctrinal issues, especially with the challenge posed by Jansenism, particularly in relation to the doctrines of grace and justification. However, Jansenism had never taken root in the Asian Catholic communities, even though some French missionaries had occasionally been accused of professing this doctrine.[76] It is truly only with the First Vatican Council that a space of doctrinal dissent was opened within South Asian Catholicism. At that point it became possible to proclaim oneself "Catholic" and at the same time oppose defining doctrines of the Roman Church. In the case of Ceylon, the marker of such an opening was precisely the Tamil and English translation of Strossmayer's apocryphal "Great Speech".

2.4 The Development of the Portuguese Mission in the 1870s

A quantitative insight can show how the influence of the *Padroado* loyalists in Ceylon grew in the decades preceding the emergence of the Independent Catholics. General statistics of the Catholic Church in India and Ceylon were produced by order of the Apostolic Vicar of Pondichéry, Clément Bonnand, in 1859. The outcome was eventually published in the *Madras Catholic Directory* in 1869.[77] It shows that the Apostolic Vicariate of Colombo had 50 faithful under the Portuguese jurisdiction against a total number of 101,222 Catholics. Rather different was the situation in the Jaffna Vicariate, with 1,000 Portuguese loyalists against a total number of 57,874 Catholics in the northern Vicariate.[78]

Proportions altered dramatically in Colombo around 1875, when the Catholics following the Goan priests reached 1,200. Facing the sharp increase of the Christians under the jurisdiction of *Padroado*, Bonjean realised that an appropriate solution was to assign a special district to the Goan priests. It was expected that defined boundaries of jurisdiction would prevent transgression and potential discord.[79] In 1877, the Apostolic Vicar in Colombo, the Sylvestrine-Benedictine monk Ilarione Sillani (1812–1879), made a formal concession of three churches to the pro-*Padroado* priests, namely the church of Our Lady of Good Death in Colombo – now known under the Italian spelling of Buona Morte – Saint Pedro in Negombo, and Boa Viagem in Duwa.[80]

The period from 1877 to 1880 was relatively peaceful for the Roman Catholic authorities in Ceylon, suggesting that the Portuguese Mission remained at a minimum level of activity. In April 1877 Bonjean even claimed the extinction of the schism from the Island:

> I have a consoling news to share with you. The schism has been rooted out in Ceylon. You already know that I was on the best of terms with the new Archbishop [of Goa, i.e. Aires de Ornelas e Vasconcelos]. He had come to see me in Jaffna, but he had no time and went from Colombo to Tuticorin, as Mgr. Canoz had invited me to go to Trichinopoly, I set out on this journey and, in spite of the fatigue I had to undergo, I am very happy to have gone. Six bishops met at Trichinopoly: the Archbishop of Goa, Mgr. Persico as envoy of Rome for this affair,

---

76 The most famous case concerned Antoine Guigues (or Guigue), convicted in Canton in 1724 of disobedience to the Constitution *Unigenitus*. H.C. LEA, *The Inquisition in the Spanish Dependencies*. Sicily, Naples, Sardinia, Milan, the Canaries, Mexico Peru, New Granada (New York 1922, 1st ed. 1908), 317–318.
77 P.N. KOWALSKY, "Die Oblatenmission von Jaffna (Ceylon) zur Zeit der apostolischen Visitation im Jahre 1860" *(Zeitschrift für Missionswissenschaft und Religionswissenschaft 1,* 1956), 209.
78 *The Madras Catholic Directory*, 1870, 221.
79 Bonjean to Propaganda 20 January 1875. In: PERNIOLA, *The Catholic Church. The British Period*. Vol. 5, 524.
80 *Negocios Externos: Documentos apresentados ás cortes na sessão legislativa de 1887 pelo ministro e secretario d'Estado dos Negocios Estrangeiros: Negociações com a Santa Sé*, Segunda parte (Lisboa 1887), 92.

Mgr. Canoz of Madura, Mgr. Meurin of Bombay, Mgr. Laouenan of Pondicherry and myself. Our meeting and our long discussions with the Archbishop were very cordial. He is a man of great intelligence, of engaging manners, of a conciliatory spirit, an ultramontane of a good sort, very devoted to the Holy See. We [Bonjean and Ornelas] have set down this *status quo* in an agreement and signed it. In it we have established some fixed rules governing the relations between the priests of the two jurisdictions. Those who have rebelled against me and those who still nurse the hope of doing so sooner or later, have lost every hope of doing so. [...] finally he has promised to send some good priests to Mannar to replace those who are there now since he finds that it is urgent to change them.[81]

We can assess Bonjean's remarks in three regards. First of all, the cordial relation between the Propaganda bishops and the Archbishop of Goa was based on an unprecedented trust at a personal level. Bonjean's description of the Portuguese Archbishop as an "ultramontane of a good sort" reveals that the *Padroado* questions in South Asia were taken for granted as an extension of the old rivalry in the European Church, as we have discussed in chapter 2. Secondly, earlier in 1877, the Archbishop of Goa, Aires de Ornelas e Vasconcelos (r. 1874–1880), visited Jaffna and showed respect to the Bishops and the Apostolic Vicars in the island. This visit announced the start of a new process of reconciliation between the *Padroado* and the prelates representing the Propaganda Fide. The "agreement" signed between Ornelas e Vasconcelos and Bonjean on the double jurisdiction might have given consolation to the Portuguese Mission in Ceylon, and therefore reduced the tensions with the Catholic authorities. Thirdly, Ornelas e Vasconcelos' reconciliation with Rome coincided with the arrival of Ignazio Persico (1823–1895), who represented the Holy See in the attempts to solve the divisions among the Catholic Suriani, at the time of Mar Mellus.[82] The gathering of six Catholic bishops in Tiruchirapalli, hosted by the Bishop of Madurai Alexis Canoz S.J., (1805–1888), involved the most active voices on the *Padroado* controversies, such as the Bishops of Bombay, Pondicherry, and Jaffna on the one side, and the Archbishop of Goa on the other. Persico was present at the meeting, as both an expert on the *Padroado* controversies and authoritative specialist on the Syrian Church of Malabar. It was a typical occasion in which parallel schisms in South Asia were jointly discussed and unavoidably compared one with each other by European prelates, for the noticeable similarity of the two affairs in terms of tension with native clergy. Further studies are required to see how the Portuguese schism or the *Padroado* controversies have been involved in the other contemporary divisions in South Asian Christianity.

The Portuguese Mission in Ceylon remained silent, but not to the extent of pacification. After Ornelas e Vasconcelos' death in 1880, voices of rebellion re-emerged in the churches under double jurisdiction across India and Ceylon, leading to the publication of the final *Concordat* in 1886, signed by Rome and Lisbon regardless of the recurrent petitions of the Goan priests and laymen. In 1887 the Portuguese Mission again became a major concern for Bonjean, when he took charge of the Archbishopric of Colombo. It was in that year that the Catholic Portuguese Mission created by Misso transformed to an Independent Catholic Mission, guided by Alvares and Lisboa Pinto, both coming from India.

---

81 Bonjean to J. Fabre, Jaffna, 11 April 1877. In: PERNIOLA, *The Catholic Church*. The British Period. Vol. 5, 626–627.
82 See Persico's trip to India in 1877 in V.J. VITHAYATHIL, *The Origin and Progress of the Syro-Malabar Hierarchy* (Kottayam 1980), 45.

Chapter 5:
Ceylon II: The Independent Catholic Mission 1887–ca. 1900

In this chapter we examine the development of the Independent Catholics centred in Colombo, Mannar, and Mantotte (i.e. Mathottam) roughly from 1887 to 1900. It is divided into three sections, considering first of all the decision for a separation from Rome as well as the first contacts with the Syrian Church of Malabar, then the adaptation process to the bourgeoisie in Ceylon of leaders who came from abroad, and finally the decline of the Mission in the early 20th century. We emphasise two aspects in the short history of this Mission. On the one hand, it was the laymen's agency and quest for religious and social changes of the Catholics in Ceylon that called for a change of subjection. The intensified coercive measures of the Propaganda bishops over the *Padroadist* congregations might have been the trigger of their identification with the global trend of the Independent Catholic movement reacting to the First Vatican Council. On the other hand, the Independent Catholics were not isolated from the dynamic social movements in Ceylon that aimed at creating a modern and industrial civil society. Such movements had attracted elites from all religious backgrounds, specifically Buddhists, Muslims, and even our Independent Catholics. This chapter proposes the flexibility and hybridity of the Independent Catholics as a main factor for their success in catching global attention through periodicals, newspapers, and other mass media, but also as the reason why their movement declined soon after the death of the lay leader Lisboa Pinto in 1898.

1. Decisive Years, 1884–1888

1.1 Despair, 1884–1887

The practical arrangement by Ilarione Sillani, Apostolic Vicar of Colombo, of formally conceding three churches to the pro-*Padroado* priests in 1877, mentioned at the end of the last chapter, might be interpreted as an attempt at an appeasement between the *Padroado* and the Propaganda Fide factions. The truce lasted less than a decade, as the publication of the new *Concordat* between Lisbon and Rome signed in 1886 triggered a final escalation and the exit of a group of *Padroadists*, centred around the Church of Our Lady of Good Death. In 1884, C. X. Alphonso, a Goan priest self-proclaimed as Vicar General, was stationed at that church. On 20 October of that year, he published an English circular addressed "To the clergy and the faithful subject to the Jurisdiction of His Grace the Archbishop of Goa in Ceylon", in which he criticised a pastoral letter published by the Vicar Apostolic of Colombo. In this letter Bishop Bonjean had proposed an offer of allowing the Goan missionaries to continue their ministry in Colombo but under his authority, to which Alphonso replied:

> I heartily reciprocate the sentiments of good will expressed by His Lordship the Vicar Apostolic of Colombo, and will always consistently with my duty co-operate with him in what regards the good of the Catholic people and the spread of Christianity in this Island.
> His Lordship the Bishop has, as stated in his Pastoral, made an offer – for which we are thankful – of continuing me and my brother priests in our present positions under his authority. Under the circumstances above set forth, it is premature to enter into such personal considerations; but if the necessity arrives, we shall, we hope, be guided by the rule of duty.
> The threatened misfortune has taken me, no less than you, by surprise, and the contemplation of our separation is all the more painful. However, I am bound in this matter to act according to the commands that may be imposed upon me by His Grace the Archbishop [of Goa], and you, I have no doubt, will equally respect his wishes. Meantime I exhort you to continue, as hitherto, in peace and in strict obedience to your superiors, and to leave the rest on this, as on all occasions, to the providence of God.[1]

In November 1884, *Padroadists* in Colombo had sent petitions to Portugal for the first time.[2] On 26 December of the same year the *Muppu*, or lay leaders, of the *Padroadist* Catholics in Mannar named Santiyago Morais and Saveu Pariyari (?) sent a petition on behalf of the church of Kumuthulasadi (?) to the Portuguese ambassador to the Holy See, the Marquês de Tomar, António Bernardo da Costa Cabral (1803–1889), who had being residing in Rome since 1870.

> We the Catholics of Mannar in Ceylon under the jurisdiction of His Grace the Archbishop of Goa beg of Your Excellency to forward the enclosed petition to His Eminence Cardinal Jacobini, Pontifical Secretary of State.[3]

Resolutions were discussed and approved on 24 May 1885, 12 September 1886, 24 October 1886, and 26 October 1886, in Colombo, Negombo, and Mannar (Oyilankulam) respectively, in the name of the "General Committee of the Roman Catholic Portuguese Mission of the Island of Ceylon." In particular, in October 1886 the Catholic Portuguese Missions held three meetings also in Goa and Bombay, against the execution of the *Concordat*.[4] It was during the last meetings in October 1886 that the decision on a delegation to Europe was made, whose expenses were to be paid entirely by the Mission in Ceylon. However, their plans and hopes vanished even before Lisboa Pinto returned from Europe. On 21 March 1887 the Patriarch of Goa, Antonio Valente, sent a telegram to Bonjean, reaffirming that "By *Concordat*, I have no more jurisdiction in Ceylon".[5] On the next day Bonjean immediately published the telegram from Goa, emphasising that according to "the telegram of the Archbishop

---

1 A circular by C. X. Alphonso, at the church of Our Lady of Good Death, Hulftsdorp, 20 October 1884. An original copy is at the Arquivo Diplomático e a Biblioteca do Ministério dos Negócios Estrangeiros (AMNE), Lisbon, *Arquivo histórico da Embaixada de Portugal junto a Santa Sé,* Caixa 39, Maço 1. Sé Oriente n. 43.
2 "The Padroadists of Ceylon" by "a padroadist", dated in Colombo on 27 May 1887. (*O Anglo-Lusitano*, 9 June 1887), 4.
3 Santiyago Morais and Saveu Pariyari to Marquês de Tomar, Colombo, 26 December 1884. AMNE, *Arquivo histórico da Embaixada de Portugal junto a Santa Sé,* Caixa 39, Maço 1. Sé Oriente n. 44.
4 ANONYMOUS [BONJEAN], *The Jacobites of Ceylon* (Colombo 1889), 8–9. Bonjean commented that the resolutions of those meetings had been published in *O Anglo-Lusitano* on 16 December 1886, without a word of condemnation. [However, I could not find those resolutions in that particular issue.]
5 Bonjean to the "Catholics late of the Jurisdiction of Goa in the Archdiocese of Colombo", Colombo, 22 March 1887, in PERNIOLA, *The Catholic Church. The British Period.* Vol. 8, 25.

of Goa to the Goa clergy here declaring that the *Concordat* having been ratified by the Portuguese Government and not having been modified, the Goa priests were free either to submit to our jurisdiction or to return to Goa."[6]

This letter might have incurred great disappointment, as if it had announced the failure of Lisboa Pinto's ongoing mission in Europe. At that moment, he was waiting to give a lecture at the Society of Geography in Lisbon, hoping to change the mind of the Portuguese government. In reaction to Bonjean's pastoral letter, the *annavy* (lay leader) Martines Pereira published a letter on 25 March on behalf of the Mission Committee, describing the administration of Propaganda Fide in Ceylon as "fresh persecutions" of the *Padroadists*, comparable to the Dutch persecutions of all Catholics:

> The Committee beg [sic], with regard to Mass and Sacrament to call to mind that the charity of the Propaganda comes too late, for the ancestors of the present Christians when suffering under the Dutch persecutions had no Mass for a very considerable period, during which the eyes of the Propaganda were fast closed. The present epoch being a period of fresh persecutions under the Propaganda the Portuguese Mission Catholics will gladly follow the footsteps of their ancestors.[7]

The following months from March 1887 to February 1888 were crucial, as it was during this period that the Portuguese Mission transformed into an Independent Mission, but one which was also in communion with the Syrian Church. We have not been able to retrieve the details from the original records, but we have to rely on the various official reports by their Catholic rival, the Archbishop of Colombo Bonjean.

In 1887 Bonjean made a detailed report on the "Goan question" to the Congregation of Propaganda Fide. The *Padroado* alliance had one church in each of these cities: Colombo, Negombo, Duwa Negombo, Pallimunay in Mannar, and Parapankandel in Mantotte. They possessed 16 chapels in various missions in Mantotte and Vanni, but all in miserable condition "with neither doors nor windows". The Goan priests visited only once a year and only for a few days each time before they moved on to other places.[8]

After sending a telegram, the Patriarch of Goa dispatched the famous Goan scholar Mons. Sebastião Rodolfo Dalgado (1855–1922), as Vicar General of Ceylon, from Goa to Colombo to formally announce the *Concordat*, putting an end to the disputes over the *Padroado* jurisdiction in Ceylon.[9] As the Portuguese Mission strongly opposed the change of jurisdiction and the "betrayal" committed by the Portuguese government with full force, Bonjean retaliated by forbidding all religious services of worship in their church. Dalgado and his fellow priests were not allowed by Bonjean, now endowed with an undivided jurisdiction, to attend to spiritual and sacramental requests made by the Christians of the Our Lady of Good Death community.

---

6   Bonjean to the "Catholics late of the Jurisdiction of Goa in the Archdiocese of Colombo", Colombo, 22 March 1887, in PERNIOLA, *The Catholic Church*. The British Period. Vol. 8, 24.
7   Martines Pereira's letter, printed in Colombo, 25th March 1887, APF, *SC Indie Orientali* vol. 32, fol. 251r–253v. It has been reprinted and published in PERNIOLA, *The Catholic Church*. The British Period. Vol. 8, 25–29.
8   Bonjean on the Goan question, dated in Colombo, 10 October 1887. In: VITO PERNIOLA, *The Catholic Church in Sri Lanka*. The British Period. Vol. 8: 1887–1899. The Archdiocese of Colombo (Dehiwala 2004), 61.
9   On this Goan priest see his biography in A. PEREIRA SJ, *Dalgado, the Man and the Scholar* (New Delhi 1983), 27. Born in Assagão (in the Bardez peninsula), Dalgado was a countryman of Lisboa Pinto, to whom he was two years senior.

In reaction, the church trustees organised a meeting under the pretext of discussing ways to celebrate the Golden Jubilee of Queen Victoria's accession to the throne, occurring in June 1887. In the assembly, the members of the congregation of Good Death agreed on the following points:

1. Public prayers for the Queen should be held in all the churches, accompanied by singing where possible.
2. The Jubilee should also be celebrated with acts of charity, such as feeding a certain number of poor and distributing clothes to destitute families.
3. The foundation stone for a statue in honour of the Venerable Joseph Vas.
4. Illuminations and fireworks at night.
5. A congratulatory telegram to Her Majesty.

As an additional consequence, trustee Stephen Silva[10] and his fellows in Colombo resorted to an emergency solution, namely to non-sacramental celebrations replacing the Holy Mass, under the direction of a lay leader. When a Mass was celebrated in the Catholic parish of St. Sebastian, located merely at one hundred meters distance, de Silva would hold "on Sundays what is called the lay religious service, which consists in ringing the bell, saying the prayers of the Mass, give a sermon, recite some litanies, etc." These Christians articulated their religious agency, in the absence of priestly services, with a para-sacramental ritual, duly advertised in local newspapers. Another example of lay devotion was the erection of a monument in honour of the highly venerated José Vaz as part of festivities for Queen Victoria's Golden Jubilee. In the ceremony, the Portuguese Consul and an English Protestant were invited to lay the foundation stone of the statue.[11]

1.2 The Establishment of the Independent Catholic Mission in February 1888

After Lisboa Pinto had fruitlessly returned to Bombay from Lisbon, his petition was finally discussed in Rome. The Congregation of Propaganda Fide submitted a report at a meeting of the Secretariat of State of the Holy See, dated on 1 December 1887. This confidential report attributed the efforts of the Bombay-Goan doctor to a Freemasonry manoeuvre and stated that the *Padroadist* community in Colombo had little impact on the Christian sphere of the metropolis. This document reveals also a crucial intervention of the Apostolic Nuncio to Portugal Vincenzo Vannutelli (in office 1883-1890), who had done intelligence work on the delegate and reduced his influence within the political circles in Portugal.

> Dr. Lisboa Pinto is a physician of Bombay, extremely well-known for his exaggerated Jansenism and for his attitude against the missionaries whom he derisively calls Propagandists. He is also suspected to be a freemason. […]

---

10 Silva's biography is still to be reconstructed. In 1894 his son, professor in the Government Technical College in Colombo, returned to the Roman Catholic Church. See PERNIOLA, *The Catholic Church*. The British Period. Vol. 8, 484.
11 Bonjean to the Congregation of Propaganda Fide on the Goan question, dated in Colombo, 10 October 1887. In: PERNIOLA, *The Catholic Church*. The British Period. Vol. 8, 67.

> Warned in time by Propaganda, Mgr Vannutelli, the Apostolic Nuncio to his most Faithful Majesty, made use of all his well-known ability to spy on every step of Dr. Pinto and to neutralize, as far as it was possible, his influence. But he could not possibly prevent Lisboa Pinto, in conversations with politicians, in public lectures and chiefly in articles published in newspapers offensive to the Holy See, from swaying public opinion in favour of the Ceylonese, describing them as people loyal to Portugal though abandoned and betrayed by Portugal, and worthy to be wrested from the yoke of Propaganda.[12]

The above-mentioned diplomatic interactions between Rome and Lisbon were confidential and appeared in none of the documents published by the *Padroadists* in India or Ceylon. No evidence has been found to suggest Ceylon *Padroadists*' involvement in the Portuguese Freemasonry or the Freemason societies in British India. The Roman theologians labelled Lisboa Pinto as a Freemanson not only out of a simplistic suspicion, but because of the fact that the Bombay doctor was able to mobilise political resources as successfully as the liberal party in Portugal. The same report presented at the Secretariat of State of the Holy See reveals that the Chamber of Peers (Câmara dos Pares, or the Senate) was in fact in favour of the Ceylon cause, for which the Nuncio to Portugal Vannutelli had to intervene again stopping it. The Ceylon cause was taken truly serious in Portugal despite its small size.

> On account of the strong arguments of Lisboa Pinto, for the first time in the Chamber of Peers and then in that of Representatives a motion was introduced in favour of the Goans of Ceylon. The Senators were planning to make use of the Throne Speech at the end of the month of May to insert a sentence which would commit the Crown and consequently the Ministry as well to make new instances to the Holy Father to bring about a modification in the Concordat with reference to Ceylon. […]
>
> The case [Ceylon motion] is truly serious. If the desire of the Portuguese Chambers were to be fulfilled, then there would follow the legalization of a rebellion of a few troublemakers in Colombo who would also inflict a new wound on the Concordat stipulated last year after the very serious wound of the cession of the five churches in Madras, of the district of Saint Warry and of the church of Poona.[13]

Back in Colombo, the community surrounding Our Lady of Good Death read an official letter that Pope Leo XIII sent to the Portuguese Parliament dated 6th December 1887, which was identical to the Propaganda Fide report and clearly influenced by the previous reports by Bonjean on the status quo of the Portuguese Mission:

> The Result of the inquiry, made by impartial person [Bonjean], points to the fact that in Ceylon there are not more than EIGHT or TEN individuals, who resolutely wish to exclude themselves from the jurisdiction of the bishops recently established there, and not more than TWENTY families who are awaiting the final result of the efforts made in Lisbon [Lisboa Pinto's petition] to decide upon their submission.[14]

In reaction to the statement of Leo XIII, on 10 February 1888 Martines Pereira, on behalf of the Portuguese Committee, published the Official Circular No. 10, declaring the establishment of a new Mission:

---

12 PERNIOLA, *The Catholic Church*. The British Period. Vol. 8, 100.
13 PERNIOLA, *The Catholic Church*. The British Period. Vol. 8, 101–102.
14 I quote the English version from the Official Circular below. An identical version of this paragraph can also be found in PERNIOLA, *The Catholic Church*. The British Period. Vol. 8, 100–101.

> From the above quotation [from Leo XIII's letter] it is more than clear, that *interested* party – holy or otherwise – with some end in view, has barefacedly misled and misinformed the Pope by the [p]erversion of the most solemn facts.
>
> Having now placed the above information before you, it is only left to the Committee to add that the congregations of the churches of Our Lady of Good Death and of St Emmanuel in Colombo, have already signified to the Committee, their determination to constitute themselves an Independent Catholic Mission under a Catholic Prelate and ministers not in communion with the See of Rome. To this end, these congregations have already taken measures to secure the services of a prelate and a staff of missionaries.[15]

In the meantime, the two churches of the dissident Catholics were placed under interdict from the Archbishop of Colombo one day before Alvares celebrated the Mass there for the first time. The interdict contained the following orders:

> I. We declare that the person who signed the above quoted "Official Circular of the Portuguese Mission" has incurred the excommunication latae sententiae, the third of those reserved in an especial manner to the Roman Pontiff in the Constitution Apostolicae Sedis, which is of the following tenor: those who pertinaciously withdraw themselves or recede from the obedience to the Pontiff for the time being. In virtue of the faculties granted us by the Holy See for a decennial period on the 23rd 1886, we reserve to ourselves the absolution of the said person after he shall have made satisfaction.
> We likewise warn all persons who, by any public act of theirs shall henceforth give or may have given their adhesion to the above circular, that they shall likewise incur, or have already incurred the same excommunication.
> II. We place the church of Our Lady of Good Death, Hultsdorf, and Emmanuel Chapel, under a sentence of interdict, that is to say, we inhibit the celebration in either of any Christian worship, and we forbid all the faithful under pain of refusal of the Sacraments and of Christian burial, to enter any of them for any purpose connected with Christian worship.
> III. We warn all the faithful that no priest, not approved by us, has any right to officiate in that church, or to administer any sacrament in his Archdiocese.[16]

1.3 Turning to the Syrian Church of Malabar in June 1888

After the official announcement of the Independent Catholic Mission in February 1888, the Committee sought for help in Goa and Bombay. It is still not clear when and how the Ceylonese congregation had the first contact with Alvares and Lisboa Pinto. However, from two letters exchanged between Stephen Silva and Mar Dionysius, the Metropolitan of the Syrian Church of Malabar, in June 1888, it can be confirmed that Alvares and Lisboa Pinto had made an agreement with the Independent Catholics for a joint application to the Syrian Church in Malabar. On the one hand these Indo-Ceylonese Catholics sought protection from the Syrian Church, stepping out of the Roman Catholic world. On the other hand, they proposed that Alvares be consecrated by the Patriarch of Antioch so that he could take on the various missions across Ceylon and India, who faced a similar situation of despair. On 6 June

---

15 "Official Circular of the Portuguese Mission, No. 10, Colombo, 11th February, 1888" is a printed document of two pages. An original copy is conserved in a private collection in Colombo. References to this important document can be also found in ANONYMOUS [Bonjean], *The Jacobites of Ceylon*, 1889, 18–19.

16 "Decree" dated in Borella, Colombo, 20 August 1888. It was written originally in English. See PERNIOLA, *The Catholic Church in Sri Lanka. The British Period, 1887–1899* Vol. VIII: 138–140.

1888, the trustee of the Committee, Stephen Silva, wrote to Mar Dionysius for the first time. In this letter Silva followed the old title of the Portuguese Mission Defence Committee of Ceylon, rather than the Independent Catholic Mission.

> May it please your Grace. I am [trustee] of the Portuguese Mission Defence Committee of Ceylon to address the following letter to you.
> The Defence Committee are informed of our worthy delegate Mr. Pedro Manuel Lisboa Pinto and our intimate patriot Rev. Fr. A. F. X. Alvares, who was lately on a visit to Your Grace, that they have appealed to Your Grace in our name and that of our brethren in India to consecrate a Bishop for Ceylon and India for the spiritual welfare of our 10,000 Christians who are excluded from pa[…]disto. I am […] to take this opportunity of informing Your Grace that our Christians belong[ing] to the 25 churches in the island are now without Mass and sacraments for upwards of 17 months and although we have used every lawful means of placing our grievances before the Holy Father, yet it is more than apparent that His Holiness has been deceived by the Propaganda not to listen to our appeal. And hence, we have after […] declaration sep[arated] ourselves from the obedience of the Church of Rome and in anticipation of an affirmative reply, we have placed ourselves under the protection of the Patriarch of Babylon.
> I am particularly requested by the Defence Committee to impress on Your Grace the impossibility of our remaining in the present state, viz. without priests, and without sacrament. Some instantaneous res[…] is greatly needed, and that we hope to receive at Your Grace hands with the least possible delay. I am particularly requested by the Defence Committee to beg of Your Grace to expedite the obtaining of the Patriarch's consent for consecrat[ing] our bishop. In conclusion I am de[…] to ask Your Grace to favour us with a reply to his letter per return post if possible.[17]

According to Silva, both Lisboa Pinto and Alvares were on a visit to Mar Dionysius and had already discussed the request from the Ceylon Independent Catholic Mission, while the Ceylon Mission presented the formal request to Kottayam.

Alvares' intervention must have been effective. Mar Dionysius' reply to Silva on 23 June 1888 promised that the Patriarch of Antioch would fulfil their requests for protection but also the episcopal consecration of Alvares as Bishop for the Independent Catholic Mission. Mar Dionysius reassured:

> Dear friend, I have great pleasure to acknowledge receipt of your letter of the 6th instant, placing the Catholic Church of Ceylon under the protection of the Syrian Patriarch and soliciting the consecration of a Bishop for Ceylon. It is unnecessary to repeat more, the pains, I am undergoing to help you, as you are already informed of the same by our esteemed friend the Rev. Alvares. Some of my subordinate bishops have entertained the doubtful opinions that your application may be a mere artful attempt to procure consecration from the Syrian Church; but I have tried to [remove] all feelings of suspicion, [reporting] my full confidence in the Rev. Alvares and Dr. Pedro whom I take to be honest gentlemen. Accordingly, I have, in congestion with His Grace the Apostolic Representative, sent an application to His Holiness the Patriarch for the necessary permission to relieve your churches, and I expect an early reply.
> I deeply sympathize with the Ceylon Churches in the hardships they endure and it is my earnest desire to […] up their wounds and relieve them. You may rest assured of help and relief, under the protection of our venerable Patriarch, who will not fail to authorise me to transact all ecclesiastical business with you.

---

17 Stephen Silva to Mar Dionysius, signed at "Fort Printing Office", Colombo, on 6 June 1888. It is a manuscript copy belonging to a private owner in Colombo. The copy that was accessible to me was only partly legible.

In conclusion, I allow you to convey these glad [news] to the Ceylon Defence Committee and to assure them in my name, of every help from the Syrian Church and her Prelates. Although I have successfully removed all feelings of suspicion, I would be very thankful if you send me an application signed by the leading representatives of the various churches in Ceylon for the satisfaction of the other Bishops and the Syrian Association over which I preside.

Finally I pray that God Almighty may stretch forth his invisible right hand and bless you and your Committee as well as the faithful Christians of Ceylon and relieve you from all your present sufferings.[18]

The consecration of a Goan ex-Catholic priest was not an uncontroversial decision, considering that the Syrian Christians were traditionally a monoethnic community giving little attention to missionary work towards non-Malayalis or non-Malayalam speakers. Not surprisingly, the cause of Alvares received objections from certain Syrian bishops, whose suspicion of Alvares might have also mixed with reluctance to subject to a foreign "Archbishop", a title totally new and alien to the terminology of the Syrian ecclesiastical hierarchy. The full title of Alvares as an "Archbishop of Ceylon, Goa and India, excluding Malabar" indicates precisely the jurisdictional divisions reassuring that Alvares' authorities would not be in any competition with other bishops or Metropolitans in Malabar.

From the perspective of the Syrian Church in Malabar, the consecration of Alvares requires more research into the local contexts of cross-confessional relations in the late nineteenth century, between the Roman Catholic Church and the Syrian Church. Curiously, in a confidential letter addressed to the Apostolic Delegate Andrea Aiuti in 1888, Mar Dionysius disclosed contacts he had with the dissenting Catholics in Ceylon. Those Christians had sent him a letter requesting him to consecrate a Goan priest so that he could be assigned as their Bishop in Ceylon. Mar Dionysius refused the request, even though the petitioners were committed to cover all expenses for the trip. Notwithstanding this refusal, the same Ceylonese committee approached the Patriarch of Antioch directly, requesting him to order the bishops of Malabar belonging to his Church to undertake the required episcopal consecration.[19] Before having received any instructions from Mardin, Mar Dionysus informed Aiuti of the Ceylonese action. The initiatives undertaken by those dissenting Catholics, as well as the channel through which the Apostolic Delegate became aware of them, suggest some considerations. First of all, the fact that a bishop of the Syrian Orthodox Church would feel the need to inform the Papal Delegate in India shows that there were effective diplomatic channels between churches officially in hostile relations. Secondly, the fact that the Ceylonese committee was able to directly approach the Primate of the Syrian Church suggests that they had succeeded to create a specific channel of communication between Colombo and Mardin. This connection can be explained in the amicable relations that the Independent Catholics had with the Tamil-speaking Muslims as well as with the Consul of Turkey, as it will be analysed in the next sections of this chapter. Thirdly, we can see clearly that it was a choice of the Ceylonese to contact the Syrian Church, rather than a proselytising initiative of the latter.

On 20 August 1888 Antonio Francisco Xavier Alvares, sent as Apostolic Prefect by the Syrian Metropolitan of Malabar Mar Dionysus, arrived at Pettah and took possession of the

---

18 From "The Most. Rev. Mar Dionysius Syrian Metropolitan of Malabar" to "Mr. Stephen Silva, secretary, Ceylon Defence Committee", Trivandrum, 23 June 1887. This is a manuscript letter with Mar Dionysius' signature in both English and Syriac, but the seal is empty. This document is in possession of a private owner in Colombo.

19 Antonio Aiuti to Giovanni Simeoni, dated in Ootacamund 16 August 1888. APF, *SC Indie Orientali* vol. 33. ff. 647r–647v, Part of Aiuti's report has been translated into English and published in PERNIOLA, *The Catholic Church*. The British Period. Vol. 8, 136–138.

church of Our Lady of Good Death. There he celebrated the first mass after 19 months since the interdict decreed by Archbishop Bonjean.[20] Two months later Stephen Silva sent a letter to Mar Dionysus to express the gratitude of the Ceylonese Christians and to update him on the recent work undertaken by Alvares. De Silva's words made it clear that the Jacobites had responded to a request made by the Independent Catholics of Ceylon:

> It is with feelings of deep gratitude that our Christians direct me to thank Your Grace for the continual kindness shown to them, and particularly at the hour of their trial.[21]

The "continual kindness" might hint at extended interactions between the group of Buona Morte and the Jacobite Church. Even though no document has been found so far explaining the specific channels through which the Independent Catholics got in touch with the Syrians of Kottayam, we have already seen that it is certain that the initiative started from Colombo. In the same letter it was reported that Alvares, as the "Vicar Prefect" of the Syrian Church, was for the moment on a visit to all the churches hitherto belonging to the *Padroado* hardliners in Mannar and Mantotte.

Between August and December Alvares and his associates visited Negombo and elsewhere.[22] Soon after the arrival of Alvares, it was the turn of Lisboa Pinto to reach Colombo on 22 October. The doctor from Bombay had been invited by the Portuguese Mission to join them in Colombo. In the journal *O Ultramar,* published in Margao, it was reported (following an article that appeared in the *The Ceylon Independent*, an English journal published in Colombo) that:

> The Mission of the Independent Catholics of Mannar, Mantotte, and Vanni, decided in a large meeting by unanimity on 28 October [1888] to offer a lancet, a pen and an inkwell of gold to Dr. Lisboa Pinto, and a collar and garland of the same metal to his most distinguished wife. They also decided to erect a monument to the above mentioned *Senhor* Pinto at the churchyard of Parappankandel as a testimony of his relevant services, and for having emancipated them from the forceful yoke of Propaganda.[23]

The arrival of Alvares and Lisboa Pinto in 1888 opened a new chapter in the history of the Roman Catholic Portuguese Mission in Ceylon since 1837. In the next decade this official title gradually gave way to that of "Independent Catholic Church", which appeared more often in their publications in the late 1890s. On the one hand, the Ceylon Independent Catholics received the pastoral care they strove for, but also social recognition through litigation success, and the personal achievement of church leaders adapting to the influential and elite groups. Their lost pride – once associated with the Portuguese Consul Misso – was now restored with a reputation projected even beyond South Asia, catching the attention of the Anglicans, the Old Catholics, and American Catholics. However, the unity of the congregations was still at stake, especially among the younger generation, who were more tempted to return to the Roman Catholic Church than their "schismatic" parents. On the other hand, the

---

20 Stephen Silva to the editor of *O Ultramar*, Colombo, 29 August 1888. (*O Ultramar*, 15 September 1888), 3.
21 A copy of a letter from Stephen Silva to Mar Dyonisus, dated on October 14, 1888, 1 page, found in a private collection in Colombo.
22 See Aiuti's report o the Congregation of Propaganda Fide again on Alvares' activities, dated in Ootacamund, 7 September1888, in PERNIOLA, *The Catholic Church*. The British Period. Vol. 8, 141–143, with reference to Alvares' visit to Negombo on page 142.
23 "Padroado em Ceylão" (*O Ultramar*, 24 November 1888), 3.

Goan priests and lay leaders had to live up to the high expectations of their Ceylonese Catholic fellows, while getting involved with other social and religious reforms that had a much larger scale than the one of the Independent Catholics. In the next section we will look at the membership and daily life of the laity through a case study of Lisboa Pinto's birthday party celebrated in 1898, shortly before his sudden death in the same year.

2. Members, Sociability, and Rivalry

2.1 Members

In this section we will have a cursory look at some of the information available on the leadership and member structure of the Independent Catholic movement. Much additional research on these questions of social history is needed.

From 1887 to the end of the nineteenth century, at least eleven priests were recruited by Alvares from Goa and sent to staff the various missions in Colombo, Mannar, Dindigul, Tuticorin, and Kallianpur. In Colombo, Alvares ordained two priests, named Kempis and W. M. Talayaratna, of Eurasian and Sinhala origin respectively, for the missions in Ceylon and India.[24] In addition to the episcopal consecration of Vilatte, Alvares ordained the English Alexander W. Stuart, former Anglican, who returned to England soon after his priestly ordination.[25]

From 1887 to 1903, Archbishop Alvares visited Ceylon at least five times, his longest stay on the island being between May 1892 and May 1893. During his absence, the Vicar General A. A. A. de Souza was in charge of the Colombo mission, while Luis Mariano Soares (?–1903) was devoted to Mannar and other missions in the north region. The *Book of Order* of the Malankara Orthodox Syrian Church enlisted four Goan subdeacons who received priestly ordinations between 30 April and 1 May 1889 at the Old Seminary in Kottayam. These include Luis Mariano Soares, Damio Lopes, A. A. A. Souza and Joseph Xavier Botelho. One month later, between 13–14 June, a Portuguese subdeacon named Jeronimo de Jesus was promoted to priest (*Kashisha*). It is possible that these priests remained in Kottayam until they attended the episcopal ordination of Alvares, which took place on 15 July of the same year at the Old Seminary.[26]

Apart from the clergy ordained by the Syrian Church, there were priests who had received ordination in Goa before they joined the Independent Catholic Mission. Avelino da Cunha, who accompanied Alvares to Colombo in 1888, was of Portuguese origin. The leader of the Kallianpur congregation Zeferino de Noronha had already been ordained as a priest when he was assigned to the Mission in South Kanara. His senior position and zeal for missionary work became the main reasons why the Ceylon congregation elected him as bishop of Mangalore to share more responsibility for the mission in India.[27]

---

24 See the letter sent by the Independent Catholics in Colombo to the Patriarch of Antioch entitled "To His Holiness Ignatius A. Messias, Patriarch of Antioch and the East", dated in Colombo, November 10, 1900.
25 See a brief biography of Stewart in ABBA SERAPHIM's *Flesh of Our Brethren,* 413 note 27.
26 See the journal of the Bethany Ashram of the Malankara Orthodox Church with the title *Bethany Masika* (ബഥനി മാസിക [or Bethany Magazine in English] 1/2, 2017), 38.
27 The Independent Catholics in Ceylon requested that the Patriarch of Antioch issue bulls and apostolic letters for the consecration of Noronha as Bishop of Mangalore. See "To His Holiness Ignatius A. Messias, Patriarch of Antioch and the East", dated in Colombo, November 10, 1900.

While Bishop Alvares and two other priests – namely A.A.A. Souza and Joseph Xavier Botelho – took care of the Colombo community, from 1888 to 1893 Soares was the only vicar in northern Ceylon, being responsible for thousands of adherents. However, the Mannar and Mantotte missions were in constant litigation with the Roman Catholic Church.

The Colombo congregation was constituted by Dutch and Portuguese Burghers, as well as Sinhalese, whose ancestors, however, may not always have belonged to the Portuguese Mission created in 1837. In comparing the list of members of the Roman Catholic Portuguese Mission from 1837–1887 and that of the Independent Catholic Mission from 1888–1898, the Passe family appeared to be the only one that joined both Missions, whereas the Misso family was not active at all in the Christian community after the death of João Bonifacio in 1844.[28] According to some rumours, he had reconciled with the Roman Catholic Church, and so had his descendants. Due to the limits of our sources, it is difficult to say how many families actually participated in both Missions. However, a generation gap acted as a counter-force against the consolidation and expansion of the Independent Catholic community and became a threat to the progress of the small mission.

A typical case was the one of the medical doctor Stephan Silva, who was the most active initiator in the pursuit of support from outside the island. Little is known about his biography except for information about his son W. C. de Silva. In the early 1890s, the young Silva studied engineering at the Royal College, the best boys' college in British Ceylon. His success and good performance at that College as well as at the Cooper's Hill Royal Indian Engineering College was often celebrated in the periodical *The Independent Catholic*.[29] However, in 1894 W. C. de Silva reconciled with the Roman Catholic Church.[30] In that year the Catholic sources reported that there were hardly 12 to 17 families belonging to the Independent Catholic Mission, out of which two families returned to the Roman Catholic faith before death.[31]

The laity played an essential role in the survival of the congregation during the two phases of Missions. The lay leaders were known as *muppu* and *annavi*. Both terms came from Tamil and were used also among the Sinhala- and English-speaking Catholics. According to OMI missionary and historian Robrecht Boudens, *muppu* referred to "chief lay officer or warden among Catholics. In the days of the Oratorian Fathers, he had charge of the temporalities."[32] *Annavi* was used to refer to a catechist "who, in absence of a priest, led the prayers and instructed the faithful."[33]

Other lay leaders were *trustees*, in charge of the finances as well as of the communication with other Churches. It was possible to have various trustees in a congregation at the same time. The most notable trustees in Colombo included Martines Pereira, Stephen Silva, Vincent W. Pereira and Louis G. Fernando.[34] Those in Mannar included J. A. Figuerado.[35] Curiously, Lisboa Pinto never appeared in any documents as a trustee of the congregation, even though he had been considered the most prominent lay leader of that group.

---

28 See Appendix 1.
29 "A young Independent Abroad" (*The Independent Catholic*, May 1892), 3.
30 Archbishop of Colombo André-Théophile Mélizan to Propaganda Fide, Colombo 16 November 1894. In: Perniola, *The Catholic Church in Sri Lanka, The British Period, 1887–1899*. Vol. 8, 484.
31 Mélizan to Propaganda Fide, Colombo 16 November 1894. In: PERNIOLA, *The Catholic Church in Sri Lanka, The British Period, 1887–1899*. Vol. 8, 484.
32 ROBRECHT BOUDENS, *The Catholic Church in Ceylon under Dutch Rule*, (Roma, 1957), 253.
33 BOUDENS, *The Catholic Church*, 252.
34 See Appendix 1.
35 See Appendix 1.

Women of the Independent Catholic community in Colombo are known merely as wives to one or the other renowned laymen. Names of women normally appeared in lists of participants to festivals and ceremonies. The first Ladies' Confraternity was founded in 1895. The responsibilities of women were defined in association with their family. In an assembly on the second Sunday of the new year 1895, Lisboa Pinto and Stephen Silva addressed them:

> Doctor Lisboa Pinto delivered a warm speech indicating the necessity of the ladies co-operating with their husbands and brothers in the good work of propagating the truth and helping and strengthening them by participating in their endeavours and offering them words of cheer. Mr. Stephen Silva also spoke at some length and lucidly explained to the ladies the past and present position of the Independent Catholics in Ceylon and called on them to work in the home circles to extend the salutary influence of Independent Catholicism in the island.[36]

A higher education for girls from Independent Catholic families, as equal to contemporary boys, was by and large discouraged. When a proposal for a college for girls was presented to the Ceylon government, the editor of *The Independent Catholic* strongly opposed it:

> We are aware that the existing girls' schools are at present unable to teach our young ladies to write a few consecutive sentences in grammatical English – we are here speaking only of the average school educated girl. But this may be remedied, without putting the Government to the expense of establishing and maintaining a new college.
> [...] But there is another and to our mind a nobler "higher education" which we wish to advocate. [...] It is the education which will give them a truer idea of their place and their mission in the world and make them realize their true duties and responsibilities. They must be taught to leave off hankering after "women's rights," and shed that happiness around the domestic hearth, which only a good and true woman can shed.[37]

This attitude was in fact not consistent with the overall vision on women expressed by the Independent Catholics. In January 1892, Lisboa Pinto extended appraisal to women scientists when two American lady doctors, Mrs. Stockham and Miss Ryder, gave lectures at the Sangamita [sic] School, developing an "important subject on female education".[38] Among the participants of the lecture, there were the lady principal of the School Mrs. Higgins, Lisboa Pinto, and other celebrated medical doctors and their wives. Meanwhile, Lisboa Pinto extended a cordial welcome to Dr. Van Lugen and her movement of "introducing lady physicians into the Island". Dr. Van Lugen's work was part of a scheme organised by Lady Havelock, wife of the Governor Arthur Havelock (r. 1890–1895).[39]

The main targets of the Independent Catholic missionary work were the *Padroadist* congregations, while occasionally Buddhists and Protestant Burghers aspired to join the congregation for specific reasons. Adult conversions took place in each mission on the island. In March 1892, *The Independent Catholic* reported that seven adults had been baptised by the Vicar General de Souza in the Independent Catholic Cathedral.[40] In November 1892 Alvares baptised a "Buddhist gentleman" from Kalutara, in South Colombo, and christened him 'K. D. F. Don Abraham'. The ceremony took place at the cathedral and lasted for forty-five

---

36 "The confraternity of Our Lady of Good Death", (*The Independent Catholic*, January 1895), 3.
37 "Higher education for our girls", (*The Independent Catholic*, March 1895), 1.
38 "Female education", (*The Independent Catholic*, February 1892), 3.
39 "Lady doctors for Ceylon" (*The Independent Catholic*, February 1892), 3.
40 *The Independent Catholic*, April 1892, 3.

minutes, with questions posed in Sinhala, likely with assistance of translation.[41] Though Roman Catholic authorities declared the Independent Catholics to be schismatics, they were not always seen in a negative way by the other native Christians. Alvares and his alternative church movement certainly was an inspiring example for the Portuguese Burghers living in Batticaloa, on the north-western coast. The Superior of the Trincomalee Mission of the Society of Jesus, John W. Lange S.J., recorded a conflict taking place in two main churches of Batticaloa in his manuscript history of the Diocese. Two Catholic churches, Saint Mary and Saint Anthony, were in a bitter rivalry. The former was constituted of the Portuguese Burghers, the Velalar cultivators, and the Barber castes, whereas the latter was exclusively for Karaiyar Fishermen. The two caste congregations competed for the smallest issues on ritual precedence, but also polarised their attitudes towards the coming of a new bishop. With little hope of reconciliation, discussions spread in Saint Mary that an alternative solution would be "breaking away from Rome and affiliating with the Portuguese Catholic Church of the Goan schismatic, Bishop Alvarez."[42] This rumour shows that even though the Independent Catholics had entered into communion with the Syrian Church, the movement was still remembered by the Ceylon Catholics more conveniently by its former title of 'Portuguese Catholic Church'.

2.2 Glimpses of Daily Life

Elements for a social history of the Independent Catholics in Colombo can be drawn from the advertisements for machines, food, drink, and books that cover up to half a page on the monthly broadsheet *The Independent Catholic*. An interesting example was the American firm Singer Manufacturing Company, whose 1892 advert called consumers' attention to "inferior German sewing machines, offered as 'Singer', 'Improved Singer' &c. They are all imitations."[43] The Singer Company had developed a global commercial network across South and Southeast Asia. Their first offices and shops in Colombo are believed to have been opened around 1885. The warning message in the advertisement was not rhetoric but out of a real concern to fight against other competitors or imitators in the Ceylon market. In 1899 Singer appeared regularly in the English daily *The Ceylon Independent*, claiming that the company owned a hundred offices in India, Burma, and Ceylon.[44] Singer's choice of *The Independent Catholic* in 1892 and 1893, a relatively new journal run by a small schismatic Catholic community, might reflect a potential readership of the small periodical who would be most capable and willing to afford a sewing machine. From 1886 to 1887, 81 machines were sold from Singer's Colombo office. According to Nira Wickramasinghe's moderate calculation of the users of Singer in 1930, when the brand had taken 90 per cent of the Ceylon market, the number of sewing machines per inhabitant can be tallied to 1 for 10 families, namely 10 percent of households.[45] Statistics of the sewing machine ownership in the late

---

41 "Noteworthy conversion" (*The Independent Catholic,* November 1892), 3.
42 DENNIS B. MCGILVRAY quotes this episode from an unpublished manuscript by J. W. LANGE S.J., entitled "The Secluded Coast: The Story of the Diocese of Trincomalee-Batticaloa, Ceylon, 1895–1970" in his chapter "The Portuguese Burghers of Eastern Sri Lanka in the Wake of Civil War and Tsunami", in: JORGE MANUEL COSTA DA SILVA FLORES (ed.), *Re-Exploring the Links*. History and Constructed Histories between Portugal and Sri Lanka (Wiesbaden, 2007), 341–342.
43 Advertisements such as "Beware of Inferior German Sewing Machines" appeared regularly in *The Independent Catholic* starting 4 August 1892.
44 N. WICKRAMASINGHE, *Metallic Modern*. Everyday Machines in Colonial Sri Lanka (New York 2014), 23.
45 WICKRAMASINGHE, *Metallic Modern*, 23–24.

19th century may not be attainable, yet the rarity was obvious and its usage was exclusive to the wealthiest families. More importantly, an advertisement was unavoidably commensurate with the social status of the owners of the newspaper that published the commercial and its readers. Singer's choice of the young *The Independent Catholic* can be seen as evidence of the Independent Catholics' readiness for a "metallic modern" lifestyle.

In the early issues of *The Independent Catholic* one sees advertisements for the sale of alcoholic beverages such as brandy, whisky, gin, handled by Framjee Bhikhajee & Company, owned by a prominent Parsi family from Bombay, who had relocated to Colombo in 1817.[46] The company was known for its importation of liquors from Europe and America but also for its recruitment of Parsis to Ceylon from India, South East Asia and even east Africa. By 1890 the Framjee Company was elected as a member of the Ceylon Chamber of Commerce.[47] Advertisements on alcohol no longer appeared in the Independent Catholic journal when Lisboa Pinto actively campaigned for Ceylon Temperance Alliance with publications in 1895.[48]

The Independent Catholic did not have a strict censorship of books published by its religious foes. A bookseller called A. W. Salgado was able to publish a column "For sale" in the issue of April 1892, stressing his specialised collections of "Roman Catholic Missals and other devotional books".[49]

Our idea of the daily life of the owners and readers of *The Independent Catholic* can be further completed if we introduce a wider context of economic and social history of industrialised Colombo. However, instead of drawing a general picture of the average life of the congregations, we would like to shed light on an individual case, such as the lay leader Lisboa Pinto, so as to explore the social relations that he developed in the first ten years after he moved from Bombay to Colombo. Through these relations, one can see into the texture of inter-religious dynamics that have not yet been highlighted in the official Catholic representations of this independent mission.

2.3 Lisboa Pinto and His Social Integration in Colombo

Inside the church of Our Lady of Good Death, there are four grave stelæ, belonging to six Christians who died between 1856 and 1875.[50] Yet many other members of the Portuguese Mission might have been buried on this ground, for the land was first used for interment before a chapel was constructed. Since early on, the Catholic authorities in both Ceylon and Goa imposed restrictions on burials of the schismatic members as an efficient measure to isolate them from other Catholics. In 1898 Lisboa Pinto was buried in the general cemetery at Borella, which until today has a clear division between the Catholic, the Protestant, and other Christian graves. In 1929 Alvares was buried in the Catholic church of Saint Ines in Panjim, but at the margins of the cemetery. It is not surprising that the local Catholic Church

---

46 It was spelt as "Pramjee" in "For sale" (*The Independent Catholic*, April 1892), 4.
47 On Framjee Bhikhajee and Company see J. HINNELLS / A. WILLIAMS (eds.), *Parsis in India and the Diaspora* (London / New York 2007), 190. For a general description of the Parsi merchants in British Ceylon see pp. 188–193. Later information on the Framjee Company can be found in STALL CEYLON OBSERVER, *Ferguson's Ceylon Directory for 1944 (eighty-sixth Year)*, revised up to May 1944 (Colombo 1944), 178, 325, & passim.
48 See P.M. LISBOA PINTO, *Alcoholic Drinks or Notes on the Medical, Social, Political and Religious Aspects of the Liquor Question* (Colombo 1895).
49 *The Independent Catholic*, April 1892, 4.
50 See Appendix 2.

intervened in the funerals and burials of the Independent Catholics or their relatives, as will be seen in the case of Lisboa Pinto's brother, who died in Goa in 1892. At the end of October 1892 Lisboa Pinto returned from Colombo to Assagão, Goa, to attend the funeral of his brother Placido Estrocio Lisboa Pinto, who died on 24 October. While staying in Goa, Lisboa Pinto published a letter of gratitude to the attendants, in which he made a satirical expression towards the Patriarch of Goa, who had denied a Roman Catholic funeral to the deceased:

> My gratitude [...] to the Revd. Fathers Pio Ribeiro and Patrocinio Monteiro for their efforts upon the very worthy Patriarch of Goa by virtue of which efforts he forbade the solemn burial and High Mass [sung Mass], because the deceased lodged in his house the Exmo. Bishop Alvares, even though he had been the president of the confraternity in this town until his death.[51]

As the schismatics were intentionally divided from the other authentic Catholics, the Catholic missionaries discouraged all contacts between Catholics and non-Catholics. This can be compared with the results of the research undertaken by the anthropologist Roderich L. Stirrat on the Catholic communities in Pallansena, near Negombo. According to Stirrat, the sense of separateness had an impact on the identity-building of the Catholics, who tended to consider themselves as an autonomous social entity in Sri Lanka. In contrast, the majoritarian religious groups – Buddhists and Hindus – were seen as "heathens", while Muslims were perceived as an Old Testament religious expression.[52] This was however not the case with the Independent Catholic congregation in Hultsdorp. We will see now how its relation with Muslims had different aspects.

As we have already seen, Pedro Manuel Lisboa Pinto was born in 1857 in Assagão, in the district of Bardez in northern Goa.[53] During his trip to Europe in 1887, he was elected a member of the Society of Geography of Lisbon. Since he moved to Colombo in 1888, he became affiliated with a number of academic institutes in Colombo, including the Royal Asiatic Society and the British Medical Association. Lisboa Pinto was certainly considered one of the most prominent Goan figures in Ceylon. In September 1893 he, together with Alvares and Mar Dionysius, received the chivalric title of Knight of the Order of the Crown of Thorns from Prince-Abbot of the Abbey- Principality of San Luigi.[54]

In the evening of 1 October 1898, birthday candles were lit in a new residence named after "St Luke", in Silversmith Street, Hultsdorf. On that occasion was celebrated the forty-one-year birthday of the house owner Dr. Lisboa Pinto. A big number of Ceylonese friends, colleagues and patients gathered at the party, eager to present gifts in gratitude for the ten-year medical service received from the Goan doctor since his first entry to the island.[55] The guest list published in the newspaper *The Ceylon Independent* in the following week revealed a noticeable "Moorish" presence in the evening at St Luke's, in addition to the names of guests with other ethnic and religious backgrounds, such as the Burghers and the Sinhalese.

---

51 "Agradecimentos" (*O Anglo-Lusitano*, 2 February 1893), 4: "aos revds. padres Pio Ribeiro e Patrocinio Monteiro pelos seus esforços junto do mui digno Patriarcha de Goa em virtude dos quaes este prohibiu enteramento solemne e missa cantada, porque o funado -que era presidente da confraria d'esta aldea até o dia do seu decesso- déra agazalheu em sua casa ao exmo. bispo Alvares...".
52 R.L. STIRRAT, *Power and Religiosity in a Post-Colonial Setting*. Sinhala Catholics in Contemporary Sri Lanka (Cambridge 1992), 14.
53 F.X. GOMES CATÃO, "Aldeia de Assagão (Goa). Subsídios para a sua história" (*Studia: Revista Semestral* 40, 1978, 279–347), 342.
54 "The Lisboa Pinto testimonial and dance" (*The Independent Catholic*, September 1893), 2.
55 This party was announced in advance as "Local & General News" (*Supplement to The Ceylon Independent*, Saturday 23 September 1898).

This circumstance suggests that a rather amicable circle of clients surrounded Lisboa Pinto, but also that a potential network of Independent Catholics gravitated to the neighbourhood of the Church of Our Lady of Good Death.

> The guests commenced to arrive from 8:30, and spent some time inspecting the Doctor's new residence and the numerous presents. After the visitors had been treated to cake and wine, Mr. Emmanuel Jayawardene, Proctor read the following address: Chevalier Dr. P.M. Lisboa Pinto, Knight of the Order of the Crown of Thorns, F.E.A., M.R.A.S., &c. &c.[56]
> Dear Doctor. -Permit us your friends and patients, to take this opportunity of your entering your new residence, to express to you our warm and grateful appreciation of the many and useful services you have rendered us.
> [...] At this stage Mr. A. C. A. Latiff, a well-known member of the Moorish Community, handed the Doctor a silk bag containing a substantial sum of money. The Doctor, who was visibly affected, said that it was very gratifying to see that at the end of ten years of labours, those labours had been appreciated. The life of a physician was no bed of roses, but it was more than a recompense to find so large a gathering present. It amply compensated for all the thorns that he had had to bear. It was really very pleasing to him to think that he should enter into this new residence under such auspicious circumstances. He concluded by thanking those friends who were kind enough to make him that very generous and substantial gift. Dancing followed, and a programme of twelve dances was gone through till midnight, the Lancashire Band supplying the music.[57]

As the newspaper itself observed, in the list of over sixty guests at St Luke's there were "prominent members of the moorish community".[58] In fact, 38 names reflected a Muslim origin. Even though the identity of each Muslim guest at the party is still unattainable, at least "the Turkish Consul" can be identified. He was Abdul Madjid Effendi (spelled also as Abdul Majeed), who served as Honorary Consul of the Ottoman Empire in Ceylon between 1891 and 1903. His father Hussain Lebbe Marikkar had been the first Honorary Consul, serving since 1864.[59] The presence of the Turkish Consul was significant in the first place, as Abdul Madjid Effendi belonged to a Muslim family so prominent that it had been considered worthy of representing the Sublime Porte in Ceylon. A further possibility to be explored is whether Lisboa Pinto and the Consul had occasions of discussing Ottoman affairs of potential interest to the physician, such as the activities of the various Orthodox Churches subject to the Caliph.

Lisboa Pinto was highly active in the intellectual circle, giving lectures on science at various academic institutes,[60] while cultivating interests in Ceylon culture and history. For instance, soon after his arrival in Ceylon in 1888, Lisboa Pinto became a member of the Ceylon Branch of the Royal Asiatic Society and Oriental Studies Society, which was established by the British government in 1845 with a purpose to "institute and promote inquiries into the History, Religion, Literature, Art and Natural Philosophy of Ceylon, together with

---

56 It is not yet clear which title the abbreviation of F.E.A. represents. M.R.A.S. stands for: Member of the Royal Asiatic Society.
57 "Dr. and Mrs Pintos at home. Interesting function" (*The Ceylon Independent*, 4 October 1898).
58 See Appendix 1: C.
59 Embassy of Sri Lanka, Ankara, Turkey, "Trading with Sri Lanka", Powerpoint at https://www.adaso.org.tr/Content/WebDosyalar/Sayfalar/Sunumlar/SR%C4%B0%20LANKA%20SUNUMU.pdf (last accessed on 24 March 2022).
60 On his lecture entitled "Leeches and counterirritants as aids to treatments" at the British Medical Association Ceylon Branch, see "Medical" (*The Independent Catholic*, September 1892, 3). On his lecture about electricity given at the School of Agriculture see "Stray thoughts for the month" (*The Independent Catholic*, July 1895), 1.

the Social condition of its present and former inhabitants."[61] The Society played an essential role in the establishment of institutes of public and academic interests, such as the Colombo Museum opened in 1877, and the Department of Archaeology launched in 1890. Since its start, the Society embraced elites and influential figures on the island, while its patron was always the Governor. Each institute published periodicals that were circulated to local schools and colleges, but even to the other British colonies.[62] Lisboa Pinto was able to adapt to the Ceylonese intellectual circles and learned society thanks to his affiliation with the Royal Asiatic Society, whose general meetings he attended regularly.[63] For instance, in a council meeting of the Society held at the Colombo Museum Library in November 1894, Lisboa Pinto attended a lecture given by lawyer and Crown Counsellor Charles Matthew Fernando entitled "The music of the mechanics of Ceylon", followed by a lecture entitled "A half-hour with two ancient Tamil poets" presented by Ponnambalam Coomaraswamy, lawyer and member of the Legislative Council of Ceylon. Lisboa Pinto participated in a discussion on the creole music and dance preserved by the Portuguese-speaking Burghers in Ceylon, the "mechanics":

> Mr. John Ferguson said it would be interesting to know whether the admixture of the native races with the Ceylon Portuguese had introduced a native element into their music.
> Mr. Fernando replied in the negative, and observed that the music was essentially European in character, and had developed among the Portuguese descendants of Ceylon in the same way that what is known as Christy Minstrelsy originated among the Negroes of America.
> [...] Dr. Pinto supported this view [of Fernando], and remarked that some of these tunes were to be heard at Bombay at the present day, and bore a strong affinity to music which he himself had heard at Lisbon.[64]

This was among the earliest scientific discussions on the music and dance of *kaffirinna* (or *kafferina, kafferinha*), *chikotti* (or *chikoti*) and *baila*, recorded at the Society.[65] As Lisboa Pinto observed, the *baila* dance was also popular among the Catholics living in Bombay and along the Konkan coast of India, distinguishing itself from any other Indian local dances. C. M. Fernando observed in his study that some creole-speaking Burghers in the eastern coast of the island preserved Portuguese tunes and ballad fragments from the 16th century.[66]

2.4 Liturgy and Feasts

One of the main concerns of the Ceylon mission was the lack of clergy. For this reason Alvares travelled often to Goa in search of adequate clerics. Some of these men, already ordained as deacons or full priests in the Catholic Church, had to receive a second ordination from the Bishops of the Jacobite Syrian Church in Malabar. The original certificate of Joseph

---

61 R.G.G. OLCOTT GUNASEKERA, "150 Years of The Royal Asiatic Society of Sri Lanka", in: G.P.S. HARISCHANDRA DE SILVA / C.G. URAGODA (eds.), *Sesquicentennial Commemorative Volume of the Royal Asiatic Society of Sri Lanka, 1845–1995* (Colombo 1995), 2.
62 TILAK KULARATNE, *History of Printing and Publishing in Ceylon, 1736–1912* (Dehiwala, Sri Lanka 2006), 168.
63 Lisboa Pinto was present at the meetings in February & August, 1893, and January & July 1894 (*Journal of the Ceylon Branch of the Royal Asiatic Society*, Volume XIII, No. 44–45, 1893–1894), 4, 9, 59, 127, 181.
64 Notes of the discussion were published in the *Journal of the Ceylon Branch of the Royal Asiatic Society*, Volume XIII, No. 44–45, 1893–1894, 202.
65 See this musical tradition in S. ARYARATNE, *Baila Kaffirinna. An Investigation* (Colombo 2001).
66 MCGILVRAY, "The Portuguese Burghers", 335.

Botelho's ordination, issued by the Bishop of Niranam, Geevargese Mar Gregorios (1848–1902), reveals the formality being used for the Goan priests entering the Syrian Church. The document, composed originally in Syriac with the attachment of a notarised English translation, was likely issued on the occasion of a Holy Qurbana celebrated in the Metropolitan Palace in Kottayam on 1 May 1889.

The statement says:

> We hereby certify that, by the power vested in us from God through the mediation of His Holiness Moran Mar Ignatius, Patriarch of the Apostolic Throne of Antioch and all the East; and with the permission of the most Reverend Fathers Simon Mar Athanasius, Delegate of the Patriarch of Antioch, and Joseph Mar Dionysius, Metropolitan of Malabar and President of the Jacobite Syrian Association of Malabar, our Spiritual son Joseph Xavier Botelho was ordained by the Holy Ghost first a Deacon and on this day a complete Priest. May God Almighty grant that his works may be honest, just and pure before men and acceptable before the exalted throne of Divine Majesty. [67]

The name "Simon Mar Athanasius" referred to Kadavil Paulose Mar Athanasius (?–1907), who was the first Metropolitan of the Angamaly Diocese and delegate of the Patriarch of Antioch in India. "Joseph Mar Dionysius" was Geevarghese Dionysius of Vattasseril or Dionysius VI, whose father was called Joseph. Acting as the president of the "Jacobite Syrian Association of Malabar", he was the prelate with direct responsibility over Álvares' mission in Ceylon. Little is known yet about the efforts made by the three Bishops for the promotion of the new mission in Ceylon. For sure the highlight of their ministry in this realm occurred in May 1892, when the three Malabar Bishops arrived in Colombo for the consecration of Vilatte to the episcopal dignity, with approval by the Patriarch of Antioch.

The Syrian Church clearly aimed at creating a Latin branch that would keep its rite intact in the most important ceremony of the new mission. Vilatte's consecration took place at the Cathedral at Hultsdorf on Sunday 29 May 1892. Alvares chanted a High Mass following the Tridentine Latin rite, while "a large and representative gatnering [sic] of ladies and gentlemen, of almost every profession and rank […] witnessed the ceremony in profound silence."[68] The choir sang Gregorian hymns and antiphons. It was reported that Vilatte was moved visibly when the Syrian Bishops imposed their hands upon him and pronounced the solemn "accipe spiritum sanctum". If the record was fully trustworthy, then the three Bishops from Malabar had pronounced the consecration formula in Latin, not in Syriac.

The Ceylonese considered Vilatte's consecration as an important occasion to attack the Roman Catholic authorities. A piece of news appeared in parallel to the consecration in Hultsdorf, reporting on the departure of Władysław Michał Zaleski from Ceylon to Calcutta for his consecration as bishop on 15 May and his appointment as Apostolic Delegate of the East Indies, replacing Andrea Aiuti. The forty-year-old bishop was referred to as "the young gentleman" and his consecration "smells queer".[69] The Archbishop of Colombo Bonjean remained on the island being "nothing less than a Metropolitan, Domestic Prelate to the Pope

---

67 ACCO, *Rubric* 109, Soriani del Malabar Varia (1894–1897)ff. 8009–8010. The Syriac title has been translated into English as "In the name of the Essential Eternal Self-existing Almighty, George Gregorios Bishop of Niranom [sic] etc. Malabar". This certificate was seized by the Archbishop of Goa Antonio Valente, who reported on 4 December 1894 to the Secretary of the Congregation of Propaganda Fide Archbishop Agostino Ciasca on the "schismatic one [Botelho] in Ceylon". Rubric 109. Soriani del Malabar Varia (1894–1897)f. 8007.
68 "News: The Consecration of Mgr. R. Vilatte" *(The Independent Catholic*, May 1892), 3.
69 "The Delegate Archbishop" (*The Independent Catholic*, May 1892), 3.

and Assistant to the Pontifical Throne! He is evidently very fastidious, that Mgr. Zaleski." By contrasting the consecrations of Vilatte and Zaleski, the Independent Catholics aimed at showing the superior spirit of communion and the higher spirituality of the Syrian Orthodox, by whom the episcopal dignity had a special esteem and was conferred with great devotion, not a profane honour.

Both Alvares and Lisboa Pinto promoted their social status on the occasion of Vilatte's consecration. Two days before the ceremony, both leaders attended a reception at the Queen's House.[70] This was one of the three official residences of the Governor of Ceylon, located in Colombo, Kandy, and Nuwara Eliya respectively. The residence in Colombo was built in 1856. Little is known yet on the social activities that took place there, but it may not be impossible that social attention would have been called to the unusual upcoming events in Hultsdorf, as people would have probably been curious about the episcopal consecration of a French Latin priest by three Indian bishops of the Syrian Orthodox Church. The presence of Alvares and Lisboa Pinto at a reception at the Governor's House might be understood as an acknowledgement of the social status achieved by the Independent Catholic community, as well as an attempt on their side to increase and secure their public standing among the elites of Colombo.

It is not yet clear to what extent the Independent Catholics followed the Syrian liturgical calendar. According to *The Independent Catholic* circulated between 1892 and 1893, the Colombo congregation celebrated Easter and Christmas with greatest solemnity. The most characteristic feast was celebrated on 13 or 14 August in honour of Our Lady of Good Death, after which the Cathedral was named.[71] Let us compare the formula of this feast as reported in 1892 and 1893:

> 1892: The novenas commence on the 5th [of August]. Solemn vespers will be chanted on Saturday the 13th, 8 pm, and there will be High Mass at 8 am, on Sunday. The sermon will be preached by the Rev. Vicar [de Souza].[72]
>
> 1893: The Novenas in the Independent Catholic Cathedral commence on the 4th of August, the feast taking place on Sunday the 13th. Every evening there will be Rosary, solemn Salve Regina, Sermon in Portuguese and Benediction, commencing at 7:30. The service will be alternatively in English, Portuguese and Sinhalese. Solemn Vespers, 12th August, 8 pm. High Mass Sermon in English, Procession, Benediction on Sunday 9 am. Procession to the Sepulchre, Sunday evening 8 o'clock.[73]

The three languages used for Mass – English, Portuguese, and Sinhala – suggest that there must have been a considerable number of Sinhala speaking Christians in the Colombo congregation, who might not have been able to converse in the two European languages. No record from the sources in the early 1890s has shown that the Goan priests were fluent in Sinhala.

---

70 "Independent Catholics at the Leyee [sic]" (*The Independent Catholic*, May 1892), 3.
71 "Portuguese-speaking Catholics have a history of familiarity with Nossa Senhora da Boa Morte. In Portugal, brotherhoods of Our Lady of the Good Death go back to the seventeenth century". D. RANCOUR-LAFERRIERE, *Imagining Mary. A Psychoanalytic Perspective on Devotion to the Virgin Mother of God*, (New York 2018), 291. It seems that the precise date of the feast was the second Sunday of August, always occurring just before the Solemnity of the Assumption of Mary on 15 August.
72 *The Independent Catholic*, July 1892, 3.
73 *The Independent Catholic*, August 1893, 3.

2.5 Rivalry With the "Romanists"

The Independent Catholics defined their adversaries as "Romanists", never as "Catholics". The motto of their official periodical declared that the latter was "in the interests of True Catholicism", implying a separation between Romanists and real Catholics, a category under which they obviously classified themselves. In their opinion the real Catholics could not be related to Rome, and they even declared that they were very much irritated if ever one called them "Roman".[74] The Romanists included the Pope, the missionaries of Propaganda Fide, as well as anyone that might be against the Portuguese royal patronage, as for instance the Jesuits[75]. Among the Propagandists, the two prelates Bonjean and Zaleski received most criticism from the Cathedral of Our Lady of Good Death.

Bonjean, whose French compatriots were mocked as "Romanists but not Catholics",[76] had the fiercest debates with the Independent Catholics in the public sphere, fulminating multiple excommunications against the Independent priests and laymen. Various Missionary Oblates of Mary Immaculate also joined their confrere Archbishop Bonjean in a polemical endeavour against the schismatics. Charles Collin (1840–1910) was one of the Oblates who was particularly concerned by the Independent Catholics.

We can find a trace of Bonjean's polemical activity in the quotation of a pseudonymous text of his, reported in an anonymous publication of his adversaries. In the pamphlet entitled *The Church Militant in Ceylon and in India: Audi Alteram Partem*, apparently published by the Independent Catholics, a strong criticism was raised against the Propagandists and their statements on the *Messenger*, the official journal of the Roman Catholic Church in Ceylon.[77] The Independent Catholic author described in the following terms the way his Roman Catholic adversary had attacked both the Syrian Church and Alvares:

> The writer spins a yarn about Syrian belief, – a really nice yarn with hardly a word of truth in it. If that is all that these people know of the Syrian church, well...... we live to learn! "By the strong family resemblance," one would suppose the same father had begotten the two: - viz: the Syrian church yarn and the other yarn about Father Álvares being a married man, having his wife and children in India, and having donned on a cassock just to come to Ceylon! *Credite posteri*![78]

Against the Roman Catholic attacks even on the press, the Independent Catholics published satires and comic anecdotes in their periodicals, mocking both Bonjean and Zaleski. A noticeable account was published under the title "Zaleski's window".[79] We have also previously

---

74 "Impotent rage" (*The Independent Catholic*, May 1892), 3.
75 It should be noticed that the Old Society of Jesus, before the suppressions in the second half of the eighteenth century, had been very closely related to Portugal and its *Padroado*. In fact, the Jesuits had been a major pillar in the Portuguese ecclesiastical jurisdiction in the East. The situation changed slightly only when French Jesuits entered Asia in the late seventeenth century, for instance establishing the Carnatic mission from their base in Pondichéry. A useful introduction into the relation of the Society of Jesus with Portugal is provided by D. ALDEN, *The Making of an Enterprise. The Society of Jesus in Portugal, Its Empire, and Beyond 1540–1750* (Stanford 1996).
76 "Impotent rage" (*The Independent Catholic*, May 1892), 3.
77 Born in Poitiers, Charles Collins came to Jaffna with his brother Jules Collins (1850-?) in 1877. He was a loyal supporter of Bonjean who ordained him in 1880. Collins worked as Vicar General, administrator of the College of Colombo and was involved in many religious associations. He also wrote numerous articles for journals. See P. DUSCHAUSSOIS, *Sous les feux de Ceylan. Chez les Singhalais et les Tamouls* (Paris 1929), 131–136.
78 A CATHOLIC, *The Church Militant in Ceylon and in India*. Audi Alteram Partem (Colombo, 1888), 15–16.
79 "Mgr. Zaleski jumps through a window!" (*The Independent Catholic*, May 1892), 2–3.

seen how Zaleski was mocked as a "young gentleman", very fastidious and whose episcopal consecration "smell[ed] queer".[80]

3. Decline

3.1 Complaints Against Alvares

The last stay of Alvares in Colombo was in 1904. In 1905 he left his Cathedral for the last time and sailed out to Kottayam. His rare presence on the island and frequent trips to the missions in India had already triggered discontent in the Colombo congregation. In the report to the Patriarch of Antioch Ignatius Messias, the Independent Ceylonese complained against their Bishop for several reasons. First of all, financial tensions rose up after the episcopal consecration of Vilatte in May 1892, leading to an open strife between Alvares and Lisboa Pinto, each of whom freely used "altar and the pulpit" to "discuss the pros and cons of this unfortunate difference".[81] Secondly, after seeing the acrimony in Colombo, Alvares left for Goa in May 1893 where he started a Portuguese weekly entitled *O Brado indiano: Semanario político, industrial e agricolo* (circulation from December 1894 to May 1895) "mostly relating to politics, which in no way helped our Mission". For this reason, the Ceylon congregation refused to continue to provide funding for Alvares' activities. Thirdly, Alvares refused to intervene in the crisis of the Mannar mission, when five of the churches there returned to the Roman Catholic Church. Instead Alvares was focused on his trip from Colombo to India, allegedly "for no reason whatever except perhaps to start his Press."[82] Fourthly, Alvares was too old for active work. As a consequence, the Ceylon Mission was at risk of losing its members to the Roman Catholics. At the end of the report, the Colombo congregation begged that someone should be sent from Malabar to Colombo to investigate the precarious situation of the Mission.

3.2 Demands of Priests

According to the Ceylon census of 1901, the total number of the Independent Catholics amounted to just 1,718 individuals, in comparison to 287,419 Roman Catholics and 60,102 Protestants.[83] The fact that the Independent Catholics in the island were then equal to 0.59 percent of the Roman Catholic population marked a clear difference from the experience of the *Iglesia Filipina Independiente*, a contemporaneous independent Catholic movement in

---

80 "The young gentleman went to Calcutta for his consecration." in "The delegate Archbishop" (*The Independent Catholic*, May 1892), 3.
81 "To His Holiness Ignatius A. Messias, Patriarch of Antioch and the East", dated in Colombo, November 10, 1900. See footnote 26.
82 "To His Holiness Ignatius A. Messias, Patriarch of Antioch and the East", dated in Colombo, November 10, 1900.
83 J. FERGUSON, *Ceylon in 1903*. Describing the Progress of the Island Since 1803, Its Present Agricultural and Commercial Enterprises, and Its Unequalled Attractions to Visitors, with Useful Statistical Information (Colombo 1903), xlvii.

the Philippines, that might have encompassed 25 percent of the entire Philippine population at approximately the same time.[84]

Between 1892 and 1900 Mar Julius travelled constantly to Independent missions along the Konkan coast and around Madurai. In June 1900 Alvares returned from his trip in India to Colombo. By that time the Independent Catholics had witnessed the loss of three leading members. First of all, Lisboa Pinto had died of a heart attack in 1898.[85] Subsequently Fr. Luis Mariano Soares (c.1858–1903), Vicar of Mar Julius, who under the name of Mar Baselios had become a bishop of the Chaldean Syrian Church of the East in 1899, died of cholera in the village of Muttalapatty (possibly today's Muthanampatti) near Dindigul in July 1903.[86] Thirdly, in 1899 Joseph René Vilatte (1854–1929) had visited Rome and sought reconciliation with the Roman Catholic Church. No agreement was found at the time (it eventually happened only in 1925), but Vilatte's attitude deeply disappointed Mar Julius, who had consecrated the turbulent Frenchman together with Mar Gregorios of Parumala (1848–1902) and Mar Anathasius Paolus in the Cathedral of Buona Morte in May 1892.

Between June and July 1900, the community at Our Lady of Good Death wrote at least two letters to Fr. Zeferino Roque Noronha (1850–1936), vicar of Mar Julius at Kallianpur, trying to persuade him to accept the consecration as Bishop of the Jacobite Church. Noronha declined the offer, for reasons that are not yet clear.[87] At any rate, this decision possibly had an impact on the growth of the Independent Catholic community, which needed bishops so as to ensure a regular flow of priestly ordinations. The scarcity of clergy was a severe problem, hence Stephen de Silva sent letters to different Orthodox churches asking for priests. One letter reached the Archimandrite Germanos Kazakis, head of the Greek Orthodox Church in Calcutta, established for Greek merchants who came to Bengal as early as in the seventeenth century. The original letter has not yet been found, but from a review of it published in 1904 in *Échos d'Orient*, a journal dedicated to Greek Christianity and Byzantine studies, we can glean details on the impressions that contemporary Greek Orthodox Christians could have had of the Independent Catholics.[88] According to the author, the Church under the leadership of Lisboa Pinto and Alvares denied three dogmas of the Roman Catholic Church, namely *Filioque*, Papal infallibility, and the Immaculate Conception. However, they retained a substantial Roman legacy both in doctrine and liturgy: they believed in Purgatory, practiced baptism by infusion (instead of immersion), used azyme bread for the Eucharist, gave communion only under one species to the laymen, maintained that clerical celibacy was compulsory, and decorated their churches with statues. All these aspects were highlighted by the French Orientalist Georges Bartas for being some of the major differences that divided the Catholic and Orthodox Churches, and as traits that, from an Orthodox perspective, could appear as innovations brought in by "Papism".[89]

---

84 P.-B. SMIT, *Old Catholic and Philippine Independent Ecclesiologies in History*. The Catholic Church in Every Place (Leiden / Boston 2011), 147.

85 "Sudden death of Dr. Lisboa Pinto" (*The Ceylon Independent*, 20 October 1898).

86 SUSAN BAYLY, *Saints, Goddesses and Kings*. Muslims and Christians in South Indian Society, 1700–1900 (Cambridge 2003), 449–452; See *The Tablet*, 15 August 1903, 248.

87 A document in a private collection in Brahmavar, Antonio Francisco Xavier Álvares Mar Julius to Zeferino Roque Noronha, Colombo, 24 July 1900, with 25 signatures.

88 *Échos d'Orient* was created at the Institut de Kadiköy, an institute established in Turkey in 1895 by Leo XIII for the education of indigenous clergymen from the Ottoman Empire, as well as for calling the Greek and Bulgarian Christians to "return" to the Roman Catholic Church. A. FAILLER, "Le centenaire de l'Institut byzantin des Assomptionnistes" (*Revue des études byzantines* 53/1, 1995), 6.

89 G. BARTAS, "Coup d'oeil sur l'Orient gréco-slave" (*Échos d'Orient* 7/49, 1904, 366–372), 371–372.

Eventually the Greek Orthodox did not support the community of Ceylon, whose desperation led to appeals in all directions. Therefore, in 1902 Stephen de Silva established a first contact with the *Iglesia Filipina Independiente*, after having learnt from "an American Magazine" about the progress of that church in Manila:

> We, who are at present called the Independent Catholics of Ceylon [...] find [it] difficult to continue in this state for we cannot get sufficient priests to work independent of Rome. Will your Lordship be able to send us two priests intelligent and good in their moral conduct. [sic] Most of our people speak Portuguese and if you can send one or two Spanish priests here will be very good as we could easily understand them.[90]

Eventually no assistance came even from the Philippines and the Independent Catholics of Ceylon had to rely on the limited forces of the Jacobite Church and later on, from 1912, of the Malankara Orthodox Church. In 1941 the Goan Fr. Joseph D'Mello left Ceylon and the Independent Catholics ended up being without any priests. Deprived of sacraments and in a context quite different from the one of the nineteenth century, the Independent Catholic community faded away, mostly reabsorbed by the Roman Catholic Church. At a micro-level, the neighborhood of Hultsdorf experienced a demographic shift, with the Muslims replacing the Christian inhabitants.

3.3 Last Days in the Twentieth Century

Statistics published in 1936 about the consistency of all Christian denominations in Ceylon show the position of the Independent Catholic Church in the Christian panorama of the island. It was the smallest denomination with only one church. Among all the minority denominations who possessed less than 10 churches, one could find the Church of Scotland with 2 churches, whereas Ceylon and India General Mission, the Friends' Mission, and the Seventh Day Adventists' Mission had 6 churches each. The largest Christian community in the whole of Ceylon was the Roman Catholic Church. With its 803 churches it represented more than half of all the 1,372 Christian places of worship on the entire island.[91]

---

90 Stephen de Silva to Gregorio Aglipay, 23 April 1903. From A. HERMANN, "Transregional Contacts between Independent Catholic Churches in Asia around 1900. The Case of the *Iglesia Filipina Independiente* and the *Independent Catholics of Ceylon*", in: C. BURLACIOIU / A. HERMANN (eds.), *Veränderte Landkarten auf dem Weg zu einer polyzentrischen Geschichte des Weltchristentums*. Festschrift für Klaus Koschorke zum 65. Geburtstag (Wiesbaden 2015), 144.

91 C. BROOKE ELLIOTT, *The Real Ceylon*. New Edition with Many Illustrations (New Delhi 2005), 128.

Chapter 6:
India: Indian Representations of the Independent Catholic Mission in Ceylon

Born in Verná, a village in the Goan peninsula of Salcete in 1836, Antonio Francisco Xavier Alvares was trained and ordained as a Roman Catholic priest. Until his fifties he ministered under the *Padroado Real* and worked as chief editor of *A Cruz*, the major newspaper of the Archdiocese of Goa since the mid-19th century. However, because of a conflict with the Archbishop of Goa and Patriarch of India, António Sebastião Valente (1846–1908), Alvares was removed from his position in the Archdiocese and excommunicated in 1882. In the next five years he allied with the *Padroadists* in Goa and in Bombay and co-organised a petition to Rome in 1886. The failure of the plan led to a decisive break from the Catholic Church. Alvares joined the Syrian Orthodox Church of Antioch in Malabar in 1887, and was consecrated as Mar Julius I, Archbishop of Ceylon, Goa, and India, excluding Malabar, in 1889. From 1888 to the end of his life in 1923 Mar Julius was active in missionary work, bringing the dissatisfied Catholics who were part of the "Goan schism" into the Syrian Orthodox Church, giving them a new identity as Independent Catholics.

In recent years, Alvares has been interpreted by historians mainly as the result of the awakened national identity shared by generations of Goan intellectuals fighting for liberation from the Portuguese colonial power. However, Alvares' unprecedented spiritual transformation from Roman Catholicism to Syrian Orthodoxy has not been studied thoroughly or analysed yet in his own words and expressions. A reason for such an omission is the precarious physical conservation of the newspapers he edited. Thanks to my recent digitization of Alvares' literary works, I can present here a first step towards a close reading of his spiritual reflections, intellectual pursuits, and social-political observations explained in his own journals such as *A Cruz* (1879–1882), *A Verdade* (1882–1885), *The Times of Goa* (1885), and *O Brado Indiano* (1894–1895). The first three newspapers were edited during the years in which Alvares was excommunicated and stranded in social and religious isolation. His fierce criticism of the colonial authority, his satires against the Jesuits, and his mockery of the Church hierarchy, as well as his anxiety of reformation deserve a careful examination in comparison with his later articles in *O Brado Indiano*, published after he found consolation in the Syrian Orthodox Church. The four periodicals, published from 1879 to 1895, contained precious ego-documents recording Alvares' continued evolution. With few exceptions, Alvares edited his newspapers mainly in Portuguese, targeting the *Padroado* Christians and the intellectual milieu of the Portuguese *Estado da Índia*. His periodicals were in frequent interaction with other Lusophone journals in Goa and Bombay such as *O Ultramar* and *O Anglo-Lusitano*, whose editors adamantly supported his ecclesiastical movement and approved of his conversion.

This chapter aims not at a general narrative of the various Independent Catholic Missions in India nor at a biography of Alvares, but will rather focus on the various reactions and perceptions of the Catholic authorities, intellectuals, and missionaries in India concerning the Ceylon Mission led by this Goan priest. In the first place, I review the research literature on the biography of Alvares, initially as a Catholic priest, then as an excommunicated journalist, in the five years that preceded his joining of the Jacobite Church. This section contributes to the existing literature on his biography with some recent discoveries at archives in Europe and India, so as to question again the reasons for his break with the Roman Catholic Church. Secondly, we move to the Indian Catholic representations of the Ceylon Independent Catholic Mission from two perspectives. On the one hand the Goan civil authorities deemed Alvares an ally of a rebellious group in Goa and for this reason put him in jail in 1895. On the other hand, the former pro-*Padroadist* newspapers in Bombay and Goa expressed sympathy for the schismatic group in Ceylon, but also disagreed about the fundamental points on the obedience to the papacy. Thirdly, I briefly examine the Independent Catholic missions in Madurai, as depicted in Jesuit sources.

1. Alvares: An Indian Prelude

1.1 The Unruly Alvares Before 1877

In 1988, the journalist Carmo Azevedo, responding to a request presented by the Syrian Orthodox communities, published the first English biography of the Goan cleric, entitled *Patriot and Saint*. In the book, the presence of Alvares in Goa as an educator, social worker, journalist, revolutionary, and political activist, was well contextualized in the social and intellectual history of the Portuguese colony.[1] Being an eyewitness, Azevedo narrated the last decades of Alvares' life and his funeral in Panjim with a particular poignancy. Pratima Kamat has so far provided the best analysis of Alvares' political vision. He was not only a leading native cleric resisting the colonial power, but also a major supporter of *swadeshi* ideology.[2] George Kurian, member of the St Mary's Church in Ribandar, Goa, made a contribution to the reconstruction of the genealogy of Alvares and his family from Verná, which helps to clarify the support networks that Alvares established throughout his ecclesiastical enterprise.[3] Newspaper clips on the funeral and in memory of Alvares prove convincingly that the social impact of this historical figure on Goan society was substantial. There are also two biographies in Kannada and Malayalam authored by K.T. Varghese and D. Mathew, respectively.[4] The public media outlet run by the Syrian Orthodox communities in Brahmavar today

---

1   C. AZEVEDO, *Patriot & Saint. The Life Story of Father Alvares/Bishop Mar Julius I* (Panjim 1988). An earlier eulogiative biography in Portuguese is the one by G. CAETANO, *Homenagem ao Pe. A. F. X. Alvares, suas notas biográficas* (Margao 1927). A brief bio-bibliography is available in A.M. DA COSTA, *Dicionário de literatura goesa*. Vol. 1 (Macau 1998), 48–49.
2   P. KAMAT, *Farar Far (Crossfire). Local Resistance to Colonial Hegemony in Goa, 1510–1912*, (Panaji 1999), 140–156; P. KAMAT, "'The Indian Cry' (O Brado Indiano) of Padre António Alvares: 'Swadeshi' or 'seditious'?" (*Indian Church History Review* 46/1, June 2012, 69–91); P. KAMAT, "The Goa-Ceylon Religious Connection. A Review of the 'The Indian Cry' of Alvares Mar Julius, Archbishop of Ceylon, Goa and India" (*Sabaragamuwa University Journal* 12/1, December 2013, 61–82); T.R. DE SOUZA, "Christianization and cultural conflict in Goa, 16th–19th centuries", in: *Congresso Internacional de História Missionação Portuguesa e Encontro de Culturas*. Actas. Vol. 4: Missionação: Problemática Geral e Sociedade Contemporânea (Braga 1993), 392–393.
3   GEORGE K. KURIAN, *Saint Alvares Mar Julius* (Ribandar, Panaji, Goa 2013).
4   From personal communication with Fr. David Crasta, MOSC Vicar in Brahmavar.

is named after Mar Alvares. Apart from live streaming events in the Cathedral and parishes, this organization also produced an informative English documentary entitled *A Forgotten Saint – A Documentary on the Life of Alvares Mar Julius*, including historical footage and interviews with members of the Alvares family.[5]

Even though path-breaking transformations took place in his 40s, the missionary aspiration and the unruly nature of Alvares surfaced as early as in his mid-30s,[6] during which he was inspired by the movements of apostolic life led by Goan clerics such as the secular priest Custodio de Rosario Caetano Barreto. In 1873 Barreto founded a new organisation, the Association of the Missionaries (1873–1883), devoted to the evangelization of the people subject to the Portuguese jurisdiction of the New Conquests, namely the territories acquired by the Lusitan crown only in the second half of the eighteenth century. In the company of Alvares and the layman Francisco Antonio D'Costa, Barreto came to settle in an old house in Uguem (South Goa) with the hope of transforming it into a new mission station. Despite the demanding chores for this establishment, Alvares was distracted by "letter writing" (it is not clear yet to whom), an activity perceived by Barreto as not related to the tasks of the Association. Furthermore, in the evenings Alvares would take a walk and return home only at 10 pm. Barreto was not pleased by Alvares' independent behaviour and set up a Statute regulating the newly founded small community in Uguem. Alvares refused to accept it, hence the small community split up and Fr. Barreto and D'Costa moved away to join another missionary society, called *Sociedade Patriotica,* and set up a new mission in the Village of Paroda. Alvares was left alone in Uguem and soon abandoned the Association of the Missionaries. Later in 1877, new members joined the group, and among the new recruits was Joseph Mariano Clemente Bento Martins, future founder of the Society of the Missionaries of St. Francis Xavier, also known as the Pilar Society.[7] After leaving the Association, Alvares came to Panjim and set up the *Associação de Caridade de Pangim*, providing help to the destitute and the poor.[8] A charitable College in honour of the *Sagrados Corações de Jesus e Maria* was then established in 1877. In the same year Alvares was entrusted with the editorial care of the newspaper of the Archdiocese of Goa, *A Cruz*. In the following years his commitment to social work in Panjim, and his intellectual engagement in the weekly newspaper exposed Alvares to a serious conflict, once again, with the person who was his superior in that moment. However, this discord became much worse than the one with the Association from which the Pilar Society emerged.

The bifurcating paths chosen by Barreto and Martins on the one hand, and by Alvares on the other during the 1870s, reveal some features of the Indian clergymen in the last quarter of the nineteenth century that deserve further studies. Despite their discords, all three priests expressed a grassroot apostolic ambition, born out of their own independent initiative rather than deriving from the command line of the Church hierarchy. The pioneers of the Pilar Society were moved by the lack of pastoral work in the Goan "New Conquests", populated by "pagans" (i.e. Hindus) and attracting lapsed runaway Christians. They committed themselves to fortify and expand the Catholic Church in marginal and neglected areas. On the contrary,

---

5 "A Forgotten Saint – A documentary on the life of Alvares Mar Julius (English)", directed by Viji Varghese with the support of Mar Julius Youth Movement for St Mary's Orthodox church (https://youtu.be/apGFkMooY3U, last accessed on 22 January 2019).
6 Personal communication from Father David Crasta, MOSC Vicar in Brahmavar.
7 GOMES CATÃO, *History of the Old and Reorganised Society*, unpublished. I am grateful to Father Cosme Jose Costa SFX for sharing this precious document with me.
8 AZEVEDO, *Patriot and Saint*, 20–21.

in that period Alvares attended to urban social demands, and especially engaged with the Goan Catholic educated groups and elites, promoting the circulation of knowledge and new ideas. In the meantime, the efforts of Barreto and Martins in the "New Conquests" led to the establishment of the Society of the Missionaries of St. Francis Xavier as an indigenous religious association, still within the Diocesan jurisdiction. Alvares, however, initially aiming at addressing problems within the Church, such as the abuse of power allegedly exerted by the Goan Archbishop, chose again not to surrender to the authority, but to stick to what he believed to be true in faith and in matters of ecclesiastical jurisdiction.

1.2 Conflicts With the Archbishop of Goa From 1877 to 1882

Soon after the crisis triggered by the Brief *Multa Præclare* in 1838, the Goan clergy started to publish a newspaper for the defense of the *Padroado* and other religious interests. Hence, the *Jornal da Santa Igreja Lusitana do Oriente* was published in 1844–1845.[9] Between 1867 and 1870, the Goan Church historian Casimiro Cristovão de Nazareth (1830–1928) was in charge of *O Oriente Catholico*, a fortnightly published under the aegis of the Archbishopric of Goa.[10] After the cessation of this journal in 1870, a religious weekly (*semanario religioso*) was promoted by the Archdiocese. This newspaper, the only ecclesiastical one published in Goa, now bore the name of *A Cruz*. The first issue appeared on 15 July 1876, finding inspiration in the motto of the Carthusian Order founded by Bruno von Köln (1027?–1101) in 1084: *Stat crux dum volvitur orbis,* i.e. *"the Cross is steady while the world is turning",* which was inscribed beneath the emblem of a Crucifix. This motto had been widely adopted by Spanish and Portuguese noble families in their coats of arms during the sixteenth and seventeenth centuries.[11]

> This journal, aspiring to be a firmly standing cross, aimed to shed light on various assumptions concerning Christianity and its discipline and regime. It is to publish what has happened and what has been written on it. It attends to a diversity of questions that occurred and have been discussed upon in the motherland and in other Catholic countries. It extends to all ends of this country, from the clergy to the last layman, from the first society to the last sphere, so that the interests of our faith remain unscathed from the hands of the enemies and pure from corruption […].[12]

---

9   EXPECTAÇÃO BARRETO, *Quadros Biographicos dos Padres Illustres de Goa*. Estudos do Padre Expectação Barreto (Bastorá 1899), 161.
10 F.J. XAVIER, *Breve noticia da Imprensa Nacional de Goa, seguida de um catalogo das obras e escriptos publicados pela mesma Imprensa desde a sua fundação* (Nova Goa 1876), 146; A.M. DA CUNHA, "A evolução do Jornalismo na Índia portuguesa", in: *A India Portuguesa*. Vol. 2 (Nova Goa 1923), 537–538.
11 The full sentence was likely "Stat crux dum volvitur orbis, mundo inconcussa supersto", in English "the Cross is steady while the world is turning, and undisturbed I [the Cross] stand upon the world." J. DE VICENTE GONZÁLEZ (ed.), *Antiguas boticas españolas y sus recipientes* (Comba, A Coruña 2009), 249.
12 *A Cruz* no. 1, 15 July 1876. "É pois, para este fim, que alguns eclesiásticos desta archidiocese de Goa pretendem fundar um novo jornal religioso, sob a denominação de SEMANARIO RELIGIOSO DO ARCEBISPADO DE GOA, com o intuito de diffundir luzes sobre vários assumptos, concernentes á religião e á sua disciplina e regímen; dar publicidade do que se passa, e se escreve a este respeito e com relação ás diversas questões, que se suscitam, e se combatem na mãe pátria, e em outros paizes catholicos; e pol-o tudo ao alcance de todos neste paiz, desde o clero, até o ultimo leigo, desde a primeira sociedade, até a sua ultima camada, de maneira que os interesses de nossa religião, incólumes de mão inimiga, e puros sem corrupção, …"

It was in defence of the purity of faith and the integrity of Christianity in the Portuguese empire that *A Cruz* was expected to exercise its influence as the only official newspaper of the Catholics in Goa. However, Alvares' appointment as editor in 1877 proved to be a challenging test for the paper.

Since 1880 the Archdiocese of Goa had become *sede vacante*, as the Archbishop Aires de Ornelas e Vasconcelos (1837–1880) returned to Portugal due to his deteriorating health. From 9 July 1880 on, the Bishop of Angola and Congo, Dom Thomaz Gomes d'Almeida, acted as Auxiliary Bishop in charge of the Archdiocese of Goa.[13] On 4 August 1881 the 35-year-old António Sebastião Valente was appointed by Pope Leo XIII as the new Archbishop of Goa. However, it was only in May 1882 that Valente eventually arrived in India. The start of the monsoon season welcomed Valente with tremendous rains, and as a consequence, petitions from flooded parishes were presented to the Archbishop Palace, requesting prayers that might stop the catastrophe.[14] Upon his arrival, the young Archbishop certainly had minimum time to get to know the 46-year old Goan priest Alvares personally, but must have learnt quickly the polemical character of the editor of the only journal under his episcopal authority.[15] One month after his entry into the Archdiocese, on 26 June 1882, he issued a pastoral letter banning *A Cruz* for these reasons:

> Even though this weekly had been initially approved and supported by Our Venerable Predecessor D. Ayres d' Ornellas e Vasconcellos, later on it was officialy censored by him, who defined it as violent and provocative, because of throwing every day most bitter insults and offences against the supreme authorities, both ecclesiastical and secular [...]. On the contrary, since then it became more audacious and arrogant either by staining in filthy ways and without loyalty the memory of Our illustrious predecessor, who was so sincerely appraised by other press organs of the State, by the good Goan people, and by its pious clergy (see the n° 144, 149, 193, and many others); either by defaming and slandering the various ecclesiastical authorities, and by consequence blowing a spirit of rebellion in the faithful subject to the same [authorities]; either lending more dishonourable [*desohradas*, sic] columns to all sort of insults and affronts addressed against whomsoever (See the n° 140, 142, 158, 176, 184, 189, 193 and many others).[16]

The issues of *A Cruz* that were highlighted in the pastoral letter covered the period between 12 November 1880 and 2 December 1881. Curiously, this is a period in which Valente was still in Portugal, while his episcopal appointment was declared only in August 1881.

---

13 *A Cruz* no. 140, 12 November 1880.
14 Archbishop of Goa to the Secretary Fr. Jose Perez Antunes, 13 June 1882, the Archbishop Palace, Goa. Church Archives of Goa (CAG), *Portaria* vol. 13 (1882–1887), 5.
15 M. DE JESUS DOS MÁRTIRES LOPES, "D. António Sebastião Valente. O homem e a obra (1846-1908). Contributo para a sua história", in: A.T. DE MATOS / J. TELES E CUNHA (eds.), *Goa passado e presente*. Vol. 2 (Lisboa 2012), 567–568.
16 CAG, *Portaria*, Vol. 13, 7–8. A letter of Archbishop of Goa to the public, Archbishop Palace, 26 June 1882. "Este semanario, apesar de no seu principio approvado e favorecido por Nosso Venerando antecessor D. Ayres d' Ornellas e Vasconcellos, foi mais tarde por elle oficialmente censurado com os epithetos de violento e incendiário, por lançar cada dia injurias e affrontas amarguíssimas contra as supremas auctoridades quer eclesiásticas, quer seculares, … Ao contrario desde esse tempo cresceu em audácia e arrogância, já maulando torpemente, e sem lealdade a memoria do Nosso ilustre predecessor, objecto dos encómios sinceros do resto da imprensa do Estado, dos carinhos do bom povo Goanense, e de seu piedoso clero (Veja os N°ˢ 144-149-193 e outros muitos.), já diffamando, e calumniando as diversas auctoridades eclesiásticas, e por consequência insustando o espirito de revolta nos fieis sujectos as mesmas, já prestando mas desohradas columnas a toda a espécie de insultos, e doestos dirigidos contra quem quer que fosse (Veja os N°ˢ 140-142-158-176-184-189-193, e outros muitos)."

Was it possible that Valente had already read *A Cruz* well before his appointment and before his departure from Portugal? How did the Archbishop, who had just arrived in Goa and was still struggling to adjust to a different climate, mature his decision of censoring the newspaper, having just one month to examine the previous 82 issues, from n° 140 to n° 222? Such a rapid assessment appears miraculous, also considering that in that specific moment life in Goa was made difficult by an unusually strong monsoon.[17]

In the four-folio sized weekly, editorials and commentaries occupied more than half of the content of each issue, reducing domestic and external news to several brief columns. Almost no advertisements were published except one by a bookshop in Bombay, the Livraria Furtado in Kalbadavia Road. In the issues cited by the new Archbishop, *A Cruz* had actually expressed a concern against the liberal and anti-clerical influence of Freemasonry in Europe and India. For such a concern against ideological adversaries of the Catholic Church, Mons. Valente should have actually praised *A Cruz*.

In examining the issues 140, 142, 158, 176, 184, 189, and 193 it has not yet been possible to find which articles were seen as containing inappropriate expressions or attacking the late Archbishop Ornelas. On the contrary, a special Latin prayer dedicated to him and entitled *Oremus pro Antistite Nostro Ayre* appeared in each issue of the newspaper for one year and a half, until April 1882. A special supplement was even published by *A Cruz*, collecting all condolence letters received from all parts of India on the occasion of the death of the Archbishop.

Despite these expressions of devotion to the late Ornelas, Valente wrote to the governor of Goa so as to cooperate in the marginalization of Alvares:

> I am to inform You that the priest Antonio Francisco Xavier Alvares, ex-editor of the periodical *A Cruz*, is now suspended from all his services. In this letter I inform you that the referred Fr. Alvares has been the Chaplain of the Prison [*capellão da cadea*]. I advise Your Excellency not to accept in any place any priest who is indicated by Fr. Alvares. If Your Excellency has no facility of finding an appropriate candidate for this job, I can suggest one.[18]

The concern for a potential revolt and the suspicion of Alvares' influence on dangerous people detained in prison continued until 1895, when Alvares was put under arrest for sedition, at a time during which the colonial authorities feared a conspiracy against the European authorities. Names of prominent Goans were listed as possible conspirators.[19] These lists even included figures such as José António Ismael Gracias (1857–1919), a high ranking government officer (*Official-maior da Secreteria do Governo*) and renowned historian.[20]

However, it is necessary to notice the tension between State and Church, as well as between the metropolis and the colony, in such a heavy handling of the printing press of Goa. The brutal decision of banning *A Cruz* failed at convincing the authorities in Lisbon, so that

---

17 CAG, *Portaria*, Vol. 13, page 5. Valente to the Secretary Monsenhor José Peres Antunes, dated in Paço Archiepiscopal de Nova Goa, on 13 June 1882.
18 "Archbishop of Goa to the Governor of Goa", dated 19 July 1882 (*A Verdade*, 24 July 1882), page 3. "Illmo. e Exmo. Sr. – Cumpre-me participar a V. Ex.a que o presbytero Antonio Fracisco Xavier Alvares, ex redactor do periódico a 'Cruz', se acha suspenso do exercicio de todas as suas ordens. Faço esta participação a V. Ex.a por saber que o referido pe. Alvares tem sido capelão da cadea; peço a V. Ex.a não aceite para este lugar nenhum presbytero indicado pelo mesmo pe. Alvares. Se V. Ex.a não tiver facilidade em encontrar quem seja idoneo, poderei eu indicar algun."
19 S. COELHO, Uma *pagina negra para os annaes da história colonial portugueza dedicada e oferecida aos seus patrícios e os verdadeiros portuguezes* (Nova Goa 1895), 64.
20 On Ismael Gracias see V. DEVI / M. DE SEABRA, *A literatura Indo-portuguesa* (Lisboa 1971), 157.

in October 1882 the Secretary of State of Foreign Affairs and Overseas Territories (*Secretaria de Estado dos Negocios da Marinha e Ultramar*) replied to the pastoral letter of Archbishop Valente claiming that the prohibition of the journal had an "exclusively religious character". For that reason, the Secretariate decreed that the newspaper continue its publication, with its original title or a new one, and its printing license should not be revoked. While the Secretary of State repealed the ban inflicted by the Archbishop and gave an official permission to Alvares to continue his publishing activities, the Secretary of State nonetheless added a marginal note suggesting that his letter not be published, so as not to "trigger fire" in that tense situation.[21]

If Alvares did not publish dangerous expressions against his superior, what was the ideology that he was fighting for in the newspaper? Particularly interesting is the long editorial in issue 142, published on 26 November 1880. It bore the title "Caution with counsellors" and was divided into two sections: "In general" and "And even in the ecclesiastical realm". The purpose of Alvares was to caution the incoming new Archbishop against the allegedly negative influence that he could encounter by lending an attentive ear to self-interested, evil advisers. In the first place Alvares extolled the qualities both of the Europeans and the Indians in general terms. As for the Europeans, Alvares did not yet question the colonial rule in any form:

> In conformity with the high designs of the Divine Providence, as India is dominated by Europe, the sons of the latter necessarily have to come to their possessions, with charges entrusted on them for sovereignty.[22]

However, if the Europeans enjoyed a right to rule India because of divine determinations, they nonetheless tended to have a fancy and unrealistic image of India:

> India is represented in Europe as an abode of pearls and diamonds; as a paradise in which abound immense spices and fragrances; as the emporium where all the riches of the wide Orient converge; as a mine that, in exchange with insignificant work, can enrich instantaneously both oneself and the Motherland; as a centre from which all the oriental civilisation flows out; finally, as a theatre of great facts and exploits.[23]

Alvares described in laudatory terms the general attitude of the Indians, as both obedient and dignified subjects of the European colonizers:

---

21 Directorate of Archives and Archaeology of Goa (DAAG), Monções do Reino, Vol. 9200, Secretaria de Estado dos Negocios da Marinha e Ultramar-Direcção Geral do Ultramar, Lisbon, 17 October 1882, fls.178r–178v "assim como a resposta que V. Ex.a deu as explicações, particularmente recebidas d'aquelle prelado sobre o caracter exclusivamente religioso da prohibição, declarando-lhe que assim a havia entendida e por isso poderia continuar a publicar-se o referido periódico, com o mesmo, ou outro titulo, tratando as mesmas matérias, sem que tivesse de mandar [cassar]-lhe a licença". Additional note on the document: "Por conveniencias d'occasião, a fim de não [aticar] o fogo na questão, guarde-se e ardi[...] sem se publicar o presente officio".
22 *A Cruz*, 26 November 1880, "Cautela com conselheiros", 1. "Por altos fins da Divina Providencia, sendo a India dominada pela Europa, teem os filhos desta de vir recessariamente a sua possessão com encargos a elles conferidos pela suzerania".
23 "Cautela com conselheiros – I Em geral" (*A Cruz*, 26 November 1880,) 1. "Na Europa é representada a India como fóco de perolas, e diamantes, - como um paraiso em que abundam immensidades de especiarias e aromas, como emporio aonde convergem todas as riquezas do vasto Oriente, -como uma mina que, á troco de insignificante trabalho, pode locupletar instantaneamente á si e á Mãe-Patria, - como um centro donde promana toda a civilização oriental, – como teatro, emfim, de grandes feitos e façanhas;-..."

> In India, in turn, the inhabitants, independent as for character, eminently peaceful as for nature, profoundly religious as for system; due to an education of almost four centuries, respectful of the European domination, based on the solid foundation of true equality, freedom and fraternity; having by nature a heart opposed to any intentions and aims of oppression and slavery; [these Indian inhabitants] welcome as a general rule their active, human and generous Western brothers, lending them – with an instinctive homage – honour, acknowledgement, dedication and sympathy.[24]

If the Europeans were "active, human and generous [...] brothers", albeit with inaccurate ideas about India, the inhabitants of that land were generally loyal subjects with great moral qualities. However, Alvares claimed that these general features, both of the Europeans and the Indians, were not verified in the concrete conditions of his own time:

> What we have said is valid as a rule; however, there are important and notable exceptions, and particularly today. It is not rare, in this current epoch in which all the world is shaken from its foundations; in which Europe is in a permanent state of sedition and subversion of the social order, threatening – as headquarters of the world – an awful general cataclysm of humankind; in which can be observed even the evidence of a deep decadence of humanity, dragged to the shameful and vile chaos of degradation and brutalisation of humankind [...].[25]

We can see how Alvares was partaking in Catholic anti-revolutionary, conservative, and possibly even reactionary discourses against European liberalism. With reference to Portugal and to the developments that occurred after the "September Revolution" of 1836, by which Portugal abandoned the moderate Constitutional Charter of 1828 (a compromise between national and monarchic sovereignty) and returned to the more radical Constitution of 1822 (firmly grounded on national sovereignty), Alvares painted a bleak scenario:

> For 44 years we are under the liberal regime. Before this unhappy age of sacrileges, vandalisms, and profanations, ecclesiastical affairs proceeded in a more brilliant way [...].[26]

Similarly, the liberal age had corrupted also the spirit of public officers, including those Europeans, namely Portuguese, sent to govern Portuguese India from the metropole:

---

24 "Cautela com conselheiros – I Em geral" (*A Cruz*, 26 November 1880), 1. "Na India, á seu turno, os seus habitantes por caracter independentes, -por índole eminentemente pacíficos, por systema profundamente refigiosos -por educação de quasi 4 seculos, respeitadores da dominação europea fundada na solida base de verdadeira igoaldade, liberdade e fraternidade, -por natureza revoltando-lhes o animo quaesquer intentos e propósitos de oppressão e escravidão, acolhem em geral os seus activos, humanos e generosos irmãos occidentaes, prestando-lhes em instinctiva homenagem a honra, o reconhecimento, a dedicação e sympathias; ".

25 "Cautela com conselheiros – I Em geral" (*A Cruz*, 26 November 1880), 1. "O que deixamos dito é em regra; - Há porém, importantes e notáveis excepções, e hoje especialmente;- Não é, pois raro, na epocha actual em que o mundo todo sente se aluido desde os alicerces, - em que a Europa está em permanente estado de sedição e subversão de ordem social, ameaçando como sede do mundo um medonho cataclismo geral do género humano, - em que nota-se até a evidencia uma decadência profunda da humanidade que é arrastada ao vergonhoso e vil cahos da degradação e embrutecimento da espécie humana, -".

26 "Cautela com conselheiros – II e ainda no ecclesiastico" (*A Cruz*, 26 November 1880), 1. "Há 44 annos que estamos sob o regímen liberal. Antes esta infeliz epocha de sacrilégios, vandalismos e profanações, os negócios eclesiásticos andavam por modos mais brilhantes: -".

In the unhappy epoch of "employment-mania" [*emprego-mania*], of this cancer that corrodes and undermines the current society, public offices are not for the service of the people, but for one's own sustainment [...].[27]

Moving from general remarks to more specific critiques, Alvares observed how such a ubiquitous corruption, both in the civil and the ecclesiastical realms, had also affected the Archiepiscopal See of Goa:

> This age of vandalism came in and swept away in Goa all that exalted the Oriental Princess, which by natural and logical consequence had to decay [...] those who stood near to our Prelates as their counsellors were not chosen among the hundreds and thousands as the most learned, holy and prudent, but they imposed themselves on them [=the Prelates] through recommendations and sycophancies, through gifts and favours.[28]

From these quotations we can see that by November 1880 Alvares was not yet criticising the Portuguese ecclesiastical authorities in India, but rather the corrupt counsellors they found in loco. Future research may help identify more precisely whom Alvares had concretely in mind. Was he referring to clerics born in India from Portuguese ancestors (the *Luso-descendentes*)? Another possibility could be that reference was made to certain Goan clerics, belonging to the Brahman and Charodo castes, who had attained positions of influence in the local ecclesiastical establishment.

Let us now consider the issue 176 of *A Cruz*, published on 5 August 1881. The tone had changed dramatically: from words of caution and from criticism of unspecified groups (i.e. the bad counsellors), now it was the turn of an exalted appeal "to the peoples of Portuguese India", to the people of Goa, Damão, and Diu. The context was the impending elections, scheduled for 21 August. Alvares made a long list of grievances of the people of Portuguese India against their government, mentioning in particular a series of heinous taxes (on fish, on salt, seals on public documents, etc.), and on top of all this he protested on the most unacceptable of all prevarications, namely the system of Government-sponsored candidates for the elections.[29] Elections were not fair, and this meant that the people of Portuguese India were not able to let their voice be heard in the Motherland, i.e. in Portugal. This was the call to action:

> Oppressed people of Goa, Damão and Diu!
> Alert! Alert!
> Repel with courageous indignation all lists imposed by your executioners, whatever be the names of the individuals therein contained; and like the Maccabees [i.e. the famous Jewish rebels that fought the Seleucids in the 2nd century BC] bring to the ballot box the names of whoever of your illustrious and patriotic sons, who abound in each of the districts [*circulos*],

---

27 "Cautela com conselheiros – I Em Geral" (*A Cruz*, 26 November 1880), 1. "Na infeliz epocha de empregomania-desse cancro que corroe e mina a sociedade actual, não são os empregos públicos para o serviço do povo, mas para o seu sustento; -".
28 "Cautela com conselheiros – II e ainda no ecclesiastico" (*A Cruz*, 26 November 1880), 1. "Chegou a era de vandalismos e varreu-se da face de Goa tudo o que sublimava a Princeza Oriental a qual em sua natural e logica consequencia teve de decair:-...que os que acercaram-se dos nossos Prelados como seus conselheiros, não foram escolhidos por entre o centenares e milhares como mais doutos, santos e prudentes, mas impuseram-se-lhes por recomendações e bajulações, por dons e obséquios."
29 Cf. M. A. COUTO, Goa. A Daughter's Story (New Delhi 2004), 236.

sons who are distinguished for their self-respecting [*briosa*] independence, and who have tasted the governmental bitterness in this unhappy crisis together with you.[30]

As we have seen, Alvares became increasingly involved in politics when Valente came to India to assume the Episcopal See of Goa. He advocated for the rights of the people in Portuguese India by using the press as a legitimate weapon. His call for a "self-respecting independence" referred to an autonomy within the Portuguese empire, rather than the Indian nationalism that developed only in a later stage. Still Alvares' audacious critique of the civil government became consistent and obvious in the next decade as will be analysed in the next section.

1.3 Alvares' Career as a Journalist From 1882 to 1895

At the time of the ban inflicted in June 1882, Fr. Alvares would have hardly expected to receive an authorization to continue to publish, sent from Portugal already in October. Immediately on 17 July J. U. Gonsalves, F. X. Rego, and J. I. Alvares launched a new periodical, *A Verdade*. Though Alvares was not among the founders, the fact that the abbreviated name "J. I. Alvares" actually stood for João Ignacio Alvares and belonged to the brother of the dissident priest suggests Alvares' involvement as co-editor by proxy. *A Verdade* ran for 42 months until December 1885 and is possibly the best source to examine the evolution of Alvares' ideas, and the formation of his vision of Christianity and politics.

While the Portuguese journal *A Verdade* was still in circulation, on 2 November 1885 Fr. Alvares launched his first English newspaper, *The Times of Goa,* in Panjim. From the only extant copy of this journal we can notice the attention given to the Church of Ceylon, which rarely caught the attention of the other Portuguese newspapers published by Alvares. In the middle of the title the coat of arms of the Kingdom of Portugal was printed, as a manifest of loyalty to his *patria*, as well of his adherence to the Portuguese *Padroado*.

O Brado Indiano was a Portuguese weekly in Goa, edited by Bernardo da Silva from 15 December 1894 to 28 September 1895. The subtitle of "Semanario político, industrial e agricolo" reveals the focus of the newspaper to be on the social development in Goa, thus shifting from the religious focus of Alvares' previous journals. The paper was mainly concerned about the current issues in Goa, such as the law on seals (*a lei de sello*), but also dealt with confrontations occurring between the Portuguese and British colonial governments. The newspaper was published by the printing house Imprensa Indiana, located at Rua 4 de Abril, n. 85, in Panjim. A great concern of the newspaper was medicine and public health. News on the Medical-Pharmaceutical Association of Goa, founded on 1 January 1895, was accompanied with a list of "Tabella de honorarios medicos" enlisting the price of each type of service. Attention was also paid to agriculture, promoting the propagation of coconut and manioca as well as wheat cultivation. José Maria da Sá published his *Coqueiro e a sua cultura* as a column article since the first issue of *O Brado Indiano* in December 1894.[31] Da Sá was a lawyer

---

30 "Aos povos da India Portuguesa" (*A Cruz*, 5 August 1881). "Opprimidos Povos de Goa, Damão e Diu! Alerta! Alerta! Repelli com corajosa indignação todas as listas impostas pela mão dos vossos verdugos, contenham ellas nomes de quaesquer indivíduos que sejam; e, quaes Machabeus, levae á urna com todo o valor os nomes de quaisquer dos vossos ilustrados e patrióticos filhos que abundam em cada um dos círculos, filhos distinctos por briosa independencia, e que nesta infeliz crize tenham saboreado convosco as amarguras governamentaes."

31 "Palabras prebias [sic]". This preamble was first published on *A Discussão* in 1887. J.M. DE SÁ, *O Coqueiro. Parte primeira historia natural e cultura* (Nova-Goa 1898), 1.

and served as president of the Agriculture Department of Ilhas of Goa. Most importantly, he was elected as secretary of the Association for the Defense of the *Padroado* in the East.

2. Indian Reactions to the Syrian Archbishop and His Independent Catholic Mission

2.1 Alvares' Trials in 1890, 1895, and 1906

Alvares' transformation from a schismatic Catholic to a Syrian Archbishop aroused considerable suspicion in Goa, leading to his imprisonment for at least three times. His entry into Goa was under systematic surveillance of the Archbishop of Goa, António Valente, whose zeal and interest in temporal issues had been highly acknowledged by King Dom Carlos I (r. 1889–1908).[32] A bundle of papers entitled "Adhesão do clero e fiéis a Sua Ex.a Rev.issima, o Senhor Arcebispo Primaz na questão d' *A Cruz*", conserved at the collection of *Papeis avulsos* in the Church Archive of Goa, reveals the institutionalised surveillance of the schismatic priests.[33] On 29 July and again on 1 September 1889, the Archbishop issued two pastoral letters ordering the clergy to report on Alvares and his fellows' activities. A priest from Mormugão complied with his duty of spying, writing on 11 June 1890:

> In response to the *Officio* of Your Reverence on 9 June in regard to the schismatic Fr. Alvares and his fellows, I am compelled to inform Your Reverence that they have distributed brochures in denial of the Primacy of Roman Pontiff. I do not know how long they will remain. They are lodged in one of the rented houses of the merchant Messias. They are four, but I am informed that at night two more came, so including Fr. Alvares, counting to six. They present themselves as ecclesiastics. One of them is called Botelho, native from Nachinolá, one called Abreo is from Piedade on the Islands, and another one European called Jeronimo. The other two came yesterday. I do not know their names, but one must be from Badem, the other one from Pilerne, respectively Soares and Noronha.[34]

The rigorous inspections led to the imprisonment of Alvares and three other clerics in 1890. They were summoned to the Court and charged for "appearing in public clad in cassock

---

32 See a positive interpretation of Valente's involvement in Goan politics and his attitude on Alvares in MARIA DE JESUS DOS MÁRTIRES LOPES, "D. António Sebastião Valente. O homem e a obra (1846–1908). Contributo para a sua história", in: A.T. DE MATOS / J. TELES E CUNHA (eds.), *Goa passado e presente*. Vol. 2 (Lisboa 2012), 569. He was elected as president of the Council of the State of Goa for five times, respectively in 1886, 1889, 1892, 1894, 1897, and 1905.

33 I thank the archivist of CAG, Mrs. Lilia Maria D'Souza, for sharing with me her unpublished article "Church records in Goa: Mirror of Goan Catholic Society", read at *The XIII International Seminar on Indo-Portuguese History* in Aix-en-Provence, 23–27 March 2010.

34 CAG, *Papeis avulsos*. A Portuguese letter by a certain priest called Francisco Rodriguez from the parish of Mormugão, dated on 11 June 1890. "Em respuesta ao officio de V. R. da 9 de corrente respecto aos scismaticos Pe. Alvares e seus sequazes, cumpre-me informar a V. Rma S. que eles distribuem folhetos que negam o Primado do Romano Pontifice, não me consta para que fim vem elles aqui. 2° não me consta quanto tempo querem demorar, estão alojados em uma das casas alugadas do negociante Messias, eles são quatro e á noite, consta-me vieram mais dois, com que ao todo, entrando o Pe. Alvares são seis, apresentam-se como eclesiásticos. Um delles é natural de Nachinolá, por nome Botelho, outro de Piedade das Ilhas chamado Abreo, outro Jeronimo europeo, autros dois que ontem vieram, não sei nomes mas devem ser um de Badem, outro de Pilerne Soares e Noronha".

(*batina*) and other clerical garments".[35] This imprisonment happened when Vasco Guedes was the Governor of the State. The judge Vieira Lisboa released Alvares on the ground that the Portuguese constitution tolerated all religions under the condition of not insurging against the religion of the State.[36]

The first trial in Goa did not discourage Alvares from returning to his homeland in the following years. His multiple trips to Goa were not only aimed at the recruitment of clergy so as to satisfy the increasing missionary demands in Ceylon and India. Alvares was also dedicated to the Goan cultural and social uplift, through his service in journalism and his popularisation of hygienic measures against pandemics. His deep involvement in Goan political and ecclesiastical affairs certainly provided him with support from allied Goan elites, but also posed a risk, as the Ceylon Independent Catholic congregations were concerned about being jeopardised by political upheavals in the Portuguese state. Perhaps due to the foreseeable persecution in Goa, Alvares might have applied to the Patriarch of Antioch for legal papers attesting his episcopal legitimacy. This precaution might be able to partly explain why Alvares sailed out from Colombo to India on 9 May 1893.[37] The first stop of his Indian trip was Niranam, whose Saint Mary's Cathedral – one of the most ancient churches in Kerala today – is believed to have been founded by Saint Thomas. The main purpose of this visit to the Metropolitan of Niranam, Mar Gregorios, was to receive a *Statikon*, which had recently arrived in India from Mardin. The Syriac term *statikon* (from the Greek συστατικόν) indicates "an official letter signed by the Patriarch who has consecrated a bishop for a diocese. It is the *statikon* that proves that the bishop was lawfully ordained and appointed to the given see."[38] When Alvares was consecrated as bishop in Kottayam on 15 July 1889, a document entitled *Bull of His Holiness Ignatius Peter III, Patriarch of the East on the Consecration of Archbishop Alvarez*, translated from Syriac to English by the secretary of the Metropolitan of Malabar J. M. Philipps on 29 July 1889, attested the legitimacy of Alvares' consecration.[39] It is possible that the *statikon* issued in 1893 served as a confirmation of the *Bull* concerning Alvares' episcopal validity, likely at the request of Alvares himself or Vilatte, as the episcopal authenticity of the latter had been put into question by the Episcopalian bishops in North America. Once ashore in Niranam, Alvares received a cordial reception from a multitude of people who came to welcome their Archbishop from Ceylon and gathered in a space of over two miles around the cathedral. Music was played by native bands, fireworks lit and flags waved, while the Archbishop was greeted by Mar Athanasius and Mar Gregorios. Alvares spent a few days with each of the two Malabar bishops, before he continued his trip by railway towards Goa on 6 June.[40]

The Syriac *statikon* certainly did not protect Alvares from persecutions against him in his Portuguese Catholic homeland. The second trial he underwent in 1895 was even more severe,

---

35 "Inquisition at Goa in 1895" (*The Independent Catholic*, September 1895), 1.
36 COELHO, *Uma pagina negra*, 61.
37 "Our Archbishop" (*The Independent Catholic*, May 1893), 2.
38 I. PERCZEL, "Accommodationist Strategies on the Malabar Coast. Competition or Complementarity?" in: I.G. ŽUPANOV / P.A. FABRE (eds.), *The Rites Controversies in the Early Modern World* (Leiden / Boston 2018), 231. I have not seen this *statikon* or copies made from it.
39 I have seen the original English translation of the *Bull* in a private collection in Brahmavar. A concise version of the English document was certified in front of the United States Consul of Ceylon W. Morey on 16th November 1892. See a published version of this certificate in *Documents Proving the Validity of the Episcopal Consecration of S. Renatus, Archbishop Vilatte* (London 1901) in Lambeth Palace Library, *F. Temple* vol.47: ff. 129r.–130r.
40 "Mgr. Alvares" (*The Independent Catholic* June 1893), 2.

coinciding with the revolt of the Maratha Sepoy troops and of the military chief Dada Rane against the Portuguese.[41] On 17 June 1893 Alvares had entered Panjim during torrential monsoon rains.[42] It had been three years since his last stay in the Portuguese metropolis. The weekly *O Ultramar* was the first to report on Alvares' return to Goa, drawing not only public attention to his activities, but also to the monitoring by the Archbishop of Goa. The Portuguese prelate scrupulously recorded in one of his letters dated 26 September 1893:

> The schismatic Alvares remains in Panjim. It is said that he tries to start a journal, but there are no ascertained clues to give credit to. He does not go out during the day. He leaves at night and goes to the house of the deceased Ferrão e José Maria da Sá. I am vigilant.[43]

Under the vigilant surveillance of the Archbishop, Alvares reduced his public exposure. However, his new Portuguese journal *O Brado indiano*, successfully launched in December 1894 brought him again to the ecclesiastical and political spotlight. The civil authorities of Goa were under pressure due to the resentment of residents in both the Old Conquests (including Bardez, Ilhas de Goa, and Salcete), and those New Conquests (Pernem, Bicholim, Sattari, Ponda, Sanquem, Quepem, and Canacona) that had been acquired in the late eighteenth century. The Captain Manuel Gomes da Costa (1863–1929), who came to Goa in 1893 to assist the newly appointed Governor of the State, and the Viscount of Vila Nova de Ourém, Elesbão José de Bettencourt Lapa (1831–1899), were among the most criticised Portuguese officers.[44] A few weeks later in September, a section of Maratha soldiers in the military quarters at Panjim escaped from their barracks and mutinied against the orders according to which they were to be sent to serve in Mozambique. Rebelling peasants from the adjacent districts in the New Conquests, and particularly from Sattari, supported the Maratha mutiny. These peasants were organised by the *Ranes*, a Rajput clan that collected revenues in the New Conquests, before the Portuguese won those territories from the Maratha Empire one century earlier. The *Ranes* protested against the Portuguese for the imposition of new taxes and the reorganisation of land rights, jeopardising their feudal privileges. The Portuguese state was under considerable pressure due to the limited army at its disposal. The government was threatened by the fact that the rebellion spread from the New Conquests up to Bardez, where dissatisfaction with the land laws was on the rise. While the rebels were negotiating with the government, all newspapers in Goa were suspended.[45] Reports on the insurgents in Goa were however published outside the Portuguese state, as for instance in *The Independent Catholic* in Colombo:

> The recent revolt of the Maharata [sic] soldiery in Goa afforded another excuse to the unscrupulous Portuguese to perpetrate all manner of atrocities in that ill fated land. Village after village has been burnt down, men and women have been arrested on mere suspicion and thrown into filthy dungeons, every native of the soil has been dismissed from Government service, men

---

41 See P. KAMAT, "Brief Account of the 1895 Rane Revolt in Goa" (*The Quarterly Journal of the Mythic Society* [Bangalore] 78, 1987, 22–32).
42 "Our Archbishop" (*The Independent Catholic* July 1893), 2.
43 CAG, *Papeis avulsos*, Archbishop of Goa, Paço Archiepiscopal, Nova Goa, 26 September 1893. "O Scismático Pe. Alvares continua a estar em Panjim. Diz-se que pretende fundar jornal, mas não há visos certos para se dar créditos. Elle não sahe de dia. Consta porém que tem sahido das noites e entrado nas casas do falecido Ferrão e José Maria de Sá. Estou vigilante."
44 See Gomes da Costa' memoir in defence of his campaign against the Goan newspapers and the Maratha revolt in M. DE OLIVEIRA GOMES DA COSTA, *A Revolta de Goa e a Campanha de 1895/1896* (Lisboa 1939).
45 R. PINTO, *Between Empires*. Print and Politics in Goa (New Delhi 2007), 143–144.

like the Viscount of Bardez, Mr. Ismail Gracias, Father Saldanha, Mr. Henriques and others have been most wantonly persecuted, and Archbishop Alvares and Mr. B. F. de Costa, Director of Public Instruction, were compelled to leave the country, and the latter gentleman only recently died in exile lamented by very [every] true son of Goa.[46]

Shortly before the revolt started, Alvares was arrested in the street and put in prison on 19 August 1895, while the printing house of *O Brado indiano* was ransacked. The lawyer Sertório Coelho came to defend Alvares but he too was put in jail. The ground for the arrest was of the same nature as the one in 1890: that the "priest" of Syrian rites "used insignia that do not belong to him."[47] Yet one day after the trial, Alvares and two others were released without any charge. The next day Gomes da Costa ordered to arrest Alvares for the second time and even violently stripped off his vestment before bringing him to jail.[48] Some reports even added more details of Alvares' sufferings as he was "taken only with his underwear to the Police lock-up, where he was put in a filthy room without a chair, table or bed and the floor smelling of urine and faeces."[49] The ground for the arrest was apostasy and sedition. Alvares was acquitted again after the second trial.

Outraged by the humiliation imposed on their fellow journalist, several leading Goans mentioned in the Colombo newspaper, such as the Viscount of Bardez Inácio Caetano de Carvalho (1843–1907) and Ismail Gracias as well as Sertório Coelho, defended Alvares by publishing pamphlets calling the Alvares' trial "a dark page (*uma pagina negra*) for the annals of the Portuguese colonial history", which became the title of a collection of articles by Coelho published in 1895. The Goan dissidents did not spare harsh, and even hyperbolic expressions in their interventions in the periodical press: the Governor of the State was held responsible for "the inquisitorial horrors in Goa", whereas the jails in Goa were like "a modern Bastille". However, despite the Portuguese violent repression, Gomes da Costa's campaign against Alvares was labelled as "another debacle".[50] The fact that many of the newspapers quoted in Sertório Coelho's *Pagina negra* are no longer available or not easy to find in public archives, made the book a favourite source for Alvares' biographers and researchers. However, the narratives selected by *Pagina negra* reflect only one particular voice from the Goan turmoils in the late nineteenth century. Thanks to Rochelle Pinto's critical reading of a series of prints published in 1895, written by a variety of political actors, we are able to review Alvares' trial with greater nuance.

First of all, Pinto discusses the early pamphlet of the Viscount Carvalho, who was employed in the local judiciary and owned several newspapers suppressed by Gomes da Costa. His support to Alvares was part of his self-defence, as he had been wrongly accused by the State of abetting and conspiring with the Goan-Syrian priest-journalist. On the one hand, he felt responsible for correcting the State's indifference to the local requests and "to suggest that it was within the rights and duties of the press to criticize the state's actions".[51] On the other hand, Carvalho helped the rebels negotiate with the government within the legal frame, even though he was supposed to represent the State in such negotiations. Pinto indicates that

---

46 "The recent revolt of the Maharata soldiery in Goa" (*The Independent Catholic*, March 1896), 2.
47 SERTORIO COELHO, *Uma pagina negra para os annaes da história colonial portugueza dedicada e oferecida aos seus patrícios e aos verdadeiros portuguezes* (Nova Goa 1895), 60.
48 COELHO, *Uma pagina negra*, 60.
49 AZEVEDO, *Patriot and Saint*, 29. I am unable to find the original sources that Azevedo quoted from. This description is widely quoted in references to Alvares' trial in 1895. PINTO, *Between Empires*, 146.
50 COELHO, *Uma pagina negra*, 1, 71, 79.
51 R. PINTO, *Between Empires*. Print and Politics in Goa (New Delhi 2007), 145.

many Goan intellectuals found themselves in similar conflicts of interests during the nineteenth century. Carvalho was both a critic and an agent of the Portuguese colonial power. This ambivalent position possibly safeguarded him from the radical suppression suffered by Alvares.

Secondly, however, the much criticised administrator Gomes da Costa understood the revolt in the context of the Brahmin-Charodo caste rivalry. In his posthumously published memoir, the Portuguese captain began his story with the reduction of Portuguese military presence in Goa in 1871, by which "an assured source of employment was lost to the chardos, while the brahmins saw a clear monopoly left to them over state positions in the bureaucracy."[52] The increased inequality perceived by the Charodos led to the polarisation of two newly established parties, the *nativistas* led by an overwhelming majority of Brahmins on the one hand, and the Charodos' *progressistas* on the other. In this respect, it is worthy to note that Alvares and all his sympathizers were Brahmin Catholic intellectuals.

Finally, Rochelle Pinto observes how an anonymous pamphlet asserted to have identified a group of Goan elite figures as the founders of *O Brado indiano*. These were Bernardo Francisco da Costa, the Viscount Carvalho, Ismael Gracias, Sertório Coelho, and Sertorio Mascarenhas, so that not only Alvares had to be pointed out, but an entire circle of the Brahmin Goan intelligentsia.[53] According to that same anonymous pamphlet, *O Brado indiano* and other censored journals were the trigger of the rebellion as the soldiers were "incapable of such an act, without a conspirational leader to impel them."[54] Indian nationalism and the aspiration to independence from European colonialism were ridiculed by the Charodos' discourse on the revolt and turbulences in Goa, for in their opinion the real danger to the Catholic society came from the privileged Brahmins only. Rochelle Pinto analyses in the following terms the debate articulated by the conflicting pamphlets:

> If one were to judge by the form and tenor of pamphlets produced by the elite and by Gomes de Costa, relations between state officials and the Goan elite appear to be almost non-hierarchized within the colony. An explicit note of deference was only visible in addresses to the invisible Portuguese Crown. While the punishment of Pe. Alvares indicates how hierarchies were swiftly established if the colonial elite were seen to have transgressed certain lines, the register in which state and elite communicated suggest rivalry rather than subordination.[55]

Pinto's analysis is coherent with our examination of the early publications by Alvares in *A Cruz*, in which deference was shown towards a somehow abstract Portuguese crown, while concerns were voiced so as to correct rather the existing government's misconduct.

After being released from jail, Alvares had to abandon his cassock and change to an attire with "long overcoat, loose black cashmere trousers and a flat hat."[56] In 1897 Alvares was pardoned from the charge of 1895. For reasons still to be uncovered, Alvares changed his Portuguese nationality to British over the next years. This seemed to be the final solution for

---

52 PINTO, *Between Empires*, 149. *Chardo, Charodo* and *Charado* are spellings of the same word. For an early modern perspective on the caste conflicts between Catholic Brahmans and Charodos, see A. BARRETO XAVIER, "David contra Golias na Goa Seiscentista: Escrita Identitária e Colonização Interna" (*Ler História* 49, 2005, 107–143).
53 PINTO, *Between Empires*, 148. This information was taken from *Apontamentos para a historia da Revolta em Goa dos soldados, ranes e satarienses em o anno de 1895* (Bombaim 1896).
54 PINTO, *Between Empires*, 148, quoting *Apontamentos*, 3.
55 PINTO, *Between Empires*, 151.
56 COELHO, *Uma Pagina negra*, 84.

his personal security in Goa. He was arrested for the third time in Panjim in 1906 "by the Governor's order and the Patriarch's request".[57] He was sent to the police station and then the District Judge's Court, where he was eventually released due to his British naturalization.

Alvares' trial in 1895 was the highlight of his biography and it requires further studies, especially through a systematic reading of *O Brado indiano*, whose last issues from September 1895 onwards are torn off from the only known copy of the journal, available in the Goa State Central Library, possibly as consequence of censorship. In the next section, we move from the Goan reaction to Alvares as an individual to the Goan representations of the Indo-Ceylon Independent Catholics as a church movement.

2.2 Goan Representation of the Indian-Ceylon Independent Catholics

Alvares joined the Jacobite Church sometime in 1887, came to Ceylon for the first time in 1888 as Apostolic Prefect to the Independent Catholics, and eventually was consecrated in Kottayam as Mar Julius I "Bishop of India, Goa and Ceylon (excluding Malabar)" in 1889. It appears clear that the years 1887–1889 were a crucial time, a turning point in the ecclesiastical history of the Luso-Asian world. While cases of apostasy from Roman Catholicism to "pagan" religions or to Protestantism had occurred several times in Asia during the previous centuries, what happened in India and Ceylon in those three years at the end of the nineteenth century was rather unheard of. It was the first time that Latin Catholics, not subject to the political constraints of a non-Catholic ruler, decided freely to join an Orthodox church. The Jesuit missionaries Cristovão Ferreira (1580–1650) and Giuseppe Chiara (1602–1685), in seventeenth-century Japan, among several other confreres, had rejected Catholicism for Buddhism only after having been subjected to unbearable torture.[58] The Coonan Cross Oath might have been considered by the Roman Catholic Church as the start of a mass apostasy by part of the Saint Thomas Christians, but by the latter it was rather understood as a bold quest for their own original faith and religious traditions, against the innovations imposed by the European missionaries, supported by a proto-colonial power.[59] Finally, under the protection granted by the Dutch *Vereenigde Oostindische Compagnie* and the Danish *Østindisk Kompagni*, Calvinist and Lutheran preachers were able to encroach on what had previously been mission territory of the *Padroado*, and obtained a substantial part of their converts among the native Catholics.

All these cases of apostasy from the Roman Catholic faith had occurred either as response to external stimuli (violent in the Japanese case, more lenient in the proto-colonial Dutch and Danish settings), or as acts of resistance against a Roman Catholic imposition, effacing previous Christian traditions. However, what happened in 1887–1889 was of a quite different nature. South Asian Roman Catholics, deeply Latin and Portuguese in their tradition and history, decided to break away from their own Church and enter in communion with an Orthodox Church that had rituals, linguistic expressions and even dogmatic definitions distinctively different. How could such a transformation have taken place? The Indo-Portuguese public sphere was puzzled and intrigued by those events. While the Catholic hierarchies had

---

57 *Homeward Mail from India, China and the East* (London 1857–1913), 17 February 1906, 195.
58 For an account of Ferreira's life, see H. CIESLIK, SJ, "The Case of Christovão Ferreira," (*Monumenta Nipponica* 29/1, 1974, 1–54). On the underground Christians in Japan, resisting to outright apostasy, see S. TURNBULL, *The Kakure Kirishitan of Japan. A Study of Their Development, Beliefs and Rituals to the Present Day* (Surrey 1998).
59 See for instance J. KOLLAPARAMBIL, *The St. Thomas Christians' Revolution in 1653* (Kottayam 1981).

an easy task in condemning the undeniable abandonment of their traditional faith and discipline by the hardliner *Padroadists* of Ceylon and the rebel priest Antonio Alvares, the reaction of the laymen, and particularly of the native elites, turned out to be much more nuanced, even understanding and sympathetic.

In November 1888 the weekly journal *O Ultramar,* published in Margao by the da Costa family since 1859 and until 1941, featured various articles dealing with the transition of the *Padroadists* of Ceylon to the Jacobite Church. *O Ultramar* was the first privately owned newspaper in Goa and was "managed by the politically prominent family [da Costa] through the century", and "set itself up decisively as a representative of the Goan people". In consistence with such a representative stance, the editor of *O Ultramar* "was frequently elected to the Portuguese parliament".[60] In 1888 the editor was António Anastasio Bruto da Costa, who later on, in 1896, had many of his colleagues "arrested or forced to flee the country [...] in the aftermath of a large rebellion".[61]

The journal defended the bold choice made by the Ceylon *Padroadists* and tried to find reasons that might justify it. The argumentation was both defensive and offensive, by defending the new religious denomination chosen by those Christians, and by attacking the specific model of Roman Catholic Church that they had deserted. An editorial published on 17 November, under the title *"Revista politica: Os padroadistas de Ceylão",* presented a both vitriolic and enlightening opposition between "the religion of Propaganda" and the one preached by the *Padroado* missionaries. The article caused a great commotion; it was translated and published anonymously into English in Ceylon, with the title *Read mark and digest*. A copy of that pamphlet was sent to Mons. Zaleski, by then *Consultore* at the Congregation de Propaganda Fide. Zaleski passed the incendiary document to the Prefect of the Congregation, Cardinal Giovanni Simeoni (1816–1892), as attachment to a report from Ootacamund, dated 16 December 1888.[62] The article, published in Margao but circulated on a global scale, presented in the following terms the religion that the Catholics of Ceylon had abandoned:

> The religion of Propaganda is not the religion of Christ; it is the most complete antithesis of it. Christ did not look to the exterior, but to the hearts; he despised the wealth and the greatness of this world; he was all meekness; he declared the gates of heaven to be open to all, rich or poor, who may seek him with their hearts; he even said that to the poor he was more easily accessible than to the rich; and he opened his arms to all sinners, who in repentance implored his divine mercy.
>
> The Propagandists on the contrary make the external rite their whole religion, the interior being to them of secondary importance. The wealth of the missions and temporal influence is the main spring that moves them; they open the gates of their heaven to those who pay most, so that he who dies poor must keep himself in Purgatory longer than the one who gives money to their congregations; to the poor, therefore, the Kingdom of Heaven is less accessible than to the rich [...] Facts prove, and our old missionaries can certify that this is the religion professed by the Propaganda.[63]

---

60 PINTO, *Between Empires*, 128, 131; on the founder of *O Ultramar* see SANDRA ATAÍDE LOBO, *O Desassossego goês*. Cultura e política em Goa do liberalismo ao acto colonial, PhD Thesis (Lisboa, Universidade Nova de Lisboa, 2013), 101–102.
61 PINTO, *Between Empires*, 52.
62 "Revista politica - Os padroadistas de Ceylão" (*O Ultramar*, 17 November 1888). APF, *SC Indie Orientali*. Vol. 33, f. 985r.
63 A reprint can be found in V. PERNIOLA, *The Catholic Church in Sri Lanka*. The British Period. Vol. 8: 1887–1899. The Archdiocese of Colombo (Dehiwala 2004), 147–148.

If the conflicts between *Padroado* and Propaganda clerics had been until then a matter of jurisdiction and power, now a surprisingly doctrinal dimension was affirmed as cleavage between the two different groups. Although all defined themselves as "Catholics", the missionaries of Propaganda were preaching a faith that was not at all the faith of Christ: they were Catholics, but they were no Christians!

It is useful to note that, ever since the seventeenth century, the sort of Roman Catholicism that the Portuguese had introduced in Asia had always appeared to Protestant observers as a religion based on exterior rituals and great pomp, embarrassingly similar to Hindu ritualism.[64] By contrast, the article published in *O Ultramar* represented true Christianity, namely the one promoted by the *Padroado* missionaries as a religion of interiority, particularly discarding social differences between rich and poor.

The Propagandists were blamed for professing an exterior and superficial religion, driven by wealth, where even the salvation of souls was subject to the logic of money. The reproach is remarkable, as the polemics against the "Goanese priests" had been developed by European missionaries on precisely the same lines. An example can clarify this attitude, spread among Catholic and Protestant missionaries alike. In a book published in 1875 by the Lutheran missionary Eduard Raimund Baierlein (1819–1901), the encounter with a *Padroado* priest in the Tamil region was recounted in the following terms:

> Not far from Virdachellum[= Virudachalam, at about 60 km south-west of Cuddalore], there is a little Church in the jungle where no Christians live. A Priest lives there, a dark one, one of the Portuguese. The Church contains a Mada (= mother), an image of the Virgin which is a great favorite with the heathen. When the child of one of the neighbouring heathens is sick, or one of their cattle, or they themselves get into trouble, they vow some thing to the Mada if she will help them. And for this purpose there exists a Church and a Priest. When asked how he could live there alone, since there were no Christians and the heathens would not hear of being converted, the Priest replied with a shrug of shoulders, "The Church has its income here; the Church has its income."[65]

The article in *O Ultramar* marked a reversal of a consolidated European trope about the "dark" and greedy "Portuguese" missionaries, not really committed to the evangelisation of the heathens. The editorial of 17 November 1888 presented the *Padroado* Catholics as followers of José Vaz, "who had struggled, as much as their power permitted, to keep themselves united to the Lusitanian Church of the East". However,

> being cast away by the Patron [i.e. the Portuguese Crown], and unwilling to submit themselves to the iron yoke of the Propagandists, not desirous of abandoning the religion of the Crucified, they call to their aid a spiritual superior [i.e. the Jacobite Patriarch] whose rite is most in harmony with that of the Indian apostle [= José Vaz] who carried to their forefathers the light of the Gospel.[66]

In a rather paradoxical turn, it appeared that the Roman Catholicism that Vaz had promoted in Ceylon against Calvinism was actually more in harmony with an Eastern Orthodox

---

64 PAOLO ARANHA examines this issue in his dissertation on the Malabar Rites controversy, about to be completed.
65 E.R. BAIERLEIN, *The Land of the Tamulians and Its Missions*, translated by J. D. B. Gribble (Madras 1875), 123.
66 PERNIOLA, *The Catholic Church. The British Period.* Vol. 8, 147.

tradition than with the faith and discipline of the missionaries sent directly from the Pope of Rome.

We should not infer that the specific decision taken by the *Padroadists* in Ceylon would be shared by all the other supporters of the Portuguese jurisdiction. For instance, in 1888 the Bombay *Padroadists* criticized the Independent Catholics in Ceylon, defining their move as the "schism in Ceylon", clearly seeing in it a betrayal of the Catholic Church. Their reaction was bold:

> We [the Bombay Catholics] can be patriots. We can be Portuguese. We can be padroadists. But we will never give up being good Catholics. We will never negate a religion that is our supreme blessing, which cradled us and will be the only comfort and consolation in the last moments of our lives.[67]

The Goan reactions to Alvares and his Ceylon church were polarised. The Archbishop of Goa and the authorities considered Alvares a traitor and arrested him in 1894. On the other side, some liberal Catholic elites expressed rather tolerant views and even endorsement, comparing him with Giordano Bruno, who was burnt at the stake by the Roman Inquisition in 1600.[68] Resentful of the Archbishop's attempts at censoring their newspaper, the editors of *O Ultramar* found a great resemblance between the Goan priest and the Italian dissident, not only for the persecutions they both suffered from the Roman Catholic authorities of their times, but also for their once supressed but eventually long-lasting ideas. Being aware of it or not, by paring Alvares with the great hero of European secularism, Alvares' sympathizers hinted at a possible link between him and Freemasonry, whose influence was strong in Portugal as well as in India. This comparison of Alvares to Bruno, which seems to have appeared only in *O Ultramar*, could have been convincing evidence in the eyes of the Archbishop of Goa and the Papal Nuncio in Portugal about Alvares' alleged masonic connections. At any rate, even beyond masonic appropriations, Bruno was a symbol of a new, liberal and unified Italy, whose birth was achieved also with the demise of the Papal States. In fact, "in nineteenth-century Italy, the mythologizing of Giordano Bruno and Galileo into nationalist and anticlerical heroes [...] was not unrelated to the political goals of the Risorgimento (the unification of Italy), which required the dismantling of papal temporal power."[69]

2.3 Goan Representations of the Syrian Character of the Independent Catholic Mission

Evidence suggests that some Christians of Persian tradition did once settle and live in Goa. The Arab traveller Ibn Battuta (1304 – ca.1369), who passed by Goa in 1342, described a Christian settlement near the city. The discovery of a Syrian Cross with a Pahlavi inscription

---

67 "Scisma em Ceylão" (*O Anglo-Lusitano*, 18 October 1888), 2: "Nós podemos ser patriotas, podemos ser portuguezes, podemos ser padroadistas, mas nunca deixando de ser bons catholicos, nunca renegando a religião que é o nosso supremo bem, que nos embalou no berço e há de ser o único conforto e consolação nos momentos derradeiros da nossa vida."
68 "Revista politica. Os representantes de Deus na terra" (*O Ultramar*, 12 October 1889), 1.
69 L.M. PRINCIPE, "Myth 11: That Catholics did not contribute to the Scientific Revolution", in: R.L. NUMBERS, *Galileo Goes to Jail. And Other Myths About Science and Religion* (Cambridge 2009), 101.

in Agasaim, near Goa, in April 2001 is considered to be convincing archaeological evidence.[70] The cross is dated between the 6th and 7th century.[71] Even though the St Thomas Christians' presence on the Konkan coast remains *terra incognita* in historiography, it is very likely that Syrian Christian merchants and travellers frequented territories that later on became strongly associated with Roman Catholicism.

A side-effect of the *Padroado* control over the Diocese of Cochin, placed in the heartland of the Thomas Christians, was the communication between priests of Latin and Syrian rites, which represented a further variable in the conundrum of jurisdictional controversies. Even Goan newspapers would be distinctively alerted to interactions between priests with different liturgical costumes and conflicting ecclesiastical allegiances. An example of this concern is shown by the reactions to the presence in Goa of the Chaldean priest Dina Barjona from Baghdad. He came to India in 1853 and made his trip to Goa in the following year. There he was sanctioned alms by the Administrator of the Bardez Council (*Administrador do Concelho de Bardez*), Emigdio Luiz Caetano de Sousa. The payment was authorised later on in 1854 by the Governor of Goa Viscount of Villa-Nova d'Ourem after his documents, attesting his priestly status, had been verified and approved.[72] The acceptance of a Chaldean Catholic priest by the civil authorities in Goa suggests an early combined effort between the Goan *Padroadists* and the Suriani Christians (who had fought vehemently against the *Padroado* in the seventeenth century, after the Synod of Diamper of 1599) in a potential alliance against the same rival of that moment, the Roman Congregation of Propaganda Fide. Barjona came to Margao in later years for the funeral of Mr. Luis Salvador Gomes, father to Dr. Francisco Luis Gomes, a leading member in the Goan *Padroado* elite. Barjona celebrated a Qurbana as one of the many services dedicated to the deceased. This certainly called the attention of the Roman Catholics. Among many participants in the Eastern Syriac Liturgy there was the editor of the Margao-based journal *O Ultramar*, Antonio da Costa. At the time of the transition of the Ceylon *Padroadists* to the Syrian Orthodox Church, Costa defended their choice by drawing on past experience of Syrian priests in Goa.[73] Costa stated that decades before, Barjona had been seen celebrating mass "like the Catholic, with small differences" and then was invited to celebrate the funeral of Luis Salvador Gomes.[74] Costa reported also another concrete case of blurred limits between the Roman Catholics and the Syrian church. The Archbishop of Goa, Ornellas e Vasconcelos had acknowledged the validity of the priestly ordinations made by the Chaldean Bishop Mar Mellus, so that priests ordained by him could be accepted into the Catholic Church without once again undergoing the rite of priestly ordination.[75]

---

70 On the Pahlavi inscription on the Saint Thomas crosses in south India see C.G. CERETI / L.M. OLIVIERI / F.J. VAZHUTHANAPALLY, "The Problem of the Saint Thomas Crosses and Related Questions. Epigraphical Survey and Preliminary Research" (*East and West* 52/1, 2002, 285–310).
71 The cross is now conserved in the Pilar Seminary Museum. C.J. COSTA, *Apostolic Christianity in Goa and in the West Coast* (Pilar, Goa 2009, 75–93).
72 *Boletim do Governo do Estado da India*, sexta-feira 14 de abril, 1854, 1. The spelling "Dina" should correspond to the Syriac *Denḥa*, which means "Epiphany" and has been the name of many oriental prelates.
73 "Revista politica: Padroado portuguez da India" (*O Ultramar*, 24 November 1888.), 1.
74 "Revista politica: Os padroadistas de Ceylão" (*O Ultramar*, 17 November 1888), 1. "Nos vimos por estes nossos olhos, enfileirar-se na nossa clerezia o padre chalden Dina Barjona pertencente a esse rito, nos funeraes de Francisco Salvador Gomes, -vi mol-o missar na egreja de Margão com ceremonias, com pequena differença, eguaes ás catholicas."
75 "Revista politica: Padroado portuguez da India" (*O Ultramar*, 24 November 1888), 1. "Aterrados com o exemplo que nos deram os ceylonezes, julgaram dever pregar e pregam deveras, que o rito syriaco não é christia-

With these examples, the editor of *O Ultramar* stressed the similarity between the Orthodox liturgy and the Catholic one, and the validity of the ordinations performed in those Oriental Churches. According to Costa there were noticeable contradictions on behalf of the Catholic Church in relation to the Orthodox churches: the former acknowledged the validity of the orders conferred by the latter ones, but then presented the *Padroadists* of Ceylon as if they had given up Christianity! On the contrary, Antonio da Costa observed striking continuities between Catholicism and Orthodoxy. Even the undeniable differences between the Latin and the oriental rites were actually tolerated by the Roman Catholic Church, once it recognized as anointed by the Lord the bishops of the Greek rites, subject to their own Patriarch. The Roman Church also allowed Greek priests (probably meaning Greek Catholic priests) to say Mass according to their rites in Latin churches. According to Costa the transition of the Ceylon *Padroadists* was marked by continuity:

> The religion which they professed under the Portuguese is essentially the same they continue to profess. What is different is the supreme terrestrial head, for ours reside in Rome, theirs in Constantinople [sic]. It is true they reject some dogmas of the Catholic Roman Church, as for example, the Pope's infallibility, which they could not accept because they do not recognize him (and to which the king of Portugal, a Catholic, did not give his placet, not admitting it therefore in his dominions), and some others, which, however, do not in the least interfere with the essence of the law of Christ. Religion is a necessity, and the Ceylonese might easily have embraced the dominant (protestant) religion which being far more different from the Roman Catholic, it is beyond doubt that those who helped them to accept the Greek rite in lieu of the one obstinately denied to them by our supreme hierarchy, have done a very meritorious action.[76]

From this passage we can see that Costa's support for the choice made by the Ceylon *Padroadists* was not based on a very thorough knowledge of the oriental tradition they had embraced. Costa confused the Syrian and the Greek traditions, believing that the "supreme terrestrial head" of the Syrian Orthodox Church was actually the Patriarch of Constantinople and not the one of Antioch.

3. Expansion in Madurai

The Italian Jesuit Roberto Nobili (1577–1656) founded a pioneering Catholic mission in Madurai under the jurisdiction of the Malabar Province of the Society of Jesus.[77] This Province was one of the territorial partitions that composed the Portuguese Assistantship, represented in Rome precisely by a General Assistant helping the *Præpositus* or General Father of the Society.[78] The mission established in Madurai and the one that followed the same accommodationist method in Mysore were an essential part of the *Padroado* system of Latin Christianity in India. With the suppression of the Jesuits and their subsequent reconstitution in 1814, the way was opened for a return of the Jesuits in the old missions that they had created two

---

nismo. Mas, ainda ha pouco, o arcebispo Ornellas aceitou no seu gremio, sem conferir novas ordens, os sacerdotes, a quem as conferiu o bispo Mellus desse mesmo rito syriaco que hoje professam os ceyloneses. Como se explica isto?"

76 PERNIOLA, *The Catholic Church*. The British Period. Vol. 8, 149.
77 The most comprehensive study on Nobili is the one by P. BACHMANN, *Roberto Nobili, 1577–1656. Ein Missionsgeschichtlicher Beitrag zum Christlichen Dialog mit Hinduismus* (Rome 1972).
78 See ALDEN, *The Making of An Enterprise,* 234–235.

centuries before.[79] However, the Jesuits that came this time were no more Portuguese, but French, and rather than being supporters of the *Padroado*, they were among the most effective troops of Propaganda Fide. This fundamental turn in ecclesiastical politics created the foundations for the explosion of *Padroado*-Propaganda conflicts even in the interior of the Tamil country during the nineteenth century. Those Catholics who disobeyed the Papal decisions in favour of the Propaganda Fide jurisdiction were in dire want of priests for the maintenance of their communities. Alvares as an ordained priest, and later on as a consecrated Bishop of the Malankara Church was among the Indian clerics who fulfilled the demands of the *Padroado* loyalists in a time of underlying schism, after the open one of the two decades 1838–1857.

From archival records, we are able to identify a number of cases in which local Catholic churches throughout South India, notwithstanding repeated conciliatory attempts between the Portuguese and Papal authorities, were widely torn up and stranded in despair. We can distinctively see this dynamic in South Canara, where the establishment of the Brahmavar Church, known today as the Malankara Syrian Orthodox Diocese of Brahmavar, in Udupi district, Karnataka, was the outcome of the commotion that occurred in Kallianpur in 1887–1889.[80] The main historiographical account of these events from a Roman Catholic perspective is a typed manuscript by a parish priest of the church of Milagres, Julian D'Souza, who was himself involved in the long-lasting rivalry with the Syriac Christian community in Brahmavar, trying to convince them to return to the Roman Church.[81] In recent years, his narrative of the "Brahmavar schism" has been challenged by scholarly efforts made by the Malankara Syrian Orthodox historians, by proposing an alternative ecclesiological perspective, and by highlighting the integration process of formerly Roman Catholic community into the Malankara Syrian Church.[82] Neither the Roman Catholic nor the Malankara Syrian Orthodox perspectives stress caste as a latent cause for the Kallianpur split. The cleavage between the *Padroado*-Propaganda parties stands alone as the main drive for the former Kallianpur "schismatics", who developed a strong identity as Syrian Christians for the next generations while retaining the Tridentine Latin Rite as their official liturgy until it was replaced by the Western Syriac rite in 1980s. Further scholarship is required to understand the century-long process of liturgical transformations undertaken by the Brahmavar Orthodox community, which was a unique and intriguing case in the history of South Asian Christianity.

In contrast, the missions established in Tamil Nadu were embedded in a set of well-studied social tensions, all stemming from the caste conflicts among Christians. At present the main scholarly reference on these little known missions are some pages from Susan Bayly's highly influential study on religious dynamics in South India between the 18th and the 20th

---

79 Several essays comparing the Old and the New Madurai mission are found in A. AMALADASS (ed.), *Jesuit Presence in Indian history.* Commemorative Volume on the Occasion of the 150th Anniversary of the New Madurai Mission, 1838–1988 (Anand [Gujarat] 1988).
80 On the "Kallianpur question", see D. KAMATH S.J. / P. FIDELIS PINTO, *Defiant Submission. A history of the Diocese of Mangalore.* Vol. 2 (Mangalore 2014, 181–202).
81 Whereas D'SOUZA's manuscript entitled *Historical Notes on Some of The Churches of The Diocese of Mangalore, S. Kanara With Special Reference to The Kallianpur-Brahmavar Schism* (Mangalore, 1951) is currently not accessible, his studies have been quoted by K.K. FARIAS, *The Christian Impact in South Kanara* (Mumbai 1999), 224–226.
82 Among recent studies there are L.D. CRASTA, "The Konkani Congregation in the Malankara Orthodox Church. An Historical Approach" (Kottayam 2001); B.M. THOMAS, "A Journey through the Life of Bishop Alvares Mar Julios: A Vigilant Promoter of Ecumenism", paper read at *Journeying Together in Faith: Ecumenical Endeavours in South India,* Church History Association of India, Southern India Branch Triennial Conference, at Sophia Center, Old Seminary, Kottayam, 31 January to 1 February 2018.

century.[83] Regrettably, Bayly resorts to problematic value judgements on the Independent Catholic leaders, almost interiorizing the Roman Catholic sources.[84] She is also unaware of the significant background of Alvares, to the point of stating that, by the time he created his Independent Catholic community, he "seem[ed] to have been an ex-seminarian", when in fact he had been a well-known and highly visible mature priest.[85] In Bayly's interpretation, the passage of Alvares and Soares to the Malankara Orthodox Church is just a further instance of a "strategy of tactical conversion[s]", through which the various Syrian Christian denominations were trying to increase their size and to represent themselves as "committed to 'progressive' social action", particularly by undertaking "vigorous shows of involvement in the 'uplift' of low-caste and untouchable Hindus".[86] Bayly seems to not be taking into account the entrenched Catholic tensions between *Padroado* and Propaganda Fide jurisdictions across the Tamil region, but attributes Alvares and Soares' work purely to an initiative of the Syrian Christian metropolitans (she uses the term of "Jacobite metran").[87] On the contrary, we have seen how it was the Padroadists who approached the Malankara Orthodox, by no means the other way round. While it is possible that the evangelical efforts of the Syrian Christians at converting people from the Pulaya, Ezhava, and Cheruma communities in Kerala might have provided "a means to assert a new form of supremacy over tenants and client labourers at a time when 'traditional' service ties were being undermined by the changing economic situation",[88] such a dynamic has little do do both with the relations established with the Independent Catholics of Goa and Ceylon, and with the missions among the dissident Catholics in Tamil Nadu. In relation to the latter communities, Bayly argues from an anthropological point of view that Alvares and Soares could be identified by the new converts with the region's charismatic cult saints and sectarian gurus, who could offer "an alternative form of endorsement to south Indian Christians who were fighting their own priests and missionaries over matters of church discipline and ceremonial precedence", allegedly avoiding "the risk of excommunication".[89] In fact, this interpretation requires a first fundamental qualification: the Catholics who chose to follow Alvares and Soares were excommunicated by the Roman Catholic church, hence an alleged avoidance of the risk of excommunication cannot be invoked to explain the conversion dynamic.

---

83 S. BAYLY, *Saints, Goddesses, and Kings.* Muslims and Christians in South Indian Society, 1700–1900 (Cambridge 1989), 316–319, 375, 449–450.
84 Soares and Alvarez are described as "two of the oddest and most colourful religious leaders", as "renegade clerics" (p. 316), as well as as "rogue clerics" (p. 450). Soares is defined once as "a near-illiterate Eurasian from Goa" and then as a "celebrated buccaneer churchman" (p. 449).
85 BAYLY, *Saints, Goddesses, and Kings,* 316. On a similar note, Joseph René Vilatte's episcopal consecration is presented as being imparted upon a "failed seminarian" (p. 318), even though the Frenchman had been ordained priest in Bern's Old Catholic Cathedral on 7 June 1885.
86 BAYLY, *Saints, Goddesses, and Kings,* 314, 316.
87 For a chronology of Alvares' missions in Ceylon and India, Bayly draws her data from C.M. AGUR's *Church History of Travancore* (New Delhi 1990, 1st ed. 1903) but obviously misplaces the factual sequence of that movement. In fact, Agur's narrative on the two Goan priests is generally correct. For example, Bayly fixed the death year of Alvares as 1895 instead of 1923. This error is even copied by MICHAEL BERGUNDER in his chapter entitled "Proselytism in the History of Christianity in India", in: R.E. FRYKENBERG / R. FOX YOUNG (eds.), *India and the Indianness of Christianity*. Essays on Understanding – Historical, Theological, and Bibliographical – in Honor of Robert Eric Frykenberg (Grand Rapids, Michigan / Cambridge 2009, 181–195, specif. 183). A "copy of registration of death" of Alvares, dated 24 September 1923, has been published by AJESH PHILIP / GEORGE ALEXANDER, *Western Rites of Syriac-Malankara Orthodox Churches. Part II* (Kerala 2019), 51.
88 BAYLY, *Saints, Goddesses, and Kings,* 314–315.
89 BAYLY, *Saints, Goddesses and Kings,* 316.

Michael Bergunder refers to Bayly's analysis, claiming furthermore that the Independent Catholic missions have to be seen in the context of the proselytistic movements between the Orthodox and the Roman Catholics in India, with the Independent Catholic being a temporary and ultimately unsuccessful passage to the Malankara Orthodox church.[90] It is certainly possible to see Alvares and his partners in this perspective, however Bergunder, just as Bayly, misses two fundamental points: the Independent Catholics were dissident Padroadists and they retained the Latin rite while being Syrian Christians, as it is clearly seen in the Brahmavar mission.

The Tamil perception of Alvares and Soares' evangelical work, however, can hardly be deemed a purely Syrian proselytism, if we rely on the records kept by the French Jesuits of the Madurai mission, whose parish diaries and correspondence deliver substantial information on the "schismatic Goans". According to their notes, the peripatetic Soares and his fellow priests had constant legal disputes with the Jesuits at Manapad,[91] Periyathalai (also spelt as Periatalai), Uvari (also Ovari),[92] Kootapuly (also Kouttapouli),[93] Thoothukudi (also Tuticorin), Tirunelveli (formerly Tinnevelly, especially in a place called Velappaty), Vadakkankulam,[94] and Dindigul (especially in Muttakapatti),[95] the last of which became a center of Soares' missionary network in the Tamil region. Many of these missions had a long history of *Padroado* controversies since the early nineteenth century. For instance, in 1853 Dindigul was reported to have 12,000 Christians, one fourth out of whom however followed a schismatic Goan priest. That priest had then

> three of the largest and the best churches, which were formerly built by the Jesuit missionaries, and which were made over to the present Fathers [i.e. the French Jesuits] by the Christians on their return to the country in 1838. They continued in their possession for some years, when, strange though it may appear, they were, by the arbitrary order of an English police magistrate, forcibly expelled from them, and being Frenchmen, their ignorance of the necessary steps prevented their obtaining redress.[96]

Dindigul case shows that the success of Alvares and Soares in Madurai was entirely dependent on the legacy of the local resistance to the Propaganda missionaries since the return of the New Society of Jesus to India in 1838.

Soares' legal cases, especially about the celebration of two Catholic marriages, called public attention in 1896, eventually winning over the Jesuit Adrian Caussanel at the District Court of Tinnevelly and then at the High Court of Madras.[97] The reason for which the Jesuits

---

90 BERGUNDER, "Proselytism in the History of Christianity in India", 183–184.
91 "Records connected with the New Mission: the disputes between the Propaganda Missionaries & Goa Missionaries on the arrival of the priests of the new mission at Manapad", 1897, at The Jesuit Archives of Madurai Province, Shembaganur (Kodaikanal), 217/143.
92 "Soares in Periatalai et Orari (Vicenti) 1896, Fr. Machabert", at The Jesuit Archives of Madurai Province, Shembaganur (Kodaikanal), 217/229.
93 LEON BESSE, *La mission du Maduré*. Historique de ses pangous (Trichinopoly 1914), 554–558.
94 On this specific locality, see BAYLY, *Saints, Goddesses and Kings*, 449–450.
95 BESSE, *La mission*, 157–158.
96 See the English Jesuit WILLIAM STRICKLAND's description on a certain schismatic priest in his *The Jesuit in India*. Addressed to All Who Are Interested in the Foreign Missions (London 1852), 201–202.
97 See Soares' victorious case in Tuticorin reported in the article "Triumph of Truth", in *The Independent Catholic*, January 1895, 3. See a report on his victory in Tinnevelly in *The Independent Catholic*, February 1895, 2. The final decision of the Madras High Court concerning Caussanel's complaint against Soares on 16 April 1896 was published in C. BOULNOIS / J. BROWN / J. G. SMITH, *Indian Law Reports*. Madras Series containing Cases

denounced Soares was that he performed the sacrament of marriage according to the Catholic liturgy while being an excommunicated Catholic priest. The very danger posed by Soares and Alvares to the local Jesuit missionaries was their strong similarity to the Roman Catholic Church, rather than their acquired Syrian otherness. To support their vicar in Tamil Nadu, the Independent Catholics in Colombo started a debate against the author of a pamphlet, a Jesuit of St Joseph's College in Trichinopoly.[98] In reaction, the Jesuits made a detailed account of all the alleged transgressions of Soares. The legal proceedings reveal the initiative of a Parava Christian community in Tinnevelly, led by a layman named Vincenti, who invited Soares to assist their group in separating from the Propaganda priests, namely the French Jesuits.[99] This detail resembles how the Ceylon *Padroado* Mission's approached Alvares and Lisboa Pinto in 1887, as well as the discussions held among the Portuguese Burghers at Batticaloa in Ceylon, as we saw in chapter 5.

For reasons still to be uncovered, in 1898 Soares left the Independent Catholic Mission and the Syrian Orthodox Church in order to join the Syro-Chaldean Church, acquiring the title of *Mar Basilius, Syro-Chaldean Metropolitan of India, Ceylon, Goa, Socotora* (or Socotra), etc.[100] Again similar to Vilatte's connection to Ceylon, the English ex-Anglican priest Vernon Herford contacted Mar Basilius, seeking an episcopal consecration.[101]

Further research on Soares and the various missions across Tamil Nadu requires much more effort, namely a systematic exploration into the local archives, Jesuit collections, as well as family records. It is fascinating to see how our existing understanding of the Independent Catholic Mission centred on church hierarchies and lay leaders is actually challenged by the evidence suggesting grassroot initiatives, embedded in community identities and caste conflicts among the Tamil Christians.

Determined by the High Court at Madras and by the Judicial Committee of the Privy Council on Appeal from that Court (Madras 1898), 273–285.
98 "The Effusions of an Old Pupil" (*The Independent Catholic*, Apil 1895), 2-3.
99 A summary of these legal proceedings was offered by S. ARULDOSS, SJ, "Jesuit Madurai Mission and the Goanese Schism with special reference to Mar Basilius", paper read at the conference *A Global and Local History of the Buona Morte Church*, 22–23 November 2018, Caritas-SEDEC & the Buona Morte Church, Colombo.
100 BESSE, *La mission*, 157.
101 See BRANDETH, *Episcopi Vagantes,* 90–94; H.S.B. MAR GREGORIUS I., *A Voyage into the Orient Being Extracts from the Diary of the Rt. Rev. Bishop Vernon Herford*. Edited with an Introduction, Footnotes, and Appendices (Hove, Anvers, Belgium 1954).

Chapter 7:
The Independent Catholic in the Ceylon Public Sphere

1. The Independent Catholic as a Cradle of Trade Unionism: A Literature Review

Similar to the movement that gave it its name, the journal called *The Independent Catholic* has received little attention in the historiography on nineteenth-century Ceylon, with the only exception of Visakha Kumari Jayawardena's *The Rise of the Labor Movement in Ceylon*, first published in 1972. The author combed through journal issues of 1892–1893, so as to trace how trade unionism was first introduced to the Crown colony shortly before 60 workers came out on a strike in Colombo in September 1893 against the British-owned publisher H. W. Cave & Co.[1] Jayawardena pointed out the immediate influence of two editorials entitled "Trades' Unions", published between July and August 1893. They reported on the upsurge of printers' rebellions, urging them "to be the first workers to unionize".[2] By describing *The Independent Catholic* as the cradle of trade unionism, Jayawardena brought the previously obscure monthly newspaper to the forefront of the labour movement, and identified it as a herald of the nascent nationalism in the British colony.

Jayawardena further remarked that those who assumed the leadership of the workers' agitation were not from the labouring classes, but rather belonged to the middle class. This social group, according to Jayawardena's analysis, included both British colonists and the indigenous elites, enjoying wealth or a relatively "high status" in the local society. Within the Ceylonese middle class we can discern a spectrum of socio-political positions according to their degree of conformity with and consent to the British imperial power. Jayawardena defines the radicals within this middle class as "a small minority of professional men who had come into contact with foreign political and social movements and were active in fostering various campaigns in Ceylon, including the Buddhist revival, the temperance and political reform movement, and working-class agitation".[3] In the early stage of the Ceylon labour movement, the radical wing of the Burghers under the influence of British rationalism and the concomitant anti-Christian discourses[4] were driven by what they called a "public spirit", by which they advocated in the first place the interests of workers, who allegedly were "not in a position to put forward their demands independently"[5]:

---

1 For a brief study on the strike in 1893 see TILAK KULARATNE, *History of Printing and Publishing in Ceylon, 1736–1912* (Dehiwala, Sri Lanka 2006), 212–213.
2 VISAKHA KUMARI JAYAWARDENA, *The Rise of the Labor Movement in Ceylon* (Durham, North Carolina 1972), 85.
3 JAYAWARDENA, *The Rise of the Labor Movement*, 74.
4 JAYAWARDENA, *The Rise of the Labor Movement*, 51–53.
5 JAYAWARDENA, *The Rise of the Labor Movement*, 89.

> We propose, then, to day to present to our readers an article on the subject of Trade-Unions, which may serve as an object lesson to illustrate to our countrymen the public spirit shown by even the working classes of other nations, and to point out to them the immense advantages to be gained from such organisations, and as our purpose is an essentially practical one, we shall also consider the necessity of Trade-Unions for Ceylon and their practicability here.[6]

In concrete terms, Jayawardena highlighted several avantgardes among the printers' trade union movement, exploring the circumstances in which the radical Burghers – who gathered around *The Independent Catholic* – partook in the labour movement, agitating not only against the British ruling class but also the conservative fraction of the Eurasian community. A debate on trade unionism that took place in the English newspapers in Colombo expressively marked the polarised visions of the Burghers concerning a modern society. On the one side of the debate stood the trade unions leader Alfred Ernest Buultjens (1865–1916), *The Independent Catholic* co-Editor Pedro Manuel Lisboa Pinto (1858–1898), together with the lawyer H. J. Charles Pereira (1858–1924)[7] and the businessman Martinus C. Pereira[8], as well as the Buddhist educationist and journalist Calutantrige Don Bastian (1852–1921)[9], who all advocated for the improvement of the payment and healthcare of workers.[10] The opposite side vehemently denied workers' precarious conditions. The popular daily *Ceylon Independent* remarked that the "native workman is, as a rule, perfectly happy".[11] Trade unions would only provoke a sedition of workers who had a good relation with the employers.[12] The development of this political split within the Ceylonese middle class has not yet been fully explored, but its influence on the public sphere of the colony was undeniable. Since 1888 the *Ceylon Independent* had been owned by the Dutch Burgher Hector van Cuylenberg and was considered the cheapest of the earliest "penny" newspapers in Ceylon. With a circulation of up to 3,270 copies per day, it claimed to be the largest newspaper across the island.[13] The anti-unionist party could also count on the major English evening daily *The Times of Ceylon*, as was shown by its campaign against the initial acquittal of a certain William, who worked as machine ruler for the production of account books by the printer H. W. Cave. William undertook a strike in September 1893 and his employer denounced him for an alleged breach of an Ordinance of 1865, under which "journeymen artificers" were not allowed to abstain from their regular work.[14] The Magistrate of the Provincial Court in Colombo initially ruled

---

6   "Trade Unions" (*The Independent Catholic*, August 1893), 1.
7   On Charles Pereira's involvement in the printers' movement see K. JAYAWARDENA, *The Rise of the Working Class in Sri Lanka & the Printers Strike of 1893* (Wellawatta, Sri Lanka 1974), 15. On Pereira's later activities in relation to the 1912 Constitutional reforms see JAYAWARDENA, *The Rise of the Labor Movement*, 137–138.
8   U. KARIYAWASAM, *Industrial Relations and the Political Process in Sri Lanka* (Geneva 1981), 37.
9   Don Bastian was known as a Buddhist educationist, journalist, Sinhala *nurti* dramatist, and temperance activist. See a brief biography in K.N.O. DHARMADASA, *Language, Religion, and Ethnic Assertiveness. The Growth of Sinhalese Nationalism in Sri Lanka* (Ann Arbor 1992), 127. On the new theatrical style of *Nurti,* inspired by touring Parsi troupes, see WICKRAMSINGHE, *Sri Lanka in the Modern Age*, 85–87.
10 "Trade Unions" (*The Independent Catholic*, August 1893), 1.
11 "Trade Union. To the Editor of *Ceylon Independent*" (*The Independent Catholic*, August 1893), 2.
12 JAYAWARDENA, *The Rise of the Labor Movement*, 85.
13 KULARATNE, *History of Printing*, 182. The appeal ruling on Cave vs. William, issued on 5 December 1893, can be found in H.L. WENDT / T.E. DE SAMPAYO / F.M. DE SARAM (eds.), *The Ceylon Law Reports. Being the Reports of Cases Decided by the Supreme Court of Ceylon* (Colombo 1897), 47–48.
14 "An Ordinance to consolidate and amend the Law relating to Servants, Labourers, and Journeymen Artificers under Contracts for Hire and Service", namely Ordinance No. 11 of 1865, can be consulted in *A Revised Edition*

out that a machine ruler worker could fall into the category of "journeyman worker", so that William's strike could not be punished. *The Times of Ceylon* sided with H. W. Cave, providing media support to the appeal promoted by the Attorney General. William's acquittal was repealed by the Supreme Court of Ceylon soon after, in December 1893.[15] *The Independent Catholic* in its second year of existence could hardly compete with the two predominant English publishers in Colombo, and its radical social proposals attracted attention only from "the rural and urban lower middle class, and the urban working class"[16], remaining at the margins of colonial society.

In her social analysis of British Ceylon, Jayawardena defined the eccentric *The Independent Catholic* as "a small radical journal" and described its contributors as part of a radical middle class.[17] Her argument rested on a comparative study of James Alfred Ernst Buultjens (1865–1916) and Pedro Manuel Lisboa Pinto, who shared a commitment to trade unionism, but promoted two separate, even contradictory religious initiatives, namely Theosophy and Independent Catholicism. Buultjens epitomized the maverick Ceylonese intellectuals. Born to a Burgher family rooted in Presbyterianism and Anglicanism, he received an exclusive English education. Since the early 19th century Burghers enjoyed the privilege of being recruited into the colonial administration, while young Burgher men attending the top Anglican schools could aspire to pass the Cambridge Local Examinations and win a government fellowship for pursuing higher education in Britain.[18] This was the path through which the 19-year-old Buultjens was able to enter St John's College at Cambridge University, where he studied Moral and Natural Sciences from 1884 to 1887. In his autobiography, Buultjens summarised his transformation during the Cambridge years as "an advancement from Christianity to materialism", and his conspicuous absence at the college chapel marked his public confrontation with Christianity.[19] Similar to many English educated Ceylonese intellectuals, he was influenced by English Liberalism, freethinkers like the militant atheist Charles Bradlaugh (1833–1891), but was also attracted by the newly established Theosophical Society, whose founders Helena Blavatsky (1831–1891) and Henry Steel Olcott (1832–1907) had visited Ceylon in 1880, where they had been officially acknowledged as Buddhists. Upon his return to Ceylon in 1888, Buultjens converted to Buddhism and devoted himself to Buddhist lay education. From 1890 to 1903, he served as the principal of the Pettah Buddhist Boys School, later renamed Ananda College, where the courses were offered in English and the syllabus was modeled on Christian schools. He was also one of the editors of a militant anti-Christian English weekly, *The Buddhist*, which was in open strife with the Anglican Church and all other Christian denominations.[20]

---

    of the Ordinances of the Government of Ceylon. Vol. 1: 1799–1882 (Colombo 1894), 377–385. § 11 of the Ordinance sanctioned the refusal to work by a "servant" or a "journeyman artificer".

15 KULARATNE, *History of Printing*, 181.
16 JAYAWARDENA, *The Rise of the Labor Movement*, 74.
17 JAYAWARDENA, *The Rise of the Labor Movement*, 84.
18 Several Sinhalese intellectuals followed the same path, such as Sir Ponnambalam Arunachalam (1853–1924) and Solomon West Ridgeway Dias Bandaranaike (1899–1959). See K. N. O. DHARMADASA, *Language, Religion, and Ethnic Assertiveness. The Growth of Sinhalese Nationalism in Sri Lanka* (Ann Arbor 1992), 321–322.
19 A.E. BUULTJENS, "Why I became a Buddhist: A Lecture Delivered by Mr. A.E. Buultjens at the Buddhist Headquarters at the Request of the Colombo YMBA, March 25 1899" (*The Buddhist* 7 and 8, March and April 1899, 102–129).
20 JAYAWARDENA, *The Rise of the Labor Movement*, 81–82.

Lisboa Pinto, the "independent-minded rebel"[21] who migrated from Bombay to Colombo in 1888, shared with Buultjens a religious assertiveness, couched in a fierce denunciation of the Roman Catholic authorities whom he had previously been subject to. On the basis of the self-statements published in *The Independent Catholic* and in an anonymous pamphlet entitled *The Church Militant in India and Ceylon*, Jayawardena argues correctly that the Indo-Portuguese medical doctor addressed grievances against the "foreign control" of Rome over the Catholic Church in Goa, but she does not delve deeper into the *Padroado* question or the Catholic Church history in South Asia.[22] Jayawardena underlined that Lisboa Pinto was a fighter against the Catholic clergy protesting against what he considered "the scandal of the Catholic religion in the East".[23] Conversely, quoting an anonymous pamphlet entitled *A Crucial Test* (Colombo: Catholic Orphan Press, 1889), Jayawardena shows how the Goan-Bombay doctor was perceived by his detractors as someone "defaming the Church and the Papacy, holding up the Catholics of Ceylon to the contempt of other religionists, and lastly, practising the credulity of his Protestant readers"[24]. While these expressions give a good sense of the sharp denominational antagonism, it is necessary to explore the mechanisms that originated them.

A Crucial Test was written in response to Lisboa Pinto's English booklet *Antioch and Rome and their Connection with St Peter*, published previously in Colombo in November 1889.[25] In this treatise Lisboa Pinto aimed at an erudite refutation of Rome's primacy over the other patriarchal sees, through a rebuttal of St Peter's apostolate and martyrdom in the Eternal City, and then of the succession of the Roman Popes from the Prince of the Apostles. The argument rested fundamentally on the lack of New Testament evidence on Peter having ministered in Rome, and on anecdotes on the alleged debauchery of certain Popes. Lisboa Pinto quoted numerous authors, both early modern and contemporary, ranging from the Jesuit theologian Roberto Bellarmino (1542–1621), to ecclesiastical historians such as the Oratorian Cardinal Cesare Baronio (1538–1607), Louis Ellies Dupin (1657–1719), James Tytler (1745–1804), John Milner (1752–1826), and Emilio Castelar y Ripoll (1833–1899), in addition to a selection of Popes and Church Fathers. The profuse quotations and assemblage of statements in the 40-page long booklet incited Lisboa Pinto's adversary to doubt his "uncommonly well-furnished library", for "most of the books referred to in the pamphlet are not to be found in the Island – at least outside Mr. P[into]'s library."[26] Given the impossibility of checking all the authorities quoted, as their books were not available in Ceylon, the anonymous author tested the accuracy of Lisboa Pinto's pamphlet through a single "crucial test", namely a check on a passage from Bellarmino's treatise *De Romano Pontifice*. He concluded that Lisboa Pinto merely relied on secondhand quotations from Protestant tracts, and hence could only understand falsely the "saintly and learned Cardinal Bellarmine".[27]

---

21 JAYAWARDENA, *The Rise of the Labor Movement*, 87.
22 JAYAWARDENA, *The Rise of the Labor Movement*, 86, footnote 47. Jayawardena interviewed Lisboa Pinto's daughter, Mrs. Patricia Lobo. It is likely through the communication with her that Jayawardena attributed the anonymous pamphlet *The Church Militant in India and Ceylon* (Colombo December 1888) to Lobo's father.
23 JAYAWARDENA, *The Rise of the Labor Movement*, 86.
24 ANONYMOUS [A Missionary Apostolic], *A Crucial Test* (Colombo 1889), 6, quoted in JAYAWARDENA, *The Rise of the Labor Movement*, 86.
25 It was published first in English and then translated into Portuguese as P.M. LISBOA PINTO, *Antiochia e Roma e sua connexão* [sic] *com S. Pedro* (Bombaim 1890). I use a copy of the Portuguese version kept at the library of the Xavier Centre of Historical Research, Alto Porvorim, Goa.
26 ANONYMOUS, *A Crucial Test*, 1–2.
27 ANONYMOUS, *A Crucial Test*, 6.

The anonymous Catholic defence perhaps represented a critique to which a wider circle of Roman Catholic readers would have been susceptible in regard to the Independent Catholics. Lisboa Pinto's recourse to Roman Catholic authors intended to strengthen the anti-Catholic arguments. However, this method had been utilised extensively by Anglican and Protestant writers in the past centuries to suit their attacks against papacy. A good example are the anthologies and rebuttals of Bellarmine's works in English in the nineteenth century, which would become part of the anti-Roman literature for the Independent Catholic authors in Ceylon.[28] The fact that the anonymous Catholic author paired Lisboa Pinto with Protestant authors and readers implied a suspicion of an alliance between the two Christian groups.

Jayawardena's assessment of Lisboa Pinto becomes contradictory to her intention of showing a resemblance between him and the "radical" Buultjens. On one side, Buultjens was consistent in his bitter attacks on the Anglican Church as well as the British government.[29] On the other side, Lisboa Pinto allegedly sided with the Protestant propaganda. Jayawardena's partial analysis of Lisboa Pinto led her to overlook the latent tensions between the two unionist leaders. Both were raised in Christian families and educated in leading English schools that opened up in the colonial metropolises, i.e. Colombo and Bombay respectively. Both travelled to Europe and gained academic recognition in British and Portuguese intellectual circles. Both expressed genuine sympathy towards the working class and were critical of the indifference of the wealthy.[30] Jayawardena also mentioned Lisboa Pinto's involvement in the temperance society, a social reform that was also promoted by the Buddhists.[31] On the other hand, however, there existed ample nuances between the two figures vis-à-vis the colonial society. The very fact that Lisboa Pinto did not renounce Catholicism – but rather changed from the Latin to the Syriac communion – makes it less convincing to label him as equally radical as Buultjens. Contrary to Buultjens' "radical fever" against the promulgation of the British Education Act in 1892,[32] Lisboa Pinto showed considerable contentment with the British governor and was active in academic institutes sponsored by the government such as the Royal Asiatic Society. Needless to say that the "foreign control", namely the Catholic authority that the Independent Catholics revolted against, was the Papacy, not the British imperial power.

This being said, Jayawardena was not totally unaware of the differences between Buultjens and Lisboa Pinto. For instance, she stressed that the former's Buddhist propaganda activities "lay in his emphasis on patriotism and national feeling"[33]. She hardly applied this assertion to the Goan-Bombay medical doctor, who did not fit squarely the role of Ceylonese proto-nationalist. The fact that the Independent Catholic Mission appeared in the spotlight of the Ceylon labour movement can provide a vantage point to re-examine the decades at the turn of century, best known for Buddhist and Muslim revivalism in Ceylon and beyond. In terms of impact on the Ceylon society, the minoritarian Independent Catholics were certainly

---

28 An early use of Bellarmine's arguments on Rome and Antioch can be found for instance in RICHARD BERNARD, *Fabulous Foundation of the Popedom, shewing* [sic] *that St Peter was never at Rome* (Oxford 1619). Bernard was a Puritan theologian in Oxford. This text was reprinted and published in S. DREW (ed.), *Imperial Magazine, or, Compendium of Religious, Moral, & Philosophical Knowledge*. Vol. 3 (London 1821), 428–436. A compilation of Anglican theologians' tracts on Bellarmine was published under the title ARCHBISHOP T. TENISON ET ALS., *Cardinal Bellarmine's Notes of the Church Examined and Refuted*. In a Series of Tracts (London 1840).
29 JAYAWARDENA, *The Rise of the Labor Movement*, 82.
30 JAYAWARDENA, *The Rise of the Labor Movement*, 89.
31 JAYAWARDENA, *The Rise of the Labor Movement*, 86–87.
32 JAYAWARDENA, *The Rise of the Labor Movement*, 83.
33 JAYAWARDENA, *The Rise of the Labor Movement*, 83.

surpassed by their celebrated contemporaries, such as the Buddhist revivalist Anagarika Dharmapala (1864–1933), the Tamil civil servant Ponnambalam Arunachalam (1853–1929), and the Ceylon "Moor" solicitor and politician M. C. Siddi Lebbe (1838–1898), whose interactions and controversies between each other accompanied the rise of a Sinhala Buddhist nationalist identity.[34] Due to the relatively relaxed censorship of publications in Ceylon, contrasting with the Goan case, the small group of Portuguese, Sinhala, and Tamil speaking Christian reformers in Ceylon were able to establish relations with other global Christian minorities through the printed press. In this chapter we continue our assessment of Jayawardena's pioneering research on the newspaper *The Independent Catholic* by re-adjusting the analytical lens from a focus on the socio-economic life in Ceylon to the global religious public sphere.[35] We examine the origin, circulation and the exchange arrangements of *The Independent Catholic* with other Ceylonese newspapers and beyond, so as to see how the small Christian movement was able to spread its voice to a global Christian audience, comparable to Dharmapala's message to the universal Buddhist world.

2. The Printing Press in Nineteenth Century Ceylon: Boom and Impacts

2.1 Journalism Boom

The Independent Catholic was born in a time of newspaper boom in British Ceylon. The second half of the nineteenth century witnessed an explosive increase in the total number of newspapers, in both English and vernacular languages. In 1832, the sixth Ceylon governor Robert Wilmot Horton (in office 1831–1837) granted a *Colombo Journal* to be printed at the Government Press, marking the commencement of the history of journalism in the island. Even though the first journal circulated for merely one year before giving up its function to the already existing *Government Gazette*, the need for public media had been widely perceived by merchants and religious institutions. Until the 1850s, at least 17 English newspapers started circulating in Ceylon, most of which lasted for only two to three years. The number rose to 140 by the end of the century, with a steep increase in the last quarter.[36] From 1832 onwards, various Protestant missions started bilingual magazines introducing Scripture

---

34 A fundamental study on the Buddhist–Christian controversy is R. Fox Young / G.P.V. Somaratna, *Vain Debates*. The Buddhist-Christian Controversies of Nineteenth-Century Ceylon (Vienna 1996). A newer book on Dharmapala is S. Kemper, *Rescued from the Nation*. Anagarika Dharmapala and the Buddhist World (Chicago 2015). See the conflicts between Arunachalam and the Muslims in Kumari Jayawardena, *Nobodies to Somebodies*. The Rise of the Colonial Bourgeoisie in Sri Lanka (London 2003), 225; and Dharmapala's anti–Muslim statements in Ameer Ali, "Four Waves of Muslim-Phobia in Sri Lanka. C.1880–2009" (*Journal of Muslim Minority Affairs* 35/4 October 2015), 489. On the Catholic conflicts with other religions see R. L. Stirrat, *Power and Religiosity in a Post-Colonial Setting*. Sinhala Catholics in Contemporary Sri Lanka (Cambridge 1992), 19–21, and Gintota Parana Vidanage Somaratna, *Kotahena Riot 1883*. A Religious Riot in Sri Lanka (Gangodawila / Nugegoda 1991).
35 For an example of Christian public sphere in nineteenth century South Africa, West Africa, and the Philippines see "Transregionale und internationale Nachrichten und Perspektiven" in Klaus Koschorke et al., *"To Give Publicity to Our Thoughts"*. Journale asiatischer und afrikanischer Christen um 1900 und die Entstehung einer transregionalen indigen-christlichen Öffentlichkeit / Journals of Asian and African Christians around 1900 and the Making of a Transregional Indigenous-Christian Public Sphere (Wiesbaden 2018), 163–202.
36 V.B. de Silva, "English Periodicals of Nineteenth Century", in: K.S. Diehl (ed.), *Historical Essays*. Primary Printed and Manuscript Sources for Sixteenth to Nineteenth Century Available in Sri Lanka (Colombo 1976), 73. Also in Kularatne, *History of Printing*, 186.

stories to English as well as Sinhala and Tamil readers.[37] Yet journals exclusively printed in Sinhala did not come into existence until 1860, when the first semi-monthly entitled *Lankālokaya* (Light of Ceylon) appeared in Galle, one of the most important ports, second only to Colombo.[38] Since then Sinhala newspapers displayed a steep increase well into the early twentieth century. Between 1888 and 1924 the total number of Sinhala newspapers counted up to 524.[39] Tamil journalism underwent a similar development, but at a smaller scale. The American Ceylon Mission started *Udayatārakai* (Morning Star) in Jaffna in 1841, first as a bilingual weekly and then as a monolingual exclusively serving a Tamil readership.[40] A Malay newspaper printed in the Arabic alphabet entitled *Alamat Lankāpuri* (News of the Island of Lanka) appeared in 1869, marking the first newspaper ever printed on a lithographic press. A distinct feature of the Malay journals was their wide circulation beyond Ceylon, reaching out to Singapore, Malacca, Penang and Java, where the Malay-speaking Muslim readers were centered.[41]

The burgeoning of Ceylon journalism represented the overall development of public media throughout South and Southeast Asia. Comparing Colombo with entrepôts such as Bombay, Madras, Calcutta, Rangoon, and Singapore, the historian Mark R. Frost points out an "information explosion" as a major characteristic of the British colonies especially between 1870 and 1920, in the light of the extension of imperial mail services and regional and international syndicates.[42] In this chapter we do not aim at a systematic comparison of modern journalism in the various regions. Instead, we only draw on the connectedness of the Ceylon press with that of India, so as to provide a glimpse of the wider context in which *The Independent Catholic* was developed in the South-Asian printing industry and journalism.

A revolution of writing materials and conservation of knowledge took place when the Dutch brought the printing press to Ceylon for the first time in 1737. Although paper was introduced to Ceylon by the Portuguese in the early 16th century, it did not challenge the manuscript tradition with talipot and palmyra leaves, or on copper and golden plates as had been used since the 3rd century BC.[43] The coming of a printing press with movable types was a turning point that led to "a series of unintended consequences".[44] It was used initially for the ordinances or proclamations in the form of *plakkaten* to be distributed to all regions under the Dutch rule, to be read or heard respectively in Dutch, Sinhala and Tamil.[45] Long before, font types for vernacular languages had been developed in India. For instance, Catholic missionaries in Portuguese India had already started printing books in Latin, Portuguese, Tamil, Malayalam, and Konkani since the sixteenth century.[46] During the Portuguese presence in Ceylon, neither the missionaries nor the administrators established printing presses

---

37 KULARATNE, *History of Printing*, 187, 204.
38 KULARATNE, *History of Printing*, 189–190
39 K.N.O. DHARMADASA, "A Nativistic Reaction to Colonialism. The Sinhala-Buddhist Revival in Sri Lanka" (*Asian Studies Journal* 12/1 April 1974), 166.
40 KULARATNE, *History of Printing*, 204; WICKRAMASINGHE, *Sri Lanka in the Modern Age*, 83–84.
41 KULARATNE, *History of Printing*, 205–206.
42 M.R. FROST, "'Wider Opportunities': Religious Revival, Nationalist Awakening and the Global Dimension in Colombo, 1870–1920" (*Modern Asian Studies* 36/4 2002), 940.
43 KULARATNE, *History of Printing*, 7.
44 WICKRAMASINGHE, *Sri Lanka in the Modern Age*, 82.
45 K.S. DIEHL, "The Dutch Press in Ceylon, 1734–96" (*The Library Quarterly. Information, Community, Policy* 42/3 1972), 330.
46 B.S. KESAVAN, *History of Printing and Publishing in India*. South Indian Origins of Printing (New Delhi 1985); ANTONIO MARIA DA CUNHA, "A evolução do Jornalismo na Índia portuguesa", in: *A India Portuguesa*. Vol. 2 (Nova Goa 1923).

in the island. Publications then came from India or from Portugal. The Danish-Halle Lutheran Pietist missions in Tranquebar started to print books in Latin, Portuguese, Danish, German, English, as well as Tamil in the early eighteenth century.[47] The Dutch Reformed Church in Colombo coordinated with the Tranquebar missions and exchanged materials, such as Portuguese and Tamil fonts as well as Tamil Bibles.[48] Sinhala, being a language exclusively spoken in Ceylon, had its fonts cast rather late. When the first printed Sinhala grammar was published in Amsterdam in 1708, Ceylon still had no Sinhala types available.[49] The necessity of having a Sinhala press in Colombo was recognised only when the Dutch candidate-minister Wilhelmus Konijn embarked on the first Sinhala translation of the Bible. The *Predikant* came to Ceylon from Amsterdam in 1704 and spent the next seven years learning Sinhala while rendering the Gospels of Matthew, Mark and John for the native converts. He worked with indigenous copyists to produce the first Sinhala exemplars of the Gospel of Matthews in Colombo in 1713.[50] However, these efforts had to wait until 1737, when a *Singaalesch Gebeede-Boek* ("Sinhalese Prayer Book") was eventually published in Colombo. Publications during the Dutch period included biblical partial translations, *belijdenisboekje* (confirmation booklet), school-books, and *predikatieboek* (anthology of sermons).[51]

With the transition of Ceylon from the Dutch to the British rule since 1796, the printing press in the island experienced a further expansion. When Ceylon was still administered under the Madras Presidency, the Calcutta Auxiliary Bible Society, South Asian branch of the British and Foreign Bible Society, supplied Ceylon with Christian literature written in Sinhala and Tamil.[52] In 1814, namely one year after the elevation of Ceylon to the status of Crown colony, a Colombo Auxiliary Bible Society was established.[53] In 1815 a highly influential and long-lasting press was established in Colombo by the Wesleyan missionaries, publishing books in Sinhala, Tamil, English and Portuguese, also on behalf of other Christian organizations.[54]

Since 1823, various Tract Societies were founded across the island, working effectively at spreading Christian literature in European and vernacular languages.[55] The Church Missionary Society (CMS) established a printing press in Kotte in 1823, and a second one in Nallur, near Jaffna, in 1826.[56] In 1834 it was the turn of the American Board of Commissioners for Foreign Missions (created in Connecticut in 1810) to establish a press in Manipay, near Jaffna.[57] Soon after, in 1841, a Baptist Mission Press was inaugurated in Kandy.[58] The Roman Catholic Church was strongly pressured by such hectic Protestant endeavours, and

---

47 S. MUTHIAH, "Giving India the Printed Word", in: A. GROSS / Y.V. KUMARADOSS / H. LIEBAU (eds.), *Halle and the Beginning of Protestant Christianity in India*. Vol. 3: Communication between India and Europe (Halle 2006, 1241–1248).
48 H. LIEBAU, *Cultural Encounters in India*. The Local Co-Workers of Tranquebar Mission, 18th to 19th Centuries, trans. by R.V. RAJAN (New Delhi 2013), 333.
49 J. VAN GOOR, *Jan Kompenie as Schoolmaster*. Dutch Education in Ceylon 1690–1795" (Groningen 1978), 84–86.
50 VAN GOOR, *Jan Kompenie as Schoolmaster*, 72–73.
51 See K.S. DIEHL, "The Dutch Press in Ceylon, 1734–96" (*The Library Quarterly: Information, Community, Policy* 42/3, 1972, 329–342); G.P.V. SOMARATNA, "The History of the Sinhala Bible" (*Journal of the Royal Asiatic Society of Sri Lanka* 34, 1989, 41–64).
52 KULARATNE, *History of Printing*, 17.
53 KULARATNE, *History of Printing*, 62.
54 KULARATNE, *History of Printing*, 69–105.
55 KULARATNE, *History of Printing*, 150–155.
56 KULARATNE, *History of Printing*, 105–124.
57 KULARATNE, *History of Printing*, 130–140.
58 KULARATNE, *History of Printing*, 124–130.

so decided to open its first printing press in Colombo in 1843, and later another one in Jaffna by 1875.[59] Protestant and Catholic missionaries, through their press apostolate and the creation of schools across the island, challenged the Buddhist majority at multiple levels and in different areas, including the world vision of intellectual professionals.

A most ironical and unintended consequence of the introduction of the printing press by the missionaries occurred when the Buddhists availed themselves of the new public media to fight back against Protestant evangelical propaganda, which tended to equate Buddhism with ignorance. A sizable number of anti-Buddhist tracts by Wesleyan Missions, such as *Man Has an Immortal Soul* (1840), *Is Buddha All-wise?* (1852) and *The Folly of Image Worship* (1852), eventually triggered a vigorous and polemical response on behalf of the Buddhist intellectuals. As Sujit Sivasundaram stated: "From its very inception therefore the Ceylonese press took up the views of particular communities, bearing out the point that the press divided rather than unified an emerging public sphere."[60]

2.2 Call for a National Church

If we consider the general dynamic of the Ceylon public sphere, it comes as no surprise that *The Independent Catholic* emerged with a polemical voice. Lisboa Pinto's involvement in the printers' movement occurred when the Independent Catholics were actively building up their own Christian identity through a handful of pamphlets. By then, their main media had been a series of *Circulars* in response to the pastoral letters by the Archbishop of Ceylon. The apologetic nature of the early publications continued in their first official newspaper *The Independent Catholic*, concerning their Christian's social responsibility in living in an unjust world.

As a "religious paper" pitted against the Roman Catholic Church, *The Independent Catholic* was questioned by its readers in regard to its vehement participation in social movements. The editor answered with a biblical quotation from the Gospel of Matthew: "Verily I say unto you, inasmuch as ye have done it unto one of the least of these my brethren, ye have done it unto me. (Matthew 25:40)".[61]

The Independent Catholic made a volley of attacks on other Christians, in particular in its early years. Their targets included first of all the *Padroadist* newspapers in Bombay, secondly the Roman Pontiff, and thirdly, the Protestants in Ceylon.

The *Padroadists* in Bombay, with their alleged "incongruities", were the first object of scorn. As they had surrendered to the *Concordat* in 1886, giving up their defence of the *Padroado* in Bombay, they were seen as even more inconsistent than their rivals, the pro-Propaganda Catholics. The Ceylon Independent Catholics ridiculed the Bombay *Padroadists*, whom they had sided with until 1888. Now the Hultsdorf-based journal urged their disappointing former fellows in India to aim at creating a national Church.[62]

> Dear friends, St. Peter's pontificate in Rome is a "figment as every student of history knows." YOU WANT A NATIONAL CHURCH. You want the Christian religion as was taught by the

---

59 KULARATNE, *History of Printing*, 140–150.
60 S. SIVASUNDARAM, *Islanded. Britain, Sri Lanka, and the Bounds of an Indian Ocean Colony* (Chicago 2013), 308.
61 "Public men of Ceylon" (*The Independent Catholic*, August 1893), 1.
62 "Incongruities" (*The Independent Catholic*, January 1892), 1–2.

> Apostoles of Christ. The earlier the better, while you have your churches, schools, seminaries &c., or at least such of them as have been mercifully left to you.[63]
>
> The only solution we could think of, is to form the whole Indian Mission into a National Independent Catholic Church and for matter jurisdiction &c. apply to the see of Antioch. This will relieve everybody from their anxiety towards the welfare of the Goanese mission.[64]

The "national church" meant here was not an indigenous, native Asian church. The sense of "national" referred rather to the extent of autonomy, namely to an independence from Rome, that would allow to fully administer the church, but also to achieve the social expectations of the community via education, imparted both through schools and seminaries. However, a Catholic Church independent from Rome would not be necessarily an autocephalic unit. The Ceylon Independent Catholics, for example, were in communion with the Antiochian Orthodox Church, while retaining the Latin liturgy and an apostolic lineage originated from the Roman Catholic Church. The necessary and legitimate supremacy of Antioch over Rome was also stressed by a certain "London friend", who was in correspondence with the Colombo newspaper. In February 1892, among the latest mail shipment from Britain, Hultsdorf received a letter from this correspondent, in which the latter reported his high opinions on the Church of Antioch as well as on the entire Oriental Orthodoxy, whose influence had expanded to Ceylon, Europe and America (reference was made to Vilatte). He stated that the Church of Antioch was open and modern, in contrast to the extremely conservative Eastern Orthodox Churches.[65] What the Antiochian Church excelled in was its *modus operandi*, allowing the American and Ceylon missions to become an exceptional Latin branch within the Syrian Orthodox Church.

> There is undoubtedly a movement in Europe and America in favour of the Orthodox Church. But unlike Rome, the Eastern Orthodox Churches have hitherto been extremely conservative. They have tried always to enforce their liturgy on those who would join them. The Apostolic Church of Antioch has lately become an honourable exception, for, by allowing Ceylon and America to be in communion with her while adopting the ancient Latin liturgy, she has decidedly taken a step in the right direction. And she has also followed the truly apostolic tradition of encouraging National Churches, in which the faith shall be one and for ever the same, but the administration and other details left to the discretion of the respective prelates.[66]

The sense of "national" mentioned in the letter might be better interpreted through the European discourse on national churches and the Old Catholic Churches. However, the anonymous authorship hinders further research. Interestingly, an editorial of *The Independent Catholic* on the estrangement of a native Catholic priest named Maver by the Oblates of Mary Immaculate in Colombo, provides an angle to further clarify the notion of a national church.

---

63 "Incongruities" (*The Independent Catholic,* January 1892), 2.
64 "The Padroado" (*The Independent Catholic,* December 1892), 1.
65 Semantically "Oriental" and "Eastern" mean the same. However, in English ecclesiastical parlance, "Oriental Orthodoxy" (including the Jacobites, the Apostolic Armenians, the Copts, and the Tewahedo churches of Ethiopia and Eritrea) recognizes only three ecumenical councils, namely the First Council of Nicea in 325, the First Council of Constantinople in 381 and the Council of Ephesus in 431. "Eastern Orthodox" (e.g. the Greek and Russian Orthodox) acknowledge four more ecumenical councils: the council of Chalcedon in 451, the second and third councils of Constantinople in 553 and 681, and finally the second council of Nicea in 787. On the ecumenical dialogue between these two major branches in Christianity see C. CHAILLOT (ed.), *The Dialogue between Eastern Orthodox and Oriental Orthodox Churches* (Volos 2016).
66 "News. The Church of Antioch" (*The Independent Catholic,* February 1892), 2.

The editor explained the reason for Maver's discrimination as "the hatred that the white priests bear to the copper-coloured ones."[67] The newspaper further indicated that not all Catholic prelates partook in the despise against native clergy. The Delegate Apostolic Zaleski, on the contrary, promoted the establishment of a seminary in Kandy, today's National Seminary at Ampitiya, precisely aimed at the education of the indigenous clergy in South Asia. The analysis went on with observations on the Catholic Church in India, where some Goan priests, for instance, deserved episcopal consecration as Bishop but were not promoted to it.

> We know of priests, [...] out a miserable existence in some arid missions, who by their piety and learning are ten times more deserving of a mitre than the white bishops who are imported to lord it over them. To speak only of one who is well known in Ceylon, there is Monsignor Dalgado D.D., D.C.L. This priest is at present at Hanover [sic! = Honnavar, in South Kanara], a place in India hardly known to anybody! And the present Delegate Apostolic in Ceylon, who is driving a pair of Australian horses in Kandy and throwing blessings, to the right and to the left, on kneeling crowds as he struts in processions, was a fellow student of the Rev. Dr. Dalgado in a college at Rome, and inferior to him![68]

By contrasting the images of the competent Sebastião Rodolfo Dalgado and the arrogant Zaleski, the author stressed the fact that the native clergymen, specifically the Goans, excelled in academic qualities, and hence deserved a position in the Church equal to that of the European priests.[69] The author took as example the British Raj, where equality between black and white men had been allegedly achieved in the higher social positions, whereas the Roman Catholic Church remained reluctant to consecrate native bishops. Once again, we see how the notion of social equality and of independence from Rome had little to do with a radical nationalist ideology or a consistent anti-colonial stance.

> In Bombay, Calcutta, and Madras under the munificent British rule, Indians have risen to the highest positions in society. There are black men as professors in the best Indian colleges, as Government Agents and Collectors, as Head-clerks and Chiefs of offices, as District and Supreme Court Judges. Only in the Romish Church they cannot even get a suffragan bishopric![70]

The Independent Catholic also commented on the Old Catholic Church in Europe. This can be attested in the consistent appraisal of Vilatte, whom the Ceylonese proudly referred to as "Our Archbishop", but also in the critical attitude towards the conservative Bishops in Utrecht, especially Heykamp. In March 1893 *The Independent Catholic* published an apologetic letter by Vilatte in reply to Bishop Brown's criticism and doubts toward him.[71]

Vilatte also updated his Ceylon congregation with his latest publications. The tract entitled *St Peter in Rome*, in which the author concluded "And our last word is a challenge to any one, Protestant or Roman to prove from the Bible that Peter ever put foot into the city of Rome."[72] The journal in Ceylon expressed its fascination with the debate between Vilatte and the Roman Catholic cardinals in this regard, and wished to have triggered attention among the Catholics in Ceylon for a public debate.

---

67 "The Padroado" (*The Independent Catholic,* April 1893), 1.
68 "The Padroado" (*The Independent Catholic,* April 1893), 1.
69 On Dalgado, see *supra*, in Chapter 4.
70 "The Padroado" (*The Independent Catholic,* April 1893), 1.
71 "An open answer and a frank statement" (*The Independent Catholic,* March 1893), 2–3.
72 "Old Catholic Tracts" (*The Independent Catholic,* April 1893), 2.

3. The Independent Catholic and Its Local and Global Perceptions

3.1 The Feuille Independent

Founded in January 1892, *The Independent Catholic* was the only official organ of the congregation of Independent Catholics in Ceylon. According to the two separate copies conserved in the National Archives of Sri Lanka, the monthly circulated throughout 1892, 1893 and 1894[73] until September 1895. It was then suspended for six months from October 1895 to February 1896, before it resumed in March 1896. The reason for this gap was deliberately omitted in the last available issue published in March 1896, as "of no interest to our readers".[74] It is not clear if the newspaper continued after the last available issue in March 1896. The paper also suffered occasional changes in staff and printing press. For this reason, the issue of December 1894 was never published.[75]

We are however certain about the prehistory of the journal. Before the full-fledged newspaper was launched in 1892, a *feuille* or a small newspaper entitled *Independent* might have circulated as early as November 1888. This can be discerned from a report that the Apostolic Delegate Andrea Aiuti (in India 1887–1890) sent to the Congregation of Propaganda Fide in Rome, while he was on a visitation to various dioceses on the subcontinent. In his lengthy report on Alvares and his followers in Colombo, Aiuti added an original quotation from the Archbishop of Colombo, Christophe-Étienne Bonjean, stressing the diminutive influence of the dissidents, both in terms of membership and of impact on public media. This report, dated 16 December 1888, has been translated from Italian and French into English by Perniola:

> At the moment in Ceylon, and chiefly in Colombo, according to Mgr Bonjean, the followers of Alvarez [sic] are few. According to the *Independent* (a new and small newspaper subsidized by the party), when the *Prefect Apostolic* and the *Vicar General* (that is how they call themselves), last Sunday celebrated High Mass at the Emmanuel Chapel there were only about 30 persons present. In spite of the sensational articles published by those wretched people in that paper, they make little impression on the public and are left well alone. Outside the narrow limits within which they move, peace is so great that one can hardly believe what the newspapers of India say regarding the schism in Ceylon. It is certain that this movement, hardly perceptible here, assumes great proportion from a distance.[76]

A brief comparison of the original correspondence and report between Bonjean, Aiuti, and Propaganda Fide, as well as Perniola's English translation, reveals clear discrepancies. The French original reads:

---

73 I am grateful to Dr. Nelanga Jayasinghe for digitising the second part (1895–1896) and Mr. Yurane for retrieving the first part (1892–1983) that had been misplaced in the National Archives until February 2018. Even though the issues in 1894 are missing, the original volume numbers that marked the issue of December 1893 as "vol. II No.12" and the one of January 1895 as "vol. V, No.1", suggest that volumes III and IV were supposedly published in 1894.
74 "Ourselves" (*The Independent Catholic*, March 1896), 2.
75 "Ourselves" (*The Independent Catholic*, January 1895), 1.
76 Aiuti to Propaganda dated in Ootacamund, 16 December 1888. It is translated from Italian and French into English by VITO PERNIOLA in his *The Catholic Church in Sri Lanka. The British Period. Vol. 8: 1887–1899. The Archdiocese of Colombo* (Dehiwala 2004), 158–159.

A la grand'messe que, d'après l'*Independent*, (nouvelle misérable petite feuille soudoyée par le parti) le "Préfect Apostolique", "le vicaire général" (c'est ainsi qu'ils se qualifient) ont célébré dimanche dernier à Emmanuel's Chapel, il n'y avait qu'une trentaine d'individus.[77]

Aiuti had retained Bonjean's words with quotation marks but had eliminated the adjective "misérable", which displayed more explicitly the derogatory attitude of the original author. Perniola omitted the quotation marks in Aiuti's sentence starting from the "*Independent*" but made an honest translation of Aiuti.

In hindsight, Bonjean's underestimation of the Independent Catholics cannot be taken at face value, as the total number of adherents in 1888 exceeded two thousand if the missions in Negombo, Mannar, and Kallianpur are all taken into account. Bonjean, who died in September 1892, did not witness the path-breaking editorials on trade unionism published in *The Independent Catholic* in July 1893. However, Bonjean's consistent and often extravagant remarks on the debility and pointlessness of the "Goan schism" could have easily convinced Aiuti and later the secretaries of the Congregation of Propaganda Fide, who had limited information channels to South Asia and hence had to rely on filtered reports. In the collection of *Scritture riferite nei Congressi, Indie Orientali* at the Archive of Propaganda Fide, documents concerning the "Goan schism" often contain newspaper clips or individual issues of newspapers such as the Bombay-based *O Anglo-Lusitano* and the Goa-based *Ultramar*, inserted by the Bishops in South Asia as attachments to their reports to Rome. These periodicals became a new interface allowing the administration of the global church to observe developments on the ground, even though its efficiency in conveying native voices was still mediated at large by many variables requiring further study.

Unfortunately, we have not been able to find in the Archive of Propaganda Fide any excerpts from *The Independent Catholic*, or its preliminary version known as *Independent*. The Archdiocese of Colombo, which should have archived Bonjean and others' papers concerning Alvares and his congregation, is at the moment of writing closed to academic use. Our further analysis is therefore limited to sources written by groups who were positively associated with the journal. In the following section, we explore the local and global printing networks through which *The Independent Catholic* was able to thrive despite its short life.

3.2 Clifton Press

From 1892 to 1896, the editorial office of *The Independent Catholic* was located in the League Hall, Hultsdorp, in the same neighbourhood as the Cathedral of Our Lady of Good Death. During this time, the printing of the monthly was entrusted to at least three different publishers in Colombo.

The first issue in January 1892 was printed at Phoenix Press, located at No. 17 at Korteboam Street, Colombo. Little is known about this press except an advertisement that appeared in the English evening journal *Examiner* in 1870 in regard to an offer of "lead cast to any size" at "Phoenix Printing Works".[78] If the two "Phoenix" are identical, it is possible that the press already existed as early as 1870.

---

[77] Bonjean to Aiuti dated in Colombo, 28 November 1888, original copy in APF, *Scritture riferite nei Congressi, Indie Orientali*, Vol. 33 (1888), fols. 991r.

[78] Tilak Kularatne quoted an advertisement of the "Phoenix Printing Works" in the *Examiner* dated on 16 March 1870, see KULARATNE, *History of Printing*, 210.

In February 1892 the second issue of *The Independent Catholic* was handed over to the Clifton Press, located in Maligakande, in central Colombo. In practice, the owner of the monthly entrusted a worker at Clifton to supervise the paper in press. These workers included Robert Peter Pereira (September–December 1892), George Simon Hamber (until May 1893), Robert Jeremey Dias (June–August 1893), and Bernard Francis Quyn (September – at least December 1893). Some of these workers were members of the Independent Catholic congregation. We take Bernard Francis Quyn as an example. On 11 January 1892, he married Laurencia Margaret Pereira at Our Lady of Good Death. The priest who presided the celebration was René Vilatte, who was at that time waiting for his episcopal consecration scheduled for following May. Quyn's wedding announcement that appeared in *The Independent Catholic* in the column of "domestic occurrences" suggests that the newlyweds in fact belonged to that congregation.[79] Those above-mentioned workers at Clifton also shared a bond with Lisboa Pinto, who was elected as the first president of the Ceylon Printer's Society in 1893 with over 200 members.

After *The Independent Catholic* ended its collaboration with Clifton at the end of 1894 for unknown reasons, the press was utilized by two other groups for printing pamphlets, respectively the arrack renters and the Theosophists. From 1895 to 1896 the press published two pamphlets by two liberal writers, M. Anthony Perera and Gabriel de Silva, addressing the so-called arrack question.[80] The historian Patrick Peebles noticed how Clifton Press was located in Moratuwa, a suburb in the southeast of Colombo, known for its *karāva* inhabitants, who not only worked as renters and distillers of arrack, but also monopolized the trade of that alcohol towards Tamil Nadu.[81] The two pamphlets, however, did not bear the location of Moratuwa. In his *History of Printing and Publishing in Ceylon*, Kularatne mentioned only the starting year of the press in 1891 without providing further information.[82]

The Independent Catholic, however, specified that the Clifton Press was located at Maligakande (road), in Maradana, Colombo. Vidyodaya Piriveṇa – a prominent college founded in 1873 for educating Buddhist monks and laymen– was located in the vicinity. The founder Hikkaḍuvē Sumaṅgala (1827–1911), a pioneer of the Buddhist Revival Movement, expected this school to "provide instruction in śāstra (South Asian technical sciences related to language, literature, medicine, and protective technologies) in a manner congruent with the teachings of the Buddha (buddhāgama)".[83] "Widdioyadda College" was written on the entrance, together with the Latin motto 'Nil Desperandum'.[84] The proximity of the Clifton Press to such a lively Buddhist educational institution suggests a possible intellectual interaction between the two. In her study of a pamphlet on the Buddhist nuns authored by an intriguing theosophist woman, Tessa J. Bartholomeusz provided solid evidence of Clifton's support to the vehement Buddhist movement. Countess Miranda de Souza, wife of the Portuguese Consul in Ceylon António de Souza Canavarro (r. 1897–?), who moved to Colombo in 1897,

---

79 *The Independent Catholic*, January 1892, 3.
80 I used two copies in The British Library: G. DE SILVA, *Arrack-farming in Ceylon* (Colombo 1895); M.A. PERERA, *The Arrack Question in Ceylon 1895–1896* (Colombo 1896).
81 On the arrack renters in Moratuwa since the 1820s and especially the leading families see PATRICK PEEBLES, *Social Change in Nineteenth Century Ceylon* (New Delhi 1995), 157–161. The location of Clifton Press is mentioned in the Bibliography on pp. 269–270.
82 KULARATNE, *History of Printing*, 248.
83 A.M. BLACKBURN, *Locations of Buddhism*. Colonialism and Modernity in Sri Lanka (Chicago 2010), 38.
84 BLACKBURN, *Locations of Buddhism*, 55.

authored a pamphlet under the name "Madame de Souza Canavarro, the Saṅghamittā Convent". The text was printed at Clifton in 1899 with an order of 200 copies.[85] Upon her arrival in Colombo, Canavarro became one of the leading figures of the Theosophical movement.[86] There is no explicit evidence showing contacts or exchanges between the three different groups in Colombo, namely, the arrack activists, the Theosophist author, and the Independent Catholic leaders. The owners of Clifton Press nevertheless might have shared with those movements a vision of social reforms across economic and religious borders.

Clifton Press had no reservations against taking a polemical position in favour of the Independent Catholics. In 1893 it published as separata an excerpt from *The Independent Catholic* entitled *A Reply to the heretical teachings of the "Ceylon Evangelist." by the editor of the "Ceylon Review"* in which the Independent Catholic Editor waged a debate with the evangelical church over doctrinal questions.[87] Clifton's support continued by publishing Alvares' anti-Roman Catholic treatise entitled *A supremacia universal na Egreja de Christo* in 1898.[88]

At any rate, the journal of the Independent Catholics was published by the Clifton Press only for two years. From January to September 1895 and again in March 1896, William Julian Alex was in charge of the printing of the monthly at the "Victoria Press" in Dam Street, Colombo. Lisboa Pinto resided in the same street until July 1898.

3.3 Perceptions in Ceylon, India and Beyond

The launch of the monthly journal in 1892 received attention in the press circles both in Ceylon and British India, in English, Portuguese, and Sinhalese newspapers. *The Independent Catholic* gladly reported on the appraisals made by two influential English newspapers, both relatively liberal, namely *The Ceylon Independent* and *The Ceylon Observer*.

The daily *The Ceylon Independent* praised the overall quality of the paper material, its printing and price, but above all acknowledged its importance among Catholics in Ceylon, considering the Independent Catholics as an integral part of it.

> The Ceylon Catholics are a large and powerful community, and we have small doubt but that the Independent section of them will give to their newspaper a large and powerful support. Goodness knows that we want a lot of brutality [sic] [...] of our local journalists, and every effort towards this end is acceptable.[89]

The fortnightly *The Ceylon Observer* defined the Independent Catholic movement as a denial of both the Portuguese patronage and the papacy. It stood not alone but allied with the Old Catholics and the late Dr. Ignaz von Döllinger (1799–1890).

---

85 BARTHOLOMEUSZ described her discovery of this pamphlet in a footnote in chapter 4 "Sanghamitta Sisterhood" of her book entitled *Women under the Bo Tree. Buddhist Nuns in Sri Lanka*, (Cambridge 1994), 224, footnote 3.
86 For a biography see T.J. BARTHOLOMEUSZ, "Real Life and Romance. The Life of Miranda de Souza Canavarro" (*Journal of Feminist Studies in Religion* 10/2 ,1994, 27–47).
87 This is a separata from a column article published in *The Independent Catholic* in October 1893.
88 I used the Portuguese copy in The British Library, A.F.X. ALVARES, JULIO I ARCEBISHOP, *A supremacia universal na Egreja de Christo, provada pela escriptura, tradição e escriptores insuspeitos a Egreja Romana*, 1898. As mentioned before, a newly edited English translation of this book is provided by M. KURIAN THOMAS (ed.), *Universal Supremacy in the Church of Christ* (Devalokam, Kottayam 2020).
89 "Our contemporaries, friends, & c." (*The Independent Catholic*, February 1892), 2.

> *The Independent Catholic* is a paper which has been started as the organ of a body who belong to neither the Papal nor the Portuguese "Padroado" body of Roman Catholics, but of persons whose sympathies are with "the Old Catholics" of whom the late Dr. Dollinger was the leader. Our sympathies are of course with protests in any form against Papal claims to infallibility and universal rule or rather tyranny over men's consciences.[90]

According to the editor at Hultsdorf, two other major English newspapers in Ceylon – the *Examiner* and the *Times of Ceylon* – also reported on the new journal. The popular Sinhala paper *Sarasavi Sandarāsa* even translated the article "The Chair of St. Peter", a criticism on Roman supremacy published in the first issue of *The Independent Catholic*, into Sinhala, spreading arguments that would be well received by the Buddhists. The initial motivation for establishing *Sarasavi Sandarāsa* had to do with the critical tone against Buddhism expressed in the official Catholic organ, the Sinhala weekly *Gnānārtha Pradīpaya* (from 1866). The Theosophists incorporated the Sinhala paper into their Society and used it for the propagation of the Ananda College, among whose founders there was Alfred Ernest Buultjens, a collaborator of Lisboa Pinto in the trade union campaign.[91] It is obvious that *The Independent Catholic* was welcomed by almost all anti-Roman Catholic communities, who saw the small Christian group with sympathy.

The Colombo Mission of the Independent Catholics was well-informed of the Christian world inside and outside Ceylon. The list of journals received by the editor shows a broad spectrum of reading interests, but also potential ideological influences. To keep an information channel with the mother church in Kottayam, the Ceylon Mission exchanged journals on a regular basis. *The Independent Catholic* reported the launch of *Malankara Edavaka Pathrika,* the first Malayalam journal, when its first issue reached Hultsdorf in March 1892.[92] Meanwhile, a handful of local newspapers were received, out of which the *Ceylon Diocesan Gazette,* an official Anglican newspaper running from 1876 to 1893, was highlighted.[93] From the Catholics in Bombay came *O Concanim*[94] and *O Boletim Indiano*[95], a Konkani-Portuguese and a Portuguese weekly respectively. From Britain, Colombo received *The London Church Times,* an Anglican weekly started in 1863 and still running. The acknowledgement of receipt of a certain *New Era* in May 1892 is a curious case.[96] It was likely shortened for *The New Era: A Review of Social Work and Movements in the Churches* (1892–?) edited by the British journalist William Harbutt Dawson (1860–1948), known for his study on *Bismarck and State Socialism* and his contribution to the establishment of a social welfare system in Britain at the end of the nineteenth century.[97] It is worthy of note that the first editorial on Trade Unions was published in *The Independent Catholic* in July 1893, having received

---

90 "Our contemporaries, friends, & c." (*The Independent Catholic*, January 1892), 2.
91 KULARATNE, *History of Printing*, 173–174.
92 *The Independent Catholic*, March 1892, 2.
93 "Acknowledgement" (*The Independent Catholic*, May 1892), 3.
94 "O Concanim" (*The Independent Catholic*, March 1892), 3. This journal also started in January 1892. See its entry in DA CUNHA, "A evolução do jornalismo", 589.
95 G. GUEDES RAFAEL / M. SANTOS (eds.), *Jornais e revistas portugueses do século XIX* (Lisboa 1998), 120–121; DA CUNHA, "A evolução do jornalismo", 594.
96 "Acknowledgement" (*The Independent Catholic*, May 1892), 3.
97 I have researched in various databases of British newspapers online and at The British Library. This journal seems the only one entitled *New Era* that was in circulation in 1892. See a study on Dawson's experience and his studies on German social policy in J. FILTHAUT, *Dawson und Deutschland. Das deutsche Vorbild und die Reformen im Bildungswesen, in der Stadtverwaltung und in der Sozialversicherung Grossbritanniens 1880–1914* (Frankfurt am Main 1994). See W.H. DAWSON: *Bismarck and State Socialism. An Exposition of the Social and Economic Legislation of Germany since 1870* (London 1890).

a plausible impact from Dawson and his German example of "State socialism". From Wisconsin, Vilatte sent his own journal entitled *The Old Catholic* to Colombo on a regular basis. According to Paolo Miraglia Gullotti (1857–1918), whom Vilatte consecrated as Bishop in 1900 in Piacenza, Vilatte started to send his journal since the time he established his initial contacts with Alvares in 1889.[98] This American journal, recognised by *The Independent Catholic* as "our sister journal",[99] was an essential source for the Colombo Mission to learn about the activities of their Archbishop in Wisconsin, but also a window towards the Old Catholic Church in Europe. A reciprocal delivery has not yet been proved by archival sources, but it is not impossible that the Colombo newspaper was regularly read in Wisconsin. Thanks to this stable and frequent exchange of journals, the reputation of *The Independent Catholic* extended to the Protestant world in Europe in the early 1890s.

For example, the launch of the Independent Catholic monthly in 1892 received attention among Christians in the predominantly Lutheran Duchy of Saxe-Weimar-Eisenach, through the *Theologischer Jahresbericht* – an annual journal edited by the evangelical theologian Heinrich Holtzmann (1832–1910) – in its twelfth volume published in Braunschweig in 1893. In a literature review entitled "Interconfessional matters" (*Interconfessionalles* [sic]), a Lutheran theologian from Denstedt, Weimar, named Oscar Kohlschmidt provided a list of publications in the previous year concerning both the Inner-Catholic (*Die innerkatholische Entwickelung* [sic]) and the Protestant developments (*Die protestantische Entwickelung* [sic]).[100] In the inner-Catholic developments, the author reported that the monthly *The Independent Catholic*, published in "Colombo (Ceylon), Phoenix-Press, No. 17 Korteboam Street" and sold at the price of "Reis 100"[101], was a recent new addition. He even provided an almost accurate information calling it the organ of a "free Catholic Church movement" (*freikatholische Kirche*), edited probably by René Vilatte, the "first Old Catholic Bishop of America", who was consecrated in Colombo.[102]

Diachronically, *The Independent Catholic* was enlisted at the end of the section named "Old Catholic Reform Movement" (*Die altkatholische Reformbewegung*), but also at the end of the Inner-Catholic section. A great part of the recent studies concerned Ignaz von Döllinger (1799–1890), who had passed away two years before. The Colombo paper was, however, the only publication neither from the Old Catholic Churches in Europe, nor from their missions in America, hence representing Döllinger's far-flung influence. Synchronically, the author paired *The Independent Catholic* with three new French journals – *Catholique national* edited by Genfer von Carrier, and the two Parisian monthlies entitled *Catholique français* and *Le vrai Catholique*. We have not studied the circulation and readership of *Theologischer Jahresbericht*, but it is not impossible that readers interested in the Old Catholic Church could have contacted the Colombo Independent Catholic paper.

In contrast to the scarcely known interactions with European journals, *The Independent Catholic* was in constant dialogue with other newspapers owned by or in favour of the various Independent Catholic missions in North America. Among those papers the New York-based *The Independent* was among the earliest that paid attention to the Colombo *Independent*

---

98 UN VECCHIO-CATTOLICO ITALIANO, *Apostolo e martire*. Ossia Monsignor G. Renato Vilatte fondatore della Chiesa Vecchio-Cattolica negli Stati Uniti d'America (Firenze 1900), 40.
99 "The Old Catholic" (*The Independent Catholic*, December 1892), 3.
100 O. KOHLSCHMIDT, "Interconfessionelles", in: H. HOLTZMANN (ed.), *Theologischer Jahresbericht*. vol. 12 (Braunschweig 1893, 330–352).
101 The masthead of *The Independent Catholic* names the price as "Rs. 1-00 a year" (and later "R1 a year"). "Reis", a Portuguese currency (*réis*), must be a misunderstanding of Rupees and 100 is a mistake or typo for 1.00..
102 KOHLSCHMIDT, "Interconfessionelles", 331, 335.

Catholic. The Independent was founded in 1848 in New York by the businessman Henry C. Bowen (1813–1896) and his associates out of an effort to end the "Plan of Union" that once had united the Congregational Churches and the Presbyterian Church. With Bowen as editor until his death in 1896, the weekly "religious newspaper" favoured articles from "denominational and other religious intelligence"[103] and was divided into various departments of religious news. The historian Frank Luther Mott considers it "one of a very small group of religious papers to hold a comparatively general audience in a period which saw most such periodicals degenerate into denominational news letters."[104] Since 1872, the newspaper had changed from its original size of a four-page folio to a thirty-two page, four-column illustrated quarto.[105]

It was into the column of "Religious Intelligence" that the editor of *The Independent* placed William Bernard Harding's article (still under his monastic name as Bro. Augustine de Angelis) entitled "The Independent Catholic Church of India and Ceylon" in its issue from 18 February 1892.[106] The ex-Oblate English priest, who had introduced Alvares and his movement to Vilatte, dedicated one-third of the narrative to the origin of the conflict between the Portuguese *Padroado* and the Congregation of Propaganda Fide in the seventeenth century. With an explicitly pro-*Padroadist* tone, Bernard urged his readers to consult a document entitled *Demonstratio Juris Patronatus*, submitted by Luís de Souza, "the learned and saintly" Archbishop of Braga, to Pope Innocent XI, advocating for the *Padroado*. To emphasise the detrimental consequences of the "invasion" of the Propaganda missionaries into the territories of the Asian missions, Bernard alluded to an alleged murder of a certain Portuguese Archbishop of Saba in China, a claim for which no historical ground can be established. It is necessary to take into account that Bernard had served in the Archdiocese of Colombo and belonged to the very Propaganda missionaries that he criticised ruthlessly in his article. He blamed his ex-confreres as usurpers of the churches built by the "holy Goa missionaries" and referred to doctrines such as papal infallibility and Immaculate Conception, as well as to the devotion to the "sacred hearts of Jesus, Joseph and Mary" that Pope Leo XIII had promoted worldwide as "blind superstitions".

It is interesting to note how the once-Propaganda missionary had become hateful of the apostolic work to which he had devoted himself. His transformation of attitude perhaps made it possible for him to be sympathetic to Alvares and Lisboa Pinto, with whom he shared the same disappointment and accusations against Rome. Harding admired Lisboa Pinto's pamphlet *Antioch and Rome and their Connection with St Peter*, which was censored immediately by Bonjean. He referred to a letter written by Lisboa Pinto, in which the censored author stated that "These excommunications [from Archbishop Bonjean] do not destroy my appetite, hence I still live." Bernard described Alvares as a "patriotic and liberal journalist", who had been editor of *A Cruz*, the *Verdade,* and the *Times of Goa*. Harding's article likely was the first detailed account of the Independent Catholic Mission presented to readers outside of India and Ceylon.

The Independent Catholic also commented on non-English papers published by Independent Catholic leaders other than Vilatte. In January 1895 it ran an article on the co-founder of the American Catholic Church, Alfons Mieczysław Chrostowski, an image and article of

---

103 F.L. MOTT, *A History of American Magazines, 1850–1865*. Vol. 2: 1850–1865 (Cambridge 2002), 367–378.
104 MOTT, *A History*, 376.
105 MOTT, *A History*, 375.
106 "Religious Intelligence. The Independent Catholic Church of India and Ceylon", (*The Independent*, 44/18, February 1892), 13.

whom had appeared in an issue of an English journal *The Greater Cleveland*, precisely published in Cleveland, where his Church was located. The splendidly engraved image and his determined remarks on his Polish National Church of America served as a mirror in which the Indo-Ceylonese Independent Catholics saw themselves not isolated in Ceylon but on the threshold of a global anti-papal cause. The fact that the Colombo paper gave a high appreciation to the Polish-American leader without him being a personal acquaintance implies that the praise was part of an ideological self-identification with the Polish American counterparts. *The Independent Catholic* observed:

> *The Greater Cleveland*, a large illustrated American paper in its issue of December 8th, 1894, publishes a splendid portrait of that fearless champion of Independent Catholicism in America, and editor of the new Polish paper, *The Morning Star*. We have not the pleasure of a personal acquaintance with Mr. Chrostowski; but, to judge from the almost faultless engraving before us, he must be a man of determination and of rare pluck. The very fact that he has resolved to stand up and fight for the liberties of his countrymen against the colossus of papal Rome is a guarantee that the following words – forming the concluding portion of a letter of his published in *The Greater Cleveland* – may be relied upon by the thousands of Polish Christians whom he has only lately emancipated from the slavery of the Church of the Infallible: "Rome will not buy me […]." […]
> The Morning Star[107] – We have been favoured with a copy of this paper, "the official organ of the Polish Independent Catholic Church of America." Its editor is Mr. Chrostowski, of Cleveland, one of the leaders of the recent movement in that city against the Church of Rome. The paper is throughout written in the Polish language, with which we are unfortunately not acquainted to be able to appreciate its contents.[108]

To sum up, the Colombo monthly was regarded in the circle of the Ceylonese commercial newspapers as a fighter against the Roman Catholic Church, understood as a corrupt authority that enslaved the Christians over the world. By assuming the role of a fighter against Rome, the "schismatic Catholics" acquired legitimacy out of their claimed "true Catholicism" in the Ceylonese public sphere. In Europe the paper represented a national Church that had consecrated Vilatte, hence it had been incorporated in the Old Catholic Movement by and large. Among the adherents to Vilatte's mission in Wisconsin, the Ceylon Independent Catholics were considered confreres and the same applied vice-versa.

4. *The Independent Catholic's Importance*

The Independent Catholic's debut as part of a popular movement probably made a significant contribution to the shaping of an Independent Catholic identity, as the former *Padroadist* groups – despite their considerable differences in caste, language, social class, educational background, and especially geographic distance – were united under a social agenda oriented towards justice and equality. Such a joint commitment brought to a new level the engagement shown at the time of the *Padroado* resistance against the Propaganda Fide jurisdictional assertions.

---

107 *Jutrzenka* [The Morning Star] was started in Pittsburg by Chrostowski in 1893. See W. KRUSZKA, *Historia Polska w Ameryce*, ed. by J.S. PULA. Vol. 1: A History of the Poles in America to 1908 (Washington D.C. 1993), 360.
108 "Mr. A Chrostowski" & "The Morning Star" (*The Independent Catholic*, January 1895), 3.

Conclusion

The preceding seven chapters have presented a little-known case of religious emancipation that emerged in colonial Sri Lanka between the nineteenth and the twentieth centuries. The 'Independent Catholics of Ceylon' (known initially as the 'Independent Catholic Mission in Ceylon', and later as the 'Independent Catholic Church in Ceylon') began in 1888 as a *movement of religious protest* against changes in the Roman Catholic administration of the local churches. This movement must be understood, inter alia, in the complex context of intraconfessional relations in India and Ceylon (Sri Lanka) over the course of the 19th century. The leader of these "Independent Catholics" was the Goan Brahman priest Antonio Alvares (1836–1923), a former Roman Catholic who later became the movement's archbishop. In the early years of the twentieth century, the Independent Catholics experienced a period of decline. While most of the congregations were discontinued or merged with other churches, the one of Kallianpur in Karnataka has survived until today. Since 2010 it has grown into the Diocese of Brahmavar of the Malankara Orthodox Syrian Church.

The existing historiography on South Asian Christianity, as well as recent studies on the religious history of Goa have given contradictory statements on the causes, leading figures, and the historical impact of the Independent Catholics. In this book the focus has been on the congregations centered in Ceylon, namely, Colombo, Negombo, and Mannar, leaving aside other communities in Karnataka, Tamil Nadu, and Kerala. At the same time, Goa and Bombay have also been discussed in relation to the provenance of the clerical and lay leaders and especially their cross-regional association in support of the Portuguese *Padroado*.

When in 1888, after tumultuous decades, a few thousands Ceylonese Roman Catholics announced their separation from the communion with Rome, they named themselves an "Independent Catholic Mission", ministered by Catholic priests who had been excommunicated by the Archbishops of Goa and Colombo. This *self-designation as "independent"* was an important aspect of their identity. On 10 February 1888, the *annavi* [catechist] Martines Pereira published an Official Circular, declaring a separation of both the Church of Our Lady of Good Death and the Chapel of St Emmanuel in Colombo from the Roman Catholic communion, designating the separatists as an "Independent Catholic Mission", to our knowledge the first instance of such kind in the history of Catholicism in South Asia. Over the course of the 1890s, rather than calling themselves a "Mission", in their official English newspaper *The Independent Catholic*, they more often labeled themselves a "Church", or referred to themselves as representing "Independent Catholicism", demonstrating a more ambitious ecclesiology, developed by an optimistic and confident community over the initial years. While from the 1880s to the 1900s the terms "Mission" and "Church" were used almost interchangeably, the adjective "independent" was a constant. In order to contextualize this movement in relation to several other efforts for emancipation in the history of Christianity in India and Ceylon over the course of the 19th century, it is therefore necessary to specify what was meant by "independent" in this specific case.

First of all, the proclamation of an "Independent Mission" was an act directed against the Roman Catholic authorities. The initial target was the Congregation of Propaganda Fide, the Papal secretariat of missions, which, according to the *Padroadists*, represented a corrupted faction within the Catholic Church and the archenemy of the traditional Portuguese *Padroado*. In 1886 the *Padroadists* in Goa and Bombay had sent a delegation to Europe, but soon after this campaign had failed, the movement rebelled against the Holy See as such. However, until its final decline, the Independent Catholic movement had hardly directed its anger against the Portuguese or the British colonial governments. Neither clergymen nor laity campaigned for the independence of Ceylon and India from the British. In the same way they were not critical of the legacies of Portuguese colonialism. Indeed, a lay pioneer of the later Independent Catholics assumed the position of Consul of Portugal in Ceylon, while many others, usually Burghers, served in the British administration in Ceylon.

Secondly, though "Independent" from Rome, the "Independent Church" was soon administered and united under the mitre of the Archbishop Antonio Alvares, however without achieving episcopal continuity. At a time in which many Orthodox churches strived to obtain autocephaly, the Independent Catholics in Ceylon could not even count on the assurance of a local episcopal structure, inevitably determining the short life of the entire movement. Additionally, the early loss of charismatic leaders such as Lisboa Pinto († 1898) and Luis Soares (who passed to the Chaldean Church and then died in 1903) was a catalyst for the decline. Through Alvares the Independent Catholic mission was in communion with the Syrian Orthodox Church, but retained its original Latin rite, while keeping Portuguese to a certain extent for prayers and homilies. Together with the Syrian Orthodox residing in Malabar, the Independent Catholics in Ceylon and India were subject to the jurisdiction of the Patriarchy of Antioch, which acted as the head of the Syrian Orthodox Church of Malabar until 1912.

Thirdly, until the mid-twentieth century and with the exception of the Kallianpur (Brahmavar) congregation, the widely spread communities of the Independent Catholics in India, Goa, and Ceylon relied on a supply of breakaway priests from Goa. Following Alvares' example, those ex-Catholic priests received re-ordination in the Syrian Orthodox Church in Kottayam, before they were allocated to different mission stations. The Independent Catholic movement in Ceylon hardly was able to recruit any Ceylonese priests.

The establishment of Independent Catholicism was thus dependent on various conditions, including the acceptance of a colonial framework, the jurisdictional submission to the Antiochian See, and the dependence on Goan clergy. While the Independent Catholics of Ceylon were independent from Rome, at the same time they were anything but self-reliant and totally self-governing.

Such a structure highlights once again the *important role of Archbishop Antonio Alvares* for the Independent Catholics. While being the most studied figure of this historical movement until now, in most "official" Roman-Catholic historical accounts (like the works of Hull[1]) he is considered nothing more than a turbulent schismatic priest, deserving to be neglected. Goan historians however, displaying a rather celebratory attitude, have labelled him "Patriot & Saint".[2] Recent publications from Malankara Orthodox biographers tell his story in triumphant terms.[3] In contrast, in the preceding chapters, Alvares has appeared as an actor in the colonial landscape of nineteenth century Goa and Sri Lanka. He was not unique in his

---

1   E.R. HULL, *Bombay Mission History: With a Special Study of the Padroado Question*, Vol. 1: 1534–1858, Vol. 2: 1858–1890 (Bombay 1927–30).
2   C. AZEVEDO. *Patriot & Saint*. The Life Story of Father Alvares/Bishop Mar Julius I (Panjim 1988).
3   A. PHILIP / G. ALEXANDER, *Western Rites of Syriac-Malankara Orthodox Churches* (Kerala 2018).

beginnings and early intentions, but his impact and the success of his activities might probably find little parallel. His legacy is multidimensional, while he appears as one of the most adventurous, and also most successful of all the rebellious priests in nineteenth-century Goa.

His local fame has only increased in the last decades. In 2008, H. H. Baselios Marthoma Didimos I, Catholicos of the Malankara Orthodox Syrian Church, published a bull declaring Alvares a local saint. Since then, every year thousands of Syrian Christian pilgrims gather in Panjim and make a pilgrimage from the original burial place at the Church of Santa Ines to the new shrine hosting the remains of Alvares at St Mary's Church in Ribandar.[4] Refraining deliberately from addressing these modern developments, this book has striven to contextualize Alvares as a historical figure, in relation with other ecclesiastical and lay leaders. Alvares appears then as a shrewd and intelligent actor who found a way for his projects despite many adversities. Our nuanced understanding of Alvares has been developed on the basis of a wider set of sources, retrieved from multiple archives. The life and work of Antonio Alvares has thus served as an orienting guide to understand a marginal community with great hopes.

In exploring the prehistory, development, and decline of the Independent Catholic movement, we have been able to shed light on the agency and creativity of a complex *multi-ethnic constellation of Christians throughout a century and across a wide territory*, consisting of Dutch and Portuguese Burghers, Parava Tamils, and Sinhalese. In addition, we have also hinted at the processes of identity formation of Christian communities in the Bombay and Madras Presidencies.

As a result, our findings present a new understanding of the *development of the Padroado identity* among the South Asian Catholics over the course of the nineteenth century. In contrast to the traditional understanding of the *Padroado*–Propaganda conflicts as an inter-European institutional rivalry that was merely superimposed on the South Asian Church, this book has demonstrated how the discontent had generated a momentum, an internal dynamic, or even an "Eigendynamik" within the Asian mission itself that led to the *formation of a local popular movement*. The native Christian agency was the main reason for the success of such a movement, and it was in tune with the various religious and social reforms undertaken at the time of high colonialism.

Multiple Catholic communities, with different ethnicities and spread across a large space, were all united by a *Padroado* identity. One of the questions to be answered is how the cross-regional movement was able to achieve such success. In fact, the outbreak of the movement was a direct outcome of the plurisecular history of the *Padroado* question, but in the context of a *distinctive native agency*. Contrary to earlier *Padroado*-Propaganda conflicts that had featured mainly European missionaries, now at the end of the nineteenth century it was both lay elites and local commoners who became the leading forces in the campaign for the conservation of the Portuguese patronage.

While most of the Catholics accepted the jurisdictional transition of their parishes and dioceses from the Portuguese *Padroado* to the Roman jurisdiction of Propaganda Fide, a minoritarian dissident faction opted for resistance. Among these hardliners, a small party of English-educated lay elites, such as the upper class diasporic Goans in Bombay and the Dutch Burghers in Colombo built up an *efficient alliance* through a reliable and rapid information network via journals and the telegraph. The dispatch of a delegation in 1887 to Lisbon to deliver a Padroadist petition can be compared to the many trips to Europe undertaken by

---

4 The cult of Alvares that emerged within the Malankara Orthodox Church is a very interesting phenomenon and deserves further studies in relation to the modernisation and diversification of the Syrian Christians in India, who have been considered until now a mono-ethnic Church.

Goan priests during the early modern age. However, the delegation led by Lisboa Pinto, a layman rather than a priest, demonstrated the confidence of the socially uprising laity and its *global connections*. To take Lisboa Pinto and his extended family as an example, their religious claims were also related to their active involvement in scientific and erudite associations, such as the Geographic Society of Lisbon and the Ceylon Branch of the Royal Asiatic Society.

In the same way, the present analysis has contributed to the historiography of Sri Lankan society during the late nineteenth century and in the early period of Ceylon's nationalist awakening. It demonstrated how the Goan and Bombay Goan Catholic elites, among migrants of other ethnic and religious groups, were gradually integrated into the *early Sri Lankan independence movement*. To take Lisboa Pinto's family for example, his descendants played a notable role in the process of Sri Lankan nation building. His nephew Armand de Souza (1874–1921) was a journalist and an advocate for constitutional reform. Armand de Souza's son Doric de Souza (1914–1987) became a senator and founder of Sri Lanka's Trotskyist party, the Lanka Sama Samaja Party. Future research may clarify how the Catholic Independent movement impacted both nationalist and Marxist movements in Ceylon through such cases of family heritage.

As this book deals with a minoritarian church movement in South Asia, whose history is little known, our first and foremost goal was to provide a *historical narrative of the Independent Catholic movement* in relation to existing narratives on Christianity in South Asia and in the rest of the world. Contextualizing the movement in various scopes allows us to draw on different academic discourses and areas of research to facilitate cross-confessional comparisons. One such perspective is a comparison with nineteenth century Protestant movements for emancipation and independence. As Klaus Koschorke has highlighted for the history of Christianity in Asia, Africa, and Latin America around the turn of 19th and 20th centuries, there were in various regions simultaneous and synchronous, but usually unconnected movements of religious independency, demanding indigenous leadership and freedom from colonial and/or missionary control.[5] Several cases deserve further reflection. For instance, in the years 1876–1879 the Ceylon Anglican Church found itself in tension with Tamil Christians from the Highland. Their petitions aimed at redressing specific grievances but were also calling for an "Independent Native Church" in the island.[6] Similar initiatives can be found also in Protestant India. The most remarkable one led to the founding of the "National Church of India" in 1886 in Madras, established by a section of Protestant intelligentsia in South India and aiming at uniting all Indian Christians, irrespectively of their denominational affiliation, in *one* Indian Church.[7] Similar movements existed also in Japan and other Asian countries in the beginning of the twentieth century, usually in protest against

---

5   K. KOSCHORKE, "The World Missionary Conference in Edinburgh 1910 and the Rise of National Church Movements in Asia and Africa", in: ID. (ed.) *Transcontinental Links in the History of Non-Western Christianity* (Wiesbaden 2002, 203–217).

6   "Ceylon: Petition for an 'Independent Native Church' (1878)", in: K. KOSCHORKE / M. DELGADO / F. LUDWIG (eds.), *A History of Christianity in Asia, Africa, and Latin America, 1450–1990. A Documentary Sourcebook* (Grand Rapids 2007), 101.

7   "India: The 'National Church of India' (Madras 1886)", in: K. KOSCHORKE / M. DELGADO / F. LUDWIG (eds.), *A History of Christianity in Asia, Africa, and Latin America, 1450–1990. A Documentary Sourcebook* (Grand Rapids 2013), 102–104.

missionary dominance or paternalism and in search for a "national form" of Asian Christianity.[8]

The Independent Catholic movement in Ceylon and India certainly shared with these movements a sense of patriotic awareness and demand for indigenous – both lay and religious – leadership. At the same time, the Independent Catholics of Ceylon demonstrate that the search for religious independency by Asian Christians was not limited to Protestant mission Churches. It could also be found in Catholic Asia around the turn from the nineteenth to the twentieth centuries. A well-known example is the "Iglesia Filipina Independiente" (IFI) established in the Philippines in 1902 in the aftermath of the anti-Spanish revolution in 1898. It came into being through the activities of the Filipino intellectual Isabelo de los Reyes (1864–1938) and the former Roman Catholic priest Gregorio Aglipay (1860–1940) and comprised in its initial years up to 20% of the Filipino population.[9] Only known to insiders, however, has been so far the very existence of the Independent Catholics of Ceylon (and Goa) which have been analyzed in this book, as a scholarly monographic study, for the very first time. One of the remarkable aspects of this story are immediate *attempts of communication and exchange of letters* between the Independent Catholics of Ceylon and the IFI documented since April 1903. This rare contact again reveals the creativity and resistance of the Independent Catholics in Ceylon, whose visions for alliance extended across the confines of the subcontinent.[10] Interestingly, the only attempt at collaboration known to us between Ceylon and Philippines Independent Catholics did not lead to any eventual joint efforts or union. Further research is required to understand the very reasons behind the disruption of the potential connections, which might lead to a deeper understanding of the networking among contemporary Christian independence movements in general.

These intra-Asian connections with other non-Roman Catholics in Asia, important as they are, represent only a section of the *much wider global context* into which the history of the Independent Catholics of Ceylon has to be placed. Chapter 3 of this book has detailed the extension of Alvares' apostolic succession through Rene Vilatte, who received episcopal consecration from Alvares and two other bishops of the Syrian Orthodox Church in Malabar. Vilatte was one of those European men who sought for apostolic lineage in the Oriental Church in South Asia, such as Alexander Steward and Ulric Vernon Herford.[11] The very complex national identities and ecclesiastical belongings of those figures somehow outweighed the latent racial prejudice, which had predominated the relation between European missionaries and native clergymen within the Roman Catholic Church. Thanks to the colonial public sphere of the time, built around periodicals and newspapers, men like Vilatte and Steward came to the conclusion that the answers to their troubles lay in far-away Ceylon.

---

8   K. KOSCHORKE, "New Maps of the History of World Christianity. Current Challenges and Future Perspectives" (*Theology Today* 71/2, 2014, 178–191), 181–185; KOSCHORKE, "The World Missionary Conference".

9   P.A. RODELL, "The Founding of the Iglesia Filipina Independiente (The 'Aglipayan' Church): An Historical Review" (*Philippine Quarterly of Culture and Society* 16/3-4, 1988, 210–234); A.M. RANCHE, "The Iglesia Filipina Independiente (IFI): A People's Movement for National Freedom, Independence and Prosperity (*Philippiniana Sacra*, 35/105, 2000, 513–534); A. HERMANN, "Publicizing Independence. Thoughts on the Filipino *ilustrado* Isabelo de los Reyes, the Iglesia Filipina Independiente, and the Emergence of an Indigenous-Christian Public Sphere" (*Journal of World Christianity* 6/1, 99–122).

10 HERMANN, "Publicizing Independence", 111–114; K. KOSCHORKE ET AL., *Discourses of Indigenous Christian Elites in Colonial Societies in Asia and Africa around 1900: A Documentary Sourcebook from Selected Journals* (Wiesbaden 2016), 441–442.

11 J. BYRNE, *The Other Catholics: Remaking America's Largest Religion* (New York 2016), S. A. THERIAULT, *Msgr. René Vilatte: Community Organizer of Religion, 1854–1929* (Berkeley ²2012): H.R.T. BRANDRETH, *Episcopi Vagantes and the Anglican Church* (Berkeley ²2006); P.F. ANSON, *Bishops at Large* (London ²2006).

Alvares' journey from the Catholic to the Syrian Orthodox Church, as well as Vilatte and Steward's Asian interludes, reflected the *intensive cross-confessional negotiations* – between various branches of the Roman Catholic Church, the Anglicans, the Oriental Churches of Western Syrian and Chaldean rites, and the Old Catholic movement – that created a space for innovations.

Another field of research on which this study sheds new light is the *history of indigenous Christian periodicals and publishing* in Asia. Much attention has been paid in the last years to the missionary press, as a source of information on non-European societies and missionary networking, not only by missionary historians, but also by cultural anthropologists and historians of globalization.[12] Even more innovative have been recent studies on journals and periodicals published by local Christian elites in order "to give publicity to our thoughts" in the colonial public sphere, and as channels of communication between likeminded Christian protagonists from various regions and different colonial or missionary contexts.[13] In many regions in Asia (as well as in Africa and Latin America), the late 19th and early 20th century saw a boom of periodical and newspaper publishing. Increasingly, the new media were being used also by local Christian groups and movements of religious dissent. These indigenous Christian journals, often overlooked or dealt with only in isolated regional contexts, have become an important source for a multifaceted understanding of processes of religious and social change in the colonial context.

So, to come back to colonial Sri Lanka, *The Independent Catholic* was not only the official newspaper of the Independent Catholic Church. It also functioned as a cradle of trade unionism, as Kumari Jayawardena has observed already in 1972 in her study on the origins of the Sri Lankan labour movement.[14] The journal's articles supported the first strikes among printers in Colombo in 1893 and the call for united labour actions. Here processes of *religious and social emancipation* were closely connected. As noticed by Adrian Hermann, similar observations can be also made, for example, with regard to the religious press of the IFI in the Philippines which was distributed on the islands jointly with a trade union periodical.[15] At the same time, in the context of the nascent Sri Lankan nationalism, *cooperation between otherwise rivalling religious groups* becomes visible. There existed connections between Independent Catholics and activists of the Buddhist revival movement. The trade union leader Alfred Ernest Buultjens (1865–1916), a staunch Theosophist and Buddhist, *The Independent Catholic* co-editor Pedro Manuel Lisboa Pinto (1858–1898), as a Christian, together with the lawyer H. J. Charles Pereira (1858–1924) and the businessman Martinus C. Pereira, as well as the Buddhist educationist and journalist Calutantrige Don Bastian (1852–1921), all advocated higher salaries and a better healthcare for workers. At the same time, they belonged to different religious camps.

---

12 F. JENSZ / H. ACHE (eds.), *Missions and Media. The Politics of Missionary Periodicals in the Long Nineteenth Century* (Stuttgart 2013); F. JENSZ, "Origins of Missionary Periodicals: Form and Function of Three Moravian Publications" (*Journal of Religious History* 36/2, 2012, 234–255); R. HABERMAS / R. HÖLZ (eds.), *Mission global. Eine Verflechtungsgeschichte seit dem 19. Jahrhundert* (Köln 2014); R. HABERMAS, "Mission im 19. Jahrhundert – Globale Netze des Religiösen" (*Historische Zeitschrift* 287, 2008, 629–678); A. JOHNSTON, *Missionary Writing and Empire, 1800–1860* (Cambridge 2003).
13 K. KOSCHORKE ET AL. (eds.), *"To give publicity to our thoughts". Journale asiatischer und afrikanischer Christen um 1900 und die Entstehung einer transregionalen indigen-christlichen Öffentlichkeit / Journals of Asian and African Christians Around 1900 and the Making of a Transregional Indigenous-Christian Public Sphere* (Wiesbaden 2018).
14 VISAKHA KUMARI JAYAWARDENA, *The Rise of the Labor Movement in Ceylon* (Durham 1972)
15 See KOSCHORKE ET AL., *Discourses*, 340; KOSCHORKE ET AL., *"To give publicity to our thoughts"*, 113.

In fighting for religious independency and social improvement, *The Independent Catholic* became an actor in the country's *colonial public sphere*. Its impact on Ceylonese journalism can be glanced by the variety of newspapers that interacted with it: both in Ceylon and British India, in English, Portuguese, and Sinhalese newspapers. Its readership also reached North America and Europe. The New York-based *The Independent* was among the earliest Western periodicals that paid attention to the Colombo *Independent Catholic*. Even in Protestant Germany, in the academic *Theologischer Jahresbericht*, the journal was referred to in 1892 as a recent addition in the Catholic world, and particularly in Catholic Asia.[16]

By studying *The Independent Catholic*, this book has been able to comment on previous research on *trade unionism in late 19th century Ceylon*. Jayawardena defined the eccentric *The Independent Catholic* as "a small radical journal" and described its contributors as part of a radical middle class.[17] Her argument rested on a comparative study between James Alfred Ernst Buultjens and Pedro Manuel Lisboa Pinto. In our analysis we have instead looked at Lisboa Pinto not primarily from the perspective of the labour movement, but we have rather located him in the context of Christian independentism. Indeed while being a Christian minority, the Independent Catholics' *alliances with other religious groups*, especially the reformed Buddhists, provided a sense of communal belonging. Strategically, by assuming the role of fighters against Rome, the "schismatic Catholics" acquired legitimacy for their claimed "true Catholicism" in the Ceylonese public sphere. The Colombo monthly was regarded in the circle of Ceylonese commercial newspapers as a fighter against the Roman Catholic Church, seen as a corrupted authority that allegedly enslaved Christians all over the world. *The Independent Catholic*'s debut as part of a popular movement probably made a significant contribution to the shaping of an Independent Catholic identity under a social agenda oriented towards justice and equality. Such a joint commitment brought to a new level the engagement shown at the time of the *Padroado* resistance against the Propaganda Fide jurisdictional assertions.

By placing the history of the Independent Catholics of Ceylon into a wider global context this study has also made a contribution to exploring *polycentricity in the history of World Christianity*, a category that has been intensively discussed in recent years.[18] Admittedly, this study began as the attempt to describe the history of a regional minoritarian Christian movement as a history in its own right, within the limited geographical frame of colonial Ceylon, in a predominantly Buddhist society under British rule between the nineteenth and the twentieth century. Nonetheless, at the same time, the history of the Independent Catholics of Ceylon from its very beginning was inseparably linked with the emergence of Independent Catholicism in colonial India, emerging from a strand of the Indo-Portuguese Catholic culture. Both these histories – in Portuguese and British India on the one hand, and in Ceylon on the

---

16 *Theologischer Jahresbericht*. Zwölfter Band enthaltend die Literatur des Jahres 1892 (Braunschweig 1893), 335.
17 JAYAWARDENA, *The Rise of the Labor Movement*, 84.
18 See KOSCHORKE, "New Maps"; K. KOSCHORKE / A. HERMANN (eds.), *Polycentric Structures in the History of World Christianity* (Wiesbaden 2014); K. KOSCHORKE "Transcontinental Links, Enlarged Maps, and Polycentric Structures in the History of World Christianity" (*Journal of World Christianity* 6/1, 2016, 28–56); D.B. DAUGHRITY, "The 'Munich School' as a Corrective in World Christianity" (*International Bulletin of Mission Research* 45/3, 2020, 221–224); M. FREDERIKS, "World Christianity: Contours of an Approach", in: M. FREDERIKS / D. NAGY (eds.), *World Christianity. Methodological Considerations* (Leiden 2020), 10–39. The framework of a polycentric perspective on World Christianity has also inspired the recent establishment of the Centre for Advanced Studies "Polycentricity and Plurality of Premodern Christianities" at the University of Frankfurt (funded by the German Research Foundation).

other – were outcomes of a plurisecular conflict between *Padroado* and Propaganda allegiances which, in India, had culminated in the so-called Goan schism in the early nineteenth century. However, the roots of this conflict already had been a determining and disturbing factor in the whole Catholic missionary enterprise in Asia and Africa soon after the very founding of the Congregation of Propaganda Fide in 1622. In addition, once having declared their independence from Rome, the Independent Catholics of Ceylon got in touch in 1903 with the IFI as another (and much more prominent) non-Roman Catholic Church in Asia and, via Rene Vilatte, at least indirectly, also with the Non-Roman Catholic milieus in the United States and globally. Through their incorporation into the Malankara Orthodox Syrian Church, the Ceylonese Independent Catholics also became linked with the ecclesial networks of the Syrian Orthodox Church in Malabar and subject to the jurisdiction of the Patriarchy of Antioch; and, through their cooperation within Ceylon's nascent trade unionism, they also got in contact with other social movements in the wider South Asian context.

Therefore, if we understand the "global history of Christianity as a history of multidirectional transcontinental interactions"[19], this history allows us to understand the Independent Catholics of Ceylon not just as a local movement, but rather as a part of the way in which the history of Christianity in South Asia should be interpreted *both* from a local and from a transregional perspective.

In sum, this monograph has attempted to provide a contribution to a future history of Christianity in a polycentric perspective. Whereas it would be quite difficult to interpret the Independent Catholics in Ceylon, differently from other more expansionist emancipatory movements of Asian or African Christians around 1900, as a "regional center of expansion" – as they only had a geographically limited constituency – what the perspective of a "polycentric approach" can help us to illuminate, is how different flows of influence, and a "multiplicity of indigenous initiatives", have contributed significantly to the history of Christianity in South Asia in the nineteenth and early twentieth centuries beyond a focus limited primarily to Western missionary activities.

---

19 KOSCHORKE, "Transcontinental Links", 42.

Appendices

Appendix 1: Lists of Names

A. The Roman Catholic Portuguese Mission, 1837–1887

Members Mentioned in Documents, in Chronological Order

August 1837: 231 Roman Catholics of Colombo belonging to the Roman Catholic Portuguese Mission [1]

1 September 1837: W. Vanderstraaten, J. Sansoni, J. B. Misso, Flanderka, S. C. de Heer, H. Van Langenbergh, P. L. Ramenaden, F. H. H. Anandappa (the last two were Heads of the R. C. Chetties).[2]

21 September 1837: J. B. Misso (Chairman), F. Daniels, P. L. Ramenaden, L. Vanderstraaten, P. B. Anandappa, H. Silvaf, P. B. Fernando, P. H. de Laharpe, G. C. Kelaart, S. C. De Heer (Secretary).[3]

4 November 1837: V. W. Vanderstraaten, E. I. Silvaf, J. B. Misso, C. A. Schwallier, A. Silvaf, L. L. Vanderstraaten; besides these six gentlemen, *1481* other Catholics of Colombo signed the Memorial.[4]

25 January 1838: J. B. Misso (chairman), Hippolyte Silvaf (member).[5]

12 February 1838: J. B. Misso (chairman), Hyppolite Silvaf, P. B. Fernando, P. L. Ramanaden, P. H. de la Harpe, L. Vanderstraaten, G. C. Kelaart, P. B. Anandappa, S. C. De Heer (Secretary).[6]

1 December 1842: J. B. Misso (president), P. B. Misso, A. E. Misso, S. Duvich, G. Welkant, V. E. Misso, P. R. Kelaart.[7]

20 October 1843: John Boniface Misso, John Baptist Daniel, Celestine Daniel, Vincent Edward Misso, Lambert Anthony Passe, Luke Raux, Francis Daniel, Tevarayname (also as Tewerayan), John Adrian Duwe, John Alexander Vanlangenberg,[8] John Wright,

---

1 "Memorial of the Catholics to the Oratorians", in PERNIOLA, *The Catholic Church*. The British Period. Vol. 1, 182.
2 "The Catholics to the Oratorians", in PERNIOLA, *The Catholic Church*. The British Period. Vol. 1, 186.
3 "Reply of the Catholics to Vicente do Rozario, Vicar General", in PERNIOLA, *The Catholic Church*. The British Period. Vol. 1, 191.
4 "Memorial to Governor R. W. Horton", in PERNIOLA, *The Catholic Church*. The British Period. Vol. 1, 192–193.
5 "J. B. Misso to D. O'Connor", in PERNIOLA, *The Catholic Church*. The British Period. Vol. 1, 203.
6 "Memorial sent to Propaganda" in PERNIOLA, *The Catholic Church*. The British Period. Vol. 1, 211.
7 "The Catholics of Colombo" sent a letter to the Pope with over 2100 signatures. See an English translation of the letter in PERNIOLA, *The Catholic Church*. The British Period. Vol. 1, 314.
8 A letter by Bishop Giuseppe Maria Bravi on a "Meeting of dissident Catholics", in PERNIOLA, *The Catholic Church*. The British Period. Vol. 1, 402. These names were classified by Bravi as the first class, namely, the main participants.

Peter Fredric Dowe, John Tissera, John D' Andriez, Cosmas Daian D' Alvis, John Henry de Jonk (later came to the Catholic Church),[9] Francis Daniel, George Passe, Henry Rozario, Cornelius Baptist Perera, Andrew Almeida, Philip Kelaart, Stephen Raux, John Wintura, Emmanuel Colyn, Lodovico Patendorff, Livio Fox.[10]

1845: Father Philip Caetano Piedade da Conceição (Vicar General of the Island of Ceylon), Father G.F. Rodrigues de Almeida (Missionary), S. C. de Heer (register), C. D. de Alvis (clerk and choir master), Henry Gonsal (sexton), Warnecoolegay Jusey Perera (native sexton), J. B. Misso, Esq. (trustee of the burial ground), F. Daniel, Esq (trustee of the burial ground), J.A. Van Langenbergh (trustee of the burial ground).[11]

31 May 1845: Father J. S. da Cunha (missionary) and Father T. G. L. R. Pinto (missionary)[12]

A Full List[13]

Laity
1. John Bonifacio Misso
2. W. Vanderstraaten
3. J. Sansoni
4. Flanderka
5. S. C. De Heer
6. H. Van Langenbergh
7. P. L. Ramenaden
8. F. H. H. Anandappa
9. Francis Daniel(s)
10. L. Vanderstraaten
11. P. B. Anandappa
12. Hyppolyte Silvaf
13. P. B. Fernando
14. P. H. de Laharpe
15. G. C. Kelaart
16. E. I. Silvaf
17. C. A. Schwallier
18. A. Silvaf
19. P. B. Misso
20. A. E. Misso
21. S. Duvich
22. G. Welkant
23. Vincent Edward Misso
24. P. R. Kelaart

---

9 These were classified by Bishop Giuseppe Maria Bravi the second class, who took active role in the meeting.
10 According to Bravi, they belonged to the third class, who were present at the meeting and signed the petition.
11 "Roman Catholic Mission in Ceylon" in PERNIOLA, *The Catholic Church. The British Period.* Vol. 2, 2–3, the original paper was published in *The Ceylon Almanac* 1845, 152.
12 Bettacchini to the Congregation of Propaganda Fide, 9 June 1845, in PERNIOLA, *The Catholic Church. The British Period.* Vol. 2, 19.
13 A circular by C.X. Alphonso, Colombo, 20 October 1884. AMNE, *Arquivo histórico da Embaixada de Portugal junto a Santa Sé,* Caixa 39, Maço 1. Sé Oriente n. 43.

25. John Baptist Daniel
26. Celestine Daniel
27. Lambert Anthony Passe
28. Luke Raux
29. Tevarayname (also as Tewerayan)
30. John Adrian Dowe
31. John Alexander Vanlangenberg
32. John Wright
33. Peter Fredric Dowe
34. John Tissera
35. John D' Andriez
36. Cosmas Daian D' Alvis
37. John Henry de Jonk
38. George Passe
39. Henry Rozario
40. Cornelius Baptist Perera
41. Andrew Almeida
42. Philip Kelaart
43. Stephen Raux
44. John Wintura
45. Emmanuel Colyn
46. Lodovico Patendorff
47. Livio Fox
48. Henry Gonsal
49. Warnecoolegay Jusey Perera

Priests
1. Philip Caetano Piedade da Conceição
2. G. F. Rodrigues de Almeida
3. J. S. da Cunha
4. T. G. L. R. Pinto
5. Miguel Philip Mascarenhas
6. C. X. Alphonso

B. The Independent Catholic Mission 1888–1900

Members Mentioned in Documents, in Chronological Order

25th March 1887: Martines Pereira (Annavy)[14]
29 August 1888: Stephen (de) Silva[15]
26 December 1891: Julius Kerner and his wife[16]

---

14 APF, *SC Indie Orientali*, vol. 32: ff. 251r–252v. He died on 14 January 1892 at the Leper Asylum, see *The Independent Catholic*, February 1892, 1.
15 *O Ultramar*, 15 September 1888, 3.
16 *The Independent Catholic*, January 1892, 1.

29 December 1891: Vincent Kulow and wife[17]
4 January 1892: Lisboa Pinto and wife[18]
January 1892: The Independent Catholic Church Carol: Caetan Fernando and Vincent Kerner (violins), J. Haekel (harmonium), Oswald Andriesz (guitar), other attendants including B. Sampayo (manager of the carol), assisted by A. Kerner, B. F. Quyn, K. D. Innocent, J. Sampayo and V. M. Fulow[19]
20 January 1892: Vincent Kerner married to Edith Clara Lovendahl[20]
11 February 1892: Laurencia Margaret Pereira married to Francis Quyn (of the Clifton Press)[21]
March 1892: A. A. A. de Souza (vicar general), Vincent W. Pereira (trustee), Louis G. Fernando (trustee), Stephen Silva (trustee)[22]
March 1892: seven adults baptised by A. A. A. de Souza in Colombo[23]
January 1893: J. A. Figuerado sent his sons to the Royal College[24]
June 1893: Susan Augusta Pereira (died at age 19), Julia (widow of the late Helier Pereira, died at age 52)[25]
March 1896: Fr. Souza, Stephen Silva, L. G. Fernando, J. B. Fernando, B. de Sampayo, R. E. Fernando, Dr. Lisboa Pinto, D.A. Passe, J. de Sampayo

A Full List

Laity
1. Martines Pereira (†1892)
2. Stephan (de) Silva (trustee)
3. Julius Kerner and wife
4. Vincent Kulow and wife
5. Lisboa Pinto and wife
6. Caetan Fernando
7. Vincent Kerner and wife Edith Clara Lovendahl
8. J. Haekel
9. Oswald Andriesz (leader of the musical band)
10. B. Sampayo (manager of the carol)
11. B. F. Quyn (Clifton Press) and wife Laurencia Margaret Pereira
12. Vincent W. Pereira (trustee)
13. K. D. Innocent
14. J. Sampayo
15. V. M. Fulow
16. Louis G. Fernando (trustee)
17. J. A. Figuerado (lay leader in Mannar)

---

17 *The Independent Catholic*, January 1892, 1.
18 *The Independent Catholic*, January 1892, 1.
19 *The Independent Catholic*, January 1892, 3.
20 *The Independent Catholic*, February 1892, 1.
21 *The Independent Catholic*, February 1892, 1.
22 *The Independent Catholic*, March 1892, 3.
23 "Adult baptisms", *The Independent Catholic*, April 1892, 3.
24 "Mr. J. A. Figuerado", *The Independent Catholic*, January 1893, 1.
25 "Domestic occurrence: Deaths" *The Independent Catholic*, June 1893, 1. "Miss Susan Augusta Pereira" *The Independent Catholic*, June 1893, 2.

18. Seven adults baptised
19. Susan Augusta Pereira (daughter of Vincent W. Pereira)
20. Julia and her late husband Helier Pereira

Priests
1. Antonio Francisco Xavier Alvares
2. A. A. A. de Souza (Colombo)
3. Luis Mariano Soares (Mannar, Dindigul, Tuticorin)
4. Avelino da Cunha (of Portuguese origin)
5. Joseph Xavier Botelho (canon, served in Colombo)
6. Zeferino Roque Noronha (1850–1936, Kallianpur)
7. Damio Lopes (Kallianpur)
8. Fr. Joseph D'Mello (in Colombo until 1941, and then in Trichy)
9. ? Kempis (a Eurasian, ordained in Colombo)[26]
10. W. M. Talayaratna (a Sinhala, replacing Soares in Mannar)[27]
11. ? Alvares (nephew of Antonio Alvares, ordained in Colombo in 1898)[28]

C. Guests and Presents at Lisboa Pinto's Birthday Party in Colombo on 1 October 1898[29]

No.	Name	Gift
1	Mr. A. C. A. Latiff	a silk bag containing a substantial sum of money
2	Mr. A. N. Saldin	architectural framework representing the temple of Aesculapius
3	Mr. M. C. Perera	butter dish
4	Mr. S. D. Abdul Careem	liqueur stand
5	Mr. A. L. Abdul Careem	gong
6	Mr. E. Jayawardene	pair of vases
7	Mr C. C. Saibo Tamby	mirror
8	Mr. and Mrs. G. E. Lewis	pair of vases
9	Mrs. Silva Wijeyeratne	centerpiece
10	Mr. and Mrs. P. J. Fernando	electroplated sugar bowl and tong
11	Mr. A. L. S. Deen Hadijiar	2 pairs of vases

---

26 "To His Holiness Ignatius A. Messias, Patriarch of Antioch and the East", dated in Colombo, November 10, 1900.
27 Ibid.
28 Ibid.
29 "Dr. and Mrs Pintos at home" *The Ceylon Independent*, 4 October 1898.

12	Mr. D. J. Wanigasooria	vase
13	Mr. and Mrs. Delilkhan	vase
14	Mr. S. L. Ismail Lebbe Maricar	pair of vases
15	Mr. and Mrs. E. de Silva	pair ebony elephants
16	Mr. S. D. Maricar Hadjiar	electroplated scent diffuser
17	Mr. and Mrs R. Nicolle	pair of vases
18	Mr. I. L. M. Mohamed Seli	pair of decanters
19	Mr. S. L. Abdul Rahiman	physician's leather bag
20	Mr. and Mrs. V. Wyrewanaden	electroplated centerpiece
21	Mr. John de Sampayo	pair of frames
22	Mr. I. L. M. H. M. Mohideen	bentwood chairs
23	Mr. Abeyratne Mohandiram and Sons	8 bentwood chairs
24	Mr. A. L. M. Uduma Lebbe Maricar	bentwood chairs
25	Mr. J. Adolphus	6 plants in pots
26	Mr. M. H. Mohamed Lebbe	bentwood chairs
27	Mr. G. F. Lobendb[ ]n	6 fretwork nadoonwood chairs
28	the Turkish Consul	bentwood chairs
29	Mr. I. L. M. Avoo Lebbe Maricar	bentwood chairs
30	Mrs. K. D. Perera	electroplated centerpiece
31	Mr. C. M. Ahamed Alli	bentwood chairs
32	Mr. A.C. Noordeen	washstand and furniture
33	Mrs. Victor Bottoni	pair of wall plates
34	Mr. M. M. H. Cassim	office clock
35	Mudaliyar and Mrs. Settinayake	pair of ebony brackets
36	Mr. Don Manuel Gomes	pair of vases
37	Mr. and Mrs. Vincent W. Perera	embroidery in gold frame
38	Mr. C. M. Meera Lebbe Maricar	pair of golden plush frames
39	Mr. A. L. M. Abdul Rahiman	pair of chain flower vases
40	Mr. S. L. Idroos	bee clock
41	Mr. S. L. M. Abdul Rahiman	gilt centre piece
42	Mr. and Mrs. A.W. Salgado	pair of vases

43	Mr. A. L. M. L. Maricar	hanging lamp
44	Mr. L. L. Abdul Cader	mirror
45	Mr. M. L. Ahamed Lebbe	pair of vases
46	Mr. M. L. Abdul Latiff	pair of vases
47	Mr. Mohamed Abubacker	gilted centerpiece
48	Mr. Mohamed Esack	gilt frame
49	Mr. S. L. Neyna Maricar	hanging lamp
50	Mr. I. L. M. Noordeen Hadjiar	table lamp
51	Mr. C. L. M. Abdul Hameed	ruby tie-pin
52	Mr. C. M. Assena Mariker	musical clock
53	Mr. I. L. M. H. Noordeen Hadjiar	table lamp
54	Mr. M. M. Mohamood	carpet
55	Mr. S. M. Mohamed Salih	carpet
56	Dr. N. M. Gandavia	cheque
57	Mr. A. Abdul Rahiman	cheque
58	Mr. Pinto	cigars and cigarettes

D. Participants at the Assembly which took place on 21 October 1886 in Panjim, Goa[30]

No.	Name	Profession
1	Dr. Bernardo Wolfgang da Silva	surgeon
2	Dr. Aureliano J. d'Assumpção Rodrigues	surgeon
3	Dr. Ignacio do Rosario S. Sequeira e Nazareth	surgeon
4	Pe. Manuel Carlos R[]ldao d'Athaide	priest and teacher at the Lyceu Nacional
5	Dr. Manuel Pedro de Souza Franklin	attorney and editor of *Correio da India*
6	Dr. José Maria de Sá	attorney and president of Camara agraria das Ilhas
7	José Maria d'Azavedo	landowner and dealer
8	Vicente Sebastião Affonso	pharmacist

---

30 "Commissão central do Comicio" in: *Acta do comicio de 21 outubro de 1886: Reunion em Nova Goa com os discursos e representações respeito a Egreja Indiana* (Nova Goa Typographia de *Times of Goa*), ix.

9	Pe. Antonio Francisco X. Alvares	priest and editor of *Times of Goa*
10	Joaquim Francisco Correia de Noronha	"capitalist"
11	Roque de Sequeira e Nazareth	"capitalist"
12	Luis Guilherme Dias	"capitalist"
13	José Manuel Barreto	dealer
14	Antonio Francisco de Miranda	landowner
15	Domingos João Fortunato de Souza	pharmacist
16	João Felippe do Rego	dealer
17	Diogo Luis da Fonseca	landowner

Appendix 2: Inscriptions of Grave Stelæ in the Church of Our Lady of Good Death

Stele 1

HIC JACENT MORTALIA
Reverendi
EZECHIELIS A CONCEP. RODRIGUS
Nativitate Goanesis
Pro Vicarius Generalis Taprobanensis
Sub Regio Lusitaniae Patronatu:
Mortuus est Taprobanae
Die 8 Septembris. An: Dni: 1856
R. I. P.

Stele 2

In memory of
LAMBERT ANTHONY
PASSE
Born 16th May 1810
Died 9th July 1865
R. I. P.

Stele 3

IN
MEMORY OF
CHARLES OLIVER
SON OF S. Daniel
Died 6th December 1856
Aged 16 Years
7 Months

F D
Died 19th May 1867
Aged 73 years

E S
Died 9th Sep: 1875
Aged 76 Years

Stele 4

In Memory of
Sir JOHN B. MISSO
First Consul General
Of Portugal in Ceylon
Born 13th April 1797
Died 7th March 1864
"Have pity on me…
At least you my friends"
JOB 19 Cap 21

Bibliography

Primary Sources

List of archives

ACCO: Archivio della Congregazione per le Chiese Orientali, Vatican City
ACDF: Archivio della Congregazione per la Dottrina della Fede, Vatican City
AMNE: Arquivo Diplomático e Biblioteca do Ministério dos Negócios Estrangeiros, Lisboa
APF: Archivio della Congregazione per l'Evangelizzazione dei Popoli, Vatican City
CAG: Church Archives of Goa (old Patriarchal Archive), Panjim
DAAG: Directorate of Archives and Archaeology of Goa, Panjim
LPL: Lambeth Palace Library, London

Archival sources

AMNE: *Arquivo histórico da Embaixada de Portugal junto a Santa Sé,* Caixa 39
ACCO: *Rubrica* 109 Soriani del Malabar Varia (1894–1897)
ACDF: *Dubia circa Ordinem sacrum* 1903
APF: *Scritture riferite nei Congressi, Indie Orientali* Vol. 32 (1887), Vol. 33 (1888), Vol. 34 (1889)
CAG: *Portaria*, Vol. 13 (1882–1887)
    Papeis avulsos
DAAG: *Monções do Reino*, Vol. 9200.
LPL: *Davidson* 83.
    F. Temple 47
The Jesuit Archives of Madurai Province, Shembaganur (Kodaikanal), 217/143 and 217/229

General periodicals or running publications

Actas das Sessões da Sociedade de Geographia de Lisboa fundada em 1875. Vol. 7, 50. Lisboa, 1887.
A Cruz, 15 July 1876, 12 November 1880, 26 November 1880, 5 August 1881
A Verdade, 24 July 1882

Annaes do Conselho Ultramarino. Parte não official, Serie II. Lisboa: Imprensa Nacional, 1867.
Boletim do Conselho Ultramarino. Legislação Novissima. Lisboa: Imprensa Nacional, 1869, Vol. 2.
Boletim do Governo do Estado da Índia, n. 1. Nova Goa: 3 January 1860.
Homeward Mail from India, China and the East. London: Messrs. Smith, Elder, & Co., 1857–1913. *Le Missioni Cattoliche: Bullettino* [sic] *settimanale dell'Opera La Propagazione della Fede*, Vol. 14, no. 7. Milano, 1885.
O Brado Indiano, 1894–1895
The Independent Catholic, 1892–1893, 1895.
The Indian Magazine by National Indian Association in Aid of Social Progress and Education in India 337, July 1890.
The Madras Catholic Directory, 1870.
Western Mail, 7 January 1899.
Guardian, October 1902.

Primary sources without named author

Apontamentos para a historia da Revolta em Goa dos soldados, Ranes e Satarienses em o anno de 1895. Bombaim: Nicol's Printing Works, 1896.
A Revised Edition of the Ordinances of the Government of Ceylon. Vol. 1: 1799–1882. Colombo: G. J. A. Skeen, Government Printer, 1894.
Diccionario Bibliographico Portuguez. Estudos de Innocencio Francisco da Silva applicaveis a Portugal e ao Brasil. Vol. 8. Lisboa: Na Imprensa Nacional, 1867.
Documents Proving the Validity of the Episcopal Consecration of S. Renatus, Archbishop Vilatte. London: Hunt, Barnard & Co., 1901.
Inventory of Church Archives of Wisconsin: Protestant Episcopal Church in the United States of America: Diocese of Fond du Lac. Madison/WI, 1941.
Lista Geral dos Officiaes e Empregados da Marinha e Ultramar referida ao 1.º de Novembro de 1850. Lisboa: Imprensa Nacional.
Memoir on the Address of His Holiness Pius IX, delivered in the Secret Consistory on 17th February 1851, etc. - Translated from the original in Portuguese, and printed for Senhor João Bonifacio Missó, Consul general of Portugal in Ceylon (Colombo, 1853).
Negocios externos: Documentos apresentados ás cortes na sessão legislativa de 1887 pelo ministro e secretario d'Estado dos Negocios Estrangeiros: Negociações com a Santa Sé, Segunda parte. Lisboa: Imprensa Nacional, 1887.
Pastoral Letter of the Right Reverend Henry Marsh Marsh-Edwards on the Appalling Advance of Rationalism in the Church of England. London: Partridge and Cooper, 1903.
Quadros Biographicos dos Padres Illustres de Goa. Estudos do Padre Expectação Barreto. Bastorá: Tipographia Rangel, 1899.
Report of a meeting of the Catholics of Bombay subject to the Jurisdiction of the Archbishop Primate of the East, held on the 12th April 1885 (Bombay).
"Personal Intelligence". In *Journal of the National Indian Association in Aid of Social Progress and Education in India* 179, November 1885, 563–564.

"O. Sr. Dr. J. C. Lisboa". In *O Ultramar*, 26 March 1887, Anno 29, Nº1460, 3.
"O Sr. Doutor Lisboa". In *O Ultramar*, 7 December 1888, 4.
"Indian intelligence". In *The Indian Magazine* by National Indian Association in Aid of Social Progress and Education in India 337, July 1890, 385.
"The Late Dr. J. C. Lisboa". In *Lancet*, Volume 149, Issue 3851, 19 June 1897, 1719.

Books, articles etc. with named authors

A CATHOLIC. *The Church Militant in Ceylon and in India*. Audi Alteram Partem. Colombo, 1888.
AGUR, C. M. *Church History of Travancore*. 1st edition in 1903. New Delhi, Madras: Asian Educational Services, 1990.
ALVARES, A. F. X. *Directions for the Treatment of Cholera ... Second Edition*. Ceylon: Victoria Press, 1896.
ALVARES, A. F. X. *Universal Supremacy in the Church of Christ ... Abridged from the Original in Portuguese*. Colombo: Clifton Press, 1898.
ALVARES, A. F. X., JULIO I. *A supremacia universal na Egreja de Christo, provada pela Escriptura, tradição e escritores insuspeitos a Egreja Romana*. Colombo: Clifton Press, 1898.
ALVARES, A. F. X., JULIO I. *Mandioca*. Bastora: Typ. Rangel 1917.
ALVARES, METROPOLITAN ANTONIO FRANCISCO XAVIER MAR YOOLIOS. *Universal Supremacy of the Church of Christ*. Edited by T. Kurian. Kottayam: MOC Publications, 2020.
ALVARES, Pe. ANTONIO FRANCISCO XAVIER. *Direcções para o tratamento do cholera*. Nova Goa: Typographia da 'Verdade', n.d.
ANONYMOUS, "Mission and Vicariate Apostolic of Madura, East Indies" (*The Rambler: A Catholic Journal of Home and Foreign Literature Politics, Science, Music and the Fine Arts* 8, 1851, London), 85.
ANONYMOUS [A Missionary Apostolic]. *A Crucial Test*. Colombo: Catholic Orphans Press, 1889.
ANONYMOUS [Bonjean]. *The Jacobites of Ceylon*. N.L. 1889.
BAIERLEIN, EDUARD RAIMUND. *The Land of the Tamulians and Its Missions*, translated by J. D. B. Gribble. Madras: Higginbotham and Company, 1875.
BARTOLI, DANIELLO. *Dell'Historia della compagnia di Giesù: L'Asia*. Parte Prima. Rome: Stamperia d'Ignatio de Lazzeri, 1653.
BERNARD, RICHARD. *Fabulous Foundation of the Popedom, shewing* [sic] *that St Peter was never at Rome*. Oxford 1619.
BESSE, LEON. *La mission du Maduré. Historique de ses pangous*. Trichinopoly: Mission Catholique, 1914.
BOCARRO, ANTÓNIO. *Livro das plantas de todas as fortalezas, cidades e povoações do Estado da India Oriental*. Tomo 4, Vol. 2. Edited by A. B. de Bragança Pereira. Bastorá, Goa 1937.
BOULLAYE-LE-GOUZ, FRANÇOIS LA. *Les voyages et observations du sieur de La Boullaye-Le-Goulz*. Paris: chez Gervais Clousier au Palais, les degrez de la Sainte Chapelle, 1653.

BOULNOIS, C., J. BROWN and J. G. SMITH. *Indian Law Reports*. Madras Series containing Cases Determined by the High Court at Madras and by the Judicial Committee of the Privy Council on Appeal from that Court 19. 1898.

BUULTJENS, A. E. "Why I became a Buddhist: A Lecture Delivered by Mr. A.E. Buultjens at the Buddhist Headquarters at the Request of the Colombo YMBA, March 25 1899". In *The Buddhist* 7 and 8 (March and April 1899), 102–109.

CAETANO, GRACIAS. *Homenagem ao Pe. A. F. X. Alvares, suas notas biográficas.* Margao 1927.

COELHO, SERTORIO. *Pagina negra para os annaes da história colonial portugueza dedicada e oferecida aos seus patrícios e aos verdadeiros portuguezes.* Nova-Goa: s.n. 1895.

CONCEIÇÃO VELOSO, JOSÉ MARIANO DA. *Memoria sobre a cultura do laureio cinamomo vulgo canelleira de Ceilaõ.* Lisboa: Officina de Simão Thaddeo Ferreira, 1798.

CORDINER, JAMES. *A Description of Ceylon.* Longman, Hurst, Rees, and Orme, 1807.

COSMAS, INDICOPLEUSTES. *Kosma Aiguptiou Monachou Christianike Topographia = The Christian Topography of Cosmas, an Egyptian Monk.* Edited by John Watson McCrindle. 1st edition in 1897. London: Hakluyt Society, 2017.

COSTA, MANUEL DE OLIVEIRA GOMES DA. *A Revolta de Goa e a Campanha de 1895/1896.* Lisboa: Livraria Popular de Francisco Franco, 1939.

DAWSON, W. H. *Bismarck and State Socialism.* An Exposition of the Social and Economic Legislation of Germany Since 1870. London: Swan Sonnenschein & Co., 1890.

DREW, S. ed. *Imperial Magazine, Or, Compendium of Religious, Moral, & Philosophical Knowledge.* Vol. 3. London: Caxton Press by Henry Fisher, 1821.

DUSCHAUSSOIS, PIERRE. *Sous les feux de Ceylan.* Chez les Singhalais et les Tamouls. Paris: B. Grasset Oeuvre des Missions O.M.I., 1929.

FERGUSON, DONALD WILLIAM. "The Discovery of Ceylon by the Portuguese in 1506". *Journal of the Royal Asiatic Society Ceylon Branch* 19, no. 59, 1907, 284–363.

FERGUSON, JOHN. *Ceylon in 1903.* Describing the Progress of the Island Since 1803, Its Present Agricultural and Commercial Enterprises, and Its Unequalled Attractions to Visitors, with Useful Statistical Information. Colombo: A.M. & J. Ferguson, 1903.

HARVARD, W.M. *A Narrative of the Establishment and Progress of The Mission to Ceylon and India founded by the Late Rev. Thomas Coke.* London: printed for the author, 1823.HERZOG, WALTER. *Bischof Dr. Eduard Herzog: Ein Lebensbild.* Laufen: Buchdruckerei ‚Volksfreund', 1935.

HOLTZMANN, H. (ed.). *Theologischer Jahresbericht.* Vol. 12. Braunschweig: C. A. Schwetschke und Sohn, 1893.

HULL, ERNEST R. *Bombay Mission History: With a Special Study of the Padroado Question*, Vol. 1: 1534–1858, Vol. 2: 1858–1890. Bombay: Examiner Press, 1927–1930.

HUNT, WILLIAM SAUNDERS. *The Anglican Church in Travancore and Cochin, 1816–1916: Operations of the Church Missionary Society in South- West India* Vol. I. Kottayam: Church Missionary Society, 1920.

HYDE, LAURENCE. *A Short Historical Review of the Sylvestrine Monks in Ceylon from 1845 to 1920.* Edited by Bede Barcatta (http://www.osbsrilanka.org/wp-content/uploads/2014/09/A-Short-Historical-Review-by-Fr.-Lawrence-Hyde-OSB.pdf).

JORDÃO, LEVY MARIA, ed. *Bullarium patronatus Portugalliae regum in ecclesiis Africae, Asiae atque Oceaniae: Bullas, brevia, epistolas, decreta actaque Sanctae Sedis ab Alexandro III ad hoc usque tempus amplectens,* Vol. I (1171–1600). Lisboa: Typographia Nationali, 1868.

LISBOA PINTO, PEDRO MANUEL. *Antiochia e Roma e sua connexão* [sic] *com S. Pedro.* Bombaim: Portuguese Printing Press, 1890.

LISBOA PINTO, PEDRO MANUEL. *Alcoholic Drinks or Notes on the Medical, Social, Political and Religious Aspects of the Liquor Question.* Colombo: 'Times of Ceylon' Steam Press, 1895.

Meurin, Leo. *The Concordat Question.* n.l., ca 1885.

MEURIN, Leo. *The Padroado Question.* n.l., ca 1885.

ORTA, GARCIA DA. *Coloquios dos simples e drogas da India.* Edited by Francisco Manuel Carlos de Mello Ficalho. Lisboa: Imprensa Nacional, 1891.

PERNIOLA, VITO. *The Catholic Church in Sri Lanka.* The Dutch period, Vol. 1: 1658–1711. Dehiwala, Sri Lanka: Tisara Prakasakayo, 1983.

PERNIOLA, VITO. *The Catholic Church in Sri Lanka.* The Portuguese Period. Vol. 1: 1505-1565. Dehiwala, Sri Lanka: Tisara Prakasakayo, 1989.

PERNIOLA, VITO. *The Catholic Church in Sri Lanka.* The Portuguese Period. Vol. 3: 1620-1658. Dehiwala, Sri Lanka: Tisara Prakasakayo, 1991.

PERNIOLA, VITO. *The Catholic Church in Sri Lanka.* The British Period. Vol. 1: 1795–1844. The Colombo Vicariate. Dehiwala, Sri Lanka: Tisara Prakasakayo, 1992.

PERNIOLA, VITO. *The Catholic Church in Sri Lanka.* The British Period. Vol. 2: 1845–1849. The Vicariates of Colombo and Jaffna. Dehiwala: Tisara Prakasakayo, 1995.

PERNIOLA, VITO. *The Catholic Church in Sri Lanka.* The British Period. Vol. 3: 1850–1855. The Vicariates of Colombo and Jaffna. Dehiwala: Tisara Prakasakayo, 2003.

PERNIOLA, VITO. *The Catholic Church in Sri Lanka.* The British Period. Vol. 4: 1856–1863. The Vicariates of Colombo and Jaffna. Dehiwala: Tisara Prakasakayo, 2001.

PERNIOLA, VITO. *The Catholic Church in Sri Lanka.* The British Period. Vol. 5: 1864–1878. The Vicariates of Colombo and Jaffna, Dehiwala: Tisara Prakasakayo, 2001.

PERNIOLA, VITO. *The Catholic Church in Sri Lanka.* The British Period. Vol. 8: 1887–1899. The Archdiocese of Colombo. Dehiwala: Tisara Prakasakayo, 2004.

PERSICO, I. / STRICKLAND S. J., W. *The Goa Schism.* Being a Short Historical Account of the Resistance Made by the Indo-Portuguese Clergy to the Institution of Apostolic-Vicariates in British India. Dublin: Gerald Bellew, 1853.

PERERA, M. ANTHONY. *The Arrack Question in Ceylon 1895–1896.* Colombo: Clifton Press, 1896.

PUCCINELLI, L. *Lo scisma Indo-Portoghese al giudizio degli Imparziali: Memorie Tre* (Roma 1853)

QUEYROZ, FERNÃO DE. *The Temporal and Spiritual Conquest of Ceylon.* Vol. 1, Book 1-2. Translated by Simon Gregory Perera. 1st edition 1930. New Delhi, Madras: Asian Educational Services, 1992.

RICHARD, W. J. *The Indian Christians of St. Thomas, Otherwise Called the Syrian Christians of Malabar: A Sketch of Their History and An Account of Their Present Condition, as Well as a Discussion of the Legend of St. Thomas.* London: Bemrose and Sons, 1908.

SÁ, JOSÉ MARIA DE. *O Coqueiro.* Parte primeira historia natural e cultura. Nova-Goa: Typographia "Fontainhas", 1898.

SILVA, GABRIEL DE. *Arrack-farming in Ceylon.* Colombo: Clifton Press, 1895.
STALL CEYLON OBSERVER. *Ferguson's Ceylon Directory for 1944 (eighty-sixth Year)*, revised up to May 1944. Colombo: The Ceylon Observer Press, 1944.
STIRRAT, R. L. *Power and Religiosity in a Post-Colonial Setting.* Sinhala Catholics in Contemporary Sri Lanka. Cambridge: Cambridge University Press, 1992.
STRICKLAND, WILLIAM. *The Jesuit in India.* Addressed to All Who Are Interested in the Foreign Missions. London: Burns & Lambert, 1852.
TENISON, ARCHBISHOP THOMAS ET ALS. *Cardinal Bellarmine's Notes of the Church Examined and Refuted.* In a Series of Tracts. London: Samuel Holdsworth, Amen Corner, 1840.
TENNENT, JAMES EMERSON. *Ceylon.* An Account of the Island, Physical, Historical, and Topographical, with Notices of Its Natural History, Antiquities and Productions. Vol. 1. London: Longman, Green, Longman, and Roberts, 1860.
TENNENT, JAMES EMERSON. *Christianity in Ceylon.* Its Introduction and Progress under the Portuguese, the Dutch, the British, and American Missions; with an Historical Sketch of the Brahmanical and Buddhist Superstitions. London: John Murray, 1850.
TRINIDADE, PAULO DA. *Conquista espiritual do Oriente.* Das coisas que as frades menores da Província de S. Tomé fizeram na conversão dos infiéis desde a ilha de Ceilão até as de Japão. Vol. 3. Lisboa: Centro de Estudos históricos ultramarinos, 1962.
UN VECCHIO-CATTOLICO ITALIANO, *Apostolo e martire.* Ossia Monsignor G. Renato Vilatte fondatore della Chiesa Vecchio-Cattolica negli Stati Uniti d'America. Firenze: Claudiana, 1900.
WENDT, H. L., T. E. DE SAMPAYO and F. M. DE SARAM, eds. *The Ceylon Law Reports.* Being the Reports of Cases Decided by the Supreme Court of Ceylon. Colombo: The "Ceylon Examiner" Press, 1897.
WICKI, JOSEF. (ed.). *Documenta Indica*, Vol. III, 1553-1557, Roma: Monumenta historica Soc. Iesu, 1954.
W. WOLSKA-CONUS (ed.). *Topographie Chrétienne.* Paris: Cerf, 1968–1973.

Secondary Literature

ABBA SERAPHIM. *Flesh of Our Brethren.* An Historical Examination of Western Episcopal Successions Originating from the Syrian Orthodox Patriarchate of Antioch. 1 Edition 2006. London: The British Orthodox Press, 2018.
ABEYASINGHE, TIKIRI. "History as Polemics and Propaganda. An Examination of Fernão de Queiros' 'History of Ceylon'". *Journal of the Royal Asiatic Society Sri Lanka Branch* 25, 1980, 26–68.
ABEYASINGHE, TIKIRI. *Jaffna under the Portuguese.* Colombo: Lake House Investments, 1986.
ABEYASINGHE, TIKIRI. *Portuguese Rule in Ceylon, 1594–1612.* Colombo: Lake House Investments, 1966.
ABRANTES, MARIA LUISA. *Arquivo da cúria patriarcal de Goa.* Goa: ARQBASE, 1993.

ALDEN, DAURIL. *The Making of an Enterprise*. The Society of Jesus in Portugal, Its Empire, and Beyond 1540-1750. Stanford: Stanford University Press, 1996.

HISLOP, ALEXANDER. *The Two Babylons,* 5th ed. Brushton, New York: TEACH Services, Inc. 2002.

ALI, AMEER. "Four Waves of Muslim-Phobia in Sri Lanka. C.1880–2009". *Journal of Muslim Minority Affairs* 35, no. 4, October 2015.

ALLEN, HUGH. *New Llanthony Abbey: Father Ignatius's Monastery at Cape-y-ffin.* Tiverton: Peterscourt Press, 2016.

AMALADASS, ANAND, ed. *Jesuit Presence in Indian History*. Commemorative Volume on the Occasion of the 150th Anniversary of the New Madurai Mission, 1838–1988. Anand: Gujarat Sahitya Prakash, 1988.

AMRITH, SUNIL S. "South Indian Migration, c. 1800–1950". In *Globalising Migration History*. The Eurasian Experience (16th–21st Centuries). Edited by Jan Lucassen and Leo Lucassen. Leiden: Brill, 2014.

ANSON, PETER F. *Bishops at Large.* 1st ed. London 1964. Berkeley : Apocryphile Press, 2006.

ANTONINUS, A. J. B. *The Martyrs of Mannar*. From Authentic Documents. Mannar: St. Joseph's Catholic Press, 1944.

ARANHA, PAOLO. "Early Modern Asian Catholicism and European Colonialism, Dominance, Hegemony and Native Agency in the Portuguese Estado da Índia". In *Polycentric Structures in the History of World Christianity / Polyzentrische Strukturen in der Geschichte des Weltchristentums.* Edited by Klaus Koschorke and Adrian Hermann, 285–306. Wiesbaden: Harassowitz Verlag, 2014.

ARANHA, PAOLO. "Gerarchie Razziali e Adattamento Culturale: La 'Ipotesi Valignano'". In *Alessandro Valignano S.I., Uomo del Rinascimento*. Ponte tra Oriente ed Occidente. Edited by Adolfo Tamburello, M. Antoni J. Üçerler and Marisa Di Russo, 76–98. Roma: Institutum Historicum Societatis Iesu, 2008.

ARANHA, PAOLO. "The Social and Physical Spaces of the Malabar Rites Controversy". In *Space and Conversion in Global Perspective.* Edited by Giuseppe Marcocci, Wietse de Boer, Aliocha Maldavsky and Ilaria Pavan, 214–232. Leiden: Brill, 2014.

ARULDOSS, S., SJ. "Jesuit Madurai Mission and the Goanese Schism with special reference to Mar Basilius". Read at *A Global and Local History of the Buona Morte Church*, Colombo: S. Godage & Bros., 2018.

ARYARATNE, SUNIL. *Baila Kaffirinna*. An Investigation. Colombo: S. Godage & Bros., 2001.

ATTYGALLE, NICHOLAS ET AL. (eds.). *History of Ceylon*. Vol. I: From the Earliest Times to 1505, Part II: From the Coḷa conquest in 1017 to the arrival of the Portuguese in 1505. Colombo: Ceylon University Press, 1960.

AUGELLO, MASSIMO M. and MARCO E. L GUIDI. *The Economic Reader*. Textbooks, Manuals and the Dissemination of the Economic Sciences during the 19th and Early 20th Centuries. Abingdon: Routledge, 2012.

AZEVEDO, CARMO. *Patriot & Saint*. The Life Story of Father Alvares/Bishop Mar Julius I. Panjim 1988.

BACHMANN, PETER R. *Roberto Nobili: 1577–1656.* Ein Missionsgeschichtlicher Beitrag zum christlichen Dialog mit Hinduismus. Bibliotheca Instituti Historici vol. 32. Roma: Institutum Historicum, 1972.

BANDARAGE, ASOKA. *Colonialism in Sri Lanka*. The Political Economy of the Kandyan Highlands, 1833–1886. Berlin: Mouton Publishers, 1983.
BARCATTA, BEDE. *A History of the Southern Vicariate of Colombo, Sri Lanka, Being Also the History of the Apostolate of the Sylvestrine-Benedictine Monks in the Island.* Vol. 1. Ampitiya: Montefano Publications, 1991–1994.
BARRETO XAVIER, ÂNGELA. "David contra Golias na Goa Seiscentista: Escrita Identitária e Colonização Interna", *Ler História* 49 (2005): 107–143.
BARRETO XAVIER, ÂNGELA. "Purity of Blood and Caste: Identity Narratives among Early Modern Goan Elites". In *Race and Blood in the Iberian World.* Edited by María Elena Martínez, Max-Sebastián Hering Torres and David Nirenberg, 125–149. Münster 2012.
BARTAS, GEORGES. "Coup d'oeil sur l'Orient gréco-slave". *Échos d'Orient* 7, no. 49, 1904, 366–372.
BARTHOLOMEUSZ, TESSA J. "Buddhist Burghers and Sinhala-Buddhist Fundamentalism". In *Buddhist Fundamentalism and Minority Identities in Sri Lanka.* Edited by Tessa J. Bartholomeusz and Chandra R. de Silva, 167–185. Albany 1998.
BARTHOLOMEUSZ, TESSA J. "Real Life and Romance. The Life of Miranda de Souza Canavarro". *Journal of Feminist Studies in Religion* 10, no. 2, 1994, 27–47.
BARTHOLOMEUSZ, TESSA J. *Women under the Bo Tree*. Buddhist Nuns in Sri Lanka. Cambridge / New York: Cambridge University Press, 1994.
BASTIN, ROHAN. *The Domain of Constant Excess*. Plural Worship at the Munnesvaram Temples in Sri Lanka. New York: Berghahn, 2002.
BAYLY, SUSAN. *Saints, Goddesses and Kings*. Muslims and Christians in South Indian Society, 1700–1900, 1st edition in 1989. Cambridge: Cambridge University Press, 2003.
BEAUMONT, JOHN, *Roads to Rome: A Guide to Notable Converts from Britain and Ireland from the Reformation to the Present Day.* South Bend, Ind.: St. Augustine's Press, 2010.
BERGMANN, H. "Vascotti". In *Österreichisches Biographisches Lexikon* - Band 15 (Lfg.68, 2017): 188.
BERGUNDER, MICHAEL. "Proselytism in the History of Christianity in India". In *India and the Indianness of Christianity*. Essays on Understanding – Historical, Theological, and Bibliographical – in Honor of Robert Eric Frykenberg. Edited by Robert Eric Frykenberg and Richard Fox Young, 181–195. Grand Rapids, Michigan / Cambridge, UK: Wm. B. Eerdmans Publishing, 2009.
BETHENCOURT, FRANCISCO. *Racisms*. From the Crusades to the Twentieth Century. Princeton: Princeton University Press, 2013.
BIEDERMANN, ZOLTÁN. *The Portuguese in Sri Lanka and South India*. Studies in the History of Diplomacy, Empire and Trade, 1500-1650. Wiesbaden: Harrassowitz, 2014.
BILLAUD, AUGUSTE. *La Petite Église dans la Vendée et les Deux-Sèvres (1800-1830).* Paris: Nouvelles Editions Latines, 1982.
BIZIOURAS, NIKOLAOS. *The Political Economy of Ethnic Conflict in Sri Lanka*. Economic Liberalization, Mobilizational Resources, and Ethnic Collective Action. London: Routledge, 2014.
BLACKBURN, ANN M. *Locations of Buddhism*. Colonialism and Modernity in Sri Lanka. Chicago / London: University of Chicago Press, 2010.
BLUSSÉ, LEONARD. *The Dutch Encounter with Asia, 1600–1950*. Amsterdam: Rijksmuseum, 2002.

BOSMA, ULBE and REMCO RABEN. *Being 'Dutch' in the Indies*. A History of Creolisation and Empire, 1500–1920. Translated by Wendie Shaffer. Singapore: NUS Press, 2008.

BOUDENS, ROBRECHT. *Catholic Missionaries in a British Colony*. Successes and Failures in Ceylon 1796–1893. Immensee: Nouvelle revue de science missionaire, 1979.

BOUDENS, ROBRECHT. *The Catholic Church in Ceylon under Dutch Rule*. Roma: Officium Libri Catholici, 1957.

BOUYER, LOUIS. *The Roman Socrates*. A Portrait of St. Philip Neri. London: Chapman, 1958.

BOYD, ROBIN H. S. *A Church History of Gujarat.* Madras: Christian Literature Society, 1981.

BRADING, D. A. *Church and State in Bourbon Mexico.* Cambridge: Cambridge University Press, 2002.

BRANDRETH, HENRY R.T. *Episcopi Vagantes and the Anglican Church*. London 1947. Berkeley 2006.

BREMOND D'ARS, NICOLAS DE, and YVES KRUMENACKER (eds.). *L' Oratoire de Jésus*. 400 ans d'histoire en France (11 novembre 1611–11 novembre 2011). Paris: Cerf, 2013.

BROCK, SEBASTIAN P. "The Nestorian Church: A Lamentable Misnomer", *Bulletin of the John Rylands Library* 78, no. 3, 1996, 23–35.

BROCK, SEBASTIAN P. "Miaphysite, Not Monophysite!", *Cristianesimo nella Storia* 37, 2016, 47–51.

BROHIER, RICHARD L. and ISMETH RAHEEM. *Changing Face of Colombo, 1505–1972*. Covering the Portuguese, Dutch, and British Periods. Colombo: Lake House Investments, 1984.

BURLACIOIU, CIPRIAN. *'Within three years the East and the West have met each other':* Die Genese einer missionsunabhängigen schwarzen Kirche im transatlantischen Dreieck USA-Südafrika-Ostafrika (1921–1950). Wiesbaden: Harrassowitz, 2015.

BUSSIERRE, MARIE-THEODORE DE. *Histoire du schisme portugais dans les Indes*. Paris: Jacques Lecoffre, 1854.

BUTOMBE, J.I. NKULU. *La question du Zaire et ses répercussions sur les juridictions ecclésiastiques: 1865-1888*. Kinshasa: Faculté de théologie catholique, 1982.

BYRNE, JULIE. *The Other Catholics: Remaking America's Largest Religion.* New York; Chichester, West Sussex: Columbia University Press, 2016).

CATÃO, FRANCISCO XAVIER GOMES. "Aldeia de Assagão (Goa). Subsídios para a sua história". *Studia. Revista semestral*, Vol. 40. Lisboa: O Centro de Estudos de História e Cartografia Antiga, 1978, 279–348.

CERETI, CARLO G., LUCA M. OLIVIERI and F. JOSEPH VAZHUTHANAPALLY. "The Problem of the Saint Thomas Crosses and Related Questions. Epigraphical Survey and Preliminary Research". *East and West* 52, no. 1, 2002, 285–310.

CHAILLOT, CHRISTINE (ed.). *The Dialogue Between the Eastern Orthodox and Oriental Orthodox Churches*. Volos: Volos Academy Publications, 2016.

CHANDRALAL, DILEEP. *Sinhala*. Amsterdam: John Benjamins Publishing, 2010.

CHAPMAN, MARK D. *The Fantasy of Reunion: Anglicans, Catholics, and Ecumenism, 1833–1882.* Oxford: Oxford University Press, 2014.

CIESLIK SJ, HUBERT. "The Case of Christovão Ferreira". *Monumenta Nipponica* 29, no. 1, 1974, 1–54.

CIFRES, ALEJANDRO (ed.). *La validez de las ordenaciones anglicanas: los documentos de la comisión preparatoria de la bula "Apostolicae curae. Los documentos de 1896*. Roma: Libreria Editrice Vaticana, 2012.

CISTELLINI, ANTONIO. *San Filippo Neri. L'oratorio e la congregazione oratoriana: storia e spiritualità*. 3 vols. Brescia: Morcelliana, 1989.
COOK, BERNARD A. *Belgians in Michigan.* East Landing: Michigan State University Press, 2007.
COSTA NUNES, M. DA. *Documentação para a história da Congregação do Oratório de Santa Cruz dos Milagres do clero natural de Goa*. Lisboa: Centro de Estudos Históricos Ultramarinos, 1966.
COSTA, ALEIXO MANUEL DA. *Dicionário de literatura goesa*. Vols. 1–3. Macau: Instituto cultural de Macau, Fundação Oriente, 1998.
COSTA, COSME JOSE. *Apostolic Christianity in Goa and in the West Coast.* Pilar, Goa: Xaverian Publication Society, 2009.
COUTO, AURORA. *Goa*. A Daughter's Story. New Delhi, Toronto : Penguin Books 2005.
CRASTA, LAWRENCE DAVID. "The Konkani Congregation in the Malankara Orthodox Church. An Historical Approach". Kottayam: Orthodox Theological Seminary, 2001.
CRAWFORD, D. G. *Roll of the Indian Medical Service 1615–1930 – Volume 1: 1615–1799*. Luton: Naval & Military Press, 2012.
CREESE, MARY R. S. *Ladies in the Laboratory II:* West European Women in Science, 1800–1900: A Survey of Their Contribution to Research. Lanham: The Scarecrow Press, 2004.
CROCE, GIUSEPPE M. "Un 'famigerato Vescovo Antifallibilista [sic]': Pio IX e Il Vescovo Strossmayer dopo la fine del Vaticano I." *Archivum Historiae Pontificiae* 35, 1997, 161–81.
CROSS, FRANK L. and ELIZABETH A. LIVINGSTONE, eds. *The Oxford Dictionary of the Christian Church*, 3rd edition. Oxford: Oxford University Press, 2009.
CRUZ, MIGUEL DA. 'O Padroado', *Didaskalia* XXXIII, 2003, 239–255.
CUNHA LEÃO, FRANCISCO G., ed. *O Índico na Biblioteca da Ajuda*. Catálogo dos manuscritos relativos a Moçambique, Pérsia, India, Malaca, Molucas e Timor. Lisboa: Biblioteca da Ajuda, 1998.
CUNHA, ANTONIO MARIA DA. "A evolução do Jornalismo na Índia portuguesa". In *A India Portuguesa*. Vol. 2. Nova Goa: Imprensa Nacional, 1923, 503–594.
DANIEL, JOSEPH. *Ecumenism in Praxis*: A Historical Critique of the Malankara Mar Thoma Syrian Church. Frankfurt am Main: Peter Lang, 2014.
D'SOUZA, JULIAN. *Historical Notes on Some of the Churches of the Diocese of Mangalore, S. Kanara with Special Reference to the Kallianpur—Brahmavar Schism.* Mangalore: s.n., 1951.
D'SOUZA, LILIA MARIA. 'Church records in Goa: Mirror of Goan Catholic Society'. Unpublished article read at *The XIII International Seminar on Indo-Portuguese History,* Aix-en-Provence in March 2010.
DALGADO, SEBASTIÃO RODOLFO. *Portuguese Vocables in Asiatic Languages: From the Portuguese Original of Monsignor Sebastião Rodolfo Dalgado.* Translated by Anthony Xavier Soares, 248-302. New Delhi, Madras: Asian Educational Services, 1988.
DAUGHRITY, D.B. "The 'Munich School' as a Corrective in World Christianity". *International Bulletin of Mission Research* 45, no. 3, 2020, 221–224.
DAVID, M. D. *History of Bombay, 1661–1708*. Bombay: University of Bombay, 1973.

DEP, ARTHUR C. *The Oratorian Mission in Sri Lanka, 1795–1874*. Being a History of the Catholic Church, 1795–1874. Colombo: Elmo Lord, Mercantile Printers & Stationers, 1987.

DEPARTMENT OF CENSUS & STATISTICS, MINISTRY OF POLICY PLANNING AND ECONOMIC AFFAIRS, Sri Lanka, *Census of Population and Housing, 2012.* (http://www.statistics.gov.lk/PopHouSat/CPH2011/Pages/Activities/Reports/FinalReport/FinalReportE.pdf, 26 August 2019).

DEVI, VIMALA and MANUEL DE SEABRA, *A literatura Indo-portuguesa.* Lisboa: Junta de Investigações do Ultramar, 1971.

DEWARAJA, LORNA SRIMATHIE. *The Muslims of Sri Lanka.* One Thousand Years of Ethnic Harmony, 900–1915. Colombo: The Lanka Islamic Foundation, 1994.

DEWARAJA, LORNA SRIMATHIE. "Revenues of the King of Kandy". *Journal of the Sri Lanka Branch of the Royal Asiatic Society* 16, 1972, 17–24.

DEWASIRI, NIRMAL RANJITH. *The Adaptable Peasant.* Agrarian Society in Western Sri Lanka under Dutch Rule, 1740–1800. Leiden: Brill, 2008.

DHARMADASA, K. N. O. "A Nativistic Reaction to Colonialism. The Sinhala-Buddhist Revival in Sri Lanka". *Asian Studies Journal* 12, no. 1, April 1974.

DHARMADASA, K. N. O. *Language, Religion, and Ethnic Assertiveness.* The Growth of Sinhalese Nationalism in Sri Lanka. Ann Arbor: University of Michigan Press, 1992.

DIEHL, KATHARINE S. (ed.). *Historical Essays.* Primary Printed and Manuscript Sources for Sixteenth to Nineteenth Century Available in Sri Lanka. Colombo 1976.

DIEHL, KATHARINE S. "The Dutch Press in Ceylon, 1734–96". *The Library Quarterly. Information, Community, Policy* 42, no. 3, 1972, 329–342.

DOBBIN, CHRISTINE E. *Urban Leadership in Western India: Politics and Communities in Bombay City, 1840–1885.* Oxford Historical Monographs. London 1972.

DOUGLAS, BRIAN. *The Eucharistic Theology of Edward Bouverie Pusey: Sources, Context and Doctrine within the Oxford Movement and Beyond.* Leiden / Boston: Brill, 2015.

DROCHON, JEAN-EMMANUEL B. *La Petite Église: Essai historique sur le schisme anticoncordataire.* Paris: Maison de la bonne Presse, 1894.

ELLIOTT, C. BROOKE. *The Real Ceylon.* New Edition with Many Illustrations. New Delhi: Asian Educational Services, 2005.EMBASSY OF SRI LANKA, ANKARA, TURKEY. "Trading with Sri Lanka" (Powerpoint). (http://www.adaso.org.tr/WebDosyalar/Sayfalar/Sunumlar/SR%C4%B0%20LANKA%20SUNUMU.pdf)

EMMONS, TERENCE. *Alleged Sex and Threatened Violence: Doctor Russell, Bishop Vladimir, and the Russians in San Francisco, 1887–1892.* Stanford, CA.: Stanford University Press, 1997.

ERNST, WALTRAUD and BISWAMOY PATI. "People, princes and colonialism". In *India's Princely States. People, Princes and Colonialism.* Edited by Waltraud Ernst and Biswamoy Pati. 1–14. New York: Routledge, 2007.

FAILLER, ALBERT. "Le centenaire de l'Institut byzantin des Assomptionnistes". *Revue des études byzantines* 53, no. 1, 1995, 5–40.

FALLER, STEFAN ALFRED. "The World According to Cosmas Indicopleustes – Concepts and Illustrations of an Alexandrian Merchant and Monk". *The Journal of Transcultural Studies* 1, June 2011, 193–232.

FARIA, ALICE SANTIAGO and SIDH LOSA MENDIRATTA. 'Goans and East-Indians: A Negotiated Catholic Presence in Bombay's Urban Space'. *InterDISCIPLINARY Journal of Portuguese Diaspora Studies* 7, 2 July 2018, 47.

FARIA, PATRICÍA SOUZA. "Mateus de Castro: Um bispo 'brâmane' em busca da promoção social no império asiático português (seculo xvii)". *Revista Eletrônica de História do Brasil* 9, no. 2, 2007, 31–43.

FARIAS, KRANTI K. *The Christian Impact in South Kanara.* Mumbai: Church History Association of India, 1999.

FENWICK, JOHN. *The Forgotten Bishops.* The Malabar Independent Syrian Church and Its Place in the Story of the St. Thomas Christians of South India. Piscataway: Gorgias Press, 2009.

FERNANDES, LUIS HENRIQUE MENEZES. 'Diferença da Cristandade. A controvérsia religiosa nas Índias Orientais holandesas e o significado histórico da primeira tradução da Bíblia em português (1642–1694)'. PhD Dissertation, Universidade de São Paulo, 2016.

FERNANDO, LEONARD. "Jesuits and India". *Oxford Handbooks Online* (published online November 2016, doi: 10.1093/oxfordhb/9780199935420.013.59).

FERNANDOPULLE, ANTHONY. *A Critical Study of the Works of Fr. Jacome Gonsalves (1676–1742).* Colombo: S. Godage and Brothers Ltd., 2017.

FERNANDOPULLE, ANTHONY. *Father Jacome Gonsalves, Sinhala Christian Literary Hero.* A Study of the Sinhala Literary Works of Fr Jacome Gonsalves (1676–1742). Colombo: St. Peter's College, 2000.

FILTHAUT, JÖRG. *Dawson und Deutschland.* Das deutsche Vorbild und die Reformen im Bildungswesen, in der Stadtverwaltung und in der Sozialversicherung Grossbritanniens 1880–1914. Frankfurt am Main u.a.: Lang, 1994.

FINDLAY, G. G. and W. W. HOLDSWORTH. *The History of the Wesleyan Methodist Missionary Society.* Vol. 5. London: The Epworth Press, 1924.

FLORES, JORGE MANUEL (ed.). *Re-Exploring the Links.* History and Constructed Histories between Portugal and Sri Lanka. Wiesbaden: Harrassowitz, 2007.

FLORES, JORGE MANUEL. "The Straits of Ceylon, 1524–1539: The Portuguese Mappilla Struggle over a Strategic Area". In *Sinners and Saints.* The Successors of Vasco da Gama. Edited by Sanjay Subrahmanyam, 57–74. Delhi: Oxford University Press, 2000.

FLORES, JORGE MANUEL. *Hum curto historia de Ceylan.* Quinhentos anos de relações entre Portugal e o Sri Lanka. Lisboa: Fundação Oriente, 2001.

FLORES, JORGE MANUEL. *Os portugueses e o Mar de Ceilão.* Trato, diplomacia e guerra (1498–1543). Lisboa: Edições Cosmos, 1998.

FRASCH, TILMAN. "A Buddhist Network in the Bay of Bengal: Relations between Bodhgaya, Burma and Sri Lanka, c. 300–1300". In *From the Mediterranean to the China Sea.* Miscellaneous Notes. Edited by C. Guilot et al. 69–92. Wiesbaden: Harrassowitz, 1998.

FREDERIKS, M. "World Christianity: Contours of an Approach". In *World Christianity.* Methodological Considerations. Edited by M. Frederiks and D. Nagy, 10–39. Leiden 2020.

FRENZ, MARGRET. "To Be or Not To Be … a Global Citizen: Three doctors, three empires, and one subcontinent". *Modern Asian Studies*, 2020, 1–42.

FROST, MARK RAVINDER. "'Wider Opportunities': Religious Revival, Nationalist Awakening and the Global Dimension in Colombo, 1870–1920". *Modern Asian Studies* 36, no. 4, 2002, 937–967.
FRYKENBERG, R.E. and R. FOX YOUNG (eds.). *India and the Indianness of Christianity*. Essays on Understanding – Historical, Theological, and Bibliographical – in Honor of Robert Eric Frykenberg. Grand Rapids: Eerdmans, 2009.
MARCOCCI, G., W. DE BOER, A. MALDAVSKY and I. PAVAN (eds.). *Space and Conversion in Global Perspective*. Leiden: Brill, 2015.
GIELEN, MARTIN. *St. Thomas: The Apostle of India*. Edited by Geevarghese Chediath. Kottayam: Oriental Institute of Religious Studies, 1990.
GOMBRICH, RICHARD F. and GANANATH OBEYESEKERE. *Buddhism Transformed*. Religious Change in Sri Lanka. Princeton: Princeton Univ. Press, 1988.
GOMBRICH, RICHARD F. *Theravāda Buddhism*. A social history from ancient Benares to modern Colombo, 2nd ed. London: Routledge, 2006.
GOMES, PAULO VALERA. "'Bombay Portuguese': Ser ou não ser Português em Bombaim no século XIX', *Revista de História das Ideias* 28, 2007, 567–608.
GOOR, JURRIEN VAN. "Jan Kompenie as Schoolmaster. Dutch Education in Ceylon 1690-1795". Dissertation. Utrecht University, 1978.
GRENIER, G. V. "'Burgher' Etymology and Some Relevant Reflections." *Journal of the Dutch Burgher Union* 56, no. 1–4, 1966, 25–30.
GROSS, A., Y.V. KUMARADOSS and H. LIEBAU, (eds.). *Halle and the Beginning of Protestant Christianity in India*. Vol. 3: Communication between India and Europe. Halle: Franckesche Stiftungen, 2006.
GUNASEKERA, R. G. G. OLCOTT. "150 Years of The Royal Asiatic Society of Sri Lanka". In *Sesquicentennial Commemorative Volume of the Royal Asiatic Society of Sri Lanka, 1845–1995*. Edited by G. P. S. Harischandra De Silva and C. G. Uragoda. Colombo: Royal Asiatic Society of Sri Lanka, 1995.
GUNAWARDANA, R. A. L. H. "Irrigation and Hydraulic Society in Early Medieval Ceylon". *Past & Present* 53, 1971, 3–27.
GUNTEN, ANDRÉ F. von, and ALEJANDRO CIFRES, (eds.) *La validité des ordinations anglicanes*. Les documents de la commission préparatoire à la lettre Apostolicae curae. Firenze: L.S. Olschki, 1997.
HABBI, JOSEPH. "Les Chaldéens et les Malabares au XIXe siècle." *Oriens Christianus* 64, 1980, 82–107.
HABERLAND, DETLEF. "François Caron and His Description of Japan". *Review of Culture* [Macau] 28, 2008, 70–85.
HABERMAS, R. "Mission im 19. Jahrhundert – Globale Netze des Religiösen". *Historische Zeitschrift* 287, 2008, 629–678.
HABERMAS, R. und HÖLZ, R. (eds.), *Mission global*. Eine Verflechtungsgeschichte seit dem 19. Jahrhundert. Köln 2014.
HAEFELI, EVAN. *Against Popery: Britain, Empire, and Anti-Catholicism*. Charlottesville and London: University of Virginia Press, 2020.
HASSANKHAN, MAURITS S., LOMARSH ROOPNARINE and HANS RAMSOEDH (eds.). *The Legacy of Indian Indenture*. Historical and Contemporary Aspects of Migration and Diaspora. Milton Park, Abingdon: Routledge, 2016.

HEADRICK, DANIEL. "A Double-Edged Sword: Communications and Imperial Control in British India". *Historical Social Research / Historische Sozialforschung* 35, no. 1, 2010, 51–65.

HERMANN, ADRIAN. "Transregional Contacts between Independent Catholic Churches in Asia around 1900. The Case of the *Iglesia Filipina Independiente* and the *Independent Catholics of Ceylon*". In *Veränderte Landkarten auf dem Weg zu einer polyzentrischen Geschichte des Weltchristentums. Festschrift für Klaus Koschorke zum 65. Geburtstag.* Edited by Ciprian Burlacioiu and Adrian Hermann. Wiesbaden: Harrassowitz Verlag, 2015.

HERMANN, ADRIAN. "Publicizing Independence. Thoughts on the Filipino *ilustrado* Isabelo de los Reyes, the Iglesia Filipina Independiente, and the Emergence of an Indigenous-Christian Public Sphere". *Journal of World Christianity* 6, no.1, 2016, 99–122.

HERRING, GEORGE. *The Oxford Movement in Practice: The Tractarian Parochial Worlds from the 1830s to the 1870s.* Oxford: Oxford University Press, 2016.

HINNELLS, JOHN and ALAN WILLIAMS (eds.). *Parsis in India and the Diaspora.* London / New York: Routledge, 2007.

HOGUE, WILLIAM M. 'The Episcopal Church and Archbishop Villatte'. *Historical Magazine of the Protestant Episcopal Church* 34, no. 1, 1965, 35–36.

HOLAND, HJALMAR RUED. *Wisconsin's Belgian Community: An Account of the Early Events in the Belgian Settlement in Northeastern Wisconsin with Particular Reference to the Belgians in Door County.* Sturgeon Bay, Wisconsin: Door County Historical Society, 1933.

HOLT, JOHN CLIFFORD (ed.). *The Sri Lanka Reader.* History, Culture, Politics. Durham: Duke University Press, 2011.

HOLT, JOHN CLIFFORD. "Hindu Influences on Medieval Sri Lankan Buddhist Culture". In *Buddhism, Conflict and Violence in Modern Sri Lanka.* Edited by Mahinda Deegalle. 38–66. London: Routledge, 2006.

HOLT, JOHN CLIFFORD. *The Buddhist Vishnu.* Religious Transformation, Politics, and Culture. New York: Columbia University Press, 2004.

ILANGASINHA, H. B. M. *A Study of Buddhism in Ceylon in the Fifteenth and Sixteenth Centuries (Circa 1400–1600)*, Ph.D. Thesis. London: University of London, 1972.

INCHAKKALODY, THOMAS. *The Christian Churches of Kerala.* Trivandrum 1952.

INDRAPALA, KĀRTTIKĒCU. "The Origin of The Tamil Vanni Chieftaincies of Ceylon". *Journal of Humanities* 1, no. 2, July 1970, 111–140.

INTIRAPĀLĀ, KĀRTTIKĒCU (ed.). *The Collapse of the Rajarata Civilization in Ceylon and the Drift to the South-West.* A Symposium. Peradeniya: Ceylon Studies Seminar, University of Ceylon, 1971.

JAMES, SERENHEDD. *The Cowley Fathers: A History of the English Congregation of the Society of St John the Evangelist.* London: Canterbury Press, 2019.

JAYAWARDENA, VISAKHA KUMARI. *Nobodies to Somebodies.* The Rise of the Colonial Bourgeoisie in Sri Lanka. London: Zed Books, 2003.

JAYAWARDENA, VISAKHA KUMARI. *The Rise of the Labor Movement in Ceylon.* Durham, North Carolina: Duke University Press, 1972.

JAYAWARDENA, VISAKHA KUMARI. *The Rise of the Working Class in Sri Lanka & the Printers Strike of 1893.* Wellawatta, Sri Lanka: Wesley Press, 1974.

JENSZ, F. "Origins of Missionary Periodicals: Form and Function of Three Moravian Publications". *Journal of Religious History* 36, no.2, 2012, 234–255.
JENSZ, F. and ACHE, H. (eds.), *Missions and Media. The Politics of Missionary Periodicals in the Long Nineteenth Century*. Stuttgart 2013.
JOHNSON, GLENN D. 'Joseph René Villatte: Accidental Catalyst to Ecumenical Dialog'. *Anglican and Episcopal History* 71, no. 1, 2002, 42–60.
JOHNSTON, A. *Missionary Writing and Empire, 1800–1860*. Cambridge: Cambridge University Press, 2003.
JONES, MARGARET. *Health Policy in Britain's Model Colony*. Ceylon, 1900–1948. New Delhi: Orient Blackswan, 2004.
KADIĆ, ANTE. "Bishop Strossmayer and the First Vatican Council". *The Slavonic and East European Review* 49, no. 116, 1971, 382–409.
KAMAT, PRATIMA. "Brief Account of the 1895 Rane Revolt in Goa". *The Quarterly Journal of the Mythic Society* (Bangalore) 78, 1987, 22–32.
KAMAT, PRATIMA. "'The Indian Cry' (O Brado Indiano) of Padre António Alvares. 'Swadeshi' or 'seditious'?". *Indian Church History Review* 46, no.1, June 2012, 69–91.
KAMAT, PRATIMA. "The Goa-Ceylon Religious Connection. A Review of the 'The Indian Cry' of Alvares Mar Julius, Archbishop of Ceylon, Goa and India". *Sabaragamuwa University Journal* 12, no. 1, December 2013, 61–82.
KAMAT, PRATIMA. *Farar Far (Crossfire)*. Local Resistance to Colonial Hegemony in Goa, 1510–1912. Panaji: Institute Menezes Braganza, 1999.
KAMATH, DEVADATTA and PIUS FIDELIS PINTO. *Defiant Submission*. A History of the Diocese of Mangalore. 2 Vols., Mangalore, 2014.
KARIYAWASAM, U. *Industrial Relations and the Political Process in Sri Lanka*. International Institute for Labour Studies, 1981.
KEARNEY, ROBERT NORMAN. *Trade unions and politics in Ceylon*. Berkeley: University of California Press, 1971.
KEMPER, STEVEN. *Rescued from the Nation*. Anagarika Dharmapala and the Buddhist World. Chicago: Chicago University Press, 2015.
KER, IAN. *John Henry Newman*: A Biography. Oxford: Oxford University Press, 2019.
KERSEY, JOHN. *Joseph-Rene Vilatte (1854–1929): Some Aspects of His Life, Work and Succession*. Roseau, Dominica: European-American University Press, 2012.
KESAVAN, BELLARY SHAMANNA. *History of Printing and Publishing in India*. South Indian Origins of Printing. India: National Book Trust, 1984.
KIDAMBI, PRASHANT. *The Making of an Indian Metropolis: Colonial Governance and Public Culture in Bombay, 1890–1920*. Historical Urban Studies. Aldershot: Ashgate, 2007.
KIRAZ, GEORGE A. 'The Credentials of Mar Julius Alvares Bishop of Ceylon, Goa and India Excluding Malabar'. *Hugoye: Journal of Syriac Studies* 7, no.1, 2007, 157–168.
KOHLSCHMIDT, OSCAR. "Interconfessionelles". In *Theologischer Jahresbericht*. Vol. 12, 330–352. Edited by H. Holtzmann. Braunschweig: C. A. Schwetschke und Sohn 1893.
KOILPARAMPIL, GEORGE. *Caste in the Catholic Community in Kerala: A Study of Caste Elements in the Inter Rite Relationships of Syrians and Latins*. Cochin: Dept. of Sociology, St. Teresa's College, 1982.

KOLLAPARAMBIL, JACOB. *The St. Thomas Christians' Revolution in 1653.* Kottayam: Catholic Bishop's House, 1981.

KOSCHORKE, KLAUS. "Holländische Kolonial- und katholische Untergrundkirche im Ceylon des 17. und 18. Jahrhunderts". In *Missionsgeschichte, Kirchengeschichte, Weltgeschichte.* Christliche Missionen im Kontext nationaler Entwicklungen in Afrika, Asien und Ozeanien. Edited by Ulrich van der Heyder and Heike Liebau, 273-280. Stuttgart: Franz Steiner, 1996.

KOSCHORKE, KLAUS. "The World Missionary Conference in Edinburgh 1910 and the Rise of National Church Movements in Asia and Africa". In *Transcontinental Links in the History of Non-Western Christianity*. Edited by Klaus Koschorke, 203–217. Wiesbaden: Harrassowitz, 2002.

KOSCHORKE, KLAUS ET AL. *A History of Christianity in Asia, Africa, and Latin America, 1450–1990.* A Documentary Sourcebook. Grand Rapids: Eerdmans, 2007.

KOSCHORKE, KLAUS (ed.). *The Dutch Reformed Church in Colonial Ceylon (18th Century).* Minutes of the Consistory of the Dutch Reformed Church in Colombo Held at the Wolvendaal Church, Colombo (1735–1797). Translated by Samuel A. W. Mottau. Wiesbaden: Harrassowitz, 2011.

KOSCHORKE, KLAUS. "New Maps of the History of World Christianity: Current Challenges and Future Perspectives". In *Theology Today* 71, no.2, 2014, 178–191.

KOSCHORKE, KLAUS / HERMANN, ADRIAN (eds.). *Polycentric Structures in the History of World Christianity*. Wiesbaden: Harrassowitz, 2014.

KOSCHORKE, KLAUS ET AL. *Discourses of Indigenous Christian Elites in Colonial Societies in Asia and Africa around 1900: A Documentary Sourcebook from Selected Journals*. Wiesbaden: Harrassowitz, 2016.

KOSCHORKE, KLAUS. 'Transcontinental Links, Enlarged Maps, and Polycentric Structures in the History of World Christianity'. In *Journal of World Christianity* 6, no. 1, 2016, 28–56.

KOSCHORKE, KLAUS ET AL. *"To Give Publicity to Our Thoughts"*. Journale asiatischer und afrikanischer Christen um 1900 und die Entstehung einer transregionalen indigen-christlichen Öffentlichkeit / Journals of Asian and African Christians around 1900 and the Making of a Transregional Indigenous-Christian Public Sphere. Wiesbaden: Harrassowitz Verlag, 2018.

KOWALSKY, NICOLA and JOSEF METZLER (eds.). *Inventory of the Historical Archives of the Congregation for the Evangelization of Peoples or 'De Propaganda Fide'*. Rome: Pontificia Universitas Urbaniana, 1988.

KOWALSKY, P. N. "Die Oblatenmission von Jaffna (Ceylon) zur Zeit der apostolischen Visitation im Jahre 1860". *Zeitschrift für Missionswissenschaft und Religionswissenschaft,* Heft 1, 1956, 209–213.

KRUMENACKER, YVES / PELLEGRIN, MARIE-FRÉDÉRIQUE / QUANTIN, JEAN-LOUIS (eds.). L'Oratoire *de Jésu*.: 400 ans d'histoire en France (11 novembre 1611–11 novembre 2011). Cerf, 2013.

KRUSZKA, WACŁAW. *Historia Polska w Ameryce*. Vol. 1: A History of the Poles in America to 1908. Edited by James S. Pula. Washington, D.C.: Catholic University of America Press, 1993.

KULARATNE, TILAK. *History of Printing and Publishing in Ceylon, 1736–1912.* Dehiwala, Sri Lanka: Sridevi Printers, 2006.

KURIAN, GEORGE K. *Saint Alvares Mar Julius.* Ribandar, Panaji, Goa: St Mary's Orthodox Syrian Church, 2013.

LATREILLE, CAMILLE. *L' Opposition religieuse au Concordat de 1792 à 1803.* Paris: Hachette, 1910.

LEA, HENRY CHARLES. *The Inquisition in the Spanish Dependencies.* Sicily, Naples, Sardinia, Milan, the Canaries, Mexico Peru, New Granada. 1st ed. 1908. New York: The Macmillan Company, 1922.

LEÃO, FRANCISCO G. CUNHA, ed. *O Índico na Biblioteca da Ajuda.* Catálogo dos manuscritos relativos a Moçambique, Pérsia, India, Malaca, Molucas e Timor. Lisboa: Biblioteca da Ajuda, 1998.

LEE, IGNACIO TING PONG. "La actitud de la sagrada congregación al Regio Patronato". In *Sacrae Congregationis de Propaganda Fide memoria rerum : 350 anni a servizio delle missioni...1622–1972.* Vol. I.1. Edited by Josef Metzler, 353–438. Rome: Herder, 1971.

LIEBAU, HEIKE. *Cultural Encounters in India.* The Local Co-Workers of Tranquebar Mission, 18th to 19th Centuries. Translated by Rekha V. Rajan. New Delhi: Social Science Press, 2013.

LOBO, SANDRA ATAÍDE. *O Desassossego goês.* Cultura e política em Goa do liberalismo ao acto colonial, PhD Thesis. Lisboa, Universidade Nova de Lisboa, 2013.

LOPES, MARIA DE JESUS DOS MÁRTIRES. "D. António Sebastião Valente. O homem e a obra (1846–1908). Contributo para a sua história". In *Goa passado e presente.* Vol. 2. Edited by Artur Teodoro de Matos and João Teles e Cunha. 567–584. Lisboa: Centro de Estudos dos Povos e Culturas de Expressão Portuguesa e Centro de História de Além-Mar, 2012.

LOPES, MARÍLIA DOS SANTOS. "'Ao cheiro desta canela': Notas para a história de uma especiaria rara". In *Mirabilia Asiatica.* Edited by Jorge Manuel dos Santos Alves, C. Guillot and Roderich Ptak. 51–63. Wiesbaden / Lisboa: Harrassowitz / Fundação Oriente, 2003.

MAHROOF, M. M. M. "The Muslims under Portuguese and Dutch Occupation 1505–1796". In *An Ethnological Survey of the Muslims of Sri Lanka.* From Earliest Times to Independence. Edited by M.M.M. Mahroof et al., 43–60. Colombo, Sri Lanka: Sir Razik Fareed Foundation, 1986.

MALALGODA, KITSIRI. *Buddhism in Sinhalese Society, 1750–1900.* A Study of Religious Revival and Change. Berkeley: University of California Press, 1976.

MALEKANDATHIL, P. "Dynamics of Trade, Faith and the Politics of Cultural Enterprise in Early Modern Kerala". In *Clio and Her Descendants.* Essays in Honour of Kesavan Veluthat. Edited by Manu V. Devadevan. 157–198. New Delhi: Primus Books, 2018.

MAR APREM. *The Chaldean Syrian Church in India.* Trichur: Mar Narsai Press, 1977.

MAR GREGORIUS I, H. S. B. *A Voyage into the Orient Being Extracts from the Diary of the Rt. Rev. Bishop Vernon Herford.* Edited with an Introduction, Footnotes, and Appendices. Hove, Anvers, Belgium: The Catholic Apostolic Church (United Orthodox Catholicate), 1954.

MATHEW, ALEX. "The Reunion Movement among the St. Thomas Christians, 19th and 20th Centuries". PhD Thesis. Kottayam: Mahatma Gandhi University, 2007.

MATOS, A.T. DE and J. TELES E CUNHA (eds.). *Goa passado e presente*. Vol. 2, Lisboa: Centro de Estudos dos Povos e Culturas de Expressão Portuguesa e Centro de História de Além-Mar, 2012.
MCCRINDLE, JOHN W. *Introduction*. In *The Christian Topography of Cosmas*. Edited by John W. McCrindle, i–xxvii. Cambridge: Cambridge University Press, 2010.
MCGILVRAY, DENNIS B. "Dutch Burghers and Portuguese Mechanics. Eurasian Ethnicity in Sri Lanka". *Comparative Studies in Society and History* 24, no. 2, April 1982, 235–263.
MCGILVRAY, DENNIS B. "The Portuguese Burghers of Eastern Sri Lanka in the Wake of Civil War and Tsunami". In *Re-Exploring the Links*. History and Constructed Histories between Portugal and Sri Lanka. Edited by Jorge Manuel Costa Da Silva Flores. 325–347. Wiesbaden: Harrassowitz, 2007.
MEEGAMA, S.A. "South Indian or Sri Lankan? The Hindu temples of Polonnaruva, Sri Lanka". *Artibus Asiae* 70, no. 1, 2010, 25–45.
MENDIS, GARRETT C. *Ceylon under the British.* Reprint of the 3rd edition of 1945. New Delhi: Asian Educational Services, 2005.
METZLER, JOSEF (ed.). *Sacrae Congregationis de Propaganda Fide memoria rerum: 350 anni a servizio delle missioni 1622–1972.* 3 vols. Rom: Herder, 1971–1976.
MEYER, ERIC. "Labour Circulation between Sri Lanka and South India in Historical Perspective". In *Society and Circulation*. Mobile People and Itinerant Cultures in South Asia, 1750–1950. Edited by Claude Markovits, Jacques Pouchepadass and Sanjay Subrahmanyam. 55–88. London: Anthem Press, 2006.
MEYER, ERIC. "The Specificity of Sri Lanka. Towards a Comparative History of Sri Lanka and India". *Economic and Political Weekly* 31, no. 7, 1996, 395–398.
MIHINDUKULASURIYA, PRABO. "Persian Christians of the Anuradhapura Period". In *A Cultured Faith*. Essays in Honour of Prof. G. P. V. Somaratna on His Seventieth Birthday, edited by Prabo Mihindukulasuriya, Ivor Poobalan and Ravin Caldera, 225–244. Colombo: CTS Publishing, 2011.
MIHINDUKULASURIYA, PRABO. *The Nestorian Cross and the Persian Christians of the Anuradhapura Period.* Kohuwela, Sri Lanka: Colombo Theological Seminary, 2012.
MILTON, ANTHONY. "Epilogue: Words, Deeds, and Ambiguities in Early Modern Anti-Catholicism". In *Against Popery: Britain, Empire, and Anti-Catholicism*. Edited by EVAN HAEFELI, Charlottesville and London: University of Virginia Press, 2020.
MIROT, LÉON. "La vie et les aventures d'un Capucin auxerro-nivernais aux Indes: le Père Ephrem de Nevers", *Buletin de la Section de Géographie du Comité des Travaux historiques et scientifiques* 60, 1945, 45–69.
MITTER, PARTHA. "The Early British Port Cities of India. Their Planning and Architecture Circa 1640–1757". *Journal of the Society of Architectural Historians* 45, no. 2, June 1986, 95–114.
MONTALBAN, FRANCISCO JAVIER. *Patronato español y la conquista de Filipinas con documentos del Archivo General de Indias*. Bibliotheca Hispana Missionum, IV. Burgos: Imprenta Aldecoa, 1930.
MORGADO DE SOUSA E SILVA, I.L. and ANGIOLINI, F. (eds.). *A ordem de Cristo (1417–1521).* Militarium ordinum analecta 6, Porto: Fundação Eng. António de Almeida, 2002.
MOTT, FRANK LUTHER. *A History of American Magazines, 1850–1865*. Vol. 2: 1850–1865. Cambridge, Massachusetts: Harvard University Press, 2002.

MUNDADAN, ANTONY MATHIAS. *History of Christianity in India.* Vol. 1 From the Beginning up to the Middle of the Sixteenth Century (up to 1542). Bangalore: Published for Church History Association of India by Theological Publications in India, 1982.

MURPHEY, RHOADS. "The Ruin of Ancient Ceylon". *The Journal of Asian Studies* 16, no. 2, February 1957, 181–200.

MUTHIAH, SUBBIAH. "Giving India the Printed Word". In *Halle and the Beginning of Protestant Christianity in India.* Vol. 3: Communication between India and Europe. Edited by Andreas Gross, Y. Vincent Kumaradoss and Heike Liebau, 1241–1248. Halle: Franckesche Stiftungen, 2006.

NETO, VÍTOR. *O estado, a igreja e a sociedade em Portugal.* 1832–1911. Lisboa: IN-CM, 2001.

NICOLINI-ZANI, MATTEO, "Jesuit Jingjiao: The 'Appropriation' of Tang Christianity by Jesuit Missionaries in the Seventeenth Century." In *Hidden Treasures and Intercultural Encounters.* Studies on East Syriac Christianity in China and Central Asia. Edited by L. Tang and D.W. Winkler, 225–240, Wien: Lit, 2014.

NIDHIRY, ABRAHAM M. *Father Nidhiry, 1842–1904: A History of His Times* 2nd ed. Kuravilangad: Nidhirickal Manikathanar Foundation, 2003.

O'NEILL, CHARLES E. *Diccionario histórico de la Compañía de Jesús.* Vol. 2. *Costa Rossetti-Industrias.* Roma: Institutum historicum S.I.; Madrid: Universidad pontificia Comillas, 2001.

O'NEILL, CHARLES E. and JOAQUÍN MARIA DOMÍNGUEZ (eds). *Diccionario histórico de la Compañía de Jesús* vol. 4 *Piatti-Zwaans.* Roma : Institutum historicum S.I. ; Madrid : Universidad pontificia Comillas 2001.

OOMMEN, M. A. "Rise and Growth of Banking in Kerala". *Social Scientist* 5, no. 3, 1976, 24–46.

ORO, JOSÉ GARCÍA and MARÍA JOSÉ PORTELA SILVA. "Felipe II y el Patronato Real en Castilla". *La Ciudad de Dios* CCXIII, 2000, 530–532.

ORZELL, LAURENCE J. "A Pragmatic Union: Bishop Kozłowski and the Episcopalians". *Polish American Studies* 44, no. 1, 1987, 5–24.

ORZELL, LAURENCE J. 'Curious Allies: bishop Antoni Kozłowski and the Episcopalians.' *Polish American Studies* 40, no. 2, 1983, 36–58.

PALLATH, PAUL. *Rome and Chaldean Patriarchate in Conflict*: Schism of Bishop Rokos in India. Changanacherry: HIRS Publications, 2017.

PANICKER, THOMAS. "Jacobites in Malabar, and Their Reunion Efforts". PhD Thesis. Rome: Pont. Univ. Urbaniana de Propaganda Fide, 1958.

PATHMANATHAN, S. *The Kingdom of Jaffna.* Part 1. Circa A.D. 1250–1450. Colombo: Arul M. Rajendran, 1978.

PEEBLES, PATRICK. *Social Change in Nineteenth Century Ceylon.* New Delhi: Navrang, 1995.

PEEBLES, PATRICK. *The History of Sri Lanka.* Westport: Greenwood Press, 2006.

PEEBLES, PATRICK. *The Plantation Tamils of Ceylon.* London: Leicester University Press, 2001.

PERCZEL, ISTVÁN. "Accommodationist Strategies on the Malabar Coast. Competition or Complementarity?". In *The Rites Controversies in the Early Modern World.* Edited by Ines G. Županov and Pierre Antoine Fabre, 191–232, Leiden: Brill, 2018.

PERCZEL, ISTVÁN. "Four Apologetic Church Histories from India", *The Harp: A Review of Syriac, Oriental and Ecumenical Studies,* 24, 2009, 189–211.

PEREIRA SJ, A. *Dalgado, the Man and the Scholar.* New Delhi: Sahitya Akademi, 1983.

PEREIRO, JAMES. "The Oxford Movement and Anglo-Catholicism". In *The Oxford History of Anglicanism.* Volume III, 187–211. Edited by Rowan Strong. Oxford: Oxford University Press, 2017.

PERERA, C. GASTON. "The First Evangelical Mission of the Franciscans to Ceylon", *Journal of the Royal Asiatic Society of Sri Lanka* 53, 2007, 153–202.

PERERA, C. GASTON. *The Portuguese Missionary in 16th and 17th Century Ceylon*. The Spiritual Conquest. Colombo: Vijitha Yapa Publ., 2009.

PERERA, NIHAL. "Indigenising the Colonial City. Late 19th-Century Colombo and Its Landscape", *Urban Studies* 39, no. 9, August 2002, 1703–1721.

PERERA, NIHAL. *Society and Space*. Colonialism, Nationalism, and Postcolonial Identity in Sri Lanka. Colorado, Oxford: Westview Press, 1998.

PERERA, SIMON GREGORY. "João Vaz Monteiro. The earliest Portuguese Tombstone in Ceylon". *Ceylon Literary Register* 4, 1935, 233–241.

PERERA, SIMON GREGORY. *Life of Father Jacome Gonçalvez*. Madura: De Nobili Press, 1942.

PERERA, SIMON GREGORY. *Life of the Venerable Father Joseph Vaz, Apostle of Ceylon*. Galle: Loyola House, 1953.

PERERA, SIMON GREGORY. *Historical Sketches (Ceylon Church History)*. Colombo: Catholic Book Depot, 1962.

PERERA, SIMON GREGORY. *The Jesuits in Ceylon in the XVI and XVII Centuries*. New Delhi: Asian Educational Services, 2004.

ഫാ. ഇയ്യോബ് (PHĀ. IYYOB / FR. JOB), "പ. പരുമല തിരുമേനിയുടെ പട്ടംകൊടകൾ- (Pa. Parumala Tirumēniyuṭe paṭṭaṅkoṭakaḷ / Ordinations Conducted by P. Parumala Tirumeni)". *ബഥനി മാസിക* (Bathani Māsika / Bethany Magazine), Vol. 1, Issue 2, November 2017, 35–42.

PHILIP, AJESH and GEORGE ALEXANDER. *Western Rites of Syriac-Malankara Orthodox Churches.* Kerala: Oriental Orthodox Christianity Publications, 2018.

PHILIP, E. M. *The Indian Church of St. Thomas.* Nagercoil: London Missionary Press, 1950.

PINTO, ROCHELLE. *Between Empires*. Print and Politics in Goa. New Delhi: Oxford Univ. Press, 2007.

PODIPARA, PLACID J. *The Hierarchy of the Syro-Malabar Church*. Alleppey: Prakasam Publications, 1976.

PONNELLE, LOUIS and LOUIS BORDET. *Der heilige Philipp Neri und die römische Gesellschaft seiner Zeit (1515–1595)*. Festgabe zum 500. Geburtstag des hl. Philipp Neri. Bonn: Verlag Nova et Vetera, 2015.

PRAKASAR, SWAMINATHAPILLAI GNANA. "Sources of the Yalpana-Vaipava-Malai". *Ceylon Antiquary and Literary Register* 6, January 1921, 135–141.

PRAKASAR, SWAMINATHAPILLAI GNANA. *A History of The Catholic Church in Ceylon.* Colombo: Messenger Press, 1924.

PRINCIPE, LAWRENCE M. "Myth 11: That Catholics Did Not Contribute to the Scientific Revolution". In *Galileo Goes to Jail and Other Myths about Science and Religion*, edited by Ronald L. Numbers, 99–106. Cambridge: Harvard University Press, 2009.

QUEEN, ANDRÉ J. *Credo: The Catechism of the Old Catholic Church.* New York: iUniverse, 2005.
RAFAEL, GINA GUEDES and MANUELA SANTOS (eds.). *Jornais e revistas portugueses do século XIX.* Lisboa: Biblioteca Nacional Portugal, 1998.
RAGHAVAN, M. D. *Tamil Culture in Ceylon.* A General Introduction. Colombo: Kalai Nilayam, 1971.
RAMANNA, MRIDULA. *Western Medicine and Public Health in Colonial Bombay*, 1845-1895. New Delhi: Orient Longman, 2002.
RAMANNA, MRIDULA. *Health Care in Bombay Presidency 1896–1930.* Delhi 2012.
RANCHE, A.M. "The Iglesia Filipina Independiente (IFI): A People's Movement for National Freedom, Independence and Prosperity, *Philippiniana Sacra*, 35/105, 2000, 513–534.
RANCOUR-LAFERRIERE, DANIEL. *Imagining Mary*. A Psychoanalytic Perspective on Devotion to the Virgin Mother of God. New York: Routledge, 2018.
REBERNIK, ALEKSANDER, GIANPAOLO RIGOTTI and MICHEL VAN PARYS, O.S.B. (eds.). *Fede e martirio.* Le chiese orientali cattoliche nell'Europa del Novecento. Atti del Convegno di storia ecclesiastica contemporanea, Città del Vaticano, 22–24 ottobre 1998. Città del Vaticano: Libreria Editrice Vaticana, 2003.
RÊGO, ANTÓNIO DA SILVA, *O Padroado Português do Oriente.* Esbôço histórico. Lisboa: Divisão de Publicações e Biblioteca, Agência Geral das Colónias, 1940.
RÊGO, ANTÓNIO DA SILVA, *O Padroado Português no Oriente e a sua historiografia (1838–1950).* Subsídios para a história portuguesa 15. Lisboa 1978.
RICHARD, Francis, "Ephrem de Nevers et Zénon de Baugé, premiers auteurs français d'ouvrages en tamoul", *Moyen-Orient et Océan Indien* 6, 1989, 151–163.
ROBERTS, MICHAEL, ISMETH RAHEEM and PERCY COLIN-THOMÉ. *People Inbetween: The Burghers and the Middle Class in the Transformations within Sri Lanka, 1790s–1960s.* Vol. 1. Ratmalana, Sri Lanka: Sarvodaya Book Publishing Services, 1989.
ROBERTS, MICHAEL. *Caste Conflict Elite Formation.* The Rise of a Karāva Elite in Sri Lanka, 1500–1931. Cambridge: Cambridge University Press, 1982.
ROBINSON, EDWARD J. *Romanism in Ceylon, India, and China.* London: Hope & Co., 1855.
RODELL, P.A. "The Founding of the Iglesia Filipina Independiente (The 'Aglipayan' Church): An Historical Review", *Philippine Quarterly of Culture and Society* 16, no. 3–4, 1988, 210–234.
ROMMERSKIRCHEN, P. JOHANNES. *Die Oblatenmissionen auf der Insel Ceylon im 19. Jahrhundert (1847–1893).* Fulda: Druck der Fuldaer Actiendruckerei, 1930.
SACHS, WILLIAM L. *The Transformation of Anglicanism: From State Church to Global Communion.* Cambridge: Cambridge University Press, 1993.
SALDANHA, ANTÓNIO VASCONCELOS DE. *De Kangxi para o Papa pela via de Portugal: memória de documentos relativos à Intervenção de Portugal e da Companhia de Jesus na questão dos ritos chineses e nas relações entre o Imperador Kangxi e a Santa Sé.* 3 vols. Macau: Instituto Português do Oriente, 2002.
SAMUEL, V. C. *Truth Triumphs: An Account of the Life and Achievements of Malankara Metropolitan Vattasseril Geevarghese Mar Dionysius.* Kerala: Malankara Orthodox Church Publications, 1986.
SANKARANARAYANAN, K. C. *The Keralites and the Sinhalese.* Madras: Centre for South and Southeast Asian Studies, 1994.

SAVERIMUTTU, NICHOLAPILLAI MARIA. *The Life and Times of Orazio Bettacchini, the First Vicar Apostolic of Jaffna, Ceylon (1810-1857).* Rome: Urbaniana University Press, 1980.
SCHMITT, CARL. *The Nomos of the Earth in the International Law of the Jus Publicum Europæum.* New York: Telos Press Publishing, 2006.
SCHRIKKER, ALICIA. *Dutch and British Colonial Intervention in Sri Lanka, 1780–1815.* Expansion and Reform. Leiden: Brill, 2007.
SCHURHAMMER, GEORG and ERNST ARTUR VORETZSCH. *Ceylon zur Zeit des Königs Bhuvaneka Bahu und Franz Xavers, 1539–1552.* Quellen zur Geschichte der Portugiesen, sowie der Franziskaner- und Jesuitenmission auf Ceylon. Leipzig: Verlag der Asia Major, 1928.
SEPTUAGENARIAN [sic]. 'Memories Grave and Gay'. *Journal of the Dutch Burgher Union of Ceylon* XXXIX, no. 3, July 1949, 87.
SERRÃO, JOEL, MARIA JOSÉ DA SILVA LEAL and MIRIAM HALPERN PEREIRA (eds.). "Ministério dos Negócios Estrangeiros". In *Roteiro de Fontes da História Portuguesa Contemporânea.* Arquivo Nacional da Torre do Tombo. Vol. 2, 221–257. Lisboa: Instituto Nacional de Investigação Científica, 1984.
SHEARER, DONALD C. 'Ignatius Cardinal Persico, O.M.Cap. (1823–1895)'. *Franciscan Studies* 10, 1932, 53–137.
SHERMAN, RICHARD MOREY. 'American Contacts with Ceylon in the 19th Century: An Introduction to Their Impact'. *Journal of the Royal Asiatic Society of Sri Lanka*, New Series 35, 1990/1991, 1–8.
SHUKRI, M. A. M., ed. *Muslims of Sri Lanka.* Avenues to Antiquity. Beruwala, Sri Lanka: Jamiah Naleemia Inst., 1986.
SILVA, ISABEL. L. MORGADO DE SOUSA E ed. *A ordem de Cristo (1417–1521).* Militarium ordinum analecta 6. Porto: Fundação Eng. António de Almeida, 2002.
SILVA, CHANDRA RICHARD DE. "The First Visit of the Portuguese to Ceylon 1505 or 1506?". In *Senerat Paranavitana Commemoration Volume.* Edited by Indrapala Prematileke and Lohuiyen Van Leeuw. 218–220. Leiden: Brill, 1978.
SILVA, CHANDRA RICHARD DE, ed. *Portuguese Encounters with Sri Lanka and the Maldives.* Translated Texts from the Age of Discoveries. Farnham: Ashgate, 2009.
SILVA, D. G. B. DE. "Hugh Nevill Memorial Lecture - II: New Light on Vanniyās and their Chieftancies based on Folk Historical Tradition as found in Palm-Leaf Mss. in the Hugh Nevill Collection". *Journal of the Royal Asiatic Society of Sri Lanka* Vol. 41, 1996, 153–204.
SILVA, G. P. S. HARISCHANDRA DE AND C. G. URAGODA (eds.). *Sesquicentennial Commemorative Volume of the Royal Asiatic Society of Sri Lanka, 1845–1995.* Colombo: Royal Asiatic Society of Sri Lanka, 1995.
SILVA, KINGSLEY MUTHUMUNI DE (ed.). *History of Ceylon.* Vol. 3: From the Beginning of the Nineteenth Century to 1948. Colombo: The Colombo Apothecaries Company, 1973.
SILVA, KINGSLEY MUTHUMUNI DE. "Resistance Movements in Nineteenth Century Sri Lanka". In *Sri Lanka.* Collective Identities Revisited. Vol. 1. Edited by Michael Roberts. Colombo: Marga Institute, 1997.
SILVA, KINGSLEY MUTHUMUNI DE. *A History of Sri Lanka.* London: C. Hurst & Co. Publishers, 1981.

SILVA, KINGSLEY MUTHUMUNI DE. *Reaping the Whirlwind*. Ethnic Conflict, Ethnic Politics in Sri Lanka. New Delhi: Penguin Books, 1999.
SILVA, R. RAJPAL KUMAR DE and W. G. M. BEUMER. *Illustrations and Views of Dutch Ceylon 1602–1796*. A Comprehensive Work of Pictorial Reference with Selected Eye-Witness Accounts. London / Leiden: Serendib Publications / E. J. Brill, 1988.
SILVA, VIJITA BIANCA DE. "English Periodicals of Nineteenth Century". In *Historical Essays*. Primary Printed and Manuscript Sources for Sixteenth to Nineteenth Century Available in Sri Lanka. Edited by Katherine S. Diehl. Colombo: Hansa, 1976.
SIVARAJAH, AMBALAVANAR. *Politics of Tamil Nationalism in Sri Lanka*. New Delhi: South Asian Publishers, 1996.
SIVASUNDARAM, SUJIT. *Islanded*. Britain, Sri Lanka, and the Bounds of an Indian Ocean Colony. Chicago: University of Chicago Press, 2013.
SMIT, PETER-BEN. *Old Catholic and Philippine Independent Ecclesiologies in History*. The Catholic Church in Every Place. Leiden / Boston: Brill, 2011.
SOMARATNA, GINTOTA PARANA VIDANAGE. *Kotahena Riot 1883*. A Religious Riot in Sri Lanka. Gangodawila / Nugegoda: Deepanee, 1991.
SOMARATNA, GINTOTA PARANA VIDANAGE. *The Political History of the Kingdom of Kōṭṭe, 1400–1521*, PhD Thesis. London: University of London, 1969.
SOMARATNA, GINTOTA PARANA VIDANAGE. "The History of the Sinhala Bible", *Journal of the Royal Asiatic Society of Sri Lanka* 34, 1989, 41–64.
SOUZA, TEOTONIO R. DE. "Christianization and Cultural Conflict in Goa, 16th–19th centuries". In *Congresso Internacional de História Missionação Portuguesa e Encontro de Culturas*. Actas. Vol. 4: Missionação Problemática: Geral e Sociedade Contemporânea. Braga: Universidade Católica Portuguesa, 1993.
SOUZA, TEOTONIO R. DE. "Xavier Centre of Historical Research". In *Handbook of Libraries, Archives & Information Centres in India*. Humanities Information Systems and Centres. Vol. 9, Part 2. Edited by B. M. Gupta. 239–242. Delhi: Aditya Prakashan, 1985.
SOUZA, TEOTÓNIO R. DE. *Discoveries, Missionary Expansion, and Asian Cultures*. New Delhi: Concept Publishing Company, 1994.
STECK, RAPHAEL. *Monseigneur Joseph René Vilatte: Une vie en image*. 2013.
STIRRAT, R. L. *Power and Religiosity in a Post-Colonial Setting*. Sinhala Catholics in Contemporary Sri Lanka. Cambridge: Cambridge University Press, 1992.
STRATHERN, ALAN. *Kingship and Conversion in Sixteenth-Century Sri Lanka*. Portuguese Imperialism in a Buddhist Land. Cambridge: Cambridge University Press, 2007.
STREIT, ROBERT. *Bibliotheca Missionum*. Vol. 6: Missionsliteratur Indiens, der Philippinen, Japan und Indochinas, 1700–1799. Roma / Freiburg / Wien: Herder, 1964.
TAYLOR, WILLIAM. *Narratives of Identity*. The Syrian Orthodox Church and the Church of England 1895–1914. Newcastle upon Tyne: Cambridge Scholars Press, 2013.
TEIXEIRA, VITOR RUI GOMES. "Fr. Paulo da Trindade, O.F.M., Cronista Macaense". *Review of Culture / Revista de Cultura* [Macau], no. 28, 2008, 6–15.
THAYIL, THOMAS. *The Latin Christians of Kerala*: A Study on Their Origins. Bangalore: Kristu Jyoti, 2003.
THEKEDATHU, JOSEPH. *The Troubled Days of Francis Garcia S.J. Archbishop of Cranganore (1641–59)*, Roma: Università Gregoriana Editrice, 1972.
THERIAULT, SERGE A. *Lettres pastorales, mandements, sermons, déclarations et circulaires de Mgr René Vilatte 1892–1925*. Berkeley: Apocryphile Press, 2017.

THERIAULT, SERGE A. *Msgr. René Vilatte: Community Organizer of Religion, 1854-1929*, 1st ed. 1997. Berkeley: Apocryphile Press, 2012.

THOMAS, B.M. 'A Journal (Journey?) through the Life of Bishop Alvares Mar Julios: A Vigilant Promoter of Ecumenism'. Paper read at *Journeying Together in Faith: Ecumenical Endeavours in South India, Church History Association of India, Southern India Branch Triennial Conference*, Kottayam, 31 January to 1 February 2018.

THOMAS, M. KURIAN (ed.). *Universal Supremacy in the Church of Christ.* Devalokam / Kottayam 2020.

THOMAS, M. KURIAN. *The Way of St. Thomas: A Brief History of the Malankara Orthodox Syrian Church.* Kottayam: MOC Publications, 2012.

TISSERANT, EUGÈNE. *Eastern Christianity in India a history of the Syro-Malabar Church from the earliest time to the present day*. London: Longmans, Green and Co., 1957.

TURNBULL, STEPHEN. *The Kakure Kirishitan of Japan*. A Study of Their Development, Beliefs and Rituals to the Present Day. Surrey: Japan Library, 1998.

VARGHESE, VIJI, DIR. *A Forgotten Saint – A documentary on the life of Alvares Mar Julius (English)*. With the support of Mar Julius Youth Movement for St Mary's Orthodox (https://youtu.be/apGFkMooY3U, 22 January 2019).

VARICATT, CHERIAN. *The Suriani Church of India: Her Quest for Autochthonous Bishops (1877–1896).* Kottayam 1992.

VASCOTTI, CLARUS. *Institutiones historiae ecclesiasticae novi foederis.* 1st edition. Roma: Puccinelli, 1851.

VÄTH, ALFONS. *Die deutschen Jesuiten in Indien: Geschichte der Mission von Bombay-Puna 1854–1920.* Regensburg: Verlag Josef Kösel Friedrich Pustet, 1920.

VERGHESE, PAUL. *The Orthodox Church in India. An Overview.* Delhi: Sophia Publ., 1982.

VIAN, GIOVANNI. "Indie Orientali, Indocina, Oceania: Il modernismo in mondi lontani', in *The Reception and Application of the Encyclical Pascendi.* The Reports of the Diocesan Bishops and the Superiors of the Religious Orders until 1914, Studi di Storia 3, Edited by Claus Arnold and Giovanni Vian, 231–245. Venezia: Edizioni Ca'Foscari, 2017.

VICENTE GONZÁLEZ, JOSÉ DE, ed. *Antiguas boticas españolas y sus recipientes.* Comba, A Coruña: tresCtres [sic], 2009.

VICENTE, FILIPA LOWNDES. 'Portuguese-Speaking Goan Women Writers in Late Colonial India (1860-1940)'. *Portuguese Studies Review* 25, no. 1, 2017, 324–327.

VISVANATHAN, SUSAN *Christians of Kerala: History, Belief and Ritual among the Yakoba.* New Delhi: Oxford Univ. Press, 1999.

VITHAYATHIL, VARKEY J. *The Origin and Progress of the Syro-Malabar Hierarchy.* Kottayam: Oriental Institute of Religious Studies, 1980.

WENZLHUEMER, ROLAND. "Indian Labour Immigration and British Labour Policy in Nineteenth-Century Ceylon". *Modern Asian Studies* 41, no. 3, 2007, 575–602.

WENZLHUEMER, ROLAND. *From Coffee to Tea Cultivation in Ceylon, 1880–1900.* An Economic and Social History. Leiden: Brill, 2008.

WICKRAMASINGHE, NIRA. *Metallic Modern.* Everyday Machines in Colonial Sri Lanka. New York: Berghahn Books, 2014.

WICKRAMASINGHE, NIRA. *Sri Lanka in the Modern Age.* A History of Contested Identities. New York: Oxford Univ. Press, 2014.

WICKREMESEKERA, CHANNA. *Kandy at War*. Indigenous Military Resistance to European Expansion in Sri Lanka 1594–1818. Colombo: Vijitha Yapa Publications, 2004.

WINIUS, GEORGE D. *The Fatal History of Portuguese Ceylon*. Transition to Dutch Rule. Cambridge, Massachusetts: Harvard University Press, 1971.

WOLSKA-CONUS, WANDA. "La 'Topographie Chrétienne' de Cosmas Indicopleustès. Hypothèses sur quelques thèmes de son illustration". *Revue des études byzantines* 48, no. 1, 1990, 155–191.

WRIGHT, ARNOLD. *Twentieth Century Impressions of Ceylon*. Its History, People, Commerce, Industries, and Resources. London: Lloyd's Greater Britain Publishing Co, 1907.

XAVIER, ÂNGELA BARRETO. "David contra Golias na Goa Seiscentista: Escrita Identitária e Colonização Interna". *Ler História* 49, 2005, 107–143.

XAVIER, ÂNGELA BARRETO. "Purity of Blood and Caste: Identity Narratives among Early Modern Goan Elites". In *Race and Blood in the Iberian World*. Edited by M.E. Martínez, M. Hering Torres and D. Nirenberg, 125–149. Münster 2012.

XAVIER, FRANCISCO JOÃO. *Breve noticia da Imprensa Nacional de Goa, seguida de um catalogo das obras e escriptos publicados pela mesma Imprensa desde a sua fundação*. Nova-Goa: Imprensa Nacional, 1876.

YOUNG, RICHARD FOX and G. P. V. SOMARATNA. *Vain Debates*. The Buddhist-Christian Controversies of Nineteenth-Century Ceylon. Publications of the De Nobili Research Library, 23. Vienna: Institut für Indologie der Universität Wien, 1996.

ZANDVLIET, K. *The Dutch Encounter with Asia, 1600–1950*. Amsterdam: Antique Collectors Club Limited, 2002.

ŽUPANOV, INES G. "Goan Brahmans in the Land of Promise. Missionaries, Spies and Gentiles in the 17th-18th Century Sri Lanka". In *Portugal – Sri Lanka*. 500 Years. Edited by Jorge Flores, 171–210. Wiesbaden: Harassowitz / Calouste Gulbenkian Foundation, 2006.

Illustrations

Fig. 1: Buona Morte Church, at the entrance to the yard.

Fig. 2: St. Sebastian Muslim Mahavidyalaya.

Fig. 3: Buona Morte Church, with "Our Lady of Good Death Pray For Us" written on the wall separating the yard from the Attorney General's Department of the Supreme Court of Sri Lanka.

Fig. 4: Buona Morte Church, the altar.

Fig. 5: Buona Morte Church. An old photo taken from: Abba Seraphim Metropolitan of Glastonbury, *Flesh of Our Brethren: An Historical Examination of Western Episcopal Successions Originating from the Syrian Orthodox Patriarchate of Antioch* (London: The British Orthodox Press, 2017), 210.

Fig. 6: Antonio Alvares' photo in *Oriente* (Nova Goa), 30 September 1929.

Fig. 7: Luis Mariano Soares' Church in Dindigul, part of the which was used as a food store in 2018.

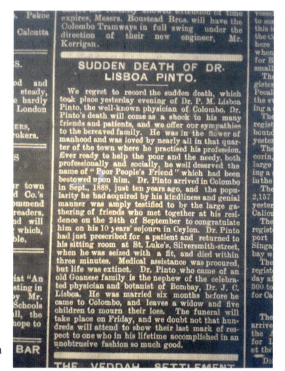

Fig. 8: "Sudden death of Dr. Lisboa Pinto", in *The Ceylon Independent*, 20 October 1898.

Fig. 9: Silversmith street, Colombo, where Lisboa Pinto's house "St Luke" was once located.

Fig. 10: The author and Mr. Sujith Varghese George's family at the St Thomas Mount National Shrine, Chennai, 4 February 2018.

Studien zur Außereuropäischen Christentumsgeschichte. Asien, Afrika, Lateinamerika / Studies in the History of Christianity in the Non-Western World

Herausgegeben von / Edited by Klaus Koschorke und / and Johannes Meier

---

33: Frieder Ludwig, Mirjam Laaser, Wilhelm Richebächer, Amélé Adamavi-Aho Ekué, Pui-Yee Pong (Eds.)

Reformation in the Context of World Christianity

Theological, political and social interactions between Africa, Asia, the Americas and Europe

2019. X, 296 pages, 3 tables, pb
170x240 mm
ISBN 978-3-447-11292-5
E-Book: ISBN 978-3-447-19914-8   each € 58,– (D)

The 500th anniversary of Luther's 95 theses in 2017 was the first such commemoration in which the global dimensions of the reformation were highlighted. This volume – the outcome of a conference held at the Fachhochschule für Interkulturelle Theologie Hermannsburg in June 2016 – reflects theological, political and social interactions between Africa, Asia, the Americas and Europe and explores new ways in which „Reformation" and „World Christianity" can be connected. It also analyzes negotiation processes in selected countries, focussing especially on the role of churches in social development, transformation processes and international discourses.

34: Klaus Koschorke

„Owned and Conducted entirely by the Native Christian Community"

Der ,Christian Patriot' und die indigen-christliche Presse im kolonialen Indien um 1900

2019. VIII, 304 Seiten, gb
170x240 mm
ISBN 978-3-447-11274-1   € 68,– (D)

Der ,Christian Patriot. A Journal of Social and Religious Progress' existierte von 1890 bis 1929 und verstand sich als „Sprachrohr" der indisch-protestantischen Gemeinschaft Südindiens. Das Blatt befand sich in „alleinigem" Besitz indischer Christen. Als solches eröffnet es ganz neue Perspektiven auf die indische und globale Christentumsgeschichte. Das Journal grenzte sich sowohl vom Paternalismus der euroamerikanischen Missionare wie von hindu-fundamentalistischen Tendenzen in der indischen Nationalbewegung ab. Dabei war es bestrebt, der Stimme indischer Christen als eigenständiger Größe in der kolonialen Öffentlichkeit des Landes Gehör zu verschaffen. Zugleich werden im Spiegel des ,Christian Patriot' transregionale Netzwerke indigen-christlicher Eliten in Asien und anderen Regionen und Kolonialgesellschaften sichtbar. Diese tragen zu einem neuen Verständnis christlicher Globalität um 1910 bei.

The 'Christian Patriot' (Madras/Chennai 1890–1929) – a journal "owned and conducted entirely" by Indian Christians – represents a new class of documents for the study of the history of World Christianity. This weekly understood itself as mouth piece of the South Indian Protestant community "as a whole" and tried to assert their independent voice in the colonial public sphere. "Christian in tone and patriotic in its aims", it criticized both missionary paternalism and Hindu fundamentalism. At the same time, the 'Christian Patriot' reflects a wide range of transregional networks of indigenous Christian elites in Asia and other regions and colonial societies. Thus, this study contributes to a new understanding of Christian globality around 1910.

The book includes an English summary.

Studien zur Außereuropäischen Christentumsgeschichte. Asien, Afrika, Lateinamerika / Studies in the History of Christianity in the Non-Western World

Herausgegeben von / Edited by Klaus Koschorke und / and Johannes Meier

---

35: Mariam Kartashyan
Zwischen kirchlicher Reform und Kulturimperialismus
Die Bulle *Reversurus* (1867) und das armenisch-katholische Schisma in seinen transnationalen Auswirkungen

*2020. 304 Seiten, 7 Abb., br
170x240 mm
ISBN 978-3-447-11401-1
⊙E-Book: ISBN 978-3-447-19972-8*   je € 58,– (D)

Als Papst Pius IX. 1867 die eigenkirchlichen Rechte der armenisch-katholischen Kirche durch die Bulle *Reversurus* einschränkte, wollte er durch eine stärkere Bindung der Kirche an Rom ihre Reform einleiten. Die päpstliche Zentralisierungspolitik führte jedoch zum armenisch-katholischen Schisma (1871–1879/81), das aufgrund der gegebenen politischen Konstellationen in Europa und im Orient das Interesse der europäischen Großmächte auf sich zog. Deren politische Ziele und Rivalitäten beeinflussten in der Folge den Verlauf des Schismas. Neben dieser komplexen politischen Gemengelage entwickelten sich jedoch auch neue zwischenkirchliche Beziehungen. Auf der Grundlage freundschaftlicher Kontakte zwischen katholischen Armeniern, Altkatholiken und Anglikanern bildete sich ein internationales Netzwerk.
Mariam Kartashyan stellt die transnationalen Auswirkungen des armenisch-katholischen Schismas im Osmanischen Reich in den Mittelpunkt ihrer Studie und analysiert sowohl die vielfältigen diplomatischen Verwicklungen als auch die daraus resultierenden zwischenkirchlichen Verbindungen. Zudem geht sie der Frage nach, inwieweit die politischen Eingriffe während der römischen Reformbestrebungen auch als Ausdruck eines Kulturimperialismus gegenüber den katholischen Armeniern zu werten sind.

36: Johannes Meier (Hg.)
Die Zeit der Reformation aus anderem Blickwinkel
Eine lateinamerikanisch-ökumenische Perspektive

*2021. X, 270 Seiten, 6 Abb., 4 Tabellen, br
170x240 mm
ISBN 978-3-447-11600-8
⊙E-Book: ISBN 978-3-447-39137-5*   je € 58,– (D)

Die Reformation in Mitteleuropa und die weltweite Ausbreitung des Katholizismus waren zwei gleichzeitige Vorgänge. Drei Tage vor der Anhörung Martin Luthers auf dem Reichstag in Worms (17./18. April 1521) taufte P. Pedro de Valderrama, Teilnehmer an der Weltumsegelung Fernando Magellans, auf der Insel Cebú das dortige Königspaar. Mit dem Taufgeschenk an die Königin, einer Figur des Jesuskindes in flämischer Tracht, in der linken Hand den Weltapfel tragend, begann auf den Philippinen dessen bis heute lebendige Verehrung.
Am selben Tag, an dem Luther noch vor Verhängung des Wormser Ediktes auf der Wartburg in Sicherheit gebracht wurde (4. Mai 1521), starb in Santo Domingo der Prior der ersten Kommunität der Dominikaner in Amerika, Pedro de Córdoba. Er war der intellektuelle und spirituelle Initiator des christlichen Kampfes für die Menschenrechte der Urbevölkerung des Doppelkontinents. Umgekehrt gelangten durch flämische und spanische Teilnehmer des Wormser Reichstags erste reformatorische Schriften in die iberische Welt.
Die in diesem Sammelband dokumentierte Magdeburger Tagung des Stipendienwerks Lateinamerika-Deutschland im Jahr 2017 hatte sich zum Ziel gesetzt, zu einer neuen Sichtweise jener Zeit vor 500 Jahren anzuregen, eine andere Perspektive in das Reformationsgedenken einzubringen. Der Band enthält zwölf Beiträge von Autoren aus Brasilien, Chile, Dänemark, Deutschland, Italien, den Niederlanden, Peru und den USA, je sechs in spanischer und deutscher Sprache mit beigegebenen Resümees in beiden Sprachen. Den Rahmen bilden eine transkontinentale Einführung in die Epoche und eine verbindende Zeittafel.